TREES

OF DELHI

A FIELD GUIDE

PRADIP KRISHEN

INTACH

Delhi Tourism

LONDON, NEW YORK, MELBOURNE,
MUNICH, DELHI

First published in 2006 by Dorling Kindersley (India)
Pvt. Limited
Copyright © 2006 Dorling Kindersley (India)
Pvt. Limited
Text copyright © 2006 Pradip Krishen
Photographs on pages 26, 30, 31 © 2006
The British Library
Photographs on pages 141, 258 © 2006
Royal Botanic Garden, Edinburgh
Photograph on page 16 (top) © 2006
Archaeological Survey of India
Photograph on page 25 (bottom) © 2006
R.S. Chundawat
Photograph on page 298 (bottom) © 2006
Suprabha Seshan
All other photographs © 2006 Pradip Krishen
Maps on pages 20, 22, 27 and 34–35 by Madhur Sharma

ISBN-13: 978-0-14400-070-8
ISBN-10: 0-14400-070-9

Book design by Mugdha Sethi
Design consultant Aparna Sharma

Printed and bound in India by
Thomson Press India Ltd, New Delhi

see our complete catalogue at

www.dk.com
www.penguin.co.in

ACKNOWLEDGEMENTS

Thank you Nishikant Jadhav, Tree Guru, for starting me off.
And Golak, Jungling Companion, for sharing the wonder
and staying the distance.

I owe a big debt of gratitude to: Dr H.B. Naithani for
sharing his knowledge of plants so generously and trawling
the FRI Herbarium for me; Henry Noltie, friend, teacher,
botanical treasure-trove; Ian Brooker of CSIRO, Canberra,
for identifying Delhi's eucalypts; John Dransfield, for
identifying some of the palms.

Shobita Punja and Dr O.P. Jain of INTACH for flicking
away obstacles and finding solutions; Arshiya Sethi and
Shreelata Prabhakaran for arranging my public tree walks
and helping to sharpen my skills; Dr J.K. Rawat of the FRI
for his kindness and hospitality; Prof. Nayanjot Lahiri, who
first told me about the sacred forest at Mangar; Dr Subodh
Pande, in a very special sense, for making it possible to
continue; Shankar Ghosh for taking me to the Delhi Golf
Course; Naresh Kumar Sharma, charioteer, and Jankidas,
maali, for their loyalty and camaraderie.

I thank the Royal Botanic Garden, Edinburgh, for
permission to reproduce two photographs from their
magnificent collection of early-19th-century Indian botanical
drawings. And the British Library (London), the National
Archives (New Delhi), the Forest Research Institute (Dehra
Dun), the Archaeological Survey of India (New Delhi) and
the Delhi State Archives (New Delhi), where I did the
research for this book.

Bena Sareen and Jaishree Ram Mohan at Penguin – it was
important to be able to rely on you. Thank you Aurobind
Patel for your generosity and infinite patience in starting off
the design process; Aparna Sharma, who brought it all
together; and Mugdha Sethi, designer par excellence and
cheerful, reliable companion throughout the gruelling
process; Madhur Sharma, for the cartography, and
Dr P.S. Mishra for valuable inputs for the map of Delhi's
eco-regions.

For love, laughter, inspiration and much else – Jojo van
Gruisen, Raghu Chundawat, Viveka Kumari, Veena and
Phil Oldenburg, Aradhana Seth, Supi Seshan, Meera and
Dr Ishwar Dass, Toby Sinclair and all my other friends in
lots of important ways.

Pia and Mithva, for their boundless love and faith and for
growing up so beautifully – and Mithva also for soaking up
so many drudge-hours on the computer.

Most earnestly – for taking me to the Ridge on a leash and
showing me its secrets, thank you Kuttuji, Bowji, Patti,
Chhutku-mal, Zizi, Ronnie and Bhondu.

And Nooni, for Everything.

TREE GUIDE

BACK OF THE BOOK

CONTENTS

INTRODUCTION

PREFACE

I've been walking on the Ridge near Sardar Patel Marg for nearly forty years now. For most of this time, I knew very little about the trees and shrubs that I saw there. The neem was probably the only tree I could recognize at a glance. I learned to tell the flame of the forest in bloom, but would have struggled to recognize it outside the flowering season. To my untrained eye, the Ridge was just a wild-looking place in the middle of the city, with lots of thorny trees and bushes.

Then something happened. It was late winter in 1995 – 16 February, to be precise. I know because I wrote it down. It is a time of year when most shrubs and trees on the Ridge have been bare for many weeks. On this particular day, I noticed that every dry twig had sprouted a tiny, pale green affirmation that it was still alive – little, glinting points of life, especially noticeable when a bush was backlit by the sun. It was like a hidden trigger had been pulled to produce the magic of a fresh shoot, not just on one plant, but everywhere I looked. I felt specially privileged, as though the forest had allowed me in on a secret event in its biological calendar.

Looking back, I am sure this was the exact moment when my interest in plants began. My earliest photographs of Delhi trees were taken in the rainy season of 1997. It must have been sometime just before then that I decided to learn as much as I could about Delhi's trees and begin the research that led to this book. As I learned more, I began to lead walks on Sunday mornings, exploring gardens and semi-wild places with groups of tree-spotters. And that is how this book slowly gathered unstoppable momentum.

NEW DELHI RIDGE in late August

I had no idea, at first, how hard it might be to track down the identity of every tree in Delhi. Native trees and those from other parts of India are not usually a problem. Unlike a natural forest, cities accumulate many ornamental trees from other parts of the world with a compatible climate. Over time, some exotic trees – like the bottlebrush and silky oak – prove their adaptability and ornamental value and become like clichés of the cultivated landscape. No problem identifying those trees.

Others fail to do well or reach full potential and are then discarded. It is these unsuccessful, forgotten exotics that can pose a challenge. I came across a small tree in Sundar Nursery (Nizamuddin) that had me puzzled for years. It had feather-compound leaves with crowded, leathery leaflets and I never found it in flower. I felt certain it wasn't an Indian tree. But where do you begin to look up the identity of an exotic tree? Without flowers, how do you assign it to a botanical family? Even if you figure out what family it belongs to, which Flora do you consult?

I came upon the same tree accidentally in the Sydney Botanic Garden three years later. The Sydney tree was tall and wide-spreading and bore little resemblance to the runt in Sundar Nursery, but something about its blunt, crowded leaflets was familiar. I brought back a leaf with me to make sure, and it was only then that I knew for certain that the Sundar Nursery specimen was a carrotwood tree from south-eastern coastal Australia.

How did it get there? Was it one of the trees that Percy-Lancaster, Delhi's Superintendent of Horticulture, planted in the 1940s? Possibly. But it wasn't the only one. In Sundar Nursery too I found a lone, forgotten specimen of a coca tree from the Peruvian Andes. I found 2 delicate-leaved Brazilian ironwood trees with wonderfully mottled bark; a magnificent khaya or Senegal mahogany; a broadleaved bottle tree, also from Australia. Each one had to be tracked down and identified.

So here it is, then – the result of a lot of detective work plus some straightforward persistence and foot-slogging. 252 trees in all, plus-minus a few subspecies. Many common ones, a few that are the only representatives of their kind in the city, and a whole lot of trees neither common nor rare. Could I possibly have accounted for every single species of tree there is in Delhi? Probably not. It is more than likely I have missed a few trees skulking in private gardens or out-of-the-way places, and I hope readers will write in and tell me if they know of missing trees that belong in this book.

WHAT IS A TREE?

The answer may seem obvious: a big, tall plant with a woody stem and rough bark, branching at the top, with lots of leaves at the ends of its twigs.

The trouble with such common-sense answers is that the world of trees is rife with awkward exceptions. Where do you draw the line separating a shrub from a tree? At 3 metres? Or 4.5 metres? It is true that all trees have woody stems, but tree bark isn't always rough or even woody. Branches? The vast majority of palm trees do not branch at all. What about leaves? Even that basic element sometimes goes missing in certain trees that have evolved substitutes or dispensed with leaves altogether.

Part of the difficulty stems from the fact that trees seem to have been independently 'invented' several times over the 420 million years or so of their evolution. That, in a nutshell, is why they present so much diversity and so many variations.

One thing that can safely be said of *all* trees is that they are perennial, woody plants with a single, well-developed trunk branching some distance above ground. From here on the quibbling begins. How much above ground must the branching be to separate a shrub from a tree? How tall? Some authors insist the minimum height of a tree is 6 m. Others specify the diameter or circumference of the trunk measured at a fixed height above the ground. Where do you place a tall, woody plant that branches very low down?

This book takes an inclusive view and I have relied on my own admittedly subjective sense of whether or not a plant seems tree-like. If you find yourself wondering why a particular shrubby plant is included here, it is because, at least sometimes, it grows unmistakably tree-like somewhere in Delhi. In other cases, when the vast majority of the specimens I have found in Delhi are either very small or multi-stemmed (like the cumquats), I have left them out. It's as simple as that. No foot rules and measuring tapes. No rigid criteria.

TREE NAMES

Many people feel intimidated or put off by difficult-sounding Latin names, and in deference to their feelings I have used common names as the principal labels for the trees in this book. It is by no means a perfect solution. While common names tend to be easier to use and remember, they are far from being standardized. The name 'aam' (for the mango), for example, does not travel well across language barriers. Even within the Hindi-speaking belt in northern India, some trees are known by several common names that are not always understood as you move from one area to the next.

Scientific names were invented to avoid precisely this sort of confusion. The trouble is they do not always work that way, because scientists have a way of changing plant names or transferring them from one genus to another. That ruins the aim of the exercise, somewhat, and I have a lot of sympathy for tree-spotters who feel completely disheartened to learn that *Haplophragma heterophyllum* has been reassigned to genus *Fernandoa*, and should henceforth be called... Learning the scientific names is hard enough – keeping up with the changes can be teeth-gnashingly frustrating.

Every tree in this book is labelled with its current scientific name as well as its common name(s) in English and local name(s). For the purpose of assigning the tree one emblematic name, however, I have picked one from its pool of common names. I hope that amateur tree-spotters will bless me for choosing uncomplicated names, and that the more botanically-minded among my readers will be reassured that most of the relevant scientific information, including author citations and recent synonyms, are in there somewhere, albeit in low profile.

Elevating one main name from the list of common names was often a simple matter of choosing the most familiar. I did not have to think hard to choose 'neem' over 'margosa', or 'babool' over 'Egyptian mimosa'. In some cases, I faced a dilemma – 'flame of the forest' and 'dhak' are both well-known names for *Butea monosperma*. I chose 'dhak' on the basis that when English and local names seemed equally compelling, I let the provenance of the tree decide – local names were given a little extra weightage if the tree is indigenous; exotics earned English names, or in certain cases, names in the language of their exoticism (Mexican names for Mexican trees) but only if these names are sufficiently well known. There are only a few exceptions, which became necessary to avoid confusion or duplication of a common name used elsewhere.

THE DHAK tree is also known locally as palash, tesu, kesu and chhichra.

THE PARTS OF A TREE

Botanists have coined an admirably precise terminology to describe the parts of plants – some 18 words to distinguish between degrees and types of hairiness! But the precision is not much use if you don't know the vocabulary and I have used simple terms, as far as possible, that everyone should understand. There are a few words which, if I had to explain each time, would make the text unbearably cumbersome. So for those of you who develop little frowns when you see words like 'style' or 'anther', here is a basic checklist of terms (in capitals) used in this book.

CANOPY or CROWN

TRUNK or BOLE

FLANGES or BUTTRESSES

LEAVES are usually arranged on the twig in characteristic ways, and are a first clue to the identity of a tree. The majority of leaves are arranged either ALTERNATELY or in OPPOSITE pairs, but they may also be SPIRALLY arranged or disposed in tufts towards the ends of branchlets

OPPOSITE leaves

ALTERNATE leaves

WHORLED BRANCHES start at the same height, like the spokes of an umbrella

SIDE-STALKS or PINNAE

LEAFLETS

COMMON LEAF STALK

COMPOUND LEAF

APEX OF LEAF

LATERAL or SECONDARY nerves

LEAF BLADE

MIDRIB

LEAF MARGIN

BASE OF LEAF

BASAL NERVES

LEAF STALK

SIMPLE LEAF

The angle formed by a leaf stalk and its twig is called an AXIL

Some leaves have tiny, raised GLANDS that can be very useful in identification

STIPULE

STIPULES are small, leafy outgrowths at the base of the leaf stalk. Fig trees have large, sheath-like stipules covering the tips of new leaves (*right*), sometimes called LEAF-BUDS

BARK TEXTURE is characteristic for most trees and is described in simple terms (prickly, papery, smooth, fissured, etc.). The word LENTICELS describes the tiny breathing pores in the bark, shown in the picture at far right.

LENTICELS are more evident on young bark, but some species have diagnostic patterns even when old

FLOWERS house a tree's sexual organs, and come in a bewildering variety of shapes and forms. You need to recognize the outermost FLOWER-CUP and the PETALS, and tell the male organs or STAMENS from the female organ or PISTIL.

PETALS are often brightly coloured, but may be absent

POLLEN is stored in the ANTHER, which is the head of the STAMEN

FILAMENT or stalk of the anther

STIGMA

STYLE is the stalk of the female organ or PISTIL, with a STIGMA at the end

SINGLE FLOWERS and clusters are either borne at the end of a twig (TERMINAL), or laterally, from the base of a leaf (AXILLARY). Loose branching clusters are called PANICLES.

terminal clusters

axillary clusters

The FLOWER-CUP is usually green, but not always. It may be divided into LOBES (segments), or it may be TUBULAR and undivided

MOST TREE FLOWERS are BISEXUAL, with both male and female parts, and are known as PERFECT FLOWERS. Others are UNISEXUAL (either male or female), and both sexes may be on the same tree or separately, on 'male' or 'female' trees. Unisexual flowers usually retain some element of the other sex, if only vestigially.

TINY FLOWERS are often clustered closely together in HEADS. The most common forms are SPHERICAL HEADS and bottlebrush-like SPIKES.

SPHERICAL HEAD of flowers

Flowers arranged in a SPIKE

FRUIT are formed when a plant's OVARIES are fertilized and reach maturity. Crucially, the fruit house the SEEDS. All the various forms of fruit are just different ways of providing packaging, protection, food and transport for the seeds inside.

woody CAPSULE fruit

ripe capsule after opening

WINGED seed

POD or LEGUME, which may or may not open on its own

fleshy fruit may have mealy or juicy pulp and contain one or many seeds

Fruit are either dry or fleshy and there are many different ways by which the seeds are freed when the fruit ripen.

MULTIPLE fruit develop from several united flowers

HOW TO USE THIS BOOK

Delhi's most common trees receive more attention, with text and pictures running to 2 pages. Less common trees have been allocated a page or only half a page, depending on their status in the city. The miniature 2-page spread (*below*) shows you how information about a common species is organized. The Leaf Key (*on the opposite page*) is a visual checklist of all the leaves belonging to a particular category. Turn to pp12-13 for the Leaf Scheme and how to use it.

DISCARDED SYNONYMS are included if they are still in popular usage. More complete listings of botanical names and recent synonyms are provided on pp343-47

FAMILIES OF TREES – familiar 'flagship' trees have been used to label Families. Go to p342 if you want to find out the botanical names of the Families

TREE PROFILES depict the typical form and the largest size of a species in Delhi. Use the human figure as a relative scale

SCIENTIFIC NAME of the tree. Author citations are provided on pp343-47

LEAF SYMBOL reminds you of the leaf-category of this species

COMMON NAME(S) in English

LOCAL NAME(S) when available. They are often missing, especially for exotic or uncommon trees

IDENTIKIT provides a summary list of the chief characters used to identify a tree

SEASONS tell you when things happen to Delhi's trees. The same species may behave very differently in other parts of India

WHERE TO SEE IT lists familiar, public places where you can find specimens of a tree. Rarer species are not always obligingly located in accessible places

---

56 JAMUN-LIKE LEAVES SIMPLE, WIDEST NEAR THE MIDDLE

GOOLAR *Ficus racemosa*

Syn: Ficus glomerata

cluster fig • country/red river/redwood/blue fig • crattock
goolar • umar • umri • trimbal • leika • dimeri • batbar • palak • daduri

mulberry/fig family

Middle-sized tree; deciduous

Bark greyish yellow or rusty, with milky sap

Leaves 18 cm long, leathery, tapering at both ends; 3 strong veins from base; toothed when young

Figs in large clusters from trunk or main branches; figs stalked, woolly, reddish when ripe

FIGS grow in large clusters directly from the trunk or main branches (unlike most other figs which grow in the axils of leafy twigs). Each fig is 2-3 cm wide with a short stalk and is more or less spherical – older figs may be somewhat flattened near their apices. Ripe figs are softly woolly with a strong skein of veins just visible under the translucent skin.

An attractive fig tree with a crooked trunk and open, spreading crown. This one is not a 'strangler' and has no aerial roots. The red, furry figs are distinctive – arranged in short, branching clusters growing from the trunk or main branches. Widely distributed especially near water, the goolar qualifies as a native Delhi tree.

young figs are green and turn red or orange when ripe

SEASONS - LEAVES evergreen near a perennial source of water. Otherwise, leaves shed in January; leafless till early March. **FIGS** often produced in 2 crops, one in March-April and the second in the rains.

WHERE TO SEE IT Seldom, if ever, cultivated but present in many parks and gardens. Once planted along the Western Jumna Canal near Bawana village and along the Mehrauli-Badarpur Road, but few survive. The largest goolar in Delhi is probably one growing next to a pond in Jaunapur village. There is a good specimen in a little garden abutting the Jama Masjid.

LEAF KEYS display all the species that belong in the same Leaf Category. Use these pages as a quick way of sorting through a category, using leaf size and the hints to help you home in on one – or a few – likely candidates for the tree you are looking to identify. Then simply go to the page(s) listed under those leaves, to see if your specimen matches the description.

LEAF-SIZES in the Leaf Keys tend towards the larger leaves of each species. Note that the leaf size (shown beneath each leaf) includes the length of the leaf stalk.

JAMUN-LIKE LEAVES 57

the leaves are arranged alternately on the twigs

LEAVES 9-13 cm long, thin and with a few irregular teeth at first, gradually becoming leathery and dark on their upper surface, duller and paler below. They lose their teeth as they mature. There are always 3 strong yellow nerves starting from the base.

the 3 basal veins are more prominent on the undersurface

young leaves with their 'baby teeth'

BARK variable in colour – creamy, yellow, pinkish, silvery grey or rusty – yet unmistakable once you have learned to recognize it. Relatively smooth, becoming somewhat scaly with age.

HABITAT According to folk wisdom, there runs a hidden stream under every goolar tree. This is not unfounded – the goolar is a 'riparian' tree, growing naturally near streams or ponds in moist, clayey loams. It is conspicuously absent in arid regions. The goolar is not a 'strangler' and is never epiphytic on other trees.

RANGE Allied species of clustering figs are found in Africa but this is the only species to have reached Asia. It has spread throughout tropical Asia from India to Australia, avoiding only the driest parts.

USES Most parts of the tree are used in traditional healing. An astringent lotion made from the bark is credited with treating deep wounds inflicted by a tiger's claws. The dried leaves are powdered as a cure for bilious afflictions. The figs are carminative and the milky latex is used to treat piles and diarrhoea. The figs are not often eaten but some forest-dwelling communities seem to relish it. The leaves make an excellent fodder. Its soft, fibrous timber is not durable except underwater. It has little practical utility but is one of the few kinds of wood prescribed in ancient Hindu scriptures for the sacrificial fire. The tree too is sacred.

CAN BE CONFUSED WITH

None of the other figs, simply because its branched clusters of figs are so distinctive. When the tree has no figs, its leaves can perhaps be mistaken for a pilkhan's but this requires a little imagination!

RANGE, HABITAT AND USES information is provided in this column for the more common trees

LEAF SYMBOLS are 'switched on' (coloured) to tell you which leaf-category you are in. The full range of leaf symbols is shown in the column on the right

>> Ever Seen the Flowers of a Peepal Tree? – see p321

THE BACK OF THE BOOK is a section where snippets of more detailed inform-ation, puzzles, doubts and intuitions, are gathered together. This symbol >> alerts you about a Back-of-the-Book item and its subject. Treat it like a hyperlink that you can visit if it interests you, but you can just as easily choose to ignore it.

CAN BE CONFUSED WITH box is provided, when necessary, to help clear up common causes of mistaken identity

THE LEAF SCHEME

As clues to the identity of a tree, leaves are more useful than flowers or fruit because they are usually there, at hand, most of the year. That's why all the trees in this book have been sorted and arranged in 10 categories (*see opposite page*) according to the shape and form of their leaves.

When you come across an unfamiliar tree in Delhi, all you need to do is decide which category its leaf belongs to. This will lead you to the pages containing a KEY to that type of leaf. The key displays all the leaves of a particular category, pointing out prominent characters and leading you – by a process of elimination – to home in on one species.

You should find the categories of SIMPLE leaves easy enough to grasp. Some of the forms of COMPOUND leaves may require some explaining, and this is provided on p14. Note that the leaf categories have nothing to do with the size, colour or texture of a leaf. These features can some- times come into play when you need to differentiate between leaves *within* the same category. But the one distinction that you must learn if you want to use leaves as diagnostic clues is the essential difference between a SIMPLE and a COMPOUND leaf.

The difference is easy to express:

A SIMPLE LEAF has its blade in one piece and is not divided up into smaller leaflets.
A COMPOUND LEAF is divided up into at least two, and often into many more, separate leaflets.

The tiny leaflets of a gulmohur leaf look like they are *organized* as part of a larger whole. It is not always this easy to spot a comp- ound leaf by the way its leaflets are arrayed.

HOW TO TELL A LEAF FROM A LEAFLET

bud growing in the axil of a simple leaf

no bud at the base of a leaflet

The problem is that a leaflet can often look confusingly just like a leaf. How do you tell if what you are looking at is a *whole* leaf or only a segment of a larger, compound leaf? LEAFLETS are clearly not the same thing as LEAVES. But in what way, precisely?

The essential test is that a leaf always has a bud growing in its AXIL – the angle formed by its leaf stalk and the twig on which it is growing.

A leaflet has no bud at its base. The bud of a compound leaf can be found at the base of its common stalk, not its leaflets.

So the leaf-bud – or its absence – offers a simple test.

Leaf-buds can sometimes be so small that you need a magnifying lens to see them. It does need a little practice to become adept at spotting a bud. But once you learn to see the difference, you will find yourself distinguishing between simple and compound leaves almost instinctively.

THE 10 LEAF CATEGORIES

SIMPLE LEAVES

JAMUN-LIKE LEAVES
widest near the middle,
pages 44-92

PEEPAL-LIKE LEAVES
widest in the lower third,
pages 93-126

FRANGIPANI-LIKE LEAVES
widest in the upper third,
pages 127-52

CHINAR-LIKE LEAVES
lobed, pages 153-59

PINE-LIKE LEAVES
long, thin or needle leaves,
pages 160-85

COMPOUND LEAVES

BAEL-LIKE LEAVES
with 2 or 3 leaflets,
pages 186-205

SEMAL-LIKE LEAVES
palmately compound,
pages 206-17

IMLI-LIKE LEAVES
feather-compound,
pages 218-63

GULMOHUR-LIKE LEAVES
twice-feathered compound,
pages 264-305

PALM-LIKE LEAVES
fan- and feather-compound,
pages 306-20

Here are some tips to help you understand the leaf-categories and put them to good use:

SIMPLE LEAVES

- Leaves are hardly ever widest at their actual apex or base. Think of a leaf in *thirds* – upper, middle and lower thirds. Now look for which third is widest. This will lead you to one of the first 3 leaf-categories that is based solely on leaf width.

  upper third

  middle

  lower third

- **CHINAR-LIKE** leaves have LOBES or SEGMENTS, and it can be hard to decide if a leaf has lobes or just outsize teeth. The important thing is that it should be undivided at its centre to qualify as 'simple'.

  lobe or segment

- **THE PINE-LIKE** category is a bit of a ragbag. It includes all the conifers, which have needles or tiny scale-like leaves, and sometimes both. It also includes all simple leaves that are long and thin – or to put a value on it, any leaf that is at least 4 times longer than its greatest width.

  scale-like leaves

  needle leaves

  long, thin leaf

COMPOUND LEAVES

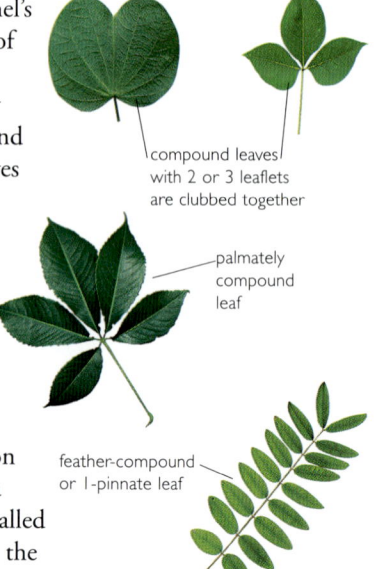

- **BAUHINIA LEAVES** – shaped like the outline of a camel's hoof – can be a little ambivalent. You can think of them as twin leaflets of a compound leaf that are fused in the middle, or as simple leaves with very large, rounded lobes. I have chosen the former, and have clubbed them together with compound leaves that have 2 or 3 leaflets.

  compound leaves with 2 or 3 leaflets are clubbed together

- The term **PALMATELY COMPOUND** describes a compound leaf whose leaflets radiate like the fingers of a hand around a central point where they are all joined.

  palmately compound leaf

- The kassod is a good example of a **FEATHER-COMPOUND LEAF** with its leaflets arranged in rows on each side of a central leaf stalk (like the veins of a feather). A feather-compound leaf is sometimes called '1-PINNATE' ('pinna' is Latin for 'feather') because the stalk divides only once.

  feather-compound or 1-pinnate leaf

- **TWICE-FEATHERED** compound leaves are like twice-divided feathers. The main leaf stalk divides once into side-stalks, and the side-stalks divide again into leaflets, so such a leaf is called 2-PINNATE or TWICE-FEATHERED. Some leaves go further and can be 3- or even 4-pinnate, but are all included here under the 2-pinnate category.

twice-feathered or 2-pinnate leaf

palm fan-leaf

- **PALM LEAVES** generally fall into one of 2 broad categories – they are either fan-leaves (shaped more or less like fans) or feather-leaves, which share much the same plan as a feather-compound leaf, except on a much bigger scale. Because palms are so distinctive, it made sense to place both sorts of palm leaves in a category of their own.

palm feather-leaf

unlobed leaf

lobed leaf

Leaves can be variable, sometimes even on the same tree. Juvenile leaves are often very different from adult foliage. What if a tree's leaves are so variable that it is hard to decide which category it belongs in? Or if the shape of a leaf is so ambiguous that it can just as easily be placed in one of 2 categories? The LEAF SCHEME handles variation and ambiguity by placing the leaf in both (or all possible) categories. The toot or mulberry, for example, has a simple leaf that is sometimes, but not commonly, deeply lobed. Because it is more usually unlobed and is widest near its base, you will find it in the PEEPAL-LIKE LEAF category. But you will *also* find it in the category of CHINAR-LIKE (lobed, simple) LEAVES. In this way, any one of the lobed or unlobed leaves will lead you to the toot tree. It's not infallible, but it works most of the time.

DELHI AS A HABITAT FOR TREES

ATHPULA BRIDGE at Khairpur – now Lodi Garden – in the years 1912 (*above*) and 2005 (*below*)

This book is about trees in the twin cities of Delhi and New Delhi which I refer to collectively as 'Delhi' (unless of course I need to make a clear distinction). Most city trees are cultivated ornamentals, found on streets, in parks and gardens, and have to a large extent supplanted the original, native flora of Delhi. Not completely, though. Here and there, it is still possible to find a native tree growing slightly out of kilter with a neat row of planted ornamentals and it can give you a buzz to realize that it could be a relict of Delhi's original flora.

Urban Delhi also includes swathes of semi-wild places (like the Ridge), and at its edges, shades off into wasteland or agricultural fields which support characteristic trees too. So this book is also about some wild tree species that live at the sufferance of the city or just beyond its destructive reach. I have done a lot of walking in such places just outside the city, searching for remnants of Delhi's original flora, especially along outliers of the hills extending southwards into Haryana. But I have had to draw the limit somewhere, and for convenience, the ambit of this book is confined to the administrative boundaries of the National Capital Territory of Delhi.

It must be hard, being a city tree, particularly so in Delhi. The air is laden with noxious gases and particles that clog leaf-pores. Unlike a natural forest, no nutrient-rich litter of dead leaves revitalizes the soil each season. The earth is either covered or packed so tight that nothing penetrates beyond the first few centimetres. Each year, the subsoil water deteriorates in quality and withdraws deeper.

But the main limiting factor for a tree growing in Delhi is the climate.

DELHI'S NATURAL ECOLOGY

Delhi receives about 60 cm of rain each year, nearly all of it in just 2 or so months of the monsoons (from mid July to early September) with an average of just 32 rainy days. Less than 50 mm of rain is recorded in each of 8 months of the year.

Delhi lies a little over 200 metres above mean sea level – not enough to matter. What does count is Delhi's insularity, far away from the sea and nudging the western desert region. Coupled with latitude (28° N), these factors combine to make Delhi scorchingly hot in summer, with temperatures touching 46° C in May and June. In winter, even if it never quite goes down to freezing, Delhi grows cold enough to cause some kinds of plants to wilt and die. Fog and mist in winter too cause sufficient loss of sunlight to make a difference to plants.

THORN FORESTS AND MONSOON FORESTS

Delhi's natural vegetation is sometimes called a 'thorn forest', which forms a transition zone where dry deciduous forest shades into desert scrub. It is a semi-arid environment, and you can see it all around Delhi, especially towards the west and south. The dominant and most common trees of thorn forests are *Acacias* and their relatives, a group of leguminous (pod-bearing) plants called 'mimosas'. Characteristic mimosas of Delhi's forests are the babool, jhand, ronjh, khair and phulai. (The kareel and ber are typical too, but are not mimosas.)

MONSOON FORESTS in northern India are close to becoming severely endangered. Much of it has already been cleared for cultivation.

From a wider perspective, thorn forests – along with dry deciduous forests and a few others – are constituents of a type of forest called a 'monsoon forest'. This term can be a little misleading because 'monsoon forest' sounds like 'rainforest', when they actually lie at opposite ends of the spectrum.

Monsoon forests are dry; rainforests are wet. The rhythm of a monsoon forest is attuned entirely to one concentrated pulse of rain that happens every year at a more or less predictable time. There is barely any rhythm in a rainforest, because it rains most of the year.

Trees of monsoon forests behave differently from rainforest trees in one very important respect – they drop their leaves in the long, dry season. It is nature's way of 'shutting down' and preventing water loss through the leaves when little or no moisture is available. Rainforest trees, by contrast, have little need of shedding their leaves and are therefore usually evergreen. The same species of tree is sometimes found in both types of forest – in which case, it behaves deciduously in a monsoon forest, and retains its leaves in the rainforest. Same tree – different responses.

The 2 kinds of forests also *look* different. Rainforests are dense and complex, with multistoreyed canopies. Monsoon forests are open and single-storeyed, and most trees have thin, feathery crowns. The natural rhythms of a monsoon forest go a long way towards helping us understand why Delhi's trees behave the way they do.

Here is a small sampling of things to notice:

- Monsoon forest trees drop their leaves in response to drought, not cold. This explains the timing of leaf-drop in Delhi, which usually begins late in January or early February, roughly 4 months after the rains have ended.
- Most monsoon forest trees tend to flower in the dry season, usually sometime between March and May, when their branches are leafless. This makes the flowers more conspicuous for pollinators and – though this is not part of nature's design – results in some magnificent massed flowering spectacles for us.
- You would expect monsoon forest trees to start new leaf only when the rains arrive. This is not so. For reasons not yet fully understood, most monsoon forest trees start new leaf many weeks before the rains. The trigger could be a slight drop in temperature or a change in day-length. Whatever the mechanism, it produces magnificent displays of bare trees cascading into new leaf, and Delhi is no exception.
- Most monsoon forest leaves go through a short phase of flushing pink or red before turning green. Does the red pigment act like a sunblock, protecting tender new leaves from harsh ultraviolet light? The precise mechanism is not fully known, but it makes for some truly beautiful sights in Delhi from March through May.

THE PEEPAL is one of many trees in Delhi that goes through a lovely pink phase when its leaves first emerge.

DELHI'S MICRO-HABITATS

Small as it is, even within the Delhi territory it is possible to distinguish ecotones, or areas with small shades of ecological difference. As far back as 1887, the Gazetteer of Delhi described Delhi district as having 4 'natural divisions' – the *kohi* or hilly tracts; the *bangar* or level main land; the *khadar* or sandy riverain of the Yamuna; and the low-lying *dabar* land that was subject to (seasonal) flooding. (These names derive from ancient terms used to assess the productivity of land.) The Delhi territory today is not identical with Delhi district as it was in the 19th century, but these 'natural divisions' are still useful descriptive labels for Delhi's micro-habitats.

KOHI

Delhi's hilly tracts correspond to 'the Ridge', which is a slightly elevated, rocky landform lying in a longitudinal axis west of and more or less parallel to the Yamuna river. Because of its underlying rock and thin, sandy soil, the Ridge is a harsh, unforgiving habitat and trees growing there need to be specially adapted to survive drought. Characteristic Ridge trees are stunted, thorny and open-canopied. They have long taproots to search for moisture deep underground, and often, shallow, spreading roots as well, to exploit dew and light rain. Few native Ridge trees are cultivated in the rest of Delhi and its trees therefore tend to be quite distinct from the rest of the city's. One prominent exception is the Central American mesquite or vilaiti keekar which has become a ubiquitous, invasive tree throughout Delhi, aggressively colonizing any patch of bare land. (More about vilaiti keekar, later.)

ROCKY HUMMOCK (with nilgai) in JNU campus – typical kohi terrain

BANGAR

The more or less level bangar is where you would expect to find Delhi's arable land. There is only a small tract of bangar to the north of the walled city – the greater part lies to the north-west and the south and takes in all of New Delhi east of the Central Ridge. The soil here is light and fertile, the subsoil

NATIVE BANGAR trees can still be seen as in these 'gallery' forests between the fairways of Delhi Golf Club.

water sweet, and left to nature this area would probably support a savannah or monsoon forest characteristic of, say, north-eastern Rajasthan or western UP. But it hasn't been left to nature, of course, because the bangar is now the heart of a modern city and lies mostly under macadam and concrete. However you can still find remnants of its natural flora wherever it has been enclosed and protected within large parks. Ber, jhand, peelu, kanju, bistendu, babool and ronjh are its most characteristic trees.

KHADAR

The 'riverain' – an old-fashioned name for the land lying between
the high banks of a river – was much more extensive in the 19th
century. The Yamuna washed the eastern flank of the walled city
and broke up into thin, braided channels meandering between
broad sandy banks as the flow declined after the rains. The
khadar had a characteristic riverine flora and was thickly forested
in places. Pig-sticking and hunting hog deer were a favourite
sport of British soldiers in the 19th century, and both wild pig
and hog deer were found rooting in patches of khadar forest.
But all that has changed. The Yamuna has been tamed between
bunds now and the sandy stretches on either side are very narrow.

DELHI'S ECOLOGICAL
subdivisions, based on
modern soil and
geological maps

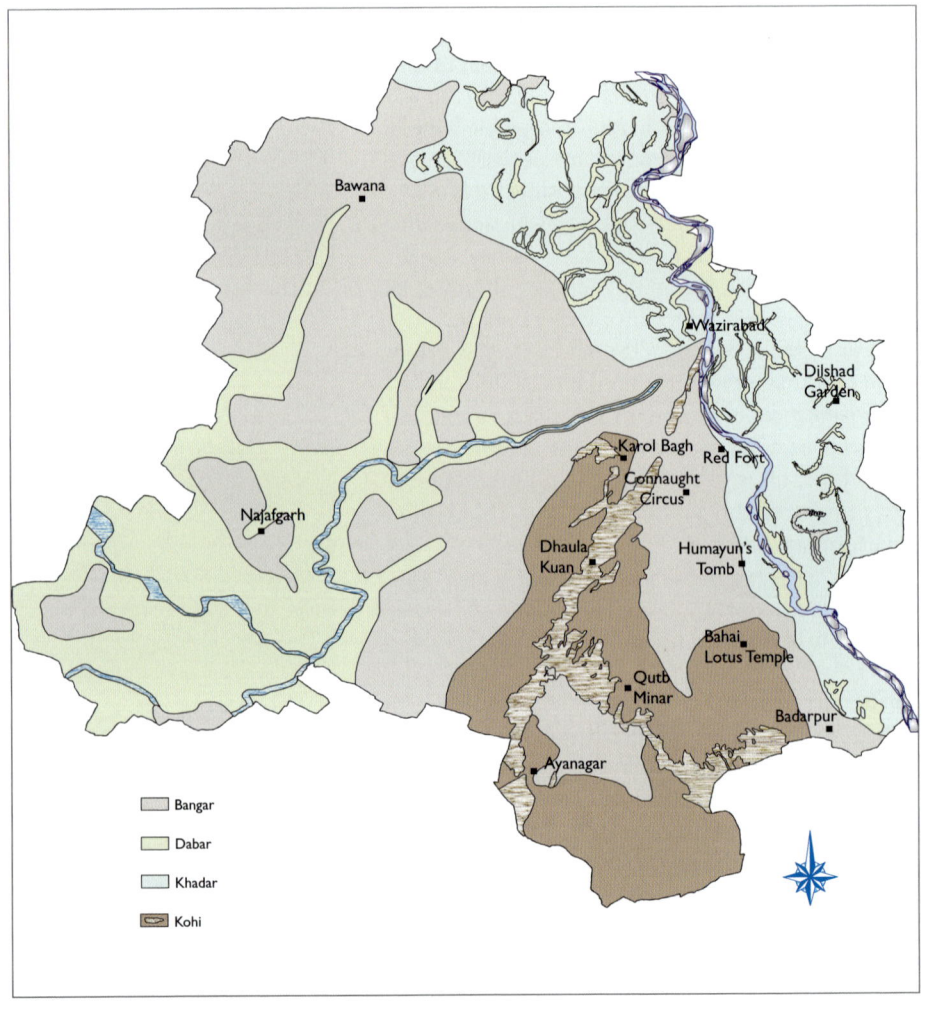

- Bangar
- Dabar
- Khadar
- Kohi

The river has also shrunk drastically in volume, and what little still trickles through is severely fouled by raw sewage and effluents. The khadar forests, not surprisingly, have completely disappeared. Nevertheless, the riverside is one of the last places in Delhi where you might find jhau (tamarisk) trees, once abundant throughout the khadar.

DABAR

The dabar or flood-prone land is a low-lying bayou or catchment extending through much of the territory west of the Ridge and south-west of the city. In years of heavy rainfall, this entire basin would become a foetid, shallow lake for some months. In many places, the soil was ruined by saltpetre rising from the waterlogged soil. Dabar land was notoriously unproductive and carried little commercial value. In 1911, planners had to give up the idea of siting the new Imperial capital north of the walled city because it was prone to becoming an unhealthy swamp every year.

The trees most often associated with dabar tracts, especially those affected by salinity, are the peelu, jhau, wild date palm and babool. But flooding and waterlogging are no longer issues today. The low-lying character of the dabar has changed, and in the years since Independence, an industrial belt of the city has spread over most of this area, so the natural character of the land is hardly apparent any more.

THE ALLUVIAL RIDGE

One micro-habitat for trees can perhaps be added to the list, though it is only a sliver and lies at the edge of Delhi. This is a part of the Southern Ridge near Jaunapur and Mandi villages, close to the border with Faridabad district. Instead of thin, rocky soil, here the sandy alluvium is piled so high that erosion has created ravines 8 m deep in places. This tract forms a unique micro-ecosystem by virtue of its deep soil. The ravines support plants and some trees – jhand, kareel, kumttha, bistendu and babool – that you expect to see in the sandy desert of western Rajasthan. A few other trees like the shisham

– native to alluvial soils in the sub-Himalayan tract – find themselves perfectly at home here, and have naturalized like a native.

BISTENDU growing in sandy alluvium at the edge of the city. Usually a small tree, it spreads out expansively here.

WHERE EXACTLY IS THE RIDGE?

Delhi's 'Ridge' is the tail-end – or the beginning, if you like – of the ancient Aravalli hills, 1500 million years old (compared to just 50 million for the Himalaya). The Aravallis stretch 800 kilometres from Gujarat through Rajasthan and Haryana, pushing into Delhi from Gurgaon to the south-west. Here, one branch bends eastwards to create the broken spurs and ravines of Tughlakabad, Jaunapur and Bhatti. The main spine of low hills continues in a north-easterly axis through Mehrauli and Vasant Vihar into Chanakyapuri. Just short of Sadar Bazar, the hills disappear only to surface again near the Barafkhana, where the road climbs steeply past the Mutiny Memorial to Hindu Rao Hospital. This low, narrow section forms the historic 'mere mound' where British soldiers dug in during the Uprising of 1857.

The Ridge finally peters out in a gentle bluff near Wazirabad to the north. In 19th-century maps of Delhi, the precise terminal point is a small rocky headland overlooking a sharp bend in the Yamuna. But the river has changed course and the ancient hills now terminate somewhat ingloriously, stranded in the middle of nothing in particular.

Delhi has not treated these hills with half the care they deserve. Large swathes of the Ridge have been lost, beginning in the second half of the 19th century when precincts such as Paharganj and Paharipur – whose names recall their hilly character – were levelled. But the great dismantling of the Ridge took place after Independence, especially since the 1970s, as the population swelled and new suburbs pushed south of the new capital city.

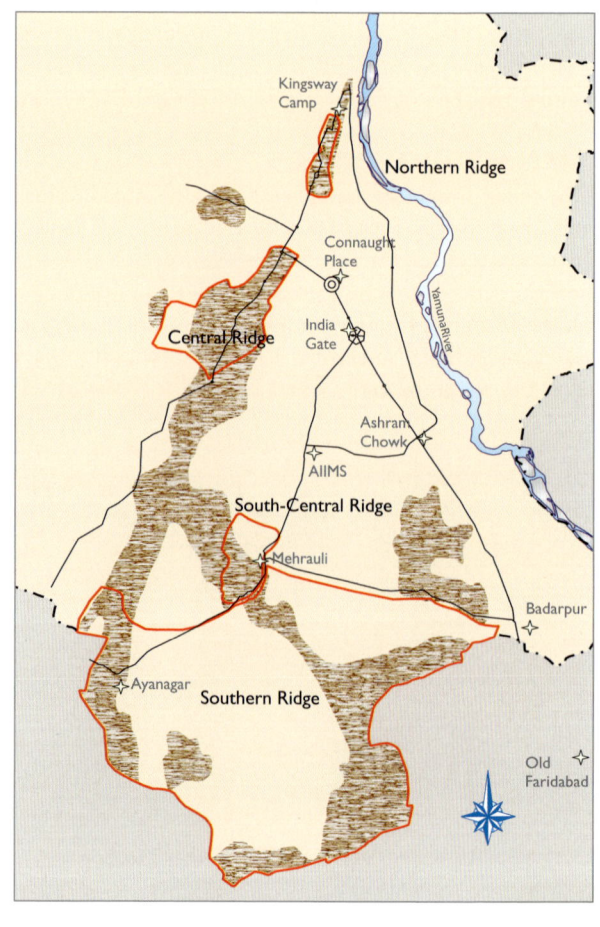

MAP showing the rocky land-form of the Ridge (shaded grey), and the notified Ridge zones (with red boundaries)

THE RIDGE TODAY for administrative reasons is divided into 4 separate zones whose boundaries and legal status, to state it plainly, are in a horrible mess. But the zones are still useful in thinking about and exploring the Ridge.

The OLD DELHI or NORTHERN RIDGE denotes the hilly area near Delhi University and is by far the smallest segment of the Ridge. Nearly 170 hectares were declared a Reserved Forest in 1915. Less than 87 hectares remain today.

The NEW DELHI or CENTRAL RIDGE was made into a Reserved Forest in 1914 and stretches from just south of Sadar Bazar to Dhaula Kuan. It extends over 864 hectares, but some bits have been nibbled away.

The MEHRAULI or SOUTH-CENTRAL RIDGE is centred on Sanjay Vana, near JNU, and encompasses 633 hectares. Large chunks have been encroached and built upon.

The TUGHLAKABAD or SOUTHERN RIDGE sprawls across 6200 hectares and includes the Asola and Bhatti wildlife sanctuaries. This is the least urban of the 4 segments of the Ridge, but a lot of it is village- or privately-owned farmland.

VILAITI KEEKAR with its twisted trunks has become the predominant tree throughout the Delhi Ridge.

NATIVE TREES OF THE DELHI RIDGE

South of Delhi, barely a few kilometres across the border
with Faridabad district, is a small, steep valley containing a
patch of forest known as 'Mangarbani'. It is only about
100 hectares or so, but is special because it is surprisingly
unspoiled by human beings and their livestock. Mangarbani
is a sacred forest, consecrated in the memory of Gudariya
Baba, a local holy man, and protected by the superstition
that anyone who breaks a branch or grazes his goats here
will suffer grievous harm.

It seems to work rather well. Gujar herdsmen with their
goats or cattle skirt the valley nervously, calling urgently or
throwing stones when an animal grazes too close to the
valley's edge. One result of this sacred conservation strategy
is that Mangarbani has become like a little outdoor museum
of what Delhi's Ridge – or at any rate, the steeper bits of it –
might have looked like without biotic pressure. In what way
is it different? Mainly in the sheer luxuriant presence of a
small, pretty tree that is locally called 'dhau'.

MANGARBANI in June,
when dhau is in new leaf.
The short, prostrate plants
in the foreground are dhau
that have been nibbled by
goats or cattle (on the
unprotected side of the
valley). All the trees in this
picture, even on the far
hillside, are dhau.

Dhau is a 'habitat specialist' and the quintessential tree of the rocky Aravallis. You can still find dhau growing in small, localized stands on the Central Ridge but it is clearly in retreat. Where it is not threatened by excessive grazing and competition – especially on steep, rocky slopes – dhau forms pure forests, defying all the pejorative value-judgements you hear about monocultures. Wonderfully pale green in new leaf at the hottest time of the year, and with beautifully mottled purple leaves just before they are shed, dhau is the most valuable tree of the Ridge flora.

The Ridge supports other trees not found in the rest of Delhi. Hingot, khair, kumttha, dhak, phulai and kareel are some of the trees superbly adapted to adverse conditions on the Ridge. But a few other Ridge species have disappeared completely. Two of them can still be seen in Mangarbani. One is the kala siris (*Albizia odoratissima*); the other is salai or the frankincense tree (*Boswellia serrata*), which only grows near the tops of steep valleys. Together with the kulu tree (*Sterculia urens*) and pisangan (*Grewia flavescens*), these are characteristic northern Aravalli trees that are certain to have once been part of Delhi's Ridge flora. Not any more.

MANGARBANI in April, when dhau is leafless. The Baba's shrine is on the right.

THE KULU tree has disappeared from the Delhi Ridge.

19TH-CENTURY DELHI

What was Delhi like before New Delhi was built? Two snapshots of Delhi – one from the mid-19th century, another early in the 1900s – will tell us enough to form a notion of how Delhi has changed, especially with regard to those places in the city where you would expect to find forests and trees.

The print (below) by A. Maclure is from the 1850s and depicts Shahjahanabad – the walled city of Delhi – from an imagined vantage point in the sky, across the river and east of the royal palace (the Red Fort today). You can clearly see the Jama Masjid and the great boulevard of Chandni Chowk stretching away to the west.

North of the city (at about 2 o'clock in relation to the palace), you can see the Northern Ridge, mostly bare and untenanted except for a military camp. East and south – in an arc between 10 and 1 o'clock to the palace – lie the ruins of earlier Delhis. Firozabad lies southwards just out of sight, but by a slight trick of perspective the Qutb is clearly seen, and Jai Singh's Jantar Mantar, like sketchy pyramids in the distance.

Contemporary accounts of the land lying south of Shahjahanabad agree that '…as far as the eye can stretch, the scene is the same – dust and crumbling stone, forgotten cities and forgotten dead'. There seems almost nothing there beyond the city walls, no forests or gardens. Fortunately, there is a corrective to this bleak picture, and it is instructive to see where Delhi's tended and untended tree-spaces lay at this time.

DELHI AND Surrounding Country by A. Maclure, 1857 (*By permission of the British Library, P-137*)

COL. JAMES SKINNER'S
GARDEN

THE RESIDENT'S
GARDEN

BAGH BEGUM
JAHANARA

ST. JAMES' CHURCH

BAGH BEGUM SAMRU

MAHTAB
BAGH

HAYAT BAKSH
BAGH

CHANDNI
CHOWK

RED FORT

JAMA
MASJID

BAGH
SHAMS-UD-DIN
KHAN

FATEHPURI
MASJID

TURKMAN
GATE

GARDENS in the
Walled City of
Shahjahanabad in
mid-19th century

INSIDE THE WALLED CITY

19th-century Delhi was heir to extensive charbaghs –
formal, rectangular Mughal gardens – laid out inside the
walled city from about the 1740s onwards. Most of these
gardens were small spaces enclosed within the high walls
of private havelis, the courtyard homes of Delhi's patrician
families. A few were large – Begum Bagh, laid out in
1650 north of Chandni Chowk by Shah Jahan's daughter
Jahanara Begum, was some 20 hectares in extent.

Inside the imperial palace lay the 2 most famous
charbaghs of Shahjahanabad – the Hayat Baksh (Life-
giving) and Mahtab Bagh (Moonlit Garden) – but by
this time they were already in a woeful state. In 1824,
Bishop Heber wrote: 'The gardens…must have been
extremely rich and beautiful… But all was, when we saw
it, dirty, lonely, and wretched: the bath and fountain dry:
the inlaid pavement hid with lumber and gardener's
sweepings, and the walls stained with the dung of birds
and bats.'

TREES OF CHARBAGHS

We know very little about
what trees were grown
inside Mughal charbaghs.
'Orange trees' are frequently
mentioned, but the term is a
loose one, and could have
referred to any one of 6 or 7
relatives or hybrids of the
orange. Like the royal
'orangeries' of 16th- and
17th-century European
gardens, charbaghs probably
grew an eclectic mix of
whichever citrus trees were
locally available. Other
likely trees would probably
have included the aam, bael,
champaka, neem, sand pear,
jamun, maulsari, lasora,
gondi, anar, kamrakh, amda,
chandni, kamini, adoo,
harshingar, badam, kachnar,
khirni and chikoo.

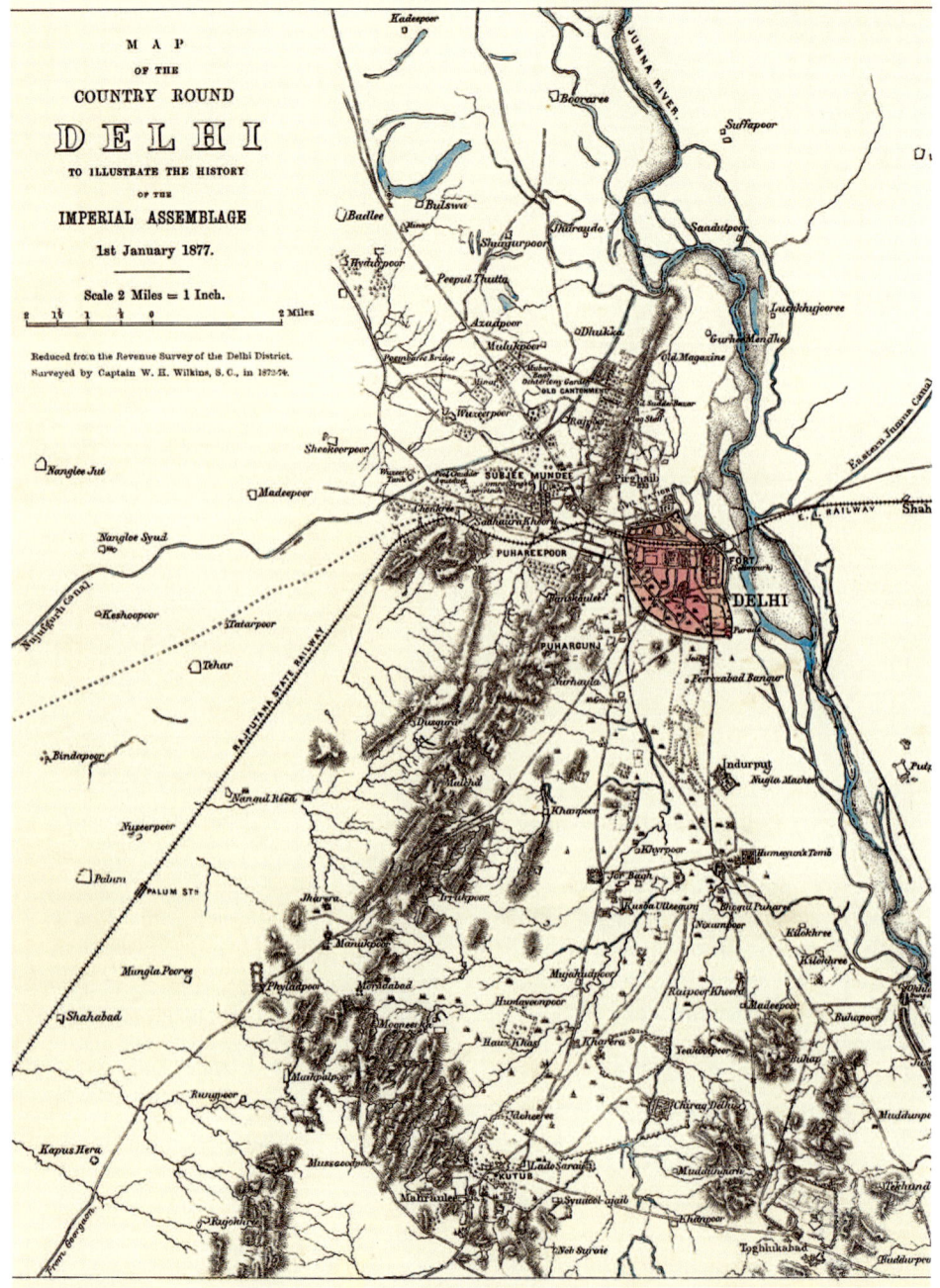

MAP OF THE COUNTRY ROUND

DELHI

TO ILLUSTRATE THE HISTORY

OF THE

IMPERIAL ASSEMBLAGE

1st January 1877.

Scale 2 Miles = 1 Inch.

Reduced from the Revenue Survey of the Delhi District.
Surveyed by Captain W. H. Wilkins, S. C., in 1873-74.

MAP OF DELHI in 1877 depicts the entire country south of the Walled City
virtually empty of habitation. The landform of the Ridge shows up prominently
along with the natural drainage which has changed significantly in the last century.

BEYOND THE CITY WALLS

By the 1850s, a few large English estates had begun to establish domain on or near the Northern Ridge. One was Thomas Metcalfe's grand residence overlooking the Yamuna, set amidst hundreds of acres – a thousand acres, according to one account – of garden. The Ridge itself was still mostly thin scrub jungle.

North-west of the walled city lay a dense patchwork of gardens and orchards forming the garden village of Sadhauran Kalan, a thousand hectares or so in extent. These gardens had come into being in the 17th century when the Mughal emperor Shah Jahan offered proprietors rent-free tenures as a deliberate incentive to plant trees on wasteland. This tract was watered by the canal bringing water to the city, and some famous Mughal gardens such as Roshanara Begum's Bagh were located here.

Two large gardens nestled up close to the city walls. Just beyond the Kabul Gate was Tees Hazari Bagh which had been planted around 1650 by Shah Jahan as a baghicha of neem trees (Could it *possibly* have had 30,000 trees, as its name suggests?). Close by, abutting Kashmiri Gate, was Qudsia Begum's Bagh, a large 18th-century walled garden along the banks of the river, with a mosque and fine baradari.

What of gardens south of the walled city? Most of them had fallen victim to unsettled times in the second half of the 18th century. Some had become small village settlements that cowered behind high walls, for safety – Humayun's tomb and Inderpat (the Purana Qila) are good examples. Mehrauli alone, by virtue of being a place of Sufi pilgrimage, held on to its baghs and tended green spaces.

1857

The Uprising was momentous for Delhi's trees because of various measures taken by the victors to fortify the city and secure it against 'another scare'. The palace (from now onwards known as 'the Fort') was emptied out and became the place of refuge for Delhi's British population. To house a permanent garrison inside, Shah Jahan's Moonlit Garden – the Mahtab Bagh – was swept away and a soldiers' barrack built in the place where it stood. There was extensive destruction at the periphery of the Fort, too. In order to gain a clear line of fire against any rebels who might think to storm the bastions, British authorities ordered the clearance of all structures in an arc 450 yards on all sides of the Fort walls (except for the river front). Before 1857, this area was dense with houses, mosques and gardens.

The same policy was adopted for the outer city walls – both Tees Hazari and Qudsia Bagh lost all trees standing within 500 yards of the ramparts. In and around Sabzi Mandi, which had been the scene of some of the fiercest fighting, thousands of trees were cut down. Sepoys had used the cover of bushes and trees from which to snipe at British positions on the Northern Ridge, and now a systematic destruction – almost a retribution – took place.

Inside the walled city, all royal properties were confiscated – among them Jahanara Begum's 20-hectare bagh north of Chandni Chowk, which now became the 'Queen's Garden' with a bandstand and serried beds of flowers 'tastefully laid out in the English style'. (In time, it acquired a 'well supplied menagerie', a cricket ground, 'a shady and picturesque promenade', and for a period, Indians were allowed in only at designated times on Wednesdays and Saturdays.)

Beyond the city walls, Roshanara Bagh was enlarged by joining it with smaller baghs, and from now on became almost an exclusive British preserve, a place for picnics, tea parties and buggy rides. Large chunks of Qudsia Bagh – badly battered in the seige – were hived off to make tennis courts and a rose garden and, nearby, a new garden was formed from land carved out from the Tees Hazari maidan.

THE EARLY 1900S

Delhi's historic gardens began to get facelifts for the first time early in the 20th century, including some gardens south of the walled city. Lord Curzon wrote to his wife in 1905:

> You remember Humayun's tomb? I had the garden restored, the water channels dug out and refilled and the whole place restored to its pristine beauty. I went to England last summer and, the eye of the master being away, the whole place has been allowed to revert. The garden has been let to a native and is now planted with turnips and the work of four years is thrown away! I shall drive out there, and woe betide the Deputy Commissioner whose apathy has been responsible...

The Hayat Baksh charbagh in the Red Fort received careful attention and work on excavating its water channels, and on its plants and shrubberies, proceeded so well that it was decided to throw a Royal Garden Party here for the Imperial Durbar of 1911.

TOMB OF the Emperor Humayun, painting by Seeta Ram – 1815 (*By permission of the British Library, Add.Or.4822*)

On 12 December 1911, King George V made the startling announcement at the Durbar that the seat of government would shift from Calcutta to 'the ancient Capital of Delhi'. At one stroke, it transformed a provincial town into an Imperial capital. At the same time, it condemned the walled city and its immediate suburbs to becoming a second-class city, eventually just 'Old Delhi'. Not all at once, of course. It would take some decades for the new city to be planned and built. But Old Delhi now suddenly seemed a poorer, more *rutputty* city in comparison, fraying at its edges and weighed down by history. A telling incident underlined its loss of stature.

CHANDNI CHOWK Painting by Seeta Ram – 1815
(*By permission of the British Library, Add.Or.4827*)

On 23 December 1912, the Viceroy, Lord Hardinge, made a ceremonial state entry into Delhi to mark the formal occupation of the new Imperial capital. His route led from the Railway Station, next to the Queen's Gardens, through the main avenue of the old Mughal city, Chandni Chowk. Hardinge and the Vicerene were seated on an elephant at the head of a grand procession. As they entered Chandni Chowk, a bomb was lobbed at his elephant and Hardinge was seriously, but not mortally, wounded. One of the direct consequences of the assassination attempt was that the rows of neem and peepal trees along Chandni Chowk were cut down and the canal flowing down its centre was bricked over. It wasn't just Shah Jahan's once-magnificent boulevard that was eviscerated. It signalled the superannuation of his capital city.

BEGUM SAMRU'S palace and tree-filled bagh are visible to the right of Chandni Chowk. Painted by Muzher Ally Khan – 1846 (*By permission of the British Library, Add.Or.4126*)

AVENUE TREES IN THE NEW CAPITAL

Captain George Swinton, Chairman of the Town-Planning Committee for the new capital, had this to say in his preliminary report (1912):

> Trees will be everywhere, in every garden however small it be, and along the sides of every roadway, and Imperial Delhi will be in the main a sea of foliage. It may be called a city, but it is going to be quite different from any city that the world has known…

Bear in mind that this was a much smaller version of New Delhi than we know today. British New Delhi – often called 'Lutyens' Delhi' after Sir Edwin Lutyens, the architect most famously associated with the grand plan – was built for a maximum of 57,000 people, including officials and subordinate staff, their families and servants, even the permanent inhabitants of bazars.

The first thing to notice about avenue trees in Lutyens' Delhi is that there are not very many species. If you discount a few species planted sparingly only along single avenues, there are only 8 kinds of trees repeated like handblock motifs.

You might also notice that many favourite north Indian avenue trees are missing. There are no mango trees, shisham or amaltas. The siris, saptaparni, semal, ashok, gulmohur, jarul, floss-silk tree and kosam – so common now – are all clearly later additions to New Delhi's avenues. There are no native Delhi trees among them either, except for the amaltas along Akbar Road – but these young trees are clearly a later addition.

So how and why did the planners and arboriculturists (clunky word, but that's what they were called then) of Imperial Delhi plumb for these *particular* tree species? Not all the details are clear, but the archival record suggests careful, premeditated intent.

AKBAR ROAD'S imli trees in April (*left*) and February (*right*) – just before the leaves are shed

When city planning went under way and the main arterial avenues of New Delhi were first being sketched in 1912-13, planners had to take into account the fact that the vistas were mostly flat and uninterrupted. South of the walled city, the eye swept 'a vast, manworn plain' littered with the crumbling debris of earlier, abandoned Delhis. All this would change, of course, when avenue trees had grown to maturity, and Capt. Swinton was well aware that 'our real difficulty in New Delhi is not going to be to hide ugly things but to prevent what we want to be seen from being hidden…' by the trees.

SOUTHEND ROAD in late May. It is the only avenue in Lutyens' Delhi planted with the mahua.

What sort of views did Swinton and Lutyens 'want to be seen'? Ancient 'architectural effects' such as Inderpat (the Purana Qila), the Lodi tombs and Safdarjang's mausoleum, mostly. Some new ones too, like the Viceroy's Palace (now Rashtrapati Bhavan). Trees were clearly desirable, but could – if they were not careful – become visual impediments, and the earliest planning documents about tree-planting in New Delhi show an awareness that the choice of species was of crucial importance.

The Final Report of the Town Planning Committee (1913) said:

> …the size of the special trees selected for the avenues determine the width of avenues in which they are to stand. For the purpose of getting the right effect from the design of an avenue both the size and shape of trees are of importance; and with this end in view the Committee have picked out 13 kinds of avenue trees out of a very large number, which will grow in Delhi… A deviation from the kind of tree selected to suit each avenue means a loss of a large general effect.

It is tempting to speculate about this shortlist of 13 species, but if you try and reconstruct the list by counting the *old* avenue trees still standing (those that were not planted within the last 50 years or so), you end up with a headcount that doesn't quite fit the magic figure of 13. (Turn to pp34-35 for a schematic map of the avenue trees in Lutyens' Delhi today, and a complete list of the tree species planted.)

What factors, other than 'size and shape', might have guided the planners in selecting these species? We can begin to understand why very large, spreading trees like the laurel fig or the kanju and banyan were (mostly) excluded from avenues and planted, if at all, only on large roundabouts. 'Too overpowering' is how one arboriculturist put it at the time. Meaning: too big, too blocky.

AVENUE TREES

The 8 mainline species:

JAMUN – on Tughlak, Rajaji, Tyagaraj Marg, etc.

NEEM – Safdarjang, Lodi, Prithviraj, Ashok Road, etc.

ARJUN – Janpath, and (mixed) on Teen Murti and M. Teresa Marg

IMLI – Akbar, Tilak, Pandit Pant Marg, and (mixed) along one stretch of M. Teresa Marg

SAUSAGE TREE – S. Bharati, Humayun, Amrita Shergil Marg, and (mixed) on Copernicus Marg

BAHEDA – Barakhamba, Sikandra, Rajendra Prasad Marg

PEEPAL – (mixed) on Baba Kharak Singh, Mandir Marg

PILKHAN - Zakir Hussain, Dalhousie Road

Less common species, confined mostly to single avenues, are:

PUTRANJIVA – Racecourse Road

MAHUA – Southend Road

JADI – Krishna Menon Marg

RIVER RED GUM – one short stretch of Tolstoy Marg

And spottily, mixed, not in 'pure' avenues:

KHIRNI – Maulana Azad and Man Singh Road

ULLOO – Copernicus Marg

BUDDHA'S COCONUT – Bishambar Das Marg

ANJAN – Pandara and Maulana Azad Marg

LAUREL FIG – one short stretch of Rajaji Marg

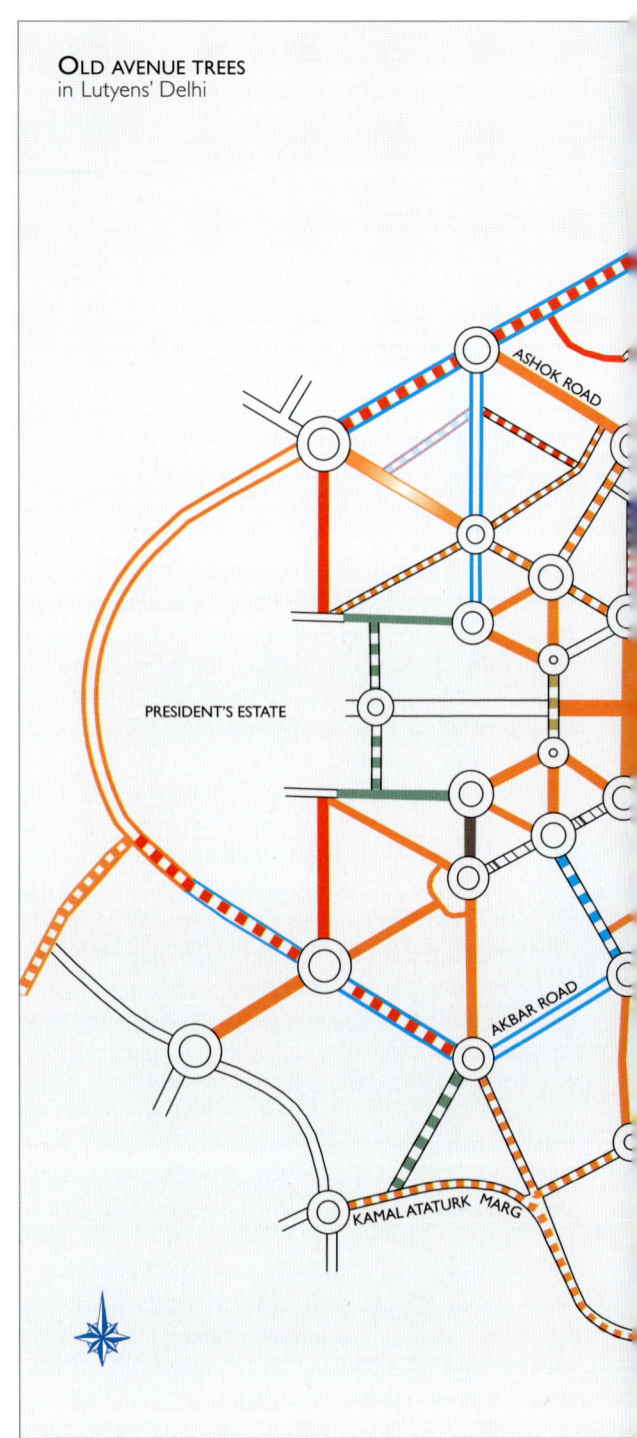

OLD AVENUE TREES
in Lutyens' Delhi

CONNAUGHT PLACE

BARAKHABHA ROAD

COPERNICUS MARG

TILAK MARG

INDIA GATE

RAJPATH

SHAHJAHAN ROAD

PRITHVIRAJ ROAD

LODI ROAD

JAMUN / RAI JAMUN

NEEM

ARJUN

IMLI

SAUSAGE TREE

BAHEDA

PEEPAL

PILKHAN

ANJAN MIXED WITH NEEM

ARJUN MIXED WITH IMLI

ARJUN MIXED WITH PEEPAL

BAHEDA MIXED WITH BUDDHA'S COCONUT

NEEM MIXED WITH JAMUN

SAUSAGE TREE MIXED WITH MAHARUKH

PUTRANJIVA

MAHUA

JADI

RIVER RED GUM

KHIRNI

CHIR

LAUREL FIG

SAPTAPARNI

NO OLD TREES LEFT

NEEM TREES on Tees January Marg (originally Albuquerque Road)

The archival record is rich with reports and memos by foresters, horticulturists – even civil servants with strong opinions – who argued for or against candidate species. One factor, above all, stands out – all their lists contain a clearly stated prejudice against deciduous trees that go bare and remain unsightly for some period in the dry season. That is clearly why the amaltas, mango, siris and shisham, for example, did not make the cut. Delhi's native trees too, remain conspicuously bare through the dry months and it is no surprise that none of them made the list. But there are many deciduous trees in the shortlist – the jamun and putranjiva excepted, all the others have a definite, albeit short, period when they shed their leaves. How might they have sneaked in? Was it, perhaps, a somewhat elastic criterion?

With hindsight, we can see that the planners and horticulturists made an elementary ecological miscalculation. Trees like the imli, arjun, neem or narikel behave like broadleaf evergreens when they are growing in moist forests or near river banks. When planted in Delhi, however, they must contend with a long period of drought. As we have seen, for most trees the most effective response to sustained drought is to drop their leaves.

So the people who planned New Delhi's avenue trees selected species that they believed to be evergreen, and weeded out candidate species that they knew to be deciduous. They got it egregiously wrong, and we are living with the consequences of their miscalculation. It is this criterion for selection that explains why some of the most familiar avenue trees of the Mughals were rejected. And why we have such a short list of avenue trees for Lutyens' Delhi.

LOOKING WEST across Lutyens' Delhi from the top of the Taj Mahal Hotel

LOOKING NORTH-EAST across the New Delhi Ridge. Rashtrapati Bhavan in the distance

THE AFFORESTATION OF THE CENTRAL RIDGE – POST-1911

The New Delhi or Central Ridge (it was called the Southern Ridge, at first) framed the new city to its west, and barely figured in initial plans until Hardinge had the impulse to place the Viceroy's residence on its highest eminence. Hardinge wrote to Lutyens in 1912:

> Can you imagine how splendid a white Government House with red tiles and a gilt dome would look in such a commanding situation, dominating the whole of the country round, while the slope from the situation of Government House down to the plain would be covered with terraces and fountains like a miniature Versailles?

Lutyens and the others on the Committee were not enthusiastic. To counter the argument that the Ridge was too barren, Hardinge asked 'the most capable forest officer [he] could find' to see if suitable trees could be identified for planting on the Ridge. The man Hardinge found was P.H. Clutterbuck, Conservator of Forests in the United Provinces.

Before the year was out, Hardinge had backed down and the Viceroy's House (Rashtrapati Bhavan) was eventually built on top of a decapitated hill at Raisena. But plans for afforesting the Ridge had been set in motion and Clutterbuck's list of 'suitable trees for the Ridge' was now ready.

Clutterbuck recommended that

> …all the usual species found in the drier parts of the sub-Himalayan forests of the UP would be suitable, but care should be taken to have a preponderance of ever-green species so that the Ridge would look green in the winter when deciduous trees are generally bare.

Even the driest parts of UP's sub-Himalayan forests are a lot wetter than the Ridge. By recommending 'a preponderance of ever-green species' for the most arid habitat in Delhi, Clutterbuck was making the same ecological miscalculation that planners had made (or were about to make) for New Delhi's avenue trees.

Shisham, for example, grows naturally in fresh alluvium deposited where Himalayan streams debouch into the plains. It tolerates drought but must have deep, loamy soil that retains moisture. It is not surprising that every attempt to plant it on the thin-soiled Ridge failed. The babool, too likes deep soil with underlying moisture and is quite at home in Delhi's dabar and khadar tracts. (Connaught Place was created by clearing a babool forest in the Maharaja of Jaipur's estate.) But on the Ridge, babool failed year after year. Foresters did not seem willing to learn from their mistakes.

Afforestation work on the New Delhi Ridge began in 1914 on an experimental plot of land only 202 acres in extent in (what is now) Chanakyapuri. By 1929, this had grown to over 1000 acres. The full story of trying to grow a forest on the New Delhi Ridge cannot be told here, but it is important to introduce one of Delhi's principal trees which made its entry through the afforestation work – this was the Central American mesquite or vilaiti keekar. The word 'vilaiti' means 'English', or loosely 'foreign', and was employed to distinguish it from the keekar, which is just another name for the babool. (The name 'vilaiti keekar' has slipped somewhat, and many people mistakenly call it 'keekar' now.) Within a very short time – no more than a few decades – vilaiti keekar would come to dominate Delhi's tree flora and become the principal cause for a number of native species on the Ridge edging towards local extinction. Its success was startling, and Delhi has paid a high price for its introduction.

DELHI TODAY

A lot has happened to Delhi in the second half of the 20th century. The population of the twin cities exploded after Independence in 1947, and the frenetic development that followed has seen the city teeter on the brink of environmental crisis. The Yamuna river is little more than a trickle of raw sewage now. The water table has plummeted, and the aquifers are dangerously tainted with toxins. Delhi's air is thick with the belched emissions of more vehicles than all the other 4 Indian metropolitan cities combined.

NEW DELHI today, seen from across the river, looking west. A modern 'Mughal perspective' by Golak Khandual

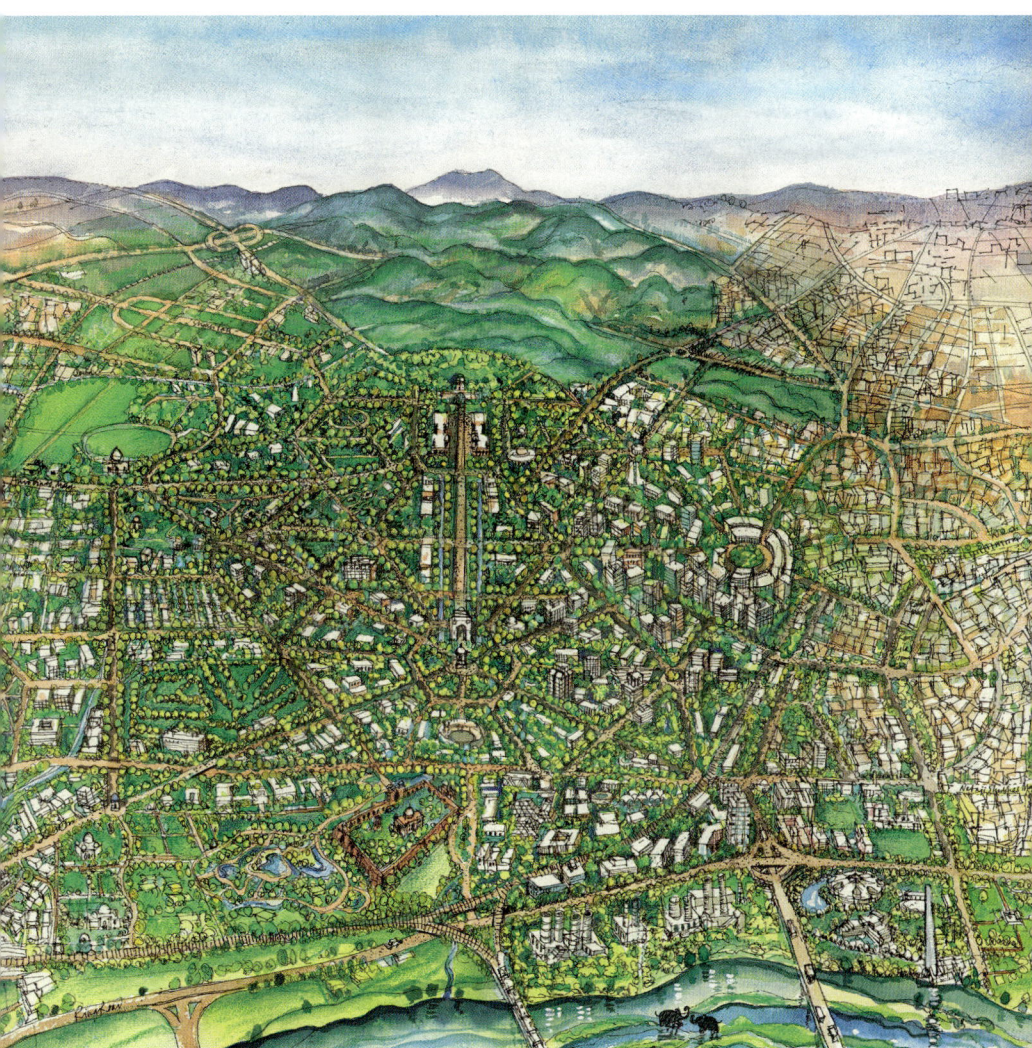

THE VIEW south-west, towards the Secretariat and Rashtrapati Bhavan

Like canaries in a mineshaft, one might expect the city's trees to have become early casualties in this dreadful unfolding of cause and effect. That this did not happen is a tribute to Delhi's civic authorities. Large parts of the city – particularly the core of Lutyens' Delhi – remain verdant and densely treed. Every one of the historic gardens that were restored early in the century has survived. This is no small achievement in the face of an intense hunger for land.

On the other hand, it is possible to see clear signs of the end of the garden city concept. As the city has expanded outwards, it is as though both trees and parks have been designed to diminish progressively and in ever-widening circles from New Delhi, the centre of power and affluence. There are hardly any trees at all where the edges of the city curl upwards into high-rise conurbations.

Trees will not, of course, solve Delhi's ecological problems. But while we search for the will and means to undo what we have done, trees are balm and salve to our mistakes. They are witnesses to our foolish tinkering with nature, embellishments of our dour cities, symbols of renewal and growth, our reasons for hope and for keeping faith. That is reason enough.

WHERE TO GO TREE SPOTTING IN DELHI

WALKS IN SEMI-WILDERNESS AREAS

The Ridge – all 4 segments of it – is easily the best place to go looking for native Delhi trees, even though vilaiti keekar has done a pernicious job of edging out a great number of its indigenous trees. The sandy ravines near village Mandi are distinctive enough from the rest of the stony Ridge to deserve a ramble, too.

Many parks have been carved out of the Ridge – Buddha Jayanti Park and Mahavir Vanasthali in the Central Ridge, Kamla Nehru Park on the Northern Ridge and Sanjay Vana in the South-central Ridge. While they are planted mostly with ornamental trees, all of them contain swathes of natural landscape.

SHADY DELL in the Central Ridge

A large portion of Hauz Khas District Park is semi-wild and contains lots of relict bangar trees. Jahanpanah city forest and pockets of JNU campus are also good places for semi-wilderness walks. Tughlaqabad can be interesting, too, but has a somewhat dangerous reputation. Asola and Bhatti wildlife sanctuaries, managed by the forest department, are not as interesting as you might expect, but will almost certainly improve gradually.

PUBLIC PARKS AND GARDENS

South Delhi

Lodi Garden is the most rewarding park to go tree-spotting in, with over 110 species of trees and a good tree-spotting map on offer. Other good places in South Delhi are Jamali Kamali and the Ladha Sarai area; the Qutb compound, which has some wonderful old

HUMAYUN'S TOMB gardens were restored in 2004, but have many old trees.

trees; all the major historic gardens like those inside the Purana Qila, Talkatora Garden, Safdarjang's Tomb and Humayun's Tomb. The latter has been lovingly restored, along with the water channels of the old charbagh.

It is also worth exploring the zoo, Hauz Khas District Park (quite apart from the semi-wild parts), Nehru Park, the Nehru Memorial Museum, Delhi Golf Club, and Siri Fort Park. Sundar Nursery is about 90 acres in extent and has a large collection of unusual trees. Pragati Maidan and Hauz Rani City Forest are of some interest. The Garden of Five Senses at Said-ul-Ajaib is young and promises much. Spread over 20 acres, and conceived as a public leisure space that evokes a sensory response, it has thematic gardens with a mix of original and introduced vegetation. The Mughal Gardens at Rashtrapati Bhavan are a big draw in February-March, but the rest of the President's Estate, even if it is hard to gain access to, is actually better for tree-spotting.

North Delhi

Roshanara Bagh is fraying at the edges, but is still a lovely place for spotting some old and unusual trees. Shalimar Gardens enclose extensive orchards which grow many kinds of fruit trees that are relatively rare in the rest of Delhi. Qudsia Bagh is worth visiting even though it has not stopped shrinking since the middle of the 19th century. The Red Fort gardens are a little too manicured, perhaps, but the contiguous Samadhi gardens stretching from Rajghat northwards to Shanti Vana and Vijay Ghat are good for an update on popular ornamental and flowering trees. Delhi University has some fine trees. The Purdah Garden, reserved for women, near the Red Fort has always intrigued me, but someone will have to tell me what lies inside.

ROSHANARA BAGH is a relict of a 17th-century Mughal estate and garden, but was reorganized and replanted to suit English tastes in the late 19th century.

TREE GUIDE

JAMUN-LIKE LEAVES *Widest near the middle*

With milky latex

pointy tip

glossy; edges wavy

maulsari
15 cm p48

tip notched or blunt

glossy, leathery

khirni
12 cm p138

pointy at both ends

chikoo
14 cm p47

tip blunt or notched

arranged in whorls

saptaparni
22 cm p142

tip pointy

secondary veins arching

batino
40 cm p47

tip blunt

glossy, leathery, darker on top

katthal
24 cm p144

softly hairy when young

short, pointy tip

mahua
24 cm p140

densely hairy, esp. below

base rounded

mysore fig
22 cm p50

blunt tip

base cup-shaped

krishna fig
20 cm p51

densely woolly when young

narrow at both ends

south indian mahua
19 cm p53

pointy tip

thin, leathery, dull

narrow at both ends

frangipani
50 cm p130

tip blunt, notched, rarely short, pointy

glossy dark-green on top

hairy or not below (depends on variety)

white frangipani
35 cm p132

blunt tip

3 nerves at base

goolar
18 cm p56

narrow at both ends

very rough on both sides

sandpaper tree
12 cm p136

pointy tip

leaves in opposite pairs

shiny on top

chandni
13 cm p129

main nerves white

3 nerves at base

pilkhan
22 cm p100

blunt tip

glossy, smooth

base narrow

laurel fig
9 cm p54

golden hairy below

base rounded

satin leaf
10 cm p53

short, pointy tip

glossy, stiff, leathery

glossy, often toothed

india rubber tree
28 cm p52

finely toothed

ban naranga
25 cm p60

rough on top, woolly below

badhal
40 cm p50

Without milky latex, margins toothed

tiny, rounded
teeth

base
often
unequal

chilla
18 cm p60

fewer
teeth near
base

pointy tips

3 nerves
at base

khirk
9 cm p61

surface
very rough

teeth large,
distant,
sometimes
absent

harshingar
13 cm p68

teeth
blunt

base deeply
heart-shaped

mahoe
24 cm p63

teeth
sharp,
forward
pointing

densely
woolly
below

grey oak
16 cm p62

teeth
blunt, soft

smooth
when
mature

chukka
30 cm p62

teeth small,
close, blunt

pania
20 cm p63

teeth
small

stalk
very
short

freshwater mangrove
21 cm p144

narrow at
both ends

teeth
very
fine

stalk
very
short

ramdhan champa
13 cm p66

leaves also
with 3
leaflets

**chestnutleaf
trumpet-bush**
18 cm p199

teeth
distant,
faint

smooth,
glossy
surface

unequal
at base

putranjiva
10 cm p108

tip blunt
or pointy

toothed
only when
young

kanju
15 cm p64

very
finely
toothed

more or
less smooth

no glands

almond
13 cm p66

dark, glossy
on top

3 nerves
at base

white,
tawny
below

ber
7 cm p67

rough and
leathery

3 basal
nerves

lasora
12 cm p75

thinly
leathery
texture

teeth
sometimes
obscure

2 round
glands at top
of short stalk

hollock
28 cm p69

JAMUN-LIKE LEAVES

Without milky latex, margins not toothed

tip usually pointy
very variable in shape
velvety when young

chamrod
20 cm p70

blunt or notched tip
hairy when young

crape myrtle
8 cm p74

tip blunt or short-pointy
firm, nearly smooth

thai crape myrtle
22 cm p76

densely hairy when young

leza
35 cm p75

tip pointy or blunt
smooth, shiny on both sides

jarul
30 cm p72

smooth on both surfaces

5-7 nerves at base

buddha's coconut
40 cm p84

smooth, shiny on top
arching, parallel nerves

kadamb
30 cm p80

curved, leathery, thick

4-6 main veins

earpod wattle
18 cm p82

thick, firm, shiny

narrow at both ends

southern magnolia
20 cm p83

pointy tip
edges wavy

golden champak
25 cm p83

shiny, paler on top
3-5 nerves at base

camphor laurel
10 cm p113

tip blunt, notched or pointy

velvety below

khasai
20 cm p85

leathery when mature
white-woolly below
2 glands

harra
23 cm p92

tip notched
citrusy smell
sometimes lobed

atalantia
10 cm p88

young leaves silky
old leaves turn red

dhau
6 cm p90

softly velvety when young
base faintly heart-shaped

bistendu
12 cm p78

softly hairy underneath
stalk very short

guava tree
15 cm p85

smooth, flat, shiny surface
veins parallel

kauri pine
15 cm p88

tip pointy or blunt
smooth, shiny, softly leathery

leaves broader than jamun's

rai jamun
22 cm p89

tip pointy or blunt
stalk often grooved

jamun
16 cm p86

smooth on top; bluish white below

benteak
10 cm p76

edges wavy
shiny on top

anar
10 cm p92

badhara bush
5 cm p159

blunt tip
lightly hairy on both sides

shareefa
15 cm p69

CHIKOO *Manilkara zapota*

sapodilla • chicle • sapote • naseberry

chikoo

chikoo family

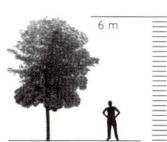

Small tree; evergreen

Bark brown or greyish, not very rough; exudes milky latex from wounds

Leaves clustered at ends of twigs, glossy, pointed at both ends; 7.5-15 cm long

Flowers small, bell-like, on slender stalks from leaf axils; petals pale green

Fruit variable, egg-shaped, about 6-10 cm in diameter; with a scurfy, brown skin; flesh soft, brownish yellow, gritty

A large evergreen tree from tropical America, with spirally arranged glossy leaves, that produces the familiar chikoo fruit. We only know it here in cultivation as a modest-sized tree. Its main commercial product is not so much the fruit as the milky latex – 'chicle' – which was once the main ingredient of chewing gum.

WHERE TO SEE IT Fairly common in private gardens, nurseries and N Delhi orchards.

BATINO *Alstonia macrophylla*

batino • hard alstonia

no local name

frangipani/oleander family

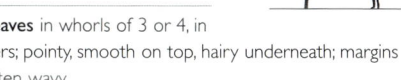

Smallish tree; evergreen

Bark greyish, relatively smooth

Leaves in whorls of 3 or 4, in tiers; pointy, smooth on top, hairy underneath; margins often wavy

Flowers small, tubular, with 5 pure-white petals

Fruit thin, bean-like, in clusters

A slender tree with a thin crown and glossy leaves, unmistakably related to the saptaparni. Its leaves are longer and thinner, but like the saptaparni, are also whorled. Native to the Malay Peninsula and Indonesia, batino was successfully introduced to Bangalore as a street tree but struggles in Delhi's climate.

WHERE TO SEE IT Lodi Garden and Nehru Park have a few trees; one prominent tree outside No. 11 Kautilya Marg.

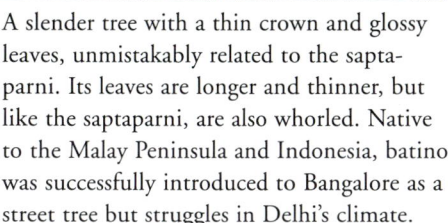

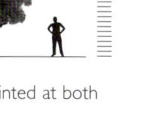

MAULSARI *Mimusops elengi*

indian medlar • spanish cherry • (asian) bulletwood

chikoo family

maulsari • maulshree • bakul

Middle-sized tree; more or less evergreen

Bark nut-brown or greyish, deeply fissured and cracked

Leaves 5-15 cm long, glossy on top; wavy-edged

Flowers white, fragrant, with numerous narrow petals

Fruit a berry, green at first, turning red-yellow when ripe

12 m

petals in the outer circle are narrow but more numerous

A middle-sized tree, branching low and forming a dense, dark, glossy head. Reputedly evergreen, it goes through a some-what lean phase in Delhi early in March. A quintessential tree of Mughal Gardens, where it is pruned and shaped to look like a toy tree. Common in Delhi's parks and gardens but not often used along avenues.

SEASONS - LEAVES nearly evergreen; most trees thin out in March. New leaf in late April, pale green, contrasting prettily with the older leaves. **FLOWERS** in May-June; another flush in the rains. **FRUIT** from February to June.

WHERE TO SEE IT The Mughal Gardens in Rashtrapati Bhavan. In the parking lot of Buddha Jayanti Park; planted along San Martin Marg (Chanakyapuri); at the western end of Rajpath, abutting Vijay Chowk. Most large parks have specimens. There are some large trees in Humayun's Tomb gardens and in the Red Fort.

FLOWERS white, 1-2 cm wide, solitary or 2-6 in a cluster, highly fragrant. The flower has a short tube crowned by 2 circles of narrow petals totalling about 24 – the inner circle with 8-10 petals, the outer with twice that number.

leaves taper at
both ends;
apex pointy

LEAVES 5-15 cm long,
smooth, glossy above, matte beneath. The
midrib often forms a deep valley, and the
edges of the leaf are conspicuously wavy.
The secondary nerves are very faint.

margins of
the leaf are
wavy

FRUIT an olive-shaped
berry about 3 cm long,
green with short, matted
hair when young, maturing
smooth, orange-red. The
yellow floury pulp inside is
edible. The pointy
segments of the flower-
cup persist on the fruit.

BARK dark brown
or greyish, deeply
cracked and ridged,
somewhat like the
bark of the khirni.

HABITAT A slow-
growing tree that does
best in warm, slightly
moist climates – Delhi
is too dry for best
results. Also found on
the coast in rocky
locations but ideally
requires deep, fertile
soil. It can withstand
waterlogging for up to
2 months in the year. It
is somewhat frost-
tender, but tolerates
shade well.

RANGE Native to the
W Ghats and Sri Lanka,
extending westwards to
the Andamans,
Myanmar, Thailand,
Malaysia and Vietnam,
and possibly parts of
Cambodia and Indo-
nesia as well. Widely
cultivated in India and
Pakistan but not much
further north than
Lahore and Delhi.

USES A traditional ittar
(perfume from the
essential oil) is distilled
from maulsari flowers.
Many parts of the tree
are used medicinally –
the leaves to treat head-
aches and sore eyes; a
decoction of the bark to
treat fevers, diarrhoea
and infections of the
gum; the unripe fruit
for fixing loose teeth;
and the crushed seeds to
cure constipation. Oil
from the seeds is used
in cooking and as a
luminant fuel. The
reddish heartwood is
hard, strong, close-
grained and durable
and is used for bridge-
building, boats, mine
props and heavy
construction.

◣ BADHAL *Artocarpus lacucha*

monkey jack • lakooch

badhal • *dheu*

mulberry/fig family

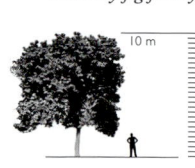

Middle-sized tree; deciduous

Bark brown, unremarkable

Leaves up to 40 cm long, rough on top, densely woolly underneath; margins have tiny rounded teeth

Flowers appear on leafless branches in March-April; male flowers fleshy, orange yellow, quickly shed; female flowers reddish, in round heads [see pic below]

Fruit up to 13 cm wide, lumpy, yellow, velvety

A middle-sized tree with densely woolly leaves, forming an untidy canopy. It bears separate male and female flowers and small, curiously misshapen, velvety fruit. Once cultivated in orchards in N Delhi, it has become rare in the city. Native to the sub-Himalayan terai, Sri Lanka and Malaysia.

WHERE TO SEE IT
Cultivated in Shalimar Bagh. 2 trees in Sapru House. Also in the NISCOM nursery (IARI) and the forest department nursery on the N Ridge.

◣ MYSORE FIG *Ficus drupacea* var. *pubescens* Syn: *Ficus mysorensis*

mysore fig • hairy fig • brown-woolly fig • drupe fig • red fig

dholobarh (assamese) • *paras peepal*

mulberry/fig family

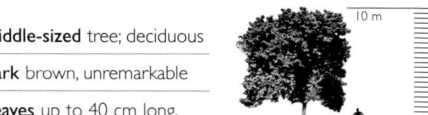

Large tree; deciduous

Aerial roots thin, few, short, not reaching the ground

Bark thick, grey, more or less smooth

Leaves and stalks densely furry, especially when young; oval, pointy, about 20 cm long; base rounded or faintly heart-shaped [see pic below]

Figs without stalks, usually in pairs, orange when ripe

A strangler fig with a large canopy, not as large as a banyan, with only a few short aerial roots wrapped around its trunk. Its new leaves and shoots are intensely hairy. Native to sub-Himalayan tracts in E India and the Deccan, the mysore fig is occasionally planted for ornament and shade.

WHERE TO SEE IT
A short row in Buddha Jayanti Park near the Bodhi tree; 2 fairly large trees in Sundar Nursery. Here and there in large parks, but not common.

KRISHNA FIG *Ficus benghalensis* var. *krishnae*

krishna fig • krishna's (butter-)cup

makkhan katora • krishna badh

Middle-sized tree; deciduous

Aerial roots occasional, thin, wiry, but no prop-roots

Bark grey, dull, with faint horizontal wrinkles

Leaves diagnostic, cup-shaped, forming a 'pocket' at base; upper surface of leaf forms the 'outside' of the pocket; underside velvety

Figs single or paired, from leaf axils, without stalks; velvety, deep rose or red when ripe

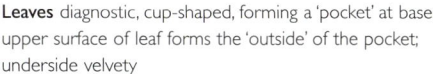

A smaller version of the banyan tree, with unique cup-forming 'pitcher' leaves. It was first described as a new species around 1900 but was later recognized to be a 'bud-sport' or mutant variety of the banyan. It is beginning to be widely grown as a 'conversation piece' in large gardens.

this is the undersurface of the leaf

LEAF POCKET found on all the leaves of the tree without exception. Unlike 'pitcher' leaves, the pocket is formed on the underside of the leaf.

>> In Which the Krishna Fig Is Identified – see p335

FIGS somewhat flattened, and grow without stalks in leaf axils, either solitary or in pairs. They are usually about 14 mm in diameter, with a soft, velvety skin.

SEASONS - **LEAVES** thin out in late February and trees look straggly till mid May.
FIGS March to June and again after the rains.

WHERE TO SEE IT Vir Bhumi has a large grove of Krishna figs. Individual trees in most large parks such as Lodi Garden and Buddha Jayanti Park.

INDIA RUBBER TREE *Ficus elastica*

(india) rubber tree • assam rubber • caoutchouc tree

no local name • *attah bor* (assamese & bengali)

mulberry/fig family

14 m

Large tree; evergreen

Aerial roots thin, scanty

Bark grey or brown, exuding milky latex when cut

Leaves firm, leathery, large, up to 30 cm long; colours of cultivars vary but natural leaf is dark, glossy green on top, dull and paler beneath; tiny point at apex; leaf-buds single, bright red, up to 15 cm long

Figs in pairs, small, stalkless, yellow-green when ripe

LEAF-BUDS – the easiest way to tell a rubber tree from another fig tree is by its leaf-bud – the thin, papery scale which sheaths the young leaf and then falls off. All other Delhi fig trees have small leaf-buds in pairs – the rubber tree has only one, and it is bright pink and so long that you can see it from a great distance.

A large evergreen strangler fig with thin aerial roots reaching 50 m or more in Assam but only about 14 m in Delhi. Its large, glossy leaves and bright-red leaf-buds are distinctive. Native to moist forests in NE India, it is seen most often in Delhi as a potted plant in various hybrid forms.

leaf-bud

secondary veins run parallel, united by a looping vein running just inside the leaf margin

>> Indoor Rubbers – see p337
A Potted History of India Rubber – see p324

AERIAL ROOTS thin and vestigial, though in its natural moist habitat, it sometimes behaves more like a strangler fig with thicker air-roots.

SEASONS - LEAVES evergreen but renewed from February onwards, right through the rainy season. The bright-red leaf-buds are particularly prominent at this time.

FIGS start to ripen in June.

WHERE TO SEE IT Talkatora swimming pool has a row of large trees on its perimeter. Grown in the hedgerow of the National Gallery of Modern Art. Common as a potted and indoor plant.

SOUTH INDIAN MAHUA *Madhuca longifolia* var. *longifolia*

south indian mahua
no local name

chikoo family

Medium-sized; semi-evergreen

Bark grey-brown with a hint of yellow

Leaves crowded at the ends of branches; 19 cm long; slender, narrowed at both ends, edges wavy; densely hairy at first, becoming smooth

Flowers creamish, succulent, fleshy, similar to mahua's

Fruit a green berry about 5 cm long; variable in shape; not seen in Delhi

A handsome tree with spreading branches and slender mango-like leaves, from moist forests in SW India and Sri Lanka. It is not well known in N India but in Shanti Vana, where it was first planted in Delhi, commands attention with its bronzed new foliage and beautiful form.

WHERE TO SEE IT 4 or 5 trees in Shanti Vana and Shakti Sthal; a solitary tree in Mahavir Vanasthali in the C Ridge.

SATIN LEAF *Chrysophyllum oliviforme*

satin leaf • damson plum • olive plum • wild star-apple
no local name

chikoo family

Smallish tree; deciduous

Bark thin, light reddish-brown, scaly; exudes milky latex when injured

Leaves stiff, about 10 cm long, more or less oval; deep green on top, silky golden brown below [see pic below]

Flowers small, white, not conspicuous [see pic at left]

Fruit olive-like, fleshy, 1-seeded, purplish

A middle-sized, ornamental tree grown mainly for its striking 2-toned leaves, stunted and unhappy in Delhi's climate. The leaves are glossy deep green on top, coppery and densely furry beneath. Native to hot, humid parts of the Caribbean, where it is sometimes planted as a street tree. Very rare in Delhi.

WHERE TO SEE IT Only one specimen, in Sundar Nursery, near the cut-flowers section.

LAUREL FIG *Ficus microcarpa*

Syn: Ficus retusa

laurel fig • indian laurel • chinese/malayan banyan • cuban laurel • curtain/glossy-leaf fig
usba • chilkhan • nandan

mulberry/fig family

Large tree; evergreen

Aerial roots thick, few, not reaching the ground or becoming prop-roots

Bark pale grey, smooth, marked with horizontal dots; exuding milky latex when bruised

Leaves about 8 cm long, glossy, oval, blunt, thick; leaf-buds small, about one cm long

Figs small, in pairs; yellow-brown when ripe

>> The Laurel Fig and Its Hybrids – see p337

FIGS less than one cm in diameter, in axillary pairs. Very pale at first, paperbag-brown when ripe, with a faint, darker aureole around the apex.

A large evergreen tree with a dominating presence, usually with a few aerial roots wrapped around the top of a short, grey trunk. The dense, glossy canopy grows to a massive size, with spreading branches cantilevered such as to defy common sense. Cultivated in Delhi mainly in roundabouts and bungalows in Lutyens' precincts.

the aureoles stand out pink when the figs are young

SEASONS - LEAVES evergreen, but new flush visible in March, distinctly pale green against the older, darker leaves. **FIGS** produced in repeated flushes from April through August.

WHERE TO SEE IT In front of Rashtrapati Bhavan, the scheme spilling over into the forecourts of the Secretariat buildings. Large specimens in some of the bungalows in Rashtrapati Bhavan and on the large roundabout in front of 10 Janpath (Windsor Circle). Stray specimens in large parks like Lodi Garden (a big one near the Sheesh Gumbad), but it is – somewhat surprisingly – hardly used else-where in Delhi as an avenue tree.

LEAVES on short stalks, about 8 cm long on average, more or less oval with a rounded or blunt apex and narrow base. The leaf blade is thick in texture, with scarcely visible veins, and is polished and shiny (when not dusty). The leaf-buds are only about one cm long.

BARK pale grey, more or less smooth. If you look closely, you will see a distinctive 'Morse code' pattern of lenticels on the bark. The aerial roots are short and thick, and are often fused with the main trunk.

THE GRAND ceremonial driveway leading from the gates of Rashtrapati Bhavan to the Jaipur Column and beyond is lined with majestic laurel fig trees.

HABITAT An epiphytic 'strangler' like the banyan, but only in the wild. In Malaysia, it is found on the banks of tidal rivers at the precise places where brackish water gives way to fresh water. There it develops elaborate prop-roots like the banyan, but this is not known to happen in Indian forests, where its aerial roots can grow into long curtains but do not reach the ground. It is reasonably drought-tolerant, and grows in a variety of well-drained soils.

RANGE Within the subcontinent, native to the sub-Himalayan tract from Kumaon eastwards to Assam, the Sundarbans, Bangladesh, Myanmar and the Andamans; southwards through C India to Sri Lanka. It extends through SE Asia and S China to tropical Australia and the islands of the SW Pacific.

USES Its pounded leaves and bark are applied as a poultice in rheumatic headaches, and to wounds and bruises. The juice of the bark (in milk) is regarded as useful in liver disease. The timber is unusual among fig trees for being moderately hard, pale reddish-grey and beautifully mottled, but is seldom used. It is best known as an evergreen avenue tree, capable of casting a dense shade over an immense area.

CAN BE CONFUSED WITH

The weeping fig. The basic differences are:
Weeping fig leaf ends in a short but prominent, pointy apex; it has few or no aerial roots; its figs are larger and bright yellow or orange-red.
Laurel fig leaves have a round or bluntly pointed apex; it has aerial roots that do not hang down; and its tiny figs are yellowish brown.

GOOLAR *Ficus racemosa*

Syn: Ficus glomerata

cluster fig • country/red river/redwood/blue fig • crattock

mulberry/fig family

goolar • umar • umri • trimbal • lelka • dimeri • batbar • palak • daduri

Middle-sized tree; deciduous

Bark greyish yellow or rusty, with milky sap

Leaves 18 cm long, leathery, tapering at both ends; 3 strong veins from base; toothed when young

Figs in large clusters from trunk or main branches; figs stalked, woolly, reddish when ripe

12 m

FIGS grow in large clusters directly from the trunk or main branches (unlike most other figs which grow in the axils of leafy twigs). Each fig is 2-3 cm wide with a short stalk and is more or less spherical – older figs may be somewhat flattened near their apices. Ripe figs are softly woolly with a strong skein of veins just visible under the translucent skin.

An attractive fig tree with a crooked trunk and open, spreading crown. This one is not a 'strangler' and has no aerial roots. The red, furry figs are distinctive – arranged in short, branching clusters growing from the trunk or main branches. Widely distributed especially near water, the goolar qualifies as a native Delhi tree.

SEASONS - LEAVES evergreen near a perennial source of water. Otherwise, leaves shed in January; leafless till early March. **FIGS** often produced in 2 crops, one in March-April and the second in the rains.

WHERE TO SEE IT Seldom, if ever, cultivated, but present in many parks and gardens. Once plant- ed along the Western Jumna Canal near Bawana village and along the Mehrauli-Badarpur Road, but few survive. The largest goolar in Delhi is probably one growing next to a pond in Jaunapur village. There is a good specimen in a little garden abutting the Jama Masjid.

young figs are green and turn red or orange when ripe •

LEAVES 9-13 cm long, thin and with a few irregular teeth at first, gradually becoming leathery and dark on their upper surface, duller and paler below. They lose their teeth as they mature. There are always 3 strong yellow nerves starting from the base.

the leaves are arranged alternately on the twigs

the 3 basal veins are more prominent on the undersurface

young leaves with their 'baby teeth'

BARK variable in colour – creamy, yellow, pinkish, silvery grey or rusty – yet unmistakable once you have learned to recognize it. Relatively smooth, becoming somewhat scaly with age.

CAN BE CONFUSED WITH

None of the other figs, simply because its branched clusters of figs are so distinctive. When the tree has no figs, its leaves can perhaps be mistaken for a pilkhan's but this requires a little imagination!

HABITAT According to folk wisdom, there runs a hidden stream under every goolar tree. This is not unfounded – the goolar is a 'riparian' tree, growing naturally near streams or ponds in moist, clayey loams. It is conspicuously absent in arid regions. The goolar is not a 'strangler' and is never epiphytic on other trees.

RANGE Allied species of clustering figs are found in Africa but this is the only species to have reached Asia. It has spread throughout tropical Asia from India to Australia, avoiding only the driest parts.

USES Most parts of the tree are used in traditional healing. An astringent lotion made from the bark is credited with treating deep wounds inflicted by a tiger's claws. The dried leaves are powdered as a cure for bilious afflictions. The figs are carminative and the milky latex is used to treat piles and diarrhoea. The figs are not often eaten but some forest-dwelling communities seem to relish it. The leaves make an excellent fodder. Its soft, fibrous timber is not durable except underwater. It has little practical utility but is one of the few kinds of wood prescribed in ancient Hindu scriptures for the sacrificial fire. The tree too is sacred.

HOW TO DISTINGUISH BETWEEN

DELHI'S FIG TREES

With 14 species, the figs are Delhi's most diverse genus of trees, though only a few are truly native to this particular region. Despite their affinities, they are not difficult to tell apart. Use this guide to distinguish between the species by looking out for certain key characters.

——— TREES WITH AERIAL ROOTS ———

BANYAN *Ficus benghalensis* (pp102-03)

Long aerial roots, forming **PROPS**
Leaves up to 20 cm long, broad, with rounded base; velvety when young
Figs without stalks, in pairs from leaf axils; **RED** when ripe

KRISHNA FIG *Ficus benghalensis* var. *krishnae* (p51)

May have slender, wiry aerial roots, but no props
Leaves 15-20 cm long, uniquely **CUP-SHAPED** at base; **BASE NARROW**; velvety, especially underneath
Figs without stalks, single or paired, from leaf axils; deep rose or red when ripe

MYSORE FIG *Ficus drupacea* (p50)

Aerial roots thin, few, short, not reaching the ground
Leaves about 20 cm long, leathery, with pointy tip; base faintly heart-shaped; leaves and leaf stalk **DENSELY HAIRY** especially when young, becoming smoother when mature
Figs without stalks, in pairs; orange when ripe

JADI *Ficus amplissima* (p98)

Aerial roots dense, wrapped around top of trunk
Bark pale **YELLOW-GREEN**
Leaves up to 20 cm, leathery, with a short-pointy tip
Figs **WITHOUT STALKS**, in pairs, deep **PURPLE** when ripe

PILKHAN *Ficus virens* (pp100-01)

Aerial roots dense, trailing or wrapped around trunk
Bark with a **SILVERY SHEEN**
Leaves up to 24 cm, leathery, with a long-pointy tip
Figs **STALKED**, in pairs, **WHITE** with red dots when ripe

LAUREL FIG *Ficus microcarpa* (pp54-55)

Few aerial roots, not reaching the ground or becoming props
Leaves **SMALL**, 8 cm long, glossy, oval, thick, with **BLUNT TIP**
Figs **SMALL**, in pairs; yellow-brown when ripe

WEEPING FIG *Ficus benjamina* (p99)

Aerial roots few, slender, not forming props
Leaves glossy, smooth, variable in size; base
rounded; **POINTY TIP, TWISTED** to one side
Figs stalkless, in pairs, **ORANGE** or **RED**
(depending on variety)

INDIA RUBBER TREE *Ficus elastica* (p52)

Aerial roots dense, forming props only in moist conditions
Leaf **FIRM**, leathery, broad, up to 30 cm long; glossy, dark green on
top; short-pointy tip; **LEAF-BUDS BRIGHT PINK**, up to 15 cm long
Figs in pairs, small, stalkless, yellow-green when ripe (not often
seen in Delhi)

TREES WITHOUT AERIAL ROOTS

GOOLAR *Ficus racemosa*
(pp56-57)

The only fig tree in Delhi
with its figs in **BRANCHING,
LEAFLESS CLUSTERS** directly
from trunk or main branches; figs woolly, pear-shaped,
red when ripe

PEEPAL *Ficus religiosa*
(pp96-97)

Leaves drooping, **WAXY**, with
WAVY MARGINS, heart-shaped
base and **ELONGATED TIP; LEAF
STALKS VERY LONG**
Figs in pairs, from leaf axils;
dark red or purple when ripe

TRIANGLE-LEAF FIG
Ficus natalensis (p136)

Leaves **TRIANGULAR**, narrow
at base, apex broad; shiny on
top, paler, dull below; **MIDRIB
FORKING** short of the apex
Figs small, single or paired,
yellow or red when ripe

ALII FIG *Ficus binnendjikii*
(p176)

Leaves long and **NARROW**,
up to 18 cm; very firm, shiny
and smooth; midrib forms a
deep valley in centre of leaf
Figs not produced in Delhi

FIDDLELEAF FIG
Ficus lyrata (p129)

Leaves **VIOLIN-SHAPED**, broad
on top; margins wavy; dark,
glossy on top; base of leaf auricled, like human ear lobes
Figs in pairs, stalkless, green
with white dots

ANJEERI *Ficus palmata*
(p95)

Leaves softly hairy on top,
rough below; often 3-5
lobed, heart-shaped at base;
margins of leaf **TOOTHED**
Figs solitary, stalked, up to
2.5 cm diameter; pear-
shaped, yellowish when ripe

BAN NARANGA *Suregada multiflora*

false lime

ban naranga

amla/castor family

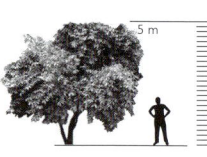
5 m

Small tree; deciduous

Bark grey, more or less smooth

Leaves up to 25 cm long, shiny and smooth, tapering at base; toothed near apex

Flowers tiny, yellowish, fragrant, male and female separate on the same tree [male flowers shown in pic below]

Fruit orange, about 2 cm in diameter, more or less round but distinctly 3-lobed [see pic at left]

A small, bushy tree from NE India and Myanmar whose glossy leaves are easily mistaken for a relative of the orange. The flowers and 3-lobed fruit, however, leave you in little doubt that this is no citrus plant. Extremely rare in Delhi, though it seems to do reasonably well here.

WHERE TO SEE IT Only one specimen seen, in Sundar Nursery, close to the wall separating it from the driveway to Humayun's Tomb.

CHILLA *Casearia tomentosa*

no english common name

chilla • chilara • bheri • bairi

chilla family

5 m

Small tree; nearly evergreen

Bark dark brown with a network of shallow cracks

Leaves up to 16 cm long, with a pointy tip and rounded base; margins minutely toothed; downy, especially underneath

Flowers small, greenish yellow, numerous, in dense clusters mostly in leaf axils [see pic below]

Fruit up to 3 cm long, ovoid, green at first, yellow when ripe; pulp reddish

A small tree with a dense canopy of interlacing branchlets and downy twigs and leaves. Native to the sub-Himalayan tract and parts of UP and Bihar, this is a little-noticed forest tree that is hardly ever cultivated. In C India, the fruit is pounded to a milky, acrid pulp used to stupefy fish.

WHERE TO SEE IT Only a single specimen found in the main timber section of Sundar Nursery.

KHIRK *Celtis tetrandra*

eastern nettle tree

elm family

khirk • khalk • kharak • adona • ku • batkar

Large tree; deciduous

Bark bluish grey, relatively smooth, speckled with raised white dots; old trees develop thin, horizontal wrinkles

Leaves 8-12 cm long, on short stalks; pale green when young, darkening later; toothed along part of the margin; 3-nerved at base; apex pointy

Flowers tiny, greenish yellow, without petals; male, female, bisexual flowers separate but on the same tree; females at the end of longer stalks in leaf axils; male and bisexual flowers at the base of short shoots below the leaves

Fruit berry-like, green turning orange-red, eventually black; about the size of a peppercorn

A fair-sized tree with a short, thick bole and speading canopy, particularly attractive in March when the new foliage is a delicate pale-green. Native to lower slopes of the Himalaya and further west. It was once widely planted in bungalows in Lutyens' Delhi and in parks, but is seldom planted now and is becoming rare.

SEASONS - LEAVES turn yellow before falling in end January; new leaf in third week of February, prime time early March. Another flush of new leaves in the rains. FLOWERING happens covertly as the leaves are renewed; female flowers develop quickly into green berries. FRUIT seen by mid April; ripen September-October.

LEAF MARGINS toothed from just above the middle, continuing almost to the short, pointy apex. Notice that the middle nerve divides the base of the leaf into very unequal halves.

WHERE TO SEE IT Large trees on Max Mueller Marg, near the bus stop outside WWF. Lodi Garden, Talkatora Garden, Sundar Nursery and Buddha Jayanti Park have good specimens. A surprisingly large number of khirk trees in the hedgerows of Teen Murti Marg and Safdarjang Road, probably planted in the 1930s. Amrita Shergil Road has quite a few, too.

MALE FLOWERS found together with bisexual flowers below the leaves. They are tiny and woolly.

>> Which *Celtis*? – see p334

GREY OAK *Quercus leucotrichophora*

Syn: Quercus incana

grey oak • white oak

oak family

banjh • ban

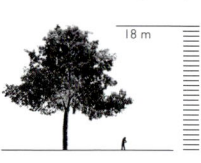

18 m

Large tree; semi-evergreen

Bark dark grey, fissured

Leaves leathery, edged with sharp teeth; mature leaves dull grey-green, smooth on top, pale and downy underneath; young leaves densely woolly, pink

Flowers male and female separate but on the same tree; male flowers in slender, drooping spikes about 8 cm long; female flowers stalkless, solitary or in short clusters

Fruit a typical acorn, with the nut enclosed by a cup, about 2 cm long; hairy at first, eventually shiny brown

A fairly large, handsome oak from the NW Himalaya, found near the upper limits of chir pine and commonly associated with the red rhododendron tree. It does not do at all well at lower elevations and it will be a horticultural feat if the lone specimen in Delhi University survives to maturity.

WHERE TO SEE IT
Only one specimen, on the road in front of the botany department, Delhi University.

CHUKKA *Croton roxburghii*

no english common name

amla/castor family

chukka • arjunna

8 m

Smallish tree; deciduous

Bark grey or greenish, smooth

Leaves crowded at ends of branches; up to 25 cm long, with blunt teeth along its margins [pic below shows a leaf just before it is shed]

Flowers male and female separate, but on the same tree; pale yellow-green, woolly, in clusters

Fruit a small, round capsule, about 12 mm across

A moderate-sized tree with pale-green, bluntly toothed leaves clustered at the ends of branchlets, turning bright orange before falling. At first sight, the leaves look fleshy or succulent, but this is illusory. Found in mixed forests from India through parts of SE Asia and S China, but not a well-known or common tree.

WHERE TO SEE IT Only a lone specimen, in the timber section of Sundar Nursery.

PANIA *Ehretia acuminata*

silky ash • churnwood • koda • heliotrope tree   *lasora family*

pania • panyan • punna • lahichan • koda • kalthaun

Small tree; deciduous

Bark greyish, rough, not deeply fissured

Leaves up to 18 cm long, with small, close-set teeth, pointed at apex

Flowers small, white, fragrant, in crowded panicles, mostly at the ends of branchlets

Fruit a small, orange berry, ripening black [see pic below]

A modest-sized tree with toothed leaves and dense panicles of small, white flowers in April. Native to the sub-Himalayan region and large tracts in tropical Asia. Pania is difficult to notice except when it is in flower. Most specimens in Delhi are found in one stretch of hedgerow in Rashtrapati Bhavan.

WHERE TO SEE IT
5 or 6 trees between gates 28 & 29 in the hedgerow of Rashtra-pati Bhavan; 4 trees in Sundar Nursery; a specimen in 94 Lodi Road, visible from the road.

MAHOE *Hibiscus tiliaceus*

mahoe • coast/sea hibiscus • coast cotton tree • yellow mallow tree   *cotton/hibiscus family*

bola • chelwa

Small tree; deciduous

Bark grey, smooth at first, becoming dark, cracked

Leaves (of subsp. *tiliaceus*) broad, heart-shaped at base with long, pointy tips; edges wavy; 9-11 nerves from the base. The other subspecies (subsp. *hastatus*) has long-fingered, lobed leaves

Flowers showy, 5 overlapping yellow petals with deep-crimson base and long staminal column; flowers last one day, turn apricot red and open out flat as they fall

Fruit capsules 1-2 cm wide, almost spherical but with a little beak

A small, unprepossessing tree found on tidal beaches and estuarine forests in India and many other parts of the world. This is the only species of hibiscus that grows tree-sized. 2 subspecies of this tree are found in Delhi, with distinctively different leaves. Both of them have beautiful yellow flowers.

WHERE TO SEE IT Subsp. *tiliaceus* on the road outside the botany department in Delhi University; in a few hedgerows on S. Bharati Marg. Subsp. *hastatus* in the School of Social Work, Delhi University.

KANJU *Holoptelea integrifolia*

indian elm

kanju • papdi • chudail/kali papdi • chilbil

elm family

25 m

Large tree; deciduous

Bark pale brown or greyish, rough in patches

Leaves smooth, with a short, blunt tip; young leaves are often toothed

Flowers tiny, greenish brown, in dense clusters; male and bisexual flowers mixed in the same cluster

Fruit a round, thin, papery disc, yellow-brown when ripe

FLOWERS very tiny, greenish brown, in dense clusters. Male and bisexual flowers are found mixed in the same cluster. Purely male flowers have 8 hairy anthers. Bisexual flowers have fewer anthers and an ovary with 2 flat 'horns' that elongate as the fruit forms.

Delhi's tallest native tree, with steeply ascending branches and a trunk usually dividing low down and buttressed at base. The flat, papery, biscuit-coloured fruit (in late April) are a useful clue to its identity. The crushed leaves and bruised bark give off a strong smell. Not often planted but can be seen here and there in large parks and common in parts of the Ridge.

fertilized bisexual flower developing into a young fruit

mostly male flowers with 8 anthers

SEASONS - LEAVES shed in March, renewed in April-May. FLOWERS appear in early March when the tree is completely bare. FRUIT form quickly, ripening and turning from green to brown in April-May.

WHERE TO SEE IT Not planted as an avenue tree anywhere in the city. Lodi Garden and Teen Murti Bhavan have some huge specimens. There are large trees next to Tamil Nadu House (on Kautilya Marg) and inside some houses on Max Mueller Marg. Scattered on the Ridge and inside JNU campus.

leaves arranged
alternately on
the twigs

rounded base

LEAVES from 8 to 15 cm long, sombre dark-green on top, paler beneath. Base rounded, tip contracting suddenly into a short, blunt point. Young leaves are often toothed and faintly downy. Older leaves are shiny and smooth, somewhat leathery, but without teeth.

blunt, pointy apex

toothed edges
of a young leaf

FRUIT thin, papery discs, nearly round, about the size of a one-rupee coin, with the seed at the centre. They start out light green and mature a biscuity brown.

very
young fruit

BARK ashy brown or grey, rough and chapped in patches, especially lower down, relatively smooth elsewhere. You can see shiny brown dots (lenticels) arranged in vertical lines all along the smooth parts.

HABITAT A 'pioneer' tree of dry deciduous forests, occurring in a rainfall zone receiving 50-200 cm of annual rain. Often found in or near cultivated fields, and frequently on disturbed sites. It prefers loamy or sandy soils and gravelly alluvium with good drainage, but suffers from frost. It is a fast grower and can reach a height of 30 m in ideal conditions, but on poor, rocky ground will remain stunted.

RANGE Throughout the sub-Himalayan tract E of the Beas river. Very common in Jammu, Kangra, Garhwal and Kumaon up to about 700 m. Scattered through much of the rest of the Indian subcontinent, extending to Sri Lanka, Nepal, Myanmar and parts of SE Asia.

USES One of those rare native trees that does not seem to have earned a high reputation in folk medicine. Its leaves are lopped for fodder and the seeds contain a fatty oil. The yellowish timber does not have any distinguishable heartwood. It is soft and light but fairly strong and is used to make cheap furniture, carts, dugouts and lightweight goods like the backs of brushes. The name 'chudail papdi' suggests the tree is feared as an abode of dark spirits.

RAMDHAN CHAMPA *Ochna obtusata*

bird's eye bush • golden champak

ramdhan champa • *kanak champa* • *khambar*

ramdhan champa family

Shrub or small tree; deciduous

Bark pale brown, smooth, without distinctive character

Leaves smooth, glossy, 7-18 cm long; variable in shape, narrowed at both ends; edges finely toothed, slightly wavy

Flowers large, showy, fragrant; petals 5-12, overlapping, bright yellow; stamens numerous, yellow

Fruit green at first, turning black; seated on a bright-red fruit-cup [see pic below]

A shrub or small tree with delicately scented bright-yellow flowers along with its new foliage in late April. Before turning green, the glossy new leaves are fleetingly touched by coppery tints, making the conjunction of new leaf and flower memorable. Native to E India, a popular garden ornamental.

WHERE TO SEE IT A small grove in Shanti Vana; Sundar Nursery has a few trees; Lodi Garden has 2 trees near Muhammad Shah's Tomb.

>> The Identity of the Ramdhan Champa – see p330

ALMOND *Prunus dulcis* var. *dulcis*

almond • sweet/domestic almond

badam

rose/peach/cherry family

Small tree; deciduous

Bark blackish, rough

Leaves narrow, finely toothed; folded in the middle to form a V-shaped valley; base tapering, pointy tip

Flowers pink or pale rose, fading to white; often in pairs, appearing before the leaves; 5 petals with pink stamens

Fruit grey-green, with a downy coat; flesh leathery; a hard, pitted stone at the centre, containing the almond

A small, bushy tree with toothed leaves and pretty pink flowers, easily mistaken for a peach tree. The almond lives inside the hard stone of its fruit. Cultivated since the Bronze Age, it is thought to originate in the dry region stretching from N Iran to the steppes of the former eastern Soviet Republics.

WHERE TO SEE IT Only a single specimen at Sundar Nursery, but there are likely to be many more in private gardens and orchards.

>> Naming the Almond – see p328

BER *Ziziphus mauritiana*

desert apple • indian jujube/plum/cherry • chinese apple/date   *ber family*

ber • bera • beri • bor • bordi

Bush or small tree; deciduous

Bark nearly black, with wavy ridges and deep, vertical furrows; inner bark red-brown

Spines in pairs, one straight, the other short and hooked

Leaves broadly oval; glossy green on top, white-downy below; margins very finely toothed; 3-nerved at base

Flowers pale greenish yellow; 5 starry segments of the flower-cup alternating with 5 tiny petals, arranged around a central cushion

Fruit cherry- or olive-like, up to 3 cm long; green at first, ripening yellow or reddish; fleshy, surrounding a hard stone. There are numerous cultivated varieties.

A smallish, spiny tree with a short bole and crooked, twisting branches forming a dense, spreading crown. The ber has been cultivated for its fruit in India for so long that no one quite knows where it was originally wild, but it is a fair guess that the dry Delhi region formed part of its native range.

SEASONS - LEAVES shed sometime between late March and early May; new leaves in late June or early July. **FLOWERS** July-August to October. **FRUIT** ripen December to March.

WHERE TO SEE IT As a relict tree on some major roads – on Aurobindo Marg, and close to Kamal cinema in Safdarjang Enclave. Common in Hauz Rani City Forest and Shalimar Bagh. The Qutb compound and Hauz Khas District Park have some fine specimens. Not as common as one might expect on the Ridge.

petal

STAR-LIKE FLOWER-CUP, forming the base of the flower, has 5 triangular segments, and between each of them an almost imperceptible, thin, white petal bends downwards.

CULTIVATED BERS are usually pruned so that main branches stay low, for ease of plucking the ripe fruit. Orchards in N Delhi have many trees like this one.

HARSHINGAR *Nyctanthes arbor-tristis*

night-blooming jasmine • tree of sorrow/sadness • coral jasmine   *olive/jasmine family [some say: teak family]*
harshingar • har • siharu • saherwa • seoli • kuri

Bush or small tree; deciduous

Bark pale or dark grey, sometimes greenish, rough, somewhat wrinkled

Leaves in opposite pairs; dark green, very rough on upper surface, paler and hairy below; margins often with large, distant teeth; apex pointy

Flowers with 5-8 white (slightly unequal) petals at the end of a brilliant orange tube about one cm long; in clusters, usually 3-5 together; highly fragrant

Fruit a flattish, round capsule just over one cm wide; bright green at first, turning brown

FLOWERS bloom at dusk and fall by early morning. There are only 2 anthers, with virtually no filaments, at the top of the orange tube.

anthers •

• orange tube

A large, untidy bush or small tree with drooping 4-angled branchlets (much like teak) and harshly scabrous leaves (also like teak, but much smaller). Cultivated in Delhi for its fragrant night-blooming flowers which carpet the ground each morning in the rains. Native to dry and moist deciduous forests throughout India.

SEASONS - LEAVES shed in February or March (depending on winter rains), renewed in June-July. FLOWERS in August, peaking in September-October. FRUIT ripen in April-May.

LEAVES 5-11 cm long. The roughness on their upper surface is caused by stiff glandular hairs with bulbous bases. The silvery hairs below are relatively soft.

WHERE TO SEE IT A fairly common tree in small gardens and parks. Buddha Jayanti Park has a dense grove. A short row is planted in front of Hindu College.

FINISHING TOUCH

Harshingar is widely distributed in natural forests in India from about 1200 m in the sub-Himalayan tracts southwards. Apart from the use of its flowers as votive offerings, its rough leaves were once used to impart a fine-grade polish to wood and ivory.

HOLLOCK *Terminalia myriocarpa*

hollock

no local name

arjun family

16 m

Large tree; semi-evergreen

Bark greyish or brown, peeling in vertical flakes

Leaves large, opposite or nearly so, margins minutely toothed; leaf stalk short, thick, with 1-2 prominent glands near top [see pic below]

Flowers small, pink, clustered on slender spikes arranged in large, branching clusters; generally rusty-hairy

Fruit yellowish, about 4 mm long but wider; has 3 angles, 2 of which are expanded into wings

A towering, large-leaved evergreen tree from moist hilly regions of NE India, hard to forget if you have seen it once in flower or fruit. It is of course stunted and severely out of joint in Delhi's climate, but still manages an impressive spectacle in flower after the rains. Its timber is valuable.

WHERE TO SEE IT Only a single specimen, in front of the department of physics and astrophysics, Delhi University.

SHAREEFA *Annona squamosa*

(scaly) custard apple • sugar apple • sweetsop

shareefa • seetaphal

custard apple family

4 m

Large shrub or small tree; deciduous

Bark greyish, not very rough

Leaves up to 15 cm long, blunt-tipped; dull green on top, pale beneath; aromatic when crushed

Flowers small, on long, drooping stalks; only 3 outer petals visible, thick and fleshy, yellow-green outside, pale yellow inside

Fruit compound and segmented, with a thick, knobbly skin, greyish or green; flesh inside creamy white, sweet, fragrant

A small fruit tree from C America whose precise origins are not known. It was brought to S India by the Portuguese in the 16th century and the familiar scaly fruit is now grown here on a large scale. The tree has a light crown with noticeably zigzag branchlets and pale-green flowers.

WHERE TO SEE IT Common in fruit orchards, small gardens and nurseries. Cultivated in the orchards around Shalimar Bagh in N Delhi. The Qutb compound has a small tree.

CHAMROD *Ehretia laevis*

no english common name

lasora family

chamrod • desi papdi • datranga • darar • koda • chambal • geen • sakar

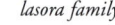
9 m

Large bush or middle-sized tree; deciduous

Trunk gnarled, knobbly and nearly always crooked

Bark yellowish or grey, not rough

Leaves variable, usually quite broad; hairy at first, becoming smooth and shiny; apex pointy

Flowers small, white, star-shaped, in loose clusters

Fruit tiny berries, bright orange, turning black when ripe

flower clusters are produced both from leaf axils and at the ends of twigs

branchlets densely mealy-hairy

Often just a small, crooked, multi-stemmed bush but it can grow into a middle-sized tree. An important part of Delhi's native flora. Recognized by its pale, knobbly trunk and in season, by loose clusters of small, white, star-shaped flowers. Bunches of small, orange berries in April are also distinctive. Common on the Ridge and occasional in parks, but nowhere cultivated.

SEASONS - LEAVES shed late in January, renewed early to mid March. **FLOWERS** at many different times. Prime time is March, but flushes in mid winter and after the first pre-monsoon showers are distinctive. **FRUIT** set very quickly after the flowers, mostly by late March. The berries turn orange in mid April.

WHERE TO SEE IT Delhi Golf Course has a large number of chamrod trees. Most large parks like Buddha Jayanti and Lodi Garden have specimens. Very common on the Ridge. Not cultivated or planted as an avenue tree anywhere in Delhi.

FLOWERS small (about 6 mm long), white, star-shaped, in loose, branching clusters. There are 5 spreading petals and 5 stamens. Often in flower out of season, triggered by a little rain.

LEAVES thin, soft and pale green when young, darkening and becoming stiffer as they mature. Both leaves and leaf stalks are hairy at first, gradually becoming perfectly smooth and shiny. Variable in form, from egg-shaped to nearly round, 6-13 cm long.

tip is usually narrowed into a tiny point •——

FRUIT in clusters. The berries are slightly larger than peppercorns, green at first, turning bright orange, eventually black and wrinkled.

BARK creamy or yellowish grey, not rough, with some scaly patches low down. The trunk is nearly always extremely knobbly.

CAN BE CONFUSED WITH

The peelu because its bark is somewhat similar in colour and texture – but the resemblance goes no further!

HABITAT Superbly drought-hardy, fire-resistant and frost-tolerant, which is why it is so successful in dry deciduous forests. It propagates by seed and also by root-suckers, making it very difficult to eradicate. It has sprung up all over Nicholson Cemetery, defying all attempts to keep the paths between the graves clear.

RANGE Common in dry forests throughout N India, ascending to about 800 m in the Shivaliks and lower Himalaya. Particularly common E of the Aravallis, extending into Gujarat and the Konkan. Beyond the subcontinent, chamrod ranges from SE Asia and S China into Australia, but this probably includes some subspecies.

USES The bark is chewed and stains the teeth red. It is also powdered and mixed with flour as a famine food. The fruit is edible but does not taste of anything in particular. The leaves are a valuable fodder resource in dry thorn forests where grass is scarce. The yellowish wood is described as being 'rather dull, straight-grained, very fine textured' and is strong and durable. It is used for construction and to make the backs of brushes and match boxes, but is not known as a timber of any value.

JARUL *Lagerstroemia speciosa*

queen's crape (or crêpe) myrtle • queen's flower • pride of india • rose of india

jarul • motabandara • arjuna

mehndi family

Small to medium-sized; deciduous

Bark pale brown, smooth or flaking thinly

Leaves large, smooth, on short, stout stalks; tapering at both ends; turning red before falling

---

Flowers mauve, pink or lilac, in large, erect clusters; petals crinkly, stamens numerous

---

Fruit nearly spherical, woody, about 2 cm long; splitting open when dry; fruit-cup with short, triangular lobes

8 m

FLOWERS pink, mauve or lilac, about 7 cm wide, in large, erect, branching clusters. Starting from the base, the flowers begin to open before dawn, but only a few at a time. Old flowers fade to pale pink or white. Each flower has 6 (rarely 7) spoon-shaped petals, very crinkly and wavy.

• the ribbed flower-cup, seen from below

The flagship species of a spectacular genus of flowering trees (and shrubs) whose rose-like flowers with crinkly petals are displayed in large, erect clusters. One of Delhi's most beautiful flowering trees, with a low, spreading crown. Native to moist forests in NE and S India, where it sometimes grows to a great size.

SEASONS - **LEAVES** start turning red and purple in December and are shed in February-March. New leaves in April. **FLOWERS** from late April to June; another flush in the rains. **FRUIT** are formed by August, remaining for long on the tree.

WHERE TO SEE IT Common in parks, gardens and traffic roundabouts. Jorbagh has many fine trees; Aurobindo Marg has a short row near Safdarjang flyover. Oddly, it is rarely planted as an avenue tree in Delhi. Absent from the Ridge.

ribbed flower buds are crowned by a short nipple

up to 200 stamens crowd the centre

petals narrowed into 'handles' at their base

leaves are nearly but not quite opposite each other on the twig

leaf stalk often twisted to one side

the arching side veins unite in a thin, wavy vein parallel to the leaf margin

LEAVES smooth, shiny, up to 26 cm long on short, strong leaf stalks. Somewhat like a mango's, only broader and longer, tapering at both ends. New foliage emerges pink; old leaves turn blotchily dark red or purple before falling.

pointy lobes of the fruit-cup

old leaves turn various shades of russet and purple

ripe fruit, dried and starting to split open to release the seed

FRUIT an oval, woody capsule about 2 cm long, crowned with a tiny spike, turning from olive green to black as it matures. The triangular lobes of the supporting fruit-cup are folded well back.

BARK pale brown or ashy, flaking thinly. Older trees develop patches of rough bark with shallow, vertical fissures.

CAN BE CONFUSED WITH

Other species of *Lagerstroemia* grown in Delhi. See the diagnostic key to the genus on page 77.

HABITAT A tree of relatively open country in moist, secondary forest or grassland, often near streams. It prefers rather more rainfall than it gets in Delhi but is evidently drought-hardy. It does not grow tall in the open but in a dense forest can reach 30 m or more with a broad, spreading canopy. Delhi's jaruls get mercilessly lopped in winter in order to induce a new flush of leaves and flowers.

RANGE Wild in the NE states and all along the W Ghats, in Sri Lanka, Bangladesh and Myanmar. Its natural range extends eastwards through Thailand and Malaysia to Indonesia, S China and the Philippines.

USES The bark and leaves have astringent and purgative proper-ties. In Indonesia the leaves are prescribed for abdominal pains and a decoction of boiled leaves has proven qualities in reducing blood sugar levels. The seeds are said to be narcotic. In 19th century Burma, jarul was the timber most highly valued after teak. It is pale red when freshly sawn, darkening to a handsome reddish brown. It is used for construction work and to make carts, wagons, boxes, panelling, gun-stocks and is also durable underwater.

CRAPE MYRTLE *Lagerstroemia indica*

crape (or crêpe) myrtle • pride of india

mehndi family

savani • cheeni mehndi • phurush

Bush or small tree; deciduous

Bark smooth, flaking off to expose grey underbark

Leaves are the smallest of Delhi's *Lagerstroemias*, broadly oval but somewhat variable; smooth; slightly paler underneath

Flowers in large, showy clusters, white, pink or mauve; 6 petals with long 'claws', crisped at edges, often frilly; stamens many, 6 outer ones longer than the rest

Fruit a woody capsule, 10-15 mm long, roundish, short-pointed on top

6 m

FLOWERS 4-5 cm wide with 6 nearly round petals intensely crisped at the edges and attached to the centre by slender 'claws'. There are up to 42 stamens, only 4-6 of which are long.

Usually hard-pruned and kept down to an ornamental bush, but if left alone it grows into a small, multi-trunked tree with an open head and profuse clusters of frilly flowers in various colours. Originally from China, it has become immensely popular worldwide and has spawned a long line of cultivated hybrids.

stamens

LEAVES are variable in size and shape, and are not reliable clues to its identity. The leaves shown here are notched and clearly broadest at their apex.

SEASONS - **LEAFLESS** through most of the dry season till mid March or later. **FLOWERING** begins in mid May and lasts through the rains. **FRUIT** start forming soon after flowering, and can remain till the next flowering season.

ENDURANCE FLOWERING

Crape myrtles are among the longest-blooming trees known to man, capable of remaining in flower for up to 120 days. They come in a dizzying array of cultivars with names such as 'Ruby lace' and 'Petite snow' and even Indian varieties such as 'Aliporensis'. The crape myrtle is sometimes successfully crossed with the jarul.

WHERE TO SEE IT A common bush planted for ornament on traffic roundabouts. Shanti Vana has a lot of bushes. There are far fewer trees in evidence, but occasionally, in not very well maintained gardens, you can get to see a crape myrtle tree that has been favoured by neglect.

LEZA *Lagerstroemia tomentosa*

leza   *mehndi family*

no local name

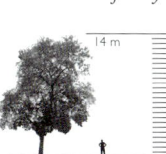

Middle-sized tree; deciduous

Bark thin, brown, peeling, with faint, vertical fissures

Leaves up to 35 cm long, rounded at base, tapering gradually to a pointy tip; surface of leaf hairy especially along nerves and underneath; margins slightly wavy; leaf stalk very short

Flowers about 5 cm wide; 6 petals, spoon shaped, white or pale pink; flower-cup has 12 or more ridges; clusters branched, terminal, the branchlets yellow-mealy

Fruit a small, ovoid, woody capsule, black when ripe

A moderate-sized tree with weak, floppy branches and long, downy leaves, easily identified by its crinkly petalled flowers as one of the crape myrtles. The flowers are white or the palest pink, produced in May-June at the ends of its branches in pyramidal, branching clusters. A native of Myanmar, S China and Thailand.

WHERE TO SEE IT A prominent row of trees is planted along a waterbody parallel to Rajpath, between Man Singh Road and India Gate. A few trees in the hedgerow of Jesus & Mary College in Chanakyapuri. Sundar Nursery has a solitary tree.

LASORA *Cordia dichotoma*

clammy cherry • indian cherry • sebestan plum • bird lime tree   *lasora family*

lasora • lasuda • bhokar • gondi • laswara

Middle-sized tree; deciduous

Bark pale or medium brown, with shallow vertical fissures

Leaves alternate, 7-12 cm long, broad-oval; margins wavy near apex, usually with 3 main nerves; rough and leathery when mature

Flowers small, white, in loose clusters, opening at night; petals curved backwards, fused into tube at base

Fruit like a pale cherry with sticky pulp, turning dark [see pic below]

A middle-sized deciduous tree with characteristic long, drooping branchlets. In moist situations, it forms a handsome, rounded crown. The bright-green leaves are broadly oval, the upper half nearly always wavy-edged. Its fruit, like a pale cherry, is pickled or eaten tender as a vegetable. An occasional tree in Delhi – possibly native, sometimes cultivated.

WHERE TO SEE IT Sundar Nursery has a few large trees. Most sizeable parks have one or 2 specimens.

◗ BENTEAK *Lagerstroemia microcarpa*   *Syn: Lagerstroemia lanceolata*

benteak • nandi tree   *mehndi family*
no local name; *nandi mara* (kannada) • *ven-tekku* (tamil, telugu)

Small tree; deciduous

Bark thin, white or very pale brown, peeling in thin flakes

Leaves broadly oval, up to 11 cm long; smooth on top, softly downy below, with arching, parallel nerves

Flowers very small, white, in large, branching clusters, but barely produced in Delhi

Fruit a small woody capsule, smaller than other Delhi *lagerstroemias*; not seen in Delhi

A common tree of lowland moist forests in the W Ghats, stranded in Delhi many miles from home. It is something of a surprise to realize that it belongs with jarul and the crape myrtle in a genus of showy, flowering trees, because its blossoms are so tiny and barely in evidence in Delhi.

WHERE TO SEE IT 5 or 6 trees in the parking lot of the Supreme Court between gates E and F, remnants of a more extensive but ill-judged planting scheme; 3 trees in Sundar Nursery.

◗ THAI CRAPE MYRTLE *Lagerstroemia floribunda*

thai or malaysian crape (or crêpe) myrtle • tabak (thai)   *mehndi family*
no local name

Small tree; deciduous

Bark thin, pale brown, flaking off to expose white or pale grey new bark

Leaves up to 22 cm long, obtuse at apex; lightly hairy when young, later smooth; new leaves pink [below]

Flowers small, in large, terminal clusters, mauve-pink fading to white; 6 crinkly petals; the bud, flower-cup and branches of the flower cluster are all yellow-scurfy

Fruit a pea-sized woody capsule, held in a scurfy fruit-cup, with faint ridges and 6 pointy lobes

A beautiful flowering tree up to 20 m tall in its native SE Asian forests, growing no higher than 5 m in Delhi. Its blossoms are like jarul flowers in miniature, distinguished by the buds and fruit-cups being covered by a yellowish mealy substance. Its new leaves are a bright brownish-pink. Rare in Delhi.

WHERE TO SEE IT 2 large trees in the Vice-Chancellor's House in Delhi University; Buddha Jayanti Park has 5 trees close to each other.

DELHI'S LAGERSTROEMIAS

Lagerstroemias can be a little confusing because their flowers are so similar, but their flower-cups and fruit capsules exhibit differences in shape, size and texture that you can rely on to distinguish between the 5 species found in Delhi. The flower-cup (calyx) forms the base of the bud and fruit and is nearly always ribbed to some degree. When the flower opens, the top of the flower-cup splits into triangular 'lobes' which spread out or fold downwards. This key will help you recognize characteristic features of each species.

THAI CRAPE MYRTLE *Lagerstroemia floribunda* p76

Flower cluster 20-40 cm long, cluster branchlets yellow-scurfy
Buds 9-10 mm long, **TOP-SHAPED**, 10-12 ribbed; **DENSELY SCURFY**
Flowers only 30 mm wide; mauve-pink
Stamens numerous, 4-6 stamens longer, red
Fruit 12-16 mm long; 5-6 valves; dark rufous brown
Fruit-cup ribbed, brown-scurfy; lobes pointy, spreading

buds yellow-scurfy, ribbed

lobes pointy, spreading

CRAPE MYRTLE *Lagerstroemia indica* p74

Flower cluster **SMALL**, 5-20 cm long, branchlets downy, **ANGLED**
Buds 5-6 mm long, **NEARLY ROUND**, **NOT RIBBED**, smooth, shiny
Flowers 40-50 mm wide; white, pink, red, purple
Stamens 36-42, 4-6 stamens stouter, longer, pink
Fruit 12-15 mm long; 4-5 valves; brown or black
Fruit-cup **SMOOTH**, lobes folded over sharply

flower-cup smooth

BENTEAK *Lagerstroemia microcarpa* p76

Flower cluster 10-35 cm long, **PENDULOUS**, grey-downy all over
Buds **ONLY 2 MM LONG**; nearly round; **NOT RIBBED**; smooth
Flowers **SMALLEST OF THE 5 SPECIES**, only 6 mm wide; pure **WHITE**
Stamens numerous, 4-6 are stouter, longer than others, white
Fruit 10-12 mm long; 3-4 valves, dark brown
Fruit-cup small, low; lobes folded over or breaking off early

apex not rounded

valves long, few

JARUL *Lagerstroemia speciosa* p72

Flower cluster 15-40 cm long; cluster branchlets ashy- or rusty-downy
Buds 7-12 mm long; 12-14 ribbed; smooth or briefly downy
Flowers **LARGE**, 50-75 mm wide; purple, pink or mauve
Stamens up to 200, mostly **EQUAL-SIZED**, purplish red; anthers yellow
Fruit 20-25 mm long, oval, 6-valved; black when ripe
Fruit-cup ribbed; smooth or downy; lobes spreading or folded over

ribbed buds

LEZA *Lagerstroemia tomentosa* p75

Flower cluster short, 6-20 cm long; branchlets yellow-downy
Buds 5-6 mm long, top-shaped; 12 or more ribbed
Flowers 40-50 mm wide, **WHITE** or very **PALE PINK**
Stamens numerous; 4-6 are longer than the others, pink
Fruit 12-17 mm long; ovoid; 5-6 valves, dark brown or black
Fruit-cup **SAUCER-SHAPED**, lobes folded over, yellow-downy

apex rounded

fruit-cup saucer-shaped

BISTENDU *Diospyros cordifolia*

mountain persimmon • bombay ebony

ebony family

bistendu • bassendu • passendu • dasaundu • kendu • lohari • temru

6 m

Smallish tree; deciduous

Bark very dark, becoming rougher as the tree ages

Branching spines may develop at ends of twigs on old trees

Leaves velvety, 5-10 cm long; base of leaf faintly heart-shaped; blade slender, tapering

Flowers tubular, with 4 creamy white petals; male and female flowers grow on separate trees

Fruit cherry-sized, yellow when ripe

Usually a small tree but capable of reaching 9 m with a short, gnarled trunk and dense, spreading canopy, often much broader than it is tall. One of Delhi's least-known native trees, with lush foliage at the driest time of the year. Found in relict pockets of original vegetation and throughout the Ridge.

SEASONS - LEAVES begin to drop in January; new leaves early in March, strikingly beautiful in April. **FLOWERS** in April. **FRUIT** set quite quickly after the flowers and remain on the tree till February or March of the following year.

WHERE TO SEE IT Fairly common on the Ridge especially in pockets of deep soil. Most large parks have specimens. A particularly tall one grows close to the Lady Willingdon Park wicket gate in Lodi Garden. A lovely double row of trees behind the mausoleum in Roshanara Bagh. Big trees inside the Qutb compound. Often trimmed into topiary bushes, such as those in front of the Secretariat at Vijay Chowk.

FLOWERS small, cup-shaped, with 4 creamy petals bent backwards. Male and female flowers grow on separate trees. Male flowers are perceptibly smaller, stalkless and are bunched together in groups of 2-6 (usually 3). Female flowers are solitary and have little stalks; they also have broader flower-cups which persist as the flower develops into a fruit.

male and female flowers are placed here together for comparison. This one is male •

the female flower is noticeably larger •

leaves are more densely velvety and paler when young

LEAVES minutely velvety on both surfaces. From a slightly heart-shaped base, the leaf elongates with nearly parallel sides, then tapers gradually to a thin or blunt point. New leaves are a lovely shade of pale green.

BARK dark grey, becoming black, rough and crusty as the tree ages.

COMPOUND SPINES may develop at the ends of twigs on old trees. This is not usually seen on younger trees.

FRUIT about the size of a cherry, growing out of the enlarged flower-cup. Smooth and green, becoming yellow or orange-tinged when ripe. The viscid pulp inside is bitter.

A TREE growing with most of its trunk inside a mosque in Paharganj. It does not seem to mind at all!

>> The Correct Name of Bistendu – see p329

HABITAT Dry, single-storeyed thorn forests like the Ridge in Delhi. It is able to find niches in washes or gullies where the soil is a little deeper. It is superbly drought-hardy and reasonably frost-hardy.

RANGE A 19th-century forester described bistendu as being 'nowhere very abund-ant and yet very widely spread' throughout the Indian subcontinent, preferring somewhat drier localities. It is reported to extend into Indo-China, the Malay Archipelago and trop-ical Australia. (This may need to be tempered by the knowledge that the species may have been confused with another closely allied tree.)

USES There is some uncertainty about whether or not its bitter fruit is poisonous to human beings. Some Adivasi communities in C India crush the fruit and drop it into fresh-water pools to stupefy fish. A 19th-century source says that bhishtis (water carriers) apply the viscid pulp of the fruit to cure boils on their hands. The twigs and leaves are lopped for fodder. The wood – related to true ebony – is seldom available in usable sizes but is said to be beautifully mottled and streaked and useful for carving and making small articles of furniture, carts and implements.

KADAMB *Neolamarckia cadamba*   <small>*Syn: Anthocephalus cadamba*</small>

cadamba • common bur-flower tree • wild cinchona   *coffee/gardenia family*
kadamb • kadam

Large tree; deciduous

Branches stiff, diverging at right angles to the trunk

Bark of old trees dark, rough, with vertical fissures

Leaves large, in opposite pairs, shiny on top, with arching, parallel secondary nerves

Flowers deep yellow, tiny, clustered in round heads

Fruit also yellow, in round heads

16 m

FLOWERS individually tiny, deep yellow or orange, clustered together in round heads about the size of an undernourished orange. The stigmas stick out like little threads, making the heads look woolly. Fragrant.

A quick-growing tree with a long, clean bole and spreading branches, reaching 36 m in its natural habitat but much shorter in Delhi. Cultivated for its glossy leaves and conspicuous flowers clustered in large woolly balls. It is popularly mistaken as the Brindavan tree associated with Lord Krishna, but that is actually a different 'kadamb'.

yellow flower buds

SEASONS - LEAVES start to drop in March; renewed between April and June. FLOWERS for a short duration late in the rains, mostly August–September. FRUIT ripen and fall in January or February.

WHERE TO SEE IT Most large parks like Lodi Garden and Nehru Park have specimens. Shanti Vana has 2 big trees and Rajghat a double row of young trees planted by named dignitaries. The Taj Palace Hotel has a row of trees out in front with the lower branches pruned brutally to make them look columnar.

white stigmas emerge as the buds open

LEAVES up to 30 cm long, with prominent secondary veins like 'quilting'. The leaves are arranged in opposite pairs – each pair is set at right angles to the pair immediately above and below it. The upper surface of the leaf is smooth and shiny, the lower minutely downy.

• smooth and shiny on top

• secondary veins arching, parallel

HABITAT Its native habitat is moist deciduous and evergreen forest where frost does not pose a danger. Kadamb grows on alluvial soil in damp places, along rivers and on swampy ground provided it is well-drained. It is a classic rapid-growing 'pioneer species', colonizing fresh forest clearings or vacant ground.

RANGE Native to the sub-Himalayan terai and low hills from Nepal eastwards into NE India, Bangladesh and Myanmar. With a conspicuous disjunct in C India, it pops up again in Andhra Pradesh, Orissa and the W Ghats. It ranges beyond the subcontinent into S China, the Malay Peninsula, Indo-China and Papua New Guinea.

USES Its fragrant flowers are offered in Hindu shrines (though I suspect this could be because of mistaken identity). The bark is used in traditional medicine to cure fevers and coughs, and the juice of the fresh bark is employed to treat inflammations of the eye. The wood is soft and light, yellowish white, with no clear distinction between heartwood and sapwood. It is not very strong and is used only in low-quality planking and for boxing materials like tea chests.

FRUIT retain the shape of the round flower heads, turning a more sombre shade of orange. The individual fruit capsules are packed tightly together. The seeds are mostly dispersed by bats.

BARK dark brown or nearly black, becoming rough and riven by vertical cracks with age.

CAN BE CONFUSED WITH

The kaim, whose flowers and fruit in spherical clusters are very similar. The obvious difference is in the leaf, which is considerably smaller in the kaim, and in its bark, which is much paler and smoother. See pages 148-49 for 'The Real Krishna Kadamb'.

EARPOD WATTLE *Acacia auriculiformis*

earpod/tan wattle • earleaf/japanese acacia • northern/darwin black wattle   *pea family – mimosa subfamily*
no local name

Medium-sized tree; evergreen

Bark grey-brown, smooth at first, becoming fissured

Leaves are actually modified appendages called 'phyllodes' [see box]; thicker, more leathery than leaves, usually curved, with 3 arching nerves

Flowers yellow, fragrant, up to about 100 tiny flowers crowded together in elongated spikes; flower-cup and petals insignificant, stamens long, intensely yellow

Fruit pods green at first, becoming intricately coiled and almost woody when ripe; pods split open on the tree

14 m

COILED FRUIT PODS split open along the edges, where the seeds dangle daintily from little orange filaments.

An unarmed evergreen acacia from New Guinea and Northern Australia that lacks the characteristic feathery foliage of Indian acacias. It has instead leathery, leaf-like 'phyllodes' which are adapted to hot, arid conditions. The tree produces spiky clusters of bright-yellow flowers in the rains. Fairly common in Delhi's parks.

filaments are part of the food source for the seeds

SEASONS - LEAVES evergreen, with fresh flushes in the rains. **FLOWERS** in the rains, mid August to early November. **FRUIT** formed by October, ripening in late April or early May, when the ground below is crunchy with fallen pods.

WHERE TO SEE IT Commonly planted in parks and gardens. Lodi Garden, Nehru Park, Talkatora Garden, Qudsia Bagh have specimens. A large semi-circle of these trees around Nehru's samadhi in Shanti Vana.

PHYLLODES have arching parallel veins, very different from the net-branching of most leaves. Look for a gland at the base of each phyllode.

BETTER THAN LEAVES

Phyllodes evolved under extreme arid conditions, where leaves were an unaffordable luxury (because of water-loss through a leaf's pores). Over millions of years, leaf stalks expanded into flattened leaf-like structures, exposing more surface area and chlorophyll to sunlight and acting just like leaf blades, without their disadvantages. Most phyllode-bearing acacias do produce 'true' acacia-like leaves when they are saplings, but not for long.

SOUTHERN MAGNOLIA *Magnolia grandiflora*

southern/evergreen magnolia • bull bay • loblolly

himchampa

magnolia family

Smallish tree; evergreen

Bark greyish, smooth at first, forming small, scaly plates

Leaves 10-20 cm long; thick, firm, glossy green above, often rusty hairy below; apex bluntly pointed; edges slightly turned under; leaf-buds large, falling as the new leaf unfurls

Flowers showy, white, cup-shaped, about 15 cm wide; petals and flower-cup segments similar, 6-12; fragrant [pic below shows the ovary after the petals have fallen]

Fruit pink to brown; with bright-red exposed seeds

An ornamental evergreen tree with deep-green, leathery leaves and large, pure-white, scented blossoms. There are several horti-cultural cultivars. In its native range in SE USA it reaches 30 m but is stunted in Delhi and hardly, if ever, sets fruit here. Planted in parks and private gardens, but not common.

WHERE TO SEE IT Lodi Garden has a short row of trees flanking the IIC wall; also here and there in private gardens.

GOLDEN CHAMPAK *Michelia champaca*

golden/yellow/orange/fragrant champaka or champak

champ • champak • champa

magnolia family

Middle-sized; semi-evergreen

Bark ashy grey; shallowly fissured; prominent lenticels

Leaves 15-25 cm long, tapering to a point at apex, edges wavy; leaf-buds softly silky, falling off early; mature leaves nearly smooth

Flowers solitary, 5 cm wide, mostly in leaf axils; segments of flower-cup and petals similar, numbering 15-21, creamy white or deep yellow to orange; highly fragrant

Fruit in a cluster, waxy and somewhat grape-like; dark brown when mature

In its natural home in elevated moist forests in the NE Himalaya and the W Ghats, the golden champak is a majestic tree with a narrow crown, towering up to 35 m. It struggles in Delhi's dry heat and remains stunted. Its chief attraction lies in its delic-iously fragrant, pale- or deep-yellow flowers.

WHERE TO SEE IT Sundar Nursery has 2 young trees in the timber section. 2 more near the department of anthropology and others scat-tered in Delhi University. The casualty rate is high; it gets easily scorched in Delhi's heat.

BUDDHA'S COCONUT *Pterygota alata* Syn: *Sterculia alata*

buddha's coconut

no local name; trade name: *narikel*

cocoa family

Large tree; deciduous

Bark grey, grey-brown or ashy, relatively smooth; shallowly fissured when old

Leaves very large, up to 40 cm, glossy and smooth; 5-7 main veins from a heart-shaped base; apex pointy or not

Flowers about 2.5 cm wide, bell-shaped; no petals; the flower-cup is densely mealy on the outside; male and female flowers are separate but on the same tree

Fruit woody, on long stalks, about as big as a fist, eccentrically round; covered with brown felt at first, becoming smoother when ripe

THE BELL-SHAPED flower-cup has 5 or rarely 6 narrow, brownish segments, beautifully purple-veined inside, densely covered with a mealy substance on the outside. There are no petals.

A towering giant of the rainforests of NE India and the W Ghats, and one of Delhi's tallest trees even though it is stunted here. With a straight, tall trunk branching very high up, and large, glossy leaves crowded near the ends of short, upturned branches, it usually takes a narrow, conical form.

SEASONS - LEAVES start to fall in mid March, starting from the top of the tree. For a short period in late April the entire tree is bare. New leaves early in May, with another flush (or two) late in the rains. FLOWERING begins in late March, as the old leaves start to fall. FRUIT ripen on the tree in April-May of the year following the flowers.

segments of the flower-cup

WHERE TO SEE IT Bishambar Das Marg (near Gol Dak Khana) has remnants of a pure avenue of Buddha's coconut trees; only a few survive. A fine tree near Muhammad Shah's tomb in Lodi Garden, a favourite perch for roosting vultures when we still had vultures. St Stephen's College has 2 trees; there are small groves inside Shanti Vana, Hauz Khas Deer Park, and outside the Crafts Museum.

FRUIT split open on one side to reveal a large number of tightly packed, winged seeds.

KHASAI *Bridelia retusa*

no english common name   *amla/castor family*

khasai • khaja

Smallish tree; deciduous

Bark grey or blackish when old, rough, cracked, flaking off in long scales

10 m

Leaves up to 20 cm long, glossy green on top, downy below; obtuse or sometimes notched at apex

Flowers tiny, greenish yellow, in long spikes; male and female on separate trees; petals about one mm broad

Fruit spherical, about 8 mm wide; fleshy, edible, purple-black when ripe [pic at left]

A moderate-sized tree widely distributed on the subcontinent and throughout SE Asia. Young trees are covered with large, conical spines that are gradually shed. In fruiting season, the khasai is a magnet for birds, especially green pigeons. Native to the Aravallis a little south of Delhi but absent from the Ridge.

WHERE TO SEE IT Only a solitary specimen in Sundar Nursery. It may have once been found on the Ridge, but I have found none there now.

GUAVA TREE *Psidium guajava*

(yellow) guava • apple guava   *jamun/eucalyptus family*

amrood

Small tree; semi-evergreen

Bark reddish brown, peeling off to expose smooth white or greenish underbark

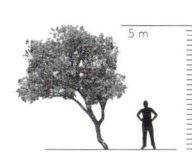
5 m

Leaves up to 15 cm long, with rounded base, apex pointy or blunt; usually downy on undersurface; edges often slightly wavy

Flowers solitary or in small clusters, from leaf axils; petals 4 or 5, pure white, fragrant; stamens numerous, crowded, white, tipped with yellow anthers [see pic at left]

Fruit round or pear-shaped, up to 10 cm long; skin green, turning yellow or pink when ripe; flesh sweet or tart, embedded with numerous tiny seeds

A small, spreading tree with an open crown and a slender, crooked stem often branching close to the ground. The thin, coppery bark peeling off the pale, bony stem is a distinctive character. Young branches are peculiarly 4-angled. The fruit are too familiar to need description. Native to tropical America, first brought to India by the Portuguese.

WHERE TO SEE IT Lots of guava trees in Hauz Rani City Forest, Rashtrapati Bhavan gardens, Shalimar Bagh and other N Delhi orchards. Common, too, in small gardens.

◣ JAMUN *Syzigium cumini*

java/malabar/portuguese or black plum • indian blackberry • jambolan
jamun • jaman • jamoa • phalinda • paiman

jamun/eucalyptus family

16 m

Large tree; more or less evergreen

Bark pale brown, flaky and rough especially on lower trunk

Leaves smooth, leathery, 7-15 cm long; secondary veins numerous, parallel, united in a marginal vein

Flowers in dense clusters; petals small, falling early; stamens numerous, conspicuous

Fruit a round or oblong berry, deep purple when ripe, with sweet or tart flesh

A beautiful, large-canopied tree native to both monsoon and moist forests in S and SE Asia. A favourite avenue tree in India largely because it retains its dense, shady crown through the dry season. Delhi's civic authorities auction the rights each year to collect the dark-purple fruit off the avenue trees.

FLOWERS only about 12 mm wide, faintly fragrant, in geometrically branched clusters usually arranged in sets of 3. Petals 4, white fading to pale pink, falling off in one piece like a cap soon after the bud opens. The numerous long, white stamens are the most conspicuous part of the flower.

cap or 'operculum'

stamens

SEASONS - **LEAVES** start to thin out in late January but are quickly replaced. The canopy looks loveliest in late March, April. **FLOWERS** in May. **FRUIT** ripen by late June or July.

WHERE TO SEE IT By far the most common avenue tree in Lutyens' Delhi – planted along Tughlak, Rajaji, Tyagaraj, Motilal Nehru, Ferozeshah, Sunehri Bagh Roads, etc. Most of the trees in the lawns of Rajpath however are not jamuns but a close relative (see p89). The tallest jamun I've seen in Delhi is inside Qudsia Bagh. CP's Central Park has lost a large number of trees to the Metro Station.

marginal vein

parallel
secondary
veins

LEAVES in opposite pairs, 7-15 cm long, with pointy tips. Upper surface dull glossy, underside paler and matte. Midrib prominent with numerous close, parallel secondary veins, united with another vein running close to the leaf margin. The leaf is aromatic when crushed.

FRUIT an edible berry 1.2-5 cm long, not quite spherical. Green at first, ripening deep purple with a thin, glossy skin. Inner pulp white or pink, juicy, sweet or with an acid tang, containing a pigment which stains the mouth blue.

the round 'crown' at the apex is the remains of the flower-cup

BARK pale grey with dark patches, cracked and flaking low down the trunk, becoming smooth higher up.

CAN BE CONFUSED WITH

The rai jamun, which is planted all along Rajpath. Some botanists are dubious about the distinction, but the jamun wallahs who harvest the fruit in Delhi are not at all equivocal – they differentiate clearly between the smaller, rounder *bhadainya* jamun or jamoa (picture above) which ripens later in the rains and the larger *ashadiya* or rai jamun (below) which matures in late June. These differences correspond to the species *Syzigium cumini* and *Syzigium nervosum* respectively. See page 89 for how to tell the 2 species apart by their field characters.

HABITAT Thrives in high rainfall, but in a dry habitat seeks out moist niches like river banks. Once established, it will survive drought but remain stunted. Tolerates a wide range of soil conditions, but prefers a clayey or sandy loam.

RANGE Throughout the Indian subcontinent except the most arid regions, up to about 1000 m elevation. Particularly abundant in S Indian moist forests where it grows to a great size. Extends eastwards through Myanmar, Malaysia and Indonesia to Northern Australia. It may have been introduced into the Philippines in prehistoric times.

USES A very popular shade tree in India. The fruit is employed in folk medicine in diabetes, dysentery and diseases of the spleen, as a tonic, and to strengthen the teeth and gums. In the wild, the fruit is eagerly devoured by jackals, civets, etc. The leaves, stem and bark are also used medicinally. The bark yields a range of durable brown dyes. The tree is one of the host plants for the tussar silkworm. It is sacred to Hindus and Buddhists. The heavy, beautiful reddish-brown heartwood is extensively used, especially for structures (like well curbs) that remain underwater.

ATALANTIA *Atalantia monophylla*

wild lime • indian atalantia

jangli nimbu

orange family

Small tree; deciduous

Bark pale brown, smooth, on deeply fluted stems [see pic below]

Leaves smooth, up to 8 cm long, shiny; apex prominently notched

Flowers white, with 4 or 5 petals; stamens 8 or 10, bundled in a tube; beautifully fragrant

Fruit like a miniature orange; not seen in Delhi

A small, spinous tree with a deeply fluted, crooked trunk and glossy leaves that smell unmistakably citrusy. The ends of the leaves are distinctively notched. It produces profuse white flowers in October, but does not seem to fruit in Delhi. Native to E and peninsular India, Sri Lanka, Myanmar and to the Malaysian region.

WHERE TO SEE IT Lodi Garden has 2 old trees close to Sheesh Gumbad; 2 tall trees in Sundar Nursery, towards the zoo.

KAURI PINE *Agathis robusta*

kauri pine • queensland kauri • smooth-bark kauri

no local name

monkey-puzzle family

Large tree; evergreen

Bark flaky, mottled with grey, brown and orange [far left]

Leaves mostly in opposite pairs, leathery, smooth, with barely visible parallel veins

Flowers male and female separate on the same tree; male cone-flowers small; female flowers on large, green, globular cones; not often seen in Delhi

Fruit cones brown, woody, with overlapping scales

A tall, imposing conifer reaching 50 m in its native forests in Northern Australia, with thick, flat leaves instead of needles. Kauri pines require rather more moisture than Delhi offers and remain stunted. For some reason, there are quite a lot of kauri pines planted in various places in Delhi University.

WHERE TO SEE IT 3 big trees in the inner garden of the department of botany, Delhi University. 3 smallish trees in a quad in the arts faculty of Delhi U; more in the garden of the faculty of music & fine arts. One largish tree and a small one in Lodi Garden. 2 trees in Talkatora Garden. One tree in the zoo, close to the director's office.

RAI JAMUN *Syzigium nervosum*

Syn: Cleistocalyx operculata

not distinguished from the jamun in english

jamun/eucalyptus family

rai jamun • piaman • dugdugia

Medium-sized tree; nearly evergreen

Bark flaky, pale grey-brown, inner bark reddish

Leaves smooth, leathery, up to 20 cm long, broadly oval; apex blunt or short-pointy; 8-12 pairs of lateral nerves

Flowers creamy white, in clusters; petals white, united and falling off in one piece like a 'cap'; stamens numerous, long, conspicuous

Fruit a dark-purple berry enclosing a single stone; usually ovoid, sometimes spherical; inner pulp sweet and tart

It may come as a surprise that most of the lovely trees on both sides of Rajpath are not jamuns but a closely allied relative known as 'rai jamuns'. They are not at all easy to distinguish from jamuns, but the fruitsellers who shake down the fruit will show you the larger, longer fruit of the earlier-maturing rai jamun.

FRUIT larger, more elongated than jamuns. They taste and smell a little different too, though the precise difference is hard to pinpoint.

SEASONS - LEAVES almost evergreen; new flush in April, some of the old leaves turning reddish before falling. **FLOWERS** much earlier than jamuns, March-April. **FRUIT** ripen by mid to late June, well before the rains.

FLOWERS in clusters, with long stamens, very hard to distinguish from the jamun's.

WHERE TO SEE IT On the lawns on both sides of Rajpath; in Sundar Nursery. (Old) Sabzi Mandi used to have some trees but they have been cut down. More common than one might think, though nearly all the avenues in Lutyens' Delhi are jamuns, not rai jamuns.

CAN BE CONFUSED WITH

The jamun (pages 86-87). The main differences are:

Jamun	Rai jamun
Leaves leathery, with many closely spaced lateral nerves; lateral veins united in a prominent marginal vein. **Fruit** rounder, distinctly smaller than rai jamuns.	**Leaves** sub-leathery, broad; only 8-12 pairs of distant lateral nerves; marginal veins not prominent, or absent. **Fruit** longer, larger than jamuns.

❧ DHAU *Anogeissus pendula*

no english common name

arjun family

dhau • dhoy • dhao • dhok • (kala) dhaukra

Middle-sized tree; deciduous

Bark silvery when young, becoming darker, rougher

Leaves small, narrowed at both ends; young leaves with silvery hairs

Flowers tiny, yellowish green, massed in round heads

Fruit also in small, round heads about 5 mm long

FLOWERS small, yellowish green, tightly clustered in round heads only about one cm wide. The sticky-out stamens give the flower heads a fuzzy, delicate look.

yellow-tipped stamens prominent ●

flower heads usually solitary, on long, unbranched stalks ●

A short, crooked tree with small, pretty leaves, silvery trunk and gracefully drooping extremities. Capable of reaching 15 m, but it stays shrubby and low when lopped or grazed. Superbly drought-hardy, this is the emblematic native tree of the Aravallis. Found now only in localized patches on the Ridge, sometimes in pure, dense stands.

SEASONS - LEAVES bare for many months from January; rain may induce short-lived new flushes. Very beautiful when fully in new leaf in mid May. **FLOWERS** June to September. **FRUIT** begin in September, remaining till February or even later.

WHERE TO SEE IT In patches on the C Ridge, especially S of Simon Bolivar Marg. Wiped out from the N Ridge and now rare in JNU and Mehrauli. 2 large trees in front of Hall No. 8 in Pragati Maidan – relics, presumably, of natural forest cleared to make the Exhibition Grounds. Sundar Nursery has a solitary tree. Dhau is in real danger of dying out completely from Delhi.

leaves up to 3 cm long, in pairs that are nearly opposite

new leaves silvery

LEAVES small, on drooping twigs. New leaves are pale with a beautiful silvery sheen from soft, silky hairs lying flat on the leaf surface. Just before dropping, the leaves acquire delicate manganese tints between purple and brown. Massed together, they are a beautiful sight.

FRUIT like the flowers, are clustered in heads. Individual fruit are flattish and more or less circular in outline, with narrow wing-like flanks.

BARK more or less smooth, pale brown with a silvery sheen particularly on young trees. The bark on older trees can sometimes be conspicuously warty, as in the picture on the right.

HABITAT Dhau is the 'habitat specialist' of the Aravalli hills, thriving on hot, dry slopes and rocky soil where most other trees would not survive. Parts of the Ridge in Delhi (where the Aravallis peter out) were once forested with dhau, but it has been heavily grazed. Dhau responds to lopping and grazing by growing shrubby and low, covering the ground in horizontally spreading mats. It has a hair-trigger response to rain in the dry season.

RANGE Confined to a limited territory bounded by the Aravallis in the W, the Delhi region in the N, stretching E to Bundelkhand and S through western MP up to the Narmada river. Common in relatively protected areas in the Aravallis and near Shivpuri, where it grows to its greatest stature.

USES Valuable for afforesting dry, rocky hills. The leaves are an excellent fodder and yield a sombre green dye that has almost been forgotten. It has only minor medicinal uses. Tannins from the bark and leaves are employed to make sheepskin whiter. The heavy wood has been rated as the toughest timber so far tested in India – even tougher than American hickory – and is especially suitable for striking tools such as mallets.

The closely allied chakwa – some botanists even regard chakwa and dhau as varieties of the same species – and differentiation is not easy. Basically, dhau is smaller, with silvery bark and more delicate leaves. Chakwa tends to be distinctively yellow-barked, with larger and hairier leaves. Fortunately, it is much too rare in Delhi to cause much confusion.

HARRA *Terminalia chebula*

black/chebulic myrobalan   *arjun family*

harra • harh • haradh

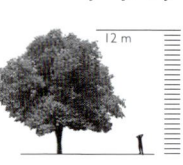

Middle-sized tree; deciduous

Bark thick, medium or dark brown with vertical furrows

Leaves up to 20 cm long, white-woolly when young, leathery when old; apex blunt to short-pointy, base rounded; 2 glands near top of leaf stalk

Flowers small, creamy, clustered in 10-cm-long spikes at ends of twigs; stamens long, no petals; smell unpleasant

Fruit pendant, more or less pear-shaped with faint ribs, about 5 cm long; green at first, turning brown and eventually black; nut hard and bony

A squat, crooked tree of deciduous forests in low hilly country, whose spreading canopy can look very pretty in new leaf. Its hard, ribbed fruit was once an important tanning agent but is now mostly just food for deer and giant squirrels. Delhi is hardly ideal harra country and it is rare here.

flowering spike •

WHERE TO SEE IT
Only 2 specimens in the nursery at Delhi University.

 # ANAR *Punica granatum*

pomegranate • chinese apple • granada   *pomegranate family*

anar

Shrub or small tree; deciduous

Bark thin, grey or grey-brown; not very rough

Leaves narrow, usually in opposite pairs, sometimes in tufts; margins slightly wavy; glossy on top

Flowers showy, funnel-shaped, about 5 cm long with a scarlet flower-cup; petals 5-8, sometimes 'double', usually orange-red; stamens numerous [pic at left]

Fruit large, globular, with a leathery shell, enclosing numerous seeds embedded in a sweet pulp [below]

A shiny-leaved bush or diminutive tree that produces one of the oldest cultivated fruit in the world. The bright-scarlet flowers (sometimes 'double' varieties) with bright yellow-capped stamens can be very beautiful. Wild at moderate altitudes in the NW Himalaya, the anar is cultivated for ornament but is seldom allowed to grow tree-sized.

WHERE TO SEE IT Fairly common as an ornamental bush in parks and private gardens; trees are much more rare. Rashtrapati Bhavan has a few.

PEEPAL-LIKE LEAVES *Widest in the lower third*

With milky latex

apex
rounded

thick,
leathery,
nearly
smooth

banyan
22 cm p102

extra
long apex

margins
wavy

smooth.
shiny

peepal
30 cm p96

very long stalk

glossy
on top

short,
prominent tip

veins
white

pilkhan
22 cm p100

shiny
on top

2 glands

chinese tallow tree
7 cm p126

apex
tapering

smooth,
glossy

veins
pale
yellow

base
v-shaped

jadi
20 cm p98

3 basal veins

leaf stalk
very long

candlenut
40 cm p155

pointy tip

smooth,
shiny
on
top

weeping fig
12 cm p99

smooth,
glossy

leaves
opposite

karaunda
8 cm p95

often lobed

**paper
mulberry**
22 cm p104

woolly,
rough

sometimes
unequal at
base

rough on both
sides; hairy
below

sometimes
3-5 lobed

anjeeri
14 cm p95

Without milky latex, margins toothed

apex long or
short, pointy

often
lobed

toot
15 cm p106

woolly
on both
sides

base
unequal

west indian elm
20 cm p104

very
rough

teeth few,
distant,
often
absent

harshingar
13 cm p68

hairy at
first; glossy
later

sand pear
17 cm p111

leaves opposite;
bluntly toothed

no teeth
near apex

arni
6 cm p155

stalk
flattened

**eastern
cottonwood**
26 cm p105

2 glands

margins
wavy

teeth
blunt

apex
blunt

bilangada
10 cm p105

teeth very
fine

smooth
above,
silky
below

indian willow
16 cm p110

smooth,
not glossy

teeth
regular;
uniform

peach tree
14 cm p111

glossy,
smooth

teeth
faint,
distant

unequal
at base

putranjiva
10 cm p108

PEEPAL-LIKE LEAVES

Without milky latex, margins not toothed

glossy,
smooth

second-
ary veins
distant

chaulmugra tree
26 cm p120

leathery,
smooth,
shiny

secondary
veins
close

gab
20 cm p113

narrow
at both
ends

hairy
below

chakwa
9 cm p112

smooth;
3-5 nerves
at base

arnatto
25 cm p112

dull grey-
green;
fleshy;
smooth

peelu
8 cm p114

smooth
above,
hairy
below

3-nerved
at base

kamala
35 cm p121

smooth,
shiny on
both
sides

stalk
very
short

ashok
25 cm p116

smooth,
leathery;
shiny on
top

wavy
edges

stalk
grooved
on top

mango tree
40 cm p118

smooth
on top,
leathery

edges may
have
minute,
rounded
teeth

2 glands

tiny stalk

arjun
25 cm p122

apex long,
usually
blunt

woolly
when
young

3-5
nerves
at base

tumri
30 cm p126

leathery
when
mature

shiny, paler
on top

camphor laurel
10 cm p113

3-5 nerves
at base

young
leaves
lobed

5-7 nerves
at base

empress tree
50 cm p121

texture soft,
velvety

5-7 nerves
at base

philippine tung tree
32 cm p119

2 glands

7 nerves
at base

margins
wavy

5-7 nerves
at base

leathery
when
mature

softly
hairy
beneath

haldu
38 cm p120

shiny on
top

**indian tulip
tree**
20 cm p119

velvety,
paler,
beneath

lobed
when
young

shiny
glands

gamhar
38 cm p124

KARAUNDA *Carissa congesta*

Syn: *Carissa carandas*

bengal currant • christ's thorn

frangipani/oleander family

karaunda

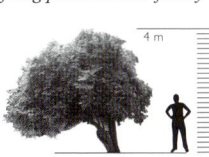

Shrub or small tree; evergreen

Bark pale brown or greyish, not very rough

Spines simple or forked, up to 5 cm long

Leaves in opposite pairs, shiny; tapering at base, rounded at apex with a tiny sharp point; new leaves red

Flowers tubular, pure white or tinged pink, at ends of twigs; petals 5, pointy, overlapping to the right

Fruit a reddish-purple berry up to 2.5 cm long; pulp juicy, acid

A straggly shrub or a small, gangly tree grown for its tart berries and sometimes as a dense, spiny, evergreen hedge. No one is quite sure where it comes from, but wild plants are reported from areas of UP and dry parts of Sri Lanka. A closely related shrub with smaller flowers is found on the Ridge.

WHERE TO SEE IT More common as a hedge (Shalimar Gardens, behind the Russian embassy); trees in fruit orchards in N Delhi.

ANJEERI *Ficus palmata*

punjab fig

mulberry/fig family

anjeeri • khemri • kaimbar • bedu • phagwara • phag • phegra • kak • kok • thapur

Tall shrub or small tree; deciduous

Bark relatively smooth, ashy or brown

Leaves stalked, broadly oval; softly hairy on top, rough below; margins toothed, apex pointy, base rounded; leaves sometimes 3-5 lobed

Figs solitary, stalked, up to 25 mm in diameter; pear-shaped, downy, yellow-purple when ripe [see pic below]

This small tree is the closest wild relative of the European fig. Usually shrubby, it is capable of growing into a small tree 8 m tall. Easily recognized because it is the only one of Delhi's fig trees with toothed leaves. Native to NW India and beyond, and a Delhi native tree as well.

WHERE TO SEE IT In the Jaunapur ravines, Hauz Khas District Park and even Teen Murti Bhavan (the epitome of a tended garden). Some trees outside the Met Office and Jorbagh Post Office.

PEEPAL *Ficus religiosa*

bo tree • sacred fig • peepal • pipal
peepal • peepli

mulberry/fig family

Large tree; deciduous

Trunk short, thick, often fluted; exudes milky latex

Bark yellowish or grey-brown, smooth, becoming scaly with age

Leaves large, with wavy margins and long stalks; heart-shaped at base with very long, pointy tip; shiny on top

Figs in pairs, from leaf axils; reddish at first, eventually deep purple when ripe

FIGS in pairs growing from leaf axils, without apparent stalks. The peepal's figs are small (for such a big tree) – only 1-1.5 cm in diameter. They are green at first, turning red, then deep purple or almost black when ripe. They are not quite spherical but slightly squashed in one plane.

A large, much-revered strangler fig lacking aerial roots. Trunks of large peepals are often fluted and sinewy. Its glossy, long-tailed leaves hanging down from extended leaf stalks are distinctive and clatter noisily in the slightest breeze. The peepal is not strictly native to Delhi but is naturalized. Common in avenues and parks.

• ripe figs can be almost black

• immature figs are sometimes spotty

SEASONS - LEAVES start to fall in January; most trees are bare by mid March. From late March to late April new leaves emerge in tints of pink, copper and cinnamon, before darkening. **FIGS** ripen around mid April, attracting hordes of birds. Some trees have a second flush, ripening in October.

WHERE TO SEE IT Delhi has many peepal avenues: Mother Teresa Marg, Mandir Marg and Panch-sheel Marg (with a double row). It is the commonest tree inside the walled city, with big specimens in Khari Baoli. Shakti Sthal has a pretty grove and individual trees are dotted about in nearly every park and yard. Present but not at all common on the Ridge.

long stalks allow the leaf to tremble and spin in the slightest breeze

wavy margin follows the scallops of the lateral veins

blade is criss-crossed by a fine network of little veins

LEAVES nearly triangular with a heart-shaped base and a long, thin tail or 'drip-tip'. The edge of the leaf is wavy. The blade (including the tail) can be up to 30 cm long, though this is an exceptional size – more usually about 14 cm. In texture the leaf is like rexine and is perfectly hairless. Dark and glossy on top, dull and paler below, with prominent yellow-green veins. The leaf stalks are exceptionally long.

CAN BE CONFUSED WITH

The gamhar. The basic difference is that gamhar leaves are velvety beneath, are not shiny and have a much shorter, pointy apex.

a peepal in the early stages of strangling a wild date palm

BARK yellowish or pale brownish-grey, more or less smooth when young, with faint patterns of horizontal 'stretch marks'. The bark becomes rough and scaly with age. The inner bark is deep pink and exudes a milky latex when injured.

>> Ever Seen the Flowers of a Peepal Tree? – see p321 – How Figs Are Pollinated – see p322

THE SACRED PEEPAL

Gautam Buddha achieved enlightenment meditating under a peepal tree and this particular tree came to be known as the 'Bodhi Tree'. The peepal is also sacred to Hindus who venerate it as the female of the banyan. (See page 323 for more on 'Sacred Peepals'.)

HABITAT A tree of hot, moist and dry forests. Like the banyan, the peepal is an epiphytic strangler. It avoids heavy, poorly drained soils but is not otherwise fussy. It is exceptionally long-lived and specimens over 2 millennia old are known.

RANGE It has been cultivated in India for so long that its original home is uncertain. Older authorities said it is truly wild only in the sub-Himalayan forests E of the Punjab, and in parts of Bengal and C India. Everywhere else it has probably run wild after 'escaping' from cultivation. Some authors claim it is also indigenous in S China, Thailand and Vietnam.

USES The root-bark is one of the 5 barks most valued by ancient Indian physicians. The juice of the bark is used as a mouthwash, for curing toothache and weak gums. The figs are laxative and are used as a remedy for asthma. The leaves and young shoots are purgative. Obstinate hiccups, 'they say', are cured by drinking water in which burnt peepal bark has been steeped. The leaves make a nutritious fodder. The greyish wood is not much used. The fibrous bark was pulped to make paper for the wonderful green Burmese umbrellas that are now an endangered art.

JADI *Ficus amplissima*

Syn: Ficus tsiela

no english common name

mulberry/fig family

jadi • (loosely) pilkhan

Middle-sized tree; deciduous

Bark pale brown or yellow with a greenish tinge, relatively smooth in texture

Leaves broadly oval with a tapering, pointy tip; 3 nerves from the base; upper surface darker and shiny

Figs in pairs, without stalks, clustered towards the ends of branches; dark purple when ripe

FIGS pear-shaped, about 12 mm in diameter, and pale green at first, before darkening to a deep purple when mature. They grow in leaf axils or from the scars of fallen leaves.

A handsome fig tree with great sinewy aerial roots that gird the top of its trunk, much like a pilkhan. It is distinguished by its yellowish bark and stalkless figs that ripen deep purple. Native to C and S India, it is planted along a few select avenues and seems to prosper in Delhi's climate.

● the figs have no stalks

AERIAL ROOTS typically strangler-like, but wrap themselves around the trunk in the absence of a 'victim'.

SEASONS - LEAVES distinctly thin through the dry season, seldom completely bare; new leaves in May. **FIGS** ripen in late March; again in August-September.

WHERE TO SEE IT Krishna Menon Marg is a pure avenue of jadi, the only one of its kind in Lutyens' Delhi. Quite a few trees planted along Ring Road near South Extension, at the foot of Link Road flyover and on Ring Road near the old JNU campus.

CAN BE CONFUSED WITH

The pilkhan, which has a distinctly silvery bark and stalked figs, which are white when ripe.

WEEPING FIG *Ficus benjamina*

weeping/java fig • java willow • benjamin tree • tropic/weeping laurel
kabra • pimpri (marathi)

mulberry/fig family

Middle-sized tree; evergreen

Aerial roots absent or thin, not prominent

Bark pale grey, dull, more or less smooth, with a characteristic pattern of lenticels

Leaves of all 3 varieties glossy, smooth, leathery, with fine secondary veins; var. *benjamina* leaves up to 12 cm long, with long, thin tails (twisted to one side); those of var. *comosa* are similar, often a bit longer, densely clustered at the ends of twigs; var. *nuda* leaves are narrower and smaller, less than 6 cm, with longer, thinner tails

Figs without stalks, in pairs, with considerable variation in size, colour and shape. Var. *benjamina*'s figs are bright red and pea-sized; those of var. *comosa* are larger and flask-shaped, bright orange or yellow when ripe; var. *nuda* bears small figs that are whitish or red-brown

VAR. *COMOSA* figs are orange, flask-shaped and larger than other varieties, up to 2 cm in diameter.

A large, handsome evergreen fig tree (in its moist, natural habitat) with a dense, spreading crown of glossy, pointy leaves and drooping branchlets. Three separate varieties of the species and numerous ornamental hybrids are distinguished, causing much confusion. Most of Delhi's outdoor trees are a variety known as '*nuda*'; the indoor plants come in an array of cultivars.

VAR. *NUDA* figs are smaller and reddish brown, up to 18 mm in diameter.

>> Varieties of the Weeping Fig – see p335

a curly leaved cultivar known as 'TooLittle', from a chance mutation discovered in 1988

SEASONS - LEAVES evergreen, with new flushes in the rains. **FIGS** of var. *comosa* ripen in July; those of var. *nuda* ripen in January, and often again in May.

WHERE TO SEE IT The oldest weeping fig (var. *comosa*) I've found in Delhi is in Lodi Garden, close to the Sheesh Gumbad. Specimens of var. *nuda* are more commonly found in parks and gardens of all sizes, and are gaining popularity.

CAN BE CONFUSED WITH

The laurel fig. The basic differences are that the leaf of the weeping fig ends in a short, prominent, pointy tail; the laurel fig's leaf is rounded or bluntly pointed. Also, the figs of the weeping fig are larger and bright yellow or orange-red; those of the laurel fig are never this colour.

PILKHAN *Ficus virens*

Syn: Ficus infectoria

grey/java/spotted/white fig

mulberry/fig family

pilkhan • pakad • pakdi • ram anjeer • khabar • palakh

Large tree; deciduous

Bark grey with a silvery aspect; with milky sap

Leaves smooth, oval with a broad base and short, pointy apex; 3 nerves start from the base

Figs in pairs, on short stalks; white speckled with tiny red dots when ripe

FIGS pea-sized, growing from the axils of leaves in pairs, on short stalks. The figs start out green, ripening white with a pinkish blush and are often speckled with red.

this is the only fig tree in Delhi with white figs

A fairly common strangler fig in Delhi with an immense, spreading canopy that displays wonderful changing tints when it renews its foliage in spring. It has long aerial roots like the banyan's but they tend to wrap themselves around the top of the trunk instead of becoming dangling prop-roots. One of Delhi's most beautiful shade trees.

SEASONS - LEAVES begin to drop in mid February with little or no synchronization. New leaf in early March, going from dusty purple to red, then through a dazzling array of russets and bronzes till they turn pale green. The Pilkhan Show continues till mid April, with another flush early in the rains. **FIGS** ripen July to September.

WHERE TO SEE IT Becoming common in Delhi now and wonderful eye-candy in April. Zakir Hussain, Dalhousie, Neeti and Nyaya Margs are purely pilkhan avenues. A short, lovely avenue inside Bu Halima's Gate (Humayun's Tomb). Constitution Club on Raisina Road has a huge specimen. Hauz Khas has some lovely trees.

• distant, arching veins form loops at their ends

LEAVES smooth, up to 16 cm long, variable but generally broadly oval with a rounded base and short, pointy apex. The leaf stalk is 4-8 cm long and distinctly channelled. The margins of the leaf are often wavy. Like all figs, the pink leaf-buds (stipules) are shed as the leaves unfurl. Beautiful red to bronzy tints as the leaves are renewed in March.

AERIAL ROOTS tend to wrap themselves around the top of the trunk like a muffler.

BARK dark grey or grey-brown with a silvery touch. Not very rough, but with odd bits of bark scaling off.

CAN BE CONFUSED WITH

The jadi, whose overall form and leaves are similar. The main difference is that jadi has smooth, distinctively greenish-yellow bark and figs without stalks that turn deep purple when they ripen.

WHICH VARIETY OF PILKHAN?

Ficus virens is among the more difficult figs to nail down and there is immense confusion about its discarded names and identity. So far as I can tell, Delhi's pilkhans are *Ficus virens* var. *virens*, and not var. *sublanceolata* or var. *wightiana* as some authors maintain. The botanical classification of the figs is intricate, turning on minute details of their microscopic flowers, and we probably need to wait until this species receives more attention to unravel its intricacies and varieties.

HABITAT A scattered tree of relatively moist forests, but adaptable and drought-hardy to a great extent. It grows in most kinds of well-drained soils and attains a great size when it is free from competition. Like other strangler figs, it often starts life as an epiphyte, growing on other trees and eventually killing them.

RANGE Fairly common in the sub-Himalayan belt across Pakistan and NW India and in the monsoon forests of C India. Uncertainty and controversy about its precise identity make it difficult to say if its range also extends into S India, but one or the other variety of this species is at home in a huge swathe of territory sprawling across SE Asia from India to the Solomon Islands and tropical Australia.

USES The leaves make an excellent fodder, particularly beloved by elephants. Its qualities of being a quick grower and providing ample shade make the pilkhan an excellent and much-used avenue tree. Because of the size of its canopy, it makes an excellent windbreak. A decoction made from the bark is used as a gargle and wash for ulcers. The greyish wood is moderately hard but not durable and is little used except to make charcoal in NW India.

BANYAN *Ficus benghalensis*

(indian) banyan tree • east indian fig-tree

mulberry/fig family

bargad • bargat • badh • bar • bor

Large spreading tree; nearly evergreen

Bark greyish, not rough; exudes milky sap when cut

Leaves leathery, up to 20 cm long, broadly oval with a rounded base; hairy at first, mostly smooth when mature

Figs without stalks, in pairs from leaf axils; large, round, faintly downy, richly red when ripe

the flowers, both male and female, lie inside the fig

With a potentially infinite system of prop-roots, the banyan forms the most extensive crown of any plant in the world. Often beginning life on another tree as a strangler, it is capable of growing to 30 m or taller and is more or less evergreen. Delhi has no outstanding specimens and has only flirted tentatively with banyans as avenue trees.

FIGS more or less spherical, about 2 cm in diameter, growing in pairs from leaf axils, without stalks. They are softly downy and dull rose-red when ripe.

soft, velvety surface

SEASONS - **LEAVES** more or less evergreen; new flush in March-April can be strikingly beautiful because of pink tints. **FIGS** ripen in April-May, but on some trees in late October.

WHERE TO SEE IT There is a short stretch of banyans on Teen Murti Marg, near the 'Bengali Lines'. Large specimens behind the Coffee Shop in Maiden's Hotel, near Kalkaji Temple, inside Olive Restaurant (Mehrauli) and in the zoo (near the crocodiles).

base rounded or faintly heart-shaped •

apex •
blunt

leaves deep • green above, paler beneath

LEAVES shielded when they first emerge by 2 large leaf-buds, which drop off as the leaves unfurl. Leaf blades up to 20 cm long (usually about 14 cm), broadly oval with a rounded or heart-shaped base. Young leaves are softly downy, becoming firm, leathery and nearly smooth when mature.

HABITAT Deciduous and semi-evergreen forests throughout India, up to 1300 m. It is semi-deciduous in very dry locations (such as the Ridge). It grows best on well-drained loamy soils, but tolerates poor soils, including shallow, stony sites and even saline lands. It will not grow in the shade.

RANGE Throughout Indian forests, but according to some authors, truly wild only in the sub-Himalayan tract and some peninsular forests. It is not found wild outside the Indian subcontinent.

USES The banyan has a host of medicinal uses: its latex is applied to bruises and cracked soles and to relieve rheumatic pains. An infusion of the bark is drunk as a tonic. The red tips of young aerial roots are eaten to cure obstinate vomiting. The leaves make good fodder, especially loved by elephants. The figs are greedily eaten by birds, bats and monkeys and are a useful famine food. The soft wood is of little value except underwater, so is used for well-curbs. The aerial roots are stronger and are used for tent-poles. The tree is worshipped by Hindus as the male consort of the peepal. It is customary to plant a silver coin under the roots of a young banyan.

• new leaves emerge a lovely shade of translucent pink

CAN BE CONFUSED WITH

The mysore fig, but the banyan is much less hairy on its leaf, stalk and around the figs.

>> Banyans and Banias
– see p323
– Ever Seen the Flowers of a Peepal Tree? – see p321
– How Figs Are Pollinated – see p322

BARK grey or silvery, relatively smooth, becoming somewhat flaky when older. The underbark is pink when exposed by a cut.

THE BANYAN'S PROP-ROOTS

A banyan's aerial roots are like pink cotton threads that start thickening only after they reach the ground. Once anchored, they grow rapidly, becoming massive props to the branches overhead. This process of infinite extension enables the banyan to produce specimens of unbelievable spread and age. See page 323 for details on 'The Biggest Banyans'.

PAPER MULBERRY *Broussonetia papyrifera*

paper mulberry • tapa cloth tree

mulberry/fig family

no local name

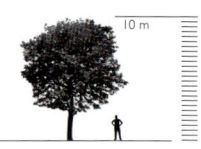

Middle-sized tree; deciduous

Bark pale grey-brown with shallow furrows and prominent lenticels; exudes milky latex

Leaves large, variable, broad with a heart-shaped base, lobed or not; rough on top, densely velvety beneath

Flowers greenish yellow, male and female on separate trees; male flowers in strings 7 cm long, females in ball-shaped clusters

Fruit round, fleshy, reddish, about 18 mm in diameter; in clusters [see pic at left]

An extremely rapid-growing, invasive East Asian tree that colonizes moist areas and can be troublesome. It is not a true mulberry but its bark has been used in Japan for 1500 years to produce high-quality paper. Mercifully rare in Delhi, because the pollen from male plants is highly allergenic.

WHERE TO SEE IT The zoo has a few trees; one grove is next to the spectacled caiman enclosure. Some trees planted in Ladha Sarai, near Jamali Kamali.

 # WEST INDIAN ELM *Guazuma ulmifolia*

west indian elm • bastard/bay cedar • pigeon wood

cocoa family

no local name

Middle-sized tree; deciduous

Bark grey-brown, cracked, rough

Leaves 6-20 cm long, hairy, markedly unequal at base; margins irregularly toothed

Flowers in clusters, about 5 mm wide, woolly-looking; 5 yellow petals topped by thread-like appendages

Fruit a capsule, cylindrical or almost round, black when ripe [immature fruit shown in pic below]

A moderate-sized tree with an irregular crown and slightly droopy branches. Briefly attractive in new leaf, otherwise somewhat unkempt-looking on account of its dusty foliage. Its small, yellow flowers are clustered in panicles. Native to tropical C America from Mexico to Paraguay and long cultivated in S India. Rare in Delhi.

WHERE TO SEE IT 4 or 5 trees inside the gate of Sector B Pocket 1, Vasant Kunj; one spent-looking specimen in Sundar Nursery; another inside Mother's International on Aurobindo Marg.

BILANGADA *Flacourtia indica*

governor's/madagascar plum • ramontchi   *chilla family*

bilangada • katai • kukai • kangu • kandi • bhanber • sherawane

Bush or small tree; deciduous

Bark ashy grey or yellowish; rough and fissured when old

Spines single, straight, up to 6 cm long, sometimes bearing leaves and flowers

Leaves smallish, with blunt teeth along the margins; apex blunt, base narrow; new leaves emerge in shades of red

Flowers about 4 mm wide, yellowish, without petals; male and female flowers on separate plants, singly or in small clusters; male plants more abundant

Fruit small, pea-sized berries, deep red or brown-purple when ripe; acid to sweetish in taste

Usually just a thorny shrub on the Ridge, it sometimes grows into a short, stiff tree armed with formidable spines and a bushy crown of small, bluntly toothed leaves. Native to hot, dry, rocky environs and widely distributed in India. Not cultivated in Delhi, though it was once used as an armed hedge.

Where to see it Very common on the Ridge, mostly in shrubby form. There's a big tree inside the Qutb compound and quite a few in JNU campus. Buddha Jayanti Park has a large male tree, very attractive in flower.

EASTERN COTTONWOOD *Populus deltoides*

eastern cottonwood • eastern/carolina poplar • necklace poplar   *willow/poplar family*

bagnu • bahar • baupeepal

Medium-sized tree; deciduous

Bark yellowish green when young, grey and deeply furrowed when mature

Leaves shaped like an equilateral triangle, the sides 7-26 cm long; shiny green above, paler beneath; apex pointed, base flat and broad; margins with rounded teeth; leaf stalk pinched flat near leaf-blade, with two round glands

Flowers in slender, hairy spikes; male and female flowers on separate trees; flowers not seen in Delhi

Fruit a small, conical, green capsule, clustered in long, drooping spikes; not seen in Delhi

A slim tree with an open crown, somewhat droopy branches and unmistakably triangular (deltoid) leaves. Native to the eastern half of the USA and renowned as the fastest-growing tree on the North American continent, it is severely stunted here. Cultivated on a huge scale in wetter climes N and NE of Delhi.

Where to see it A prominent row of cottonwood trees near Rajiv Gandhi's samadhi (Vir Bhumi). Planted on stretches of Lodi Road, flanking Lodi Garden and further west.

◗ TOOT *Morus alba*

white/chinese/silkworm/russian mulberry

mulberry/fig family

toot • tootri • shahtoot • chinni • choon • kandi

Smallish tree; deciduous

Bark brown, rough, with vertical furrows

Leaves variable, mostly oval, often lobed; base heart-shaped, margins toothed

Flowers tiny, greenish, in spikes; male and female flowers separate but on the same tree

Fruit succulent berries crowded together on short spikes; ripe fruit can be white, red or deep violet

FLOWERS tiny, greenish, crowded on slender spikes. Male and female flowers are separate but grow on the same tree, on different branches. It takes practice to tell the sexes apart: male flower spikes are longer (about 2 cm) and fall off in great quantity when they have finished producing pollen. Female spikes are half as long, with individual flowers packed together more closely.

• female flower spikes are shorter

A modest tree with a spreading, irregular crown, sometimes cultivated for its fruit in Delhi but more often self-sown and growing untended in unplanned spaces. This is the silkworm mulberry, originally from China but cultivated in India for so long that it has become naturalized, with a number of dissimilar forms and recognized varieties.

male flower spikes are longer and more loosely
• arranged

SEASONS - LEAVES shed December to January; new leaves in late February, canopy renewed by late March. FLOWERS just before the new leaves in February. Male flowers shed by early March. FRUIT start to develop early in April (depending on variety) and can continue into early May.

WHERE TO SEE IT Common as a self-sown, relict tree in gardens or vacant plots all over the city, seldom planted with intent. There are 2 outsize specimens inside the National Archives compound. Most parks have them. Conspicuously absent from the Ridge.

basal veins

unlobed leaf

lobed leaf

HABITAT Toot grows on a variety of well-drained soils but requires rather a lot of water. It spreads through the agency of birds. It tolerates shade, severe frost and high levels of sulphur pollution, but is short-lived and develops a hollow trunk and ragged crown after about 20 years.

RANGE Originally wild in hilly regions of C and E China and in Japan. Cultivated from antiquity in N India and still widely grown for silkworms. In India it is common as a self-sown tree in the plains and is grown up to 3000 m in the hills.

LEAVES extremely variable, from about 5 cm long (common) to 18 cm. Usually oval with a heart-shaped base and pointy tip, but some leaves (especially on young shoots) can be deeply lobed. There are 3-5 veins starting from the base and the edges of the leaf are irregularly toothed – the teeth may be sharp, forward pointing, blunt or rounded.

FRUIT compound, comprising lots of individual berries packed together. Each little female flower swells up and becomes sweet and juicy. Cultivated mulberries can be 5 cm long, wild ones shorter. The name 'white mulberry' is misleading – the fruit may be white, pink, lavender, violet or nearly black.

the part of each individual flower which becomes succulent is actually the flower-cup

BARK dark or medium brown, rough, with shallow, vertical furrows, becoming accentuated with age.

USES Silkworms have been reared on the leaves of this tree in China from very remote times. The fruit is considered laxative and is used by Unani hakeems to treat sore throats, dyspepsia and melancholia. The bark and roots have med-icinal uses too. The sweet fruit is eaten raw or is processed to make juice, vinegar or wine. The leaves are a nutri-tious fodder. The pale sapwood is of little use but the nut-brown heartwood is fine-grained, medium-heavy and is widely used in the sports goods industry and for light construction and joinery. It has excellent turning and bending properties and can be brought to a fine finish.

OTHER SPECIES OF MULBERRY

Writers describing the mulberry in India say that at least 2 species are commonly found in the plains – the white and the Indian mulberry – but it is very difficult to tell these 2 species apart. For the differences, and more about other species of Indian mulberries, see page 338.

PUTRANJIVA *Drypetes roxburghii* *Syn: Putranjiva roxburghii*

child-life tree • lucky bean tree • wild olive

amla/castor family

putranjiva • putra jiva • jiaputa • putjia • putajan • patji • joti • juti

Middle-sized tree; evergreen

Bark corky, grey or yellowish, studded with white dots

Leaves glossy on top, narrowed at both ends; edges very finely toothed

Flowers tiny; male and female flowers on separate trees

Fruit small, nearly round; dun-coloured when ripe

solitary female flower, long-stalked ●

A handsome evergreen tree with long, drooping branchlets bearing dark, glossy leaves. Lacking conspicuous flowers, the attraction of this tree lies in the grace and geometry of its foliage. Native to moist evergreen forests, it does surprisingly well in Delhi. It is often kept clipped down to form a beautiful, dense hedge.

FLOWERS tiny, without petals. Male and female flowers grow from leaf axils, on separate trees. Male flowers are yellowish and crowded in dense clusters, on short stalks. Female flowers are greenish, solitary or in 2s or 3s, growing at the ends of slightly longer stalks.

SEASONS - LEAVES evergreen, with paler new flushes in April and again in early July. FLOWERS in early April. FRUIT form quickly (only on female trees) after the flowers but do not ripen till February or March of the following year.

WHERE TO SEE IT Racecourse Road, where the PM lives, is the only putranjiva avenue in Lutyens' Delhi. Lots on the road leading to Rashtrapati Bhavan from INS India. 2 pruned trees in front of Teen Murti Bhavan. Shakti Sthal has a dense grove. Most parks have specimens. Often seen as an 'accidental' tree that has escaped from hedgerows of government bungalows throughout Lutyens' Delhi.

male flowers are densely clustered ●

leaf tapering at
base and apex

base is often
asymmetrical

LEAVES up to 13 cm long, thin-
textured, dark green and glossy on
top, paler and dull beneath. New
leaves start out conspicuously lighter
green. The edge of the leaf is very finely
toothed and usually wavy as well. The base
of the leaf is noticeably asymmetrical.

edge of leaf is
very minutely
toothed

FRUIT small, one-seeded, green
at first, turning dun or pale grey
as it ripens. The stone inside is
wrinkled and very hard.

BARK grey or yellowish,
somewhat corky, not very
rough. Studded with tiny
white lenticel specks
arranged in horizontal ranks.

HABITAT Primary moist
evergreen forests up to
about 1000 m.
In drier forests, it seeks
out shady river banks or
swampy ground. In dry
climates (like Delhi's),
putranjiva remains
somewhat stunted but
otherwise shows no ill-
effects. It is frost-hardy.

RANGE Moist evergreen
forests on the sub-
continent, chiefly in the
submontane tracts at
the base of the Him-
alaya and the southern
peninsula. Fairly
common but not
abundant or gregarious.
Also in Sri Lanka,
Myanmar, parts of the
Malay Peninsula and
Indo-China. Cultivated
in warm climates, but
not very common.

USES Putranjiva makes
one of the best clipped
evergreen hedges of all
Indian plants. In trad-
itional medicine, the
leaves and crushed
stones of the fruit are
used to treat colds,
fevers and rheumatism.
The oil from the seeds
was once used as a lamp
fuel. The leaves make a
good cattle fodder. The
hard stones are strung
together in rosaries and
necklaces worn by
children, to keep them
in health and ward off
evil. The wood is grey
and not particularly
attractive but is
moderately hard and
close-grained. It finds
some use locally in
making tool handles,
small articles, for house-
building and turnery.

INDIAN WILLOW *Salix tetrasperma*

indian willow

willow/poplar family

bains • bilsa • laila

Smallish tree; deciduous

Bark brown or grey, rough with deep, vertical fissures

Leaves slim, tapering to a point; undersurface paler; often hairy at first; margins of leaf minutely, irregularly toothed

Flowers tiny, densely crowded in bottlebrush-like 'spikes', male and female on separate trees; male flowers yellowish, faintly scented, in spikes up to 10 cm long; female spikes slightly longer, greenish

Fruit a small, green capsule splitting open to release long, silky hairs; not seen in Delhi

7 m

MALE FLOWERS have 5-10 stamens of varying lengths, with bright-yellow anthers.

A characteristic, slim-leaved willow found naturally on river banks and in moist, swampy places in India and much of SE Asia. Curiously, only male trees are seen on Delhi's streets, partly by design (female trees produce messy fruit) but also because willows are propagated from 'cuttings', and a unisex population easily becomes self-perpetuating.

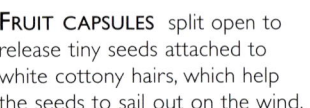

the bark has strong vertical ridges and furrows

SEASONS - LEAVES shed in end December; renewed in late January. **FLOWERING** begins between the middle and end of January, and individual trees (late starters?) may still be in flower in late February. **FRUIT** not seen in Delhi, because there are no female trees here.

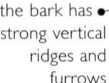

FRUIT CAPSULES split open to release tiny seeds attached to white cottony hairs, which help the seeds to sail out on the wind.

WHERE TO SEE IT Planted on Mathura Road near the NSCI, on Ring Road, near Naraina and on Ring Road near Indira Gandhi Stadium. Rao Tula Ram Marg, opposite West End, has a short stretch of willows, and there are lots around the lake east of Vir Bhumi, in the samadhi gardens.

RANGE OF THE INDIAN WILLOW

The Indian willow has an extremely wide distribution from Afghanistan in the W to Indonesia and the Philippines in the E. It grows up to about 2000 m in the Himalaya but is scarce or absent from dry tracts in C and W India.

PEACH TREE *Prunus persica*

peach tree

adoo

rose/peach/cherry family

Small tree; deciduous

Bark grey with a silvery sheen and horizontal bands of orange lenticels; fissured

Leaves smooth, slender; up to 15 cm long; long-pointed at tip, tapering at base; margins finely toothed

Flowers showy, 5-petalled (if single-flowered); usually bright pink, but darker, paler or even white forms exist

Fruit oval with a small knob at apex; outer skin velvety, green or yellow flushed with red (on the side facing the sun); fleshy and succulent inside; stone deeply sculpted

A small tree branching low down and forming a thin, irregular crown. Peach trees have been cultivated in China since before recorded history. There are hundreds of cultivars, bred for their flowers or for fruiting quality but seldom both together. Delhi is too hot to grow good fruiting varieties.

WHERE TO SEE IT In small gardens and, not very commonly, in public parks. Planted as an understorey tree along stretches of Shanti Path.

SAND PEAR *Pyrus pyrifolia*

sand pear • japanese/chinese/asian pear • asian apple-pear • nashi

nakh

rose/peach/cherry family

Small tree; deciduous

Bark rough, with pale lenticels

Leaves broadly oval, 7-17 cm long, faintly hairy at first, becoming smooth; base tapering, apex long-pointy; margins with short, sharp teeth

Flowers in clusters of 6-9, with 5 pure-white, broad petals; long-stalked; stamens many, anthers black

Fruit round or apple-shaped, about 8 cm in diameter; on long, slender stalks; skin green turning yellow, speckled brown; flesh hard, gritty [see pic below]

A small deciduous tree that looks its best in new leaf, with pretty white flowers. Native to China and Japan where they have been cultivated for over 3000 years, Asian pears are small and round, with a crisp, gritty texture. This is the only kind of pear grown in the hot, dry plains of N India.

WHERE TO SEE IT A small grove of 3 trees in Lodi Garden, near Muhammad Shah's tomb. Cultivated in orchards and gardens.

◗ CHAKWA *Anogeissus acuminata*

button tree

arjun family

chakwa (bengali) • *kardahi* • *yon* (burmese and trade name)

20 m

Large tree; deciduous

Bark mottled, dark, on a yellowish base, lightly peeling

Leaves up to 7 cm long, densely silver-hairy on new shoots; apex pointy

Flowers tiny, yellowish, in round heads [see pic below]

Fruit flattish, also clustered in round heads

A tall, graceful tree with a light canopy and slender, drooping branchlets, outstanding in new leaf in April. The flowers and fruit in round heads are easily mistaken for dhau, to which it is closely related. Native to E India and SE Asia; rare in Delhi even though it appears to tolerate a dry climate well.

WHERE TO SEE IT
2 large trees near the Bada Gumbad in Lodi Garden; many trees in the MCD Nursery near Roshanara Bagh; a solitary tree in Qudsia Bagh; 2 trees in Sundar Nursery, widely separated.

Some authors refer to this tree as *Anogeissus acuminata* var. *acuminata*.

◗ ARNATTO *Bixa orellana*

arnatto • annatto • lipstick tree • bixa

arnatto family

latkan • *lotpan* • *raktabeeja* • *sinduria*

3 m

Bush or small tree; deciduous

Leaves thin, smooth, up to 20 cm, on long stalks; base not quite heart-shaped, tip long-tapering, pointy

Flowers white or pale pink, large, in clusters

Fruit a heart-shaped, brown, spiny pod; fruit split open to reveal bright-red pulp and seeds [see pic below]

A small, ornamental tree with shiny leaves, showy pink-white flowers and prickly pods, native to the West Indies and tropical S and C America. It has been cultivated in India for many centuries for the orange-yellow dye obtained from its seeds, which is still used as a safe colouring agent for foods.

WHERE TO SEE IT
Royle found it growing in the Resident's garden in Delhi in the 1840s. Becoming rare now. One small tree in Sundar Nursery; here and there in small private gardens.

GAB *Diospyros malabarica*

Syn: Diospyros embryopteris

gaub • gaub persimmon

ebony family

gab • kumbh • kala tendu • kusi

Middle-sized tree; evergreen

Bark very dark, becoming rougher, cracked, with age

Leaves dark, shiny, firm, up to 20 cm long; new leaves start red, turn slowly to green

Flowers ivory white, male and female on separate trees; males in clusters of 3-6; females larger, solitary or in pairs

Fruit slightly bigger than a pingpong ball; covered with rusty powder when young, ripening yellow; pulp glutinous, clear

A spreading evergreen tree with a dense crown of long, shiny leaves that are startlingly red when new. Its distinctive fruit are covered with a rusty, powdery substance at first. Native to moist spots in the Himalayan foothills and S India, it adapts well to Delhi's conditions but needs lots of watering.

WHERE TO SEE IT
A large, old tree in front of the VC's office in Delhi Univ. A small grove in Buddha Jayanti Park. Sundar Nursery; inside AIIMS campus.

CAMPHOR LAUREL *Cinnamomum camphora*

camphor laurel • camphor tree • ho wood

cinnamon family

kapoor • karpoor

Small tree; semi-evergreen

Bark greyish, cracked into small plates; outer bark tastes faintly of cinnamon

Leaves broadly oval, about 6 cm long, usually with 3 basal veins; shiny on top, dull below, with a pointy tip nearly always bent to one side; look for conical leaf-buds

Flowers small, whitish or greenish, in branching clusters

Fruit small berry-like fruit resembling peppercorns

A large, handsome near-evergreen tree from China and Japan, with a dense, billowing crown. It does not like Delhi's dryness and is stunted here. The dark leaves are shiny on top, dull and paler below, and smell of camphor when crushed. The small, greenish-white flowers are not conspicuous.

WHERE TO SEE IT Buddha Jayanti Park has 2 short (but not very young) trees close together (not far from the baobab tree). One tree glimpsed in a garden at D409 Defence Colony. Not common in Delhi.

PEELU *Salvadora persica*

mustard tree • toothbrush tree • saltbush

peelu • chhota peelu • jal • meettha/kauri jal • dhalu

peelu family

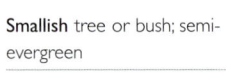

Smallish tree or bush; semi-evergreen

Bark pale, irregularly rough

Leaves smooth, lance-shaped, in opposite pairs; base broad, apex bluntly pointy

Flowers tiny, greenish to yellow, in loose clusters

Fruits tiny berries, pink to scarlet, sweet and peppery

the apex is usually blunt but can sometimes be pointy or notched

Native Delhi trees of great character with wonderfully gnarled trunks and dark foliage arranged on long, drooping branchlets. A quintessential desert tree, ranging from Arabia into dry parts of N and W India. Becoming rare in Delhi now and confined to relict patches of original forest that have somehow escaped development.

SEASONS - LEAVES nearly evergreen but with a distinctly thin phase in February. FLOWERS sometime between December and April, erratically and differing widely from tree to tree. FRUIT appear very quickly after the flowers.

WHERE TO SEE IT Delhi Golf Course is sanctuary for hundreds of peelu trees; one hapless specimen (nicknamed 'Susan') stands in the middle of a fairway. Look for: a relict tree near Golf Links Post Office; many trees in the graveyards behind B. Shah Zafar Marg; old specimens in the Qutb compound; peelu bushes growing on the mounds close to the Delhi Durbar site.

slender leaf stalks are paler than the leaves

LEAVES in opposite pairs, each leaf up to 7 cm long, shaped like a lance with a broad base tapering to a (usually) blunt apex. Smooth in texture and somewhat fleshy so that the veins are only faintly visible.

terminal flower cluster with a few pink fruit

FLOWERS greenish or yellow, very small, arranged in loose, branching clusters mostly near the ends of the branchlets. With a hand lens you might just be able to make out the tiny lobed petals and 4 protruding stamens.

FRUIT tiny, round, single-seeded berries, varying from pale, transparent pink to deep ruby-red. They are sweet with a somewhat surprising but not unpleasant peppery tang.

BARK pale brown or grey, irregularly warty and rough but not deeply fissured.

HABITAT A characteristic tree of hot, arid parts of India but only where water is available, such as stream banks and marshes. It shows a marked tolerance for clayey and saline soils, where it is capable of growing where few other species will survive.

RANGE Within the subcontinent, in dry areas from Sindh and Baluchistan in the W to Patna in the E, and S to dry, coastal Sri Lanka. It extends across the Middle-East into Saudi Arabia and Egypt and large parts of N and E Africa.

USES Young branches and the leaves are prized as camel and sheep fodder and are believed to be an antidote to various sorts of poisons. Across its range, the tree is chiefly known for the chewing sticks which are made from its twigs, which are believed to prevent tooth decay and diseases of the gums. A decoction of the root and bark is employed to treat gonorrhoea and diseases of the spleen and stomach. The timber is white, soft and easy to work but is little used, not even for fuel. It is believed that termites will not attack it. Because of its special tolerances, the tree is often used to reclaim saline lands and is planted as a shelterbelt tree to arrest marching sand dunes.

CAN BE CONFUSED WITH

The other *Salvadora* – khabbar – which is much rarer in Delhi. The easiest way of telling them apart is by their leaves – khabbar's are narrow and never more than 1.3 cm wide; peelu's are lance-shaped and wider than 1.5 cm. Further, khabbar flowers have no stalks and its fruit ripen yellow. Peelu flowers are stalked and its fruit are pink or red when ripe.

ASHOK *Polyalthia longifolia*

(indian) mast tree • indian fir • cemetery tree

ashok • devdaru • ashupal

custard-apple family

Medium-sized; nearly evergreen

Bark grey-brown, becoming darker, scabby and cracked with age

Leaves slim, long, with wavy edges and extended pointy tips; glossy on both sides

Flowers in clusters with 6 long, narrow, pale-green petals

Fruit grape-sized, in clusters growing from a common stalk; dark purple when ripe

>> Varieties of the Ashok – see p333

FLOWERS star-shaped, pale greenish-yellow, in dense clusters along the branchlets. Each flower has a slender stalk about 2 cm long, a flower-cup of 3 short, triangular segments and 6 narrow, pointy petals up to 2.5 cm long. The flowers are usually well hidden within the foliage.

A tall, erect, near-evergreen tree from the monsoon forests of Sri Lanka, usually cultivated in a narrowly conical form with short, drooping branches somewhat like a cypress. Its long, narrow, glossy leaves with wavy edges are distinctive, but the flowers and fruit are concealed within the foliage and are seldom noticed.

long, pointy petals

SEASONS - **LEAVES** renewed in late March or early April. Another green flush in the rains. **FLOWERS** in late March or early April but last only a short time. **FRUIT** ripen between late June and early August.

WHERE TO SEE IT The Red Fort has large specimens. Also in Lodi Garden, Humayun's Tomb Gardens and other historic monuments where it was planted (in the early 1900s) as a substitute for the slow-growing Italian cypress. Used as an avenue tree on the Outer Ring Road near Panchsheel Park. The small-leaved variety is less common – there are 2 large specimens inside the Supreme Court compound.

wavy margins

HABITAT It is found scattered as an understorey or main canopy tree in both evergreen and monsoon forests, sometimes along riverine systems. It is fairly drought-hardy and quick-growing and makes a good city tree because it remains near-evergreen even in very dry conditions.

LEAVES arranged alternately, narrow, up to 28 cm long with distinctive wavy margins. The tip of each leaf is long drawn-out and gently tapering, the base broadly v-shaped. Smooth on both surfaces, slightly glossier above. The midrib is prominent but the side-veins are very faint.

RANGE Native to drier parts of Sri Lanka and to a few restricted localities in S India where it is doubtfully found in the wild any more. Widely cultivated throughout India and in SE Asia, especially the narrow, conical form known as 'variety *pendula*' (though this name has been questioned).

FRUIT in clusters of 8-20 growing from the end of a common stalk, the entire cluster produced from a single flower. Each fruit is about the size of a small grape, shiny and smooth, green at first, turning deep purple.

USES The ripening fruit is avidly eaten by flying foxes, birds and monkeys, and apparently is safe for human consumption too. The bark is used medicinally to allay fevers. The startlingly white, even-grained wood is hollowed out to make drums in S India and for making pencils and small boxes. Hindus often employ the leaves in marriage ceremonies and to decorate gateways, though the origins of this sanctified use are obscure. Widely cultivated throughout India for ornament.

BARK grey-brown, dark, becoming scabby and vertically fissured with age.

WHAT IS THE 'TRUE' ASHOK?

The name 'ashok' is also used for the sita-ashok (*Saraca asoca*) and causes much confusion. *Polyalthia longifolia* however is so much more common in Delhi and the name 'ashok' so deeply entrenched here that it seems churlish to resist popular usage. I have consistently used the names 'ashok' and 'sita-ashok' to distinguish between these separate trees in this book.

MANGO TREE *Mangifera indica*

mango tree

mango/cashew family

aam • amri • ambi

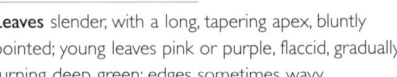

Small to medium-sized tree; semi-evergreen

Bark grey-brown, rough, with shallow cracks

Leaves slender, with a long, tapering apex, bluntly pointed; young leaves pink or purple, flaccid, gradually turning deep green; edges sometimes wavy

Flowers tiny, strongly scented, in huge, branched clusters (of up to 6000 flowers); yellowish green, with 4-5 yellow petals; most flowers are male, the rest bisexual

Fruit smooth-skinned, waxy, in various colours; flesh fibrous or pulpy; stone flattened, kidney-shaped

MANGO LEAVES

are produced in 'flushes' on a few branches at a time. A tree is seldom entirely leafless. Young leaves hang limply downwards, in delicate shades of pink or purple – gradually becoming firm and erect, turning deep green with slightly paler undersides.

In its wild form and on favourable sites, the mango can grow to 35 m with a massive trunk and a huge, dome-shaped canopy. Cultivated mango trees are much more modest in size, but with long, glossy leaves and a semi-evergreen habit, make attractive urban trees. They are nowhere near as common in Delhi as one might expect.

SEASONS - LEAVES shed mostly in January, renewed in March; new leaves limp, very pale. **FLOWERS** ('baur') first seen in mid February, reaching a peak in March. **FRUIT** ripen May-June-July, depending on variety.

WHERE TO SEE IT A favourite Mughal avenue tree that lines no major roads in Delhi. Delhi's biggest trees are inside Roshanara Bagh. Lots of trees in Lutyens' Delhi, inside the compounds of the sahibs' bungalows. Fairly common in large parks.

FLOWERS have 4-5 orange-streaked yellow petals. The flowers open at dusk and emit a strong, nutty scent. They are pollinated by flies, beetles and other small insects.

>> Cultivated Mangoes *and* How Big Can a Mango Grow? – see p326

WHAT WILD MANGOES NEED

Wild mangoes are trees of moist, shady places in monsoon forests. They need lots of moisture but must have hot, dry conditions in which to flower. They fruit in pronounced 'on' and 'off' years, a good crop usually followed by a poor one. Trees need to rest, to replenish the huge carbohydrate reserves needed to produce fruit.

PHILIPPINE TUNG TREE *Reutealis trisperma*

philippine tung tree • soft lumbang tree

no local name

amla/castor family

Small tree; deciduous

Bark grey-brown, relatively smooth

Leaves large, about 16 cm broad, glossy, with deep heart-shaped base; a pair of prominent glands at the end of an uncommonly long leaf stalk running to 28 cm

Flowers in branched clusters in late March-early April; male and female flowers separate, on the same tree; 5-7 white petals, flushed with pink [see pic below]

Fruit more or less spherical, grooved, densely velvety

A small tree with a dense crown of glossy, heart-shaped leaves on extremely long leaf stalks. Male and female flowers look similar with pinkish-white petals, but are functionally distinct – they are found on the same tree. Native to the Malaysian archipelago and the Philippine islands; rare in Delhi.

WHERE TO SEE IT The only specimens I have found are in Lodi Garden: 4 trees growing on the northern boundary of the rose garden.

INDIAN TULIP TREE *Thespesia populnea*

indian tulip tree • seaside mahoe • portia tree • umbrella tree • pacific rosewood

bhendi • *paraspeepal*

cotton/hibiscus family

Medium-sized tree; deciduous

Bark dark brown, rough and deeply cracked and fissured

Leaves almost triangular with a broad base, up to 15 cm long; apex long-pointy, base heart-shaped; smooth, shiny

Flowers about 8 cm long, bell-shaped, singly or in pairs; 5 lemon-yellow, crinkly, overlapping petals with a deep-maroon centre, fading to pink [see pic near left]

Fruit a slightly flattened sphere with a pointy apex, about 4 cm wide; green at first, turning black [see pic far left]

A densely branched, crooked tree with showy yellow flowers, native to coastal tracts and tidal forests in S India, Africa and the Pacific Isles. A common avenue tree in sea-side cities like Mumbai where it is evergreen, the Indian tulip tree struggles through Delhi's long drought and goes bare for a few months.

WHERE TO SEE IT A short row behind the lion enclosure in the zoo. Purana Qila and Buddha Jayanti Park have groves. Not common.

CHAULMUGRA TREE *Gynocardia odorata*

chaulmugra tree

chilla family

chaulmugra • chavalmungri

Smallish tree; evergreen

Bark brown or greenish, somewhat warty

Leaves up to 26 cm long, glossy, leathery, with a short leaf stalk and pointy tip

Flowers pale yellow, 5-petalled, fragrant; male and female flowers on separate trees, growing straight from the trunk or old branches [see pic]

Fruit nearly round, yellowish brown, about 10 cm in diameter; woody

An unusual tree from evergreen forests of NE India. Adapted to growing in moist, swampy places, it is surprising to find it growing in Delhi's climate. The oil from its fruit was widely used in the 19th century to treat leprosy. The yellow flowers, growing straight from the trunk in dense clusters, are deliciously fragrant.

WHERE TO SEE IT Only one tree found in Delhi, next to the botany department in Delhi University.

HALDU *Haldina cordifolia*

Syn: *Adina cordifolia*

no english common name

coffee/gardenia family

haldu • hardu • kadami • karam

Middle-sized tree; deciduous

Trunk grey, pale, scarred and pitted where pieces of bark have flaked off [see pic below]

Leaves broadly oval, in opposite pairs; deeply heart-shaped at base, pointy at apex; more or less smooth

Flowers tiny, yellowish, clustered in round heads, like those of kadamb and kaim [see pic at left]

Fruit in round heads, like the flower form

One of the largest trees of deciduous forests in India, with a massive, fluted trunk and horizontal branches, but severely stunted in Delhi. Its flowers are clustered in round heads and are produced in early June. Native to the sub-Himalayan tract and peninsular India, ranging through large tracts in SE Asia.

WHERE TO SEE IT Only 2 specimens found in Delhi, in Sundar Nursery.

🍃 KAMALA *Mallotus philippensis*

kamala tree • monkey face tree • red berry
kamala • kambal • kumila • sindoor • rora • roli • ruen

amla/castor family

8 m

Smallish tree; evergreen

Bark grey to black, rough, with shallow, vertical fissures

Leaves long-stalked, up to 35 cm long, with 3 main nerves from base; young leaves toothed; smooth, dark green on top, hairy and paler beneath; tiny red dots (glands) on undersurface

Flowers small, lacking petals, yellowish, in clusters; male [see pic at left] and female flowers on separate trees

Fruit 3-lobed, 6-8 mm wide; covered when ripe with a bright-crimson powdery substance [see pic below]

A large, handsome evergreen shrub or small tree common in the Shivaliks and widely distributed in the understorey of dry forests in India, SE Asia and N Australia. Easily recognized by its dark-crimson capsule-fruit (in late winter) on female trees. New leaves emerge in beautiful shades of pink (in July).

WHERE TO SEE IT
Only a single crooked (male) tree in the timber section of Sundar Nursery, about 7 m tall.

🍃 EMPRESS TREE *Paulownia tomentosa*

empress tree • princess tree • royal paulownia
no local name

paulownia family

10 m

Middle-sized tree; deciduous

Bark grey-brown, with shallow fissures and prominent lenticels

Leaves opposite, up to 30 cm long; 3-lobed when young, later heart-shaped at base, paler and hairy below

Flowers in terminal clusters up to 25 cm long; flowers bell-shaped, 5 cm long, pale purple, ending in 5 unequal lobes [see pic below]

Fruit a pointy, woody capsule up to 4 cm long, brown when ripe

A middle-sized, ornamental tree from C and W China, famed for its rapid growth. It produces large, upright clusters of bell-shaped flowers, pale purple or tinged with violet, before the leaves appear. The leaves are faintly lobed or toothed at first, becoming large and densely hairy underneath.

WHERE TO SEE IT
Only in the forest department nursery at Hauz Rani.

ARJUN *Terminalia arjuna*

arjun

arjun • arjan

arjun family

Large tree; deciduous

Bark smooth, pale greenish-grey, flaking thinly

Leaves opposite or nearly so; tip rounded or slightly pointy, faintly heart-shaped at base

Flowers tiny, creamy yellow, crowded in long spikes; no petals; flower-cup and long stamens prominent

Fruit ovoid, woody, up to 6 cm long, with 5 thin, flat 'wings' running along its length

24 m

FLOWERS tiny, only about 4 mm wide, densely clustered on bristly, cylindrical spikes borne (mostly) towards the ends of branchlets. There are no petals. Some people notice a pleasant honey-scent – others wrinkle their noses at the smell.

star-shaped flower-cup and long stamens are prominent

A massive tree with a broad, oval crown, smooth bark and buttressed trunk, usually found growing along watercourses in dry forests. Though noticeably stunted in the city, it still is one of the largest trees lining some of New Delhi's broadest avenues. Arjun trees can be 'noisy' because they are a favourite roost for flying foxes.

tiny flowers crowded together on spikes

flower spikes grow from leaf axils or at the ends of

SEASONS - LEAVES shed towards mid April, renewed in late April or May. FLOWERS in late April, lasting through most of May. FRUIT ripen nearly a year after flowering, dropping sometime between February and June.

WHERE TO SEE IT Janpath is a nearly pure arjun avenue; Mother Teresa Marg and Teen Murti Marg are mixed avenues. Avenue #1 in IARI campus (Pusa) is impressive. Tughlak Crescent Park has 2 magnificent specimens. There are some large trees outside Safdarjang's Tomb.

LEAVES smooth, leathery, dully shiny, 8-25 cm long, arranged opposite each other or nearly so. Blunt or only slightly pointy at apex, shallowly heart-shaped at base. Margins often faintly, bluntly toothed.

● look for 2 knobbly glands near the top of the leaf stalk, visible from underneath

base of leaf slightly heart-shaped ●

● secondary veins arching, more or less parallel

FRUIT a fibrous, woody nut up to 6 cm long, with 5 (sometimes 6) thin, leathery wings like longitudinal flanges. Green at first, ripening deep brown, tinged with rust.

BARK thin, smooth, pale, greenish grey but flaking off to reveal colours varying with the size of the tree and time of year.

HABITAT Relatively dry, lowland forests with a clear preference for moist, alluvial situations. It grows even on rocky ground if moisture is at hand. It is often possible to chart the course of a stream from the air by the presence of arjun trees growing thickly along its banks. Young plants are prone to frost and drought. Fire and wind are the chief enemies of mature trees.

RANGE Fairly common in dry, riverine forests of the subcontinent and Sri Lanka, avoiding only the most arid and more rainy areas. Possibly introduced into the Punjab and sub-Himalayan tract.

USES The bark and gum are highly valued in Ayurveda as a tonic and cure for a host of cancer, heart, skin, urinary and gynaecological disorders. The bark was once used to produce a brown dye and is used as a tanning agent. The leaves are a choice feed for tussar silkworms. The timber is hard and heavy but has a tendency to split. The sapwood is pinkish, the heartwood nutbrown with darker streaks. It is not an easy wood to work and finish but finds some use in rural house building and in making carts, implements and boats.

GAMHAR *Gmelina arborea*

white/kashmir teak • chandahar tree • yemane (trade name)
gamhar • gamari • khamar • khamer • kumar • sewan

teak family

Medium-sized tree; deciduous

Bark pale grey, smooth, flaking off in large plates

Twigs distinctly flattened, square in section

Leaves in opposite pairs on long stalks; broadly heart-shaped at base; smooth on top, velvety beneath

Flowers trumpet-shaped, yellow tinged with brown

Fruit like a small olive, 2.5 cm long, yellow when ripe

14 m

An imposing tree with a large, shady crown towering to 40 m in its natural humid forests. Delhi is much too dry for it to flourish here and it has had only limited success as a roadside tree. The city's specimens have fat, crooked trunks with thin crowns and are sometimes mistaken for peepal trees.

SEASONS - LEAVES start dropping in February and trees look thin and straggly into March. New leaves in April; canopy renewed by mid May. **FLOWERS** appear with the new leaves, lasting till mid April. **FRUITING** not seen in Delhi.

WHERE TO SEE IT 'B' Avenue and Brig. Hoshiar Singh Road in Vinay Nagar are lined with gamhar (and peepal). Shanti Niketan, Anand Niketan and parts of Hauz Khas have some gamhar; there are scattered trees in Sundar Nagar, Panchsheel Enclave and a lone spindly tree behind Khan Market.

FLOWERS in narrow, branching clusters towards the ends of twigs. The flower is trumpet-shaped, 3-4 cm long, predominantly yellow tinged with brown. The trumpets widen into a gaping mouth with 5 distinct lobes.

one yellow lobe is larger than the others and stands upright. The smaller lobes tend to be ruddy brown

LEAVES 10-38 cm long and nearly as broad, in opposite pairs on long, grooved stalks. Young leaves are often lobed. Mature leaves are matte dark green, smooth and papery on top, pale grey-green and velvety below and, in general, thin and limp. Where it joins the stalk, the base of the leaf suddenly tapers into a narrow delta to accommodate 2 more veins.

HABITAT A rainforest tree capable of adapting to drier conditions in mixed deciduous forests. It reaches its grandest size in humid, fertile valleys in Myanmar, where it sometimes attains 40 m. In drier conditions, it remains stunted and its trunk becomes fat and crooked. It prefers rich, deep, well-drained soils.

RANGE Moist forests in the sub-Himalayan tract, NW India and Myanmar. Also found in drier areas such as C India and the Aravallis, near Ajmer. Occurs in Indo-China and Malesia, but is doubtfully wild there.

3 basal veins are more easily seen on the underside of the leaf

narrow delta at base of leaf

FRUIT up to 2.5 cm long. Smooth, dark green, turning yellow as they ripen. The juice leaves a long-lasting yellow stain on the fingers.

USES The wood ash and fruit yield a yellow dye. Many parts, especially the root, find use in Ayurveda for treating indigestion, fevers and gout. The leaves are lopped for fodder and are used for rearing silkworms. Gamhar is best known for its lustrous, silky timber – called 'white teak' – which, paradoxically, combines lightness and softness with close grain and strength. Heartwood and sapwood are not clearly distinct. The wood is creamy yellow, darkening to a pale reddish-brown. It is used for furniture, drums, door panels and lacquered boxes. It is the wood of choice for Adivasis in C India and Bihar for carving figurines.

BARK ashy grey, more or less smooth, tending to break off in fairly large plates, leaving lighter-coloured, shallow depressions on the trunk.

CAN BE CONFUSED WITH

The peepal, perhaps. Peepal leaves are shiny and smooth, firm and leathery, with very long, pointy 'tails' at their apices. Gamhar leaves are not shiny but dull and velvety beneath; they are also bi-coloured (paler below) and thin in texture, with only a short, pointy apex. Further, peepal leaves are placed *alternately* on the twig; gamhar leaves are arranged in *opposite* pairs.

TUMRI *Trewia nudiflora*

false white teak   *amla/castor family*

tumri • gamhar • bhillaura

Medium-sized tree; deciduous

Bark more or less smooth, pale grey, often silvery

Leaves up to 24 cm long, densely downy at first, becoming smooth; base broad or heart-shaped with 3-5 basal nerves; apex long-pointy

Flowers male and female on separate trees; male flowers yellow in spiked clusters, with long stamens; females greenish, solitary or in 2s or 3s

Fruit a somewhat flattened, round berry, smooth, green, succulent

A good-looking tree with large, pointy leaves, easily mistaken for gamhar and sometimes called by the same Hindi name. Found in hot, damp sites in India, Myanmar and Malaysia. In favourable situations such as river banks, it sometimes forms pure stands to the exclusion of other species.

WHERE TO SEE IT
Only one tall (male) tree in Sundar Nursery growing in the main timber section.

CAN BE CONFUSED WITH

The gamhar. Tumri leaves are narrower, less pale underneath and also noticeably less heart-shaped at base.

CHINESE TALLOW TREE *Sapium sebiferum*

chinese tallow tree • vegetable tallow • white waxberry   *amla/castor family*

pahadi shisham

Small tree; deciduous

Bark pale brown or grey, with shallow ridges; exudes milky sap when injured

Leaves like shisham leaflets, broadly oval with a long, pointy tip; 2 small glands at top of leaf stalk

Flowers small, green-yellow, in clusters at ends of shoots; male flowers near the top, female flowers below

Fruit a nearly round capsule, 9-15 mm wide; black when ripe; contains 3 seeds

A small, ornamental tree native to C China and Japan that has become naturalized in the lower Himalaya. It has pretty leaves that turn red before falling. Delhi is not an ideal place to grow the Chinese tallow tree, but I was pleasantly surprised to find 3 trees doing reasonably well here.

WHERE TO SEE IT
3 young trees in the plant nursery of Hauz Khas District Park.

CAN BE CONFUSED WITH

The shisham, but its leaf is compound; the Chinese tallow tree's is simple. The 2 small glands at the top of the leaf stalk are also diagnostic.

FRANGIPANI-LIKE LEAVES

Widest in the upper third – with milky latex

violin-shaped leaves

margins wavy

short, pointy tip

apex blunt, sometimes notched

leaf thick, fleshy

dark, glossy on top

surface dull

shiny on top

base narrowly v-shaped

margins often wavy

leathery, thick; shiny on top

tapering towards base

midrib thick; side veins many

chandni
13 cm p129

fiddleleaf fig
35 cm p129

white frangipani
35 cm p132

thor
24 cm p135

often toothed near apex

harshly rough on both surfaces

pointy apex

marginal vein prominent

midrib splits into 2 before reaching apex

stalk very short

surface smooth, dull

triangular shape

apex notched or pointy

sandpaper tree
12 cm p136

triangle-leaf fig
10 cm p136

apex usually notched

shiny above, pale, dull below

arranged in whorls of 4-8 leaves

leaves clustered at branch ends

shiny, smooth on top

khirni
11 cm p138

saptaparni
22 cm p142

frangipani
50 cm p130

apex short-pointy

hairy below, especially when young

apex broad, with tiny point

usually softly downy

veins dark green

glossy, deep green on top

side-veins 10-12 pairs

almost no leaf stalk

stalk 2-4 cm long

veins pale yellow

mahua
24 cm p140

doodhi
15 cm p137

katthal
24 cm p144

FRANGIPANI-LIKE LEAVES

Widest in the upper third – without milky latex

leaves
crowded at
ends of twigs

often
growing
from
spines

leathery,
grey-green

tip blunt or
very short-
pointy

shiny, dark
green on top;
pale below

upper half
wavy or
toothed

edge
finely
toothed

edge
sometimes
finely
toothed

kankera
7 cm p145

base
narrow; stalk
very short

leathery,
harsh when
mature

gondi
15 cm p146

parallel
secondary
nerves end in
sharp teeth

freshwater mangrove
18 cm p144

tip blunt
or short-
pointy

tip bluntly
pointy

chalta
35 cm p146

leaf often compound
with 3 leaflets

base
gradually
tapering

shiny, firm,
leathery

leaves
pale, thin
texture

leaves turn
red before
falling

coca tree
4 cm p147

shiny, dark
green on
top

gourd tree
15 cm p199

torch tree
15 cm p147

australian almond
10 cm p152

in opposite
pairs

short,
pointy tip

in opposite
pairs; silver-
white below

shape
very
variable

thick,
leathery

smooth
on top;
lightly
hairy
below

very rough on
top; paler and
hairy below

olive tree
8 cm p177

kaim
17 cm p148

shiny,
smooth

tip blunt
or
pointy

tip short-
pointy,
blunt or
notched

in opposite
pairs

base
narrow;
stalk stout

teak
60 cm p152

rai jamun
22 cm p89

smooth,
dull; grey-
blue to
bluish green

baheda
28 cm p150

FIDDLELEAF FIG *Ficus lyrata*

fiddleleaf fig • banjo fig

no local name

mulberry/fig family

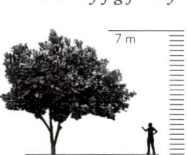

Smallish tree; evergreen

Bark grey, slightly cracked and rough when old

Leaves large, violin-shaped, with wavy margins; dark and glossy on top, dull beneath; base of leaf auricled, like a human ear lobe; apex very broad, rounded, up to 25 cm wide

Figs usually in pairs, stalkless, green with white dots

An exotic, large-leaved fig tree reaching 24 m in its native habitat in tropical W Africa, but not exceeding 7 m in Delhi. Unmistakable for its broad, glossy, violin-shaped leaves up to 30 cm long, with prominent white veins on the undersurface. A relatively recent introduction to Delhi's repertoire of ornamental plants.

WHERE TO SEE IT A prominent tree on the left as you enter the inner gate of the Qutb compound. Grown in farmhouses and in large private gardens. One Chhatarpur farmhouse has used it innovatively to make a tall boundary hedge.

CHANDNI *Tabernaemontana divaricata*

crêpe jasmine/gardenia • east indian rosebay • pinwheel flower • carnation of india

chandni • tagar • jangli chameli

frangipani/oleander family

Bush or small tree; evergreen

Bark grey, studded with raised lenticels; exudes a milky latex

Leaves in opposite pairs, up to 15 cm long; smooth, shiny, pointy at apex, base narrowed into a short leaf stalk; variegated colours also common

Flowers in clusters at ends of twigs; 5 white pin-wheel petals on a long tube; mouth of tube yellow

Fruit a pair of cylindrical follicles, curved at their beaks, up to 5 cm long

Usually a leggy bush but sometimes a small tree with a thin, crooked trunk. Planted for its evergreen foliage and white pinwheel flowers and regarded as a downmarket jasmine, though it is unrelated. Native to the sub-Himalayan tract E of the Yamuna and also to Myanmar, Thailand and S China.

WHERE TO SEE IT In gardens of all sizes. The end of Sardar Patel Marg closest to Palam has a row of relatively leggy chandni trees on both sides.

❧ FRANGIPANI *Plumeria rubra*

white/mexican frangipani • temple tree • pagoda tree

frangipani/oleander family

champa

Small tree; deciduous

Bark very thin, shiny, greenish brown; exudes milky sap

Leaves large, smooth, tapering at both ends, with a pointy tip; not shiny

Flowers fragrant, in loose clusters; colours various, mostly white with a yellow centre; 5 petals, overlapping

Fruit pods in pairs, joined in the centre, deep green

6 m

FLOWERS strongly scented in loose, upright clusters from a long common stalk. The flowers range from pink to deep crimson (often with yellow) to (most commonly) white with a golden centre and throat.

A small, deciduous, low-branching garden tree with leaves crowded at the ends of soft, blunt branches. There are many forms and hundreds of hybrids differing mainly in flower colour but the smooth, pointy leaves tapering at both ends are diagnostic. Native to tropical C America.

• 5 petals, slightly overlapping; the left edge is slightly curled

SEASONS - LEAVES start to fall in December; most trees remain bare till mid March. Leaves fully renewed in April-May. FLOWERS from May to July, with another flush late in the rains. FRUIT not always formed in Delhi; ripen in February or March.

WHERE TO SEE IT One of the most common ornamental garden trees in Delhi. Particularly good specimens in Humayun's Tomb gardens, Buddha Jayanti Park, Shakti Sthal.

• stamens hidden deep inside the throat – not visible from the outside

apex tapered, less narrowly than base •

• leaf is widest in the upper third or the middle

• side veins run parallel at first, then merge with a vein running close to the margin

• base of leaf forms a narrow V and sits on top of the leaf stalk

LEAVES clustered at the tips of the branches, up to 55 cm (longer than other *Plumerias*). Most forms are hairless and smooth when mature. The leaves are darker on top and dull, without gloss.

FRUIT a leathery pod that comes in pairs, joined at the centre, 12-15 cm long. The pods are deep green and slightly shiny, but in Delhi are not often formed even on mature trees.

BARK like a thin skin, brown with some green, shiny, becoming warty in places. It exudes a milky latex when cut or bruised.

HABITAT This species of frangipani originates in lowland regions with a distinct dry period and well-drained soil. Unlike the white frangipani, this is a deciduous tree whose dormancy coincides with the dry season, though blooming usually begins just before the rains. It does not withstand frost well.

RANGE Different forms of this species come from slightly different regions with little or no overlap, but all of them are native to a hot tropical territory stretching from S Mexico, Panama and the West Indies to northern S America. It was probably first brought to India by the Portuguese – Dr Hove found the tree 'growing abundantly on Malabar Hill' in Bombay in 1787.

USES In Bengal, the frangipani (especially forma *acutifolia*) is credited with a number of medicinal uses. The skin of the root is used as an effective purgative and the bark is used to treat fevers and gastric problems. The crushed leaves are applied to the skin to reduce swellings. The flower buds are mixed with betel-leaves to cure the ague and the milky latex is used along with coconut oil to treat skin troubles. The flowers, of course, are used as votive offerings of worship.

TEMPLE TREES, FRANGIPANIS AND CHAMPAS

Many people find it difficult to distinguish between the 2 species of *Plumeria* found in Delhi and it certainly does not help that the same common names are used indiscriminately for both species. See 'How to Distinguish between Delhi's Frangipanis' on page 134. See also 'Making Sense of the Frangipanis' on pages 339-40.

❧ WHITE FRANGIPANI *Plumeria obtusa*

white/cuban frangipani • singapore plumeria • temple tree • lily of the coast   *frangipani/oleander family*

khair champa • safed champa • champa

4 m

Small tree; nearly evergreen

Bark greyish brown with thin skin; trunk very knobbly and warty; exudes milky sap

Leaves up to 35 cm long; apex broad with a notch or only a tiny point; one variety is densely hairy below

Flowers in clusters at the ends of branches; 5 narrow white petals with a yellow 'eye', hardly or not overlapping

Fruit a pair of dark, shiny pods, joined in the centre

FLOWERS in large, terminal clusters from a long common stalk. Buds may be tinged pink but there is seldom any vestige of pink in the open flower. Not as fragrant, but slightly larger than the flowers of the frangipani, with narrower petals. The petals of the white frangipani scarcely overlap if at all.

A small near-evergreen frangipani bearing clusters of fragrant flowers with narrow, pure-white petals and a deep-yellow throat in the centre. There are 2 main varieties (*obtusa* and *sericifolia*) and dozens of cultivars but as the botanical name suggests, all forms have rounded, blunt leaves which help to distinguish it from other frangipanis.

flowers pure white with a brilliant yellow 'eye' at top of throat

petals narrow, not overlapping

5 spreading petals on a long, narrow tube

SEASONS - LEAVES almost but not quite evergreen. In late February or early March, the leaves may blacken and fall if there's a dry, cold snap. FLOWERS in April, peaking in May and again in the rains. FRUIT seen in May.

WHERE TO SEE IT Most parks and gardens in Delhi have specimens. It is a popular ornamental tree even in small plots and traffic islands. Nehru Park has a few groves of the white frangipani and Le Meridien Hotel has it lining a ramp running towards the back entrance.

LEAVES up to 35 cm long, often shorter. All forms are dark green with a soft shine on top and paler, without gloss, below. The edges of the leaf have a tendency to roll under. One variety has nearly parallel sides and is densely hairy below. The more common variety is almost smooth below, but you can see the hair on the leaf stalk and along the main rib with a hand lens.

apex broad and rounded, either notched or with a minuscule point at the tip •

side-veins • parallel to the edge, then united in a marginal vein

• base of leaf forms a narrow V

FRUIT a pair of pods joined in the centre, up to 23 cm long. Dark, shiny green on the outside, studded with raised brown dots. Trees rarely set fruit in Delhi.

fruit pod • after it has split open, showing the seeds

BARK brown or grey, with a thin outer skin. Conspicuously warty from the scars of fallen branches. A milky sap wells up from cuts in the bark.

TEMPLE TREES, FRANGIPANIS AND CHAMPAS

Both species of *Plumeria* in Delhi tend to be called by the same common names and with the huge number of garden varieties in cultivation, it is not at all easy to distinguish between the species and their varieties. See 'How to Distinguish between Delhi's Frangipanis' on page 134, and 'Making Sense of the Frangipanis' on pages 339–40.

HABITAT Like the frangipani, it is native to hot, coastal regions that enjoy a distinct dry season. Much of its native habitat is on small islands in the Atlantic Ocean. As one might expect, it likes sandy or stony soil and is distinctly drought-hardy. It suffers from and will not survive frost.

RANGE Essentially meso-American, mostly on islands lying off the eastern seaboard of the American continent. Of the 2 main varieties that we find in Delhi, variety *obtusa* is found wild in Cuba, Belize, the Bahamas and the Greater Antilles. Variety *sericifolia* is native to Yucatan in Mexico and the Greater Antilles. (The common name 'Singapore Plumeria' is grossly misleading and merely refers to the origin of a particular cultivar that became very famous as an ornamental garden plant.)

USES Surprisingly, there are no reported uses for this tree in India except for Dr Watt's statement in 1889 that 'the blunt-ended branches are introduced into the uterus to procure abortion'. The milky latex is, of course, known to be poisonous and may account for any damage it causes in the womb.

HOW TO DISTINGUISH BETWEEN

DELHI'S FRANGIPANIS

There are only 2 species of frangipani in Delhi, and while it is not difficult to learn how to tell them apart, it is much harder trying to make sense of their many different forms and cultivars. Use this key page in conjunction with 'Making Sense of the Frangipanis' on pages 339-40 to learn how to distinguish between the most common varieties.

FRANGIPANI *Plumeria rubra* (pp130-31)

Large leaf tapers narrowly at base, more gently at its apex; surface is more or less smooth (at least when mature) and dull; it has fewer secondary nerves connecting the midrib to a nerve running just inside the leaf margin

secondary nerves

The frangipani has 4 major forms, sorted by the colour of their flowers. In all cases, the broad petals are overlapping and strongly spiralled:

forma *acutifolia* flower is white, splashed with gold

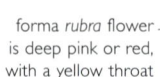

forma *rubra* flower is deep pink or red, with a yellow throat

forma *tricolor* petals are partly pink and white, with gold in the throat

forma *lutea* is similar to forma *acutifolia*, but with more gold at the base of the petals

WHITE FRANGIPANI *Plumeria obtusa* (pp132-33)

Leaf is smaller; also V-shaped at base, but the apex is noticeably broad and rounded, and is either notched or has only a minute pointy tip; the leaf is dark green on top, with a faint but distinct gloss.

The white frangipani comes in 2 main varieties which are differentiated purely by their leaves:

var. *obtusa* leaf is up to 22.5 cm long, more or less SMOOTH (lightly hairy on stalk and along nerves underneath)

var. *sericifolia* leaf is less than 15 cm long, with dense silky hairs underneath, especially along the nerves; the tip is usually notched; the sides are often parallel near the middle of the blade

The flowers of both varieties are white with yellow throats, 9-10 cm in diameter. The petals are NOT, OR SCARCELY, SPIRALLED; narrow, with NO OVERLAP. The long common stalk from which the flowers emerge is GREEN.

slender petals are not overlapping

THOR *Euphorbia neriifolia*

indian spurge • hedge euphorbia • oleander spurge

thor • thoohar • thoora • sehund

amla/castor family

Shrub or small tree; deciduous

Bark on old main stems grey and cracked, corky

Spines sharp, black, in divergent pairs; conical, seated on small corky knobs

Leaves few, fleshy, near branch-ends; apex broad with a tiny point, tapering towards base

Flowers in yellowish-green heads, in leaf axils; male and female separate; lacking petals

Fruit a smooth, 3-lobed capsule about 12 mm wide, red or pale brown; often absent

A spiny, succulent bush or small tree often mistaken for a cactus. All along its green, fleshy branches are little corky knobs arranged spirally, making the branches look angled and twisted. The smooth leaves are all bunched towards the ends of the branches. Native to dry, rocky habitats in India, stretching E to China and SE Asia.

THE FLOWERS are a complex structure (called a 'cyathium') peculiar to certain euphorbias — here, a cluster of male flowers in the middle are flanked by bisexual flowers.

male flower, surrounded by 5 bracts

paired spines on corky knobs, called 'spine shields'

SPIRALLY arranged spines are a useful way of distinguishing this species from other cactus-like euphorbias. Most others have their spines along ridges of angled stems.

SEASONS - LEAVES fall in January, renewed in May-June. FLOWERS between March-May. FRUIT in July, often absent.

WHERE TO SEE IT Large specimens in Talkatora Garden and Nehru Park; stray plants as 'escapes' or hedges all over the city.

◤ SANDPAPER TREE *Streblus asper*

sandpaper tree • siamese rough bush

siora • dahia • choriya • kuchna • rusa

mulberry/fig family

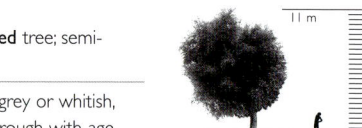

11 m

Middle-sized tree; semi-evergreen

Bark pale grey or whitish, becoming rough with age

Leaves with milky latex; dark green, hairless when mature but harshly rough on both sides; margins minutely toothed; apex pointy, base frequently asymmetric

Flowers small, yellowish green, inconspicuous, male and female flowers on separate trees

Fruit a small pea-sized berry, pale yellow to orange when ripe [see pic]; pulp sweet, edible

A somewhat stiff, densely branched tree native to dry monsoon forests in India and SE Asia. In medieval times, its rough leaves were used to impart the last fine-grade polish to ivory. This is almost certainly a Delhi native tree but I have found only 2 specimens in an old Mughal garden.

WHERE TO SEE IT
2 lovely trees in Roshanara Bagh – one inside the garden, the other on the periphery, in the children's Traffic Training Park.

TERMITE-FRIENDLY

The seeds of the sandpaper tree are known to be dispersed by termites, who drag them into their nests, where they germinate.

◤ TRIANGLE-LEAF FIG *Ficus natalensis* subsp. *leprieurii*

triangle-leaf fig • natal fig

no local name

mulberry/fig family

3 m

Small tree; evergreen

Bark brown, very slightly flaky

Leaves stalked, firm, feel like rexine; narrow at base, with broadly rounded apex; shiny on top, paler and dull beneath; midrib forking short of the apex [pic below]

Figs small, single or paired, yellow or red when ripe

A smallish fig tree from S and C Africa easily confused with the mistletoe-fig (*Ficus deltoidea*), another ornamental fig with triangular leaves from SE Asia. In suitable conditions it can grow into a large strangler like its parent Natal fig in Africa. This one is grown as a curiosity in Delhi.

WHERE TO SEE IT
Sundar Nursery has some specimens; often grown in small private gardens.

DOODHI *Wrightia tinctoria*

sweet indrajau • dyer's oleander • pala indigo • milky way • toothache plant

doodhi • karu • indrajau • khirni

frangipani/oleander family

Small tree; deciduous

Bark grey or pale brown, becoming fissured with age

Leaves pointy, in opposite pairs, softly downy, up to 15 cm long; leaf stalk very short

Flowers fragrant, white, about 3 cm wide; 5 slim, twisty petals; stamens form a cone at the centre; distinctive lacy threads around the cone

Fruit a pair of long, slender cylinders, hanging down and joined below at the tips when young; deep green

8 m

FLOWERS have a 'corona' at the centre, made of narrow scales interspersed with the stamens and surrounded by a white 'beard'. The flowers smell of vanilla.

A slender, inconspicuous tree that becomes very beautiful when it flowers at the hottest time of the year. Native to dry deciduous forests in NW and C India and a characteristic tree of the Delhi Ridge but, like many other indigenous species in Delhi, it is in retreat from more aggressive, exotic species.

SEASONS - **LEAVES** fall in December or January, renewed in April-May. **FLOWERS** soon after the leaves, mid May to late June. **FRUIT** conspicuous in November, ripening by the following summer.

WHERE TO SEE IT The N Ridge is the best place to see this tree though large, old specimens are rare. The C Ridge and Buddha Jayanti Park are good too. Lodi Garden and Humayun's Tomb have some relict trees, too small and neglected to notice.

• corona surrounded by delicate threads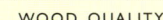

FRUIT hang down like outsize earrings. Their dark-green skin is speckled with white.

WOOD QUALITY

The ivory-pale wood of doodhi is prized for making toys and small articles because of the ease with which it turns on a lathe, and for its perfectly smooth finish even on cross- or end-grain.

KHIRNI *Manilkara hexandra*

ceylon ironwood

chikoo family

khirni • khir • rayan • raini

Large tree; semi-evergreen

Bark dark grey to black, rough, furrowed; sap milky

Leaves 5-13 cm long, shiny, stiff and leathery; rounded and often notched at apex; dark green, paler beneath

Flowers white or cream, about 6 mm wide; petals many, very small, numerous, arranged in 2 circles

Fruit about 1.5 cm long, olive-shaped; yellow or yellow-red when ripe

16 m

new leaves clustered at the ends of twigs

A slow-growing, stiff tree with shiny, leathery leaves forming a dense, spreading canopy. Only moderate-sized in Delhi, khirnis can grow very large and live to a great age. Not strictly native to Delhi but planted along avenues and in gardens. A possible candidate for Delhi's oldest living tree.

the petals in the outer circle are distinctly narrower

SEASONS - LEAVES more or less evergreen, with a lean period in February-March; new leaves in May or June. **FLOWERING** erratic in Delhi but most trees seem to flower in January. **FRUIT** seen at various times between April and June.

WHERE TO SEE IT Maulana Azad Marg and Jai Singh Road are mixed khirni avenues. Rashtrapati Bhavan has a khirni avenue; Roshanara Bagh has large specimens. One squat, spreading tree opposite the National Museum and some very old trees in Ladha Sarai, Mehrauli.

FLOWERS white or creamy, only about 6 mm wide, solitary or in clusters of 3-6. The petals are arranged in 2 circles in multiples of 6 – usually 18, sometimes 24. There are 6-8 stamens.

LEAVES firm and leathery, smooth, 5-13 cm long, crowded towards the ends of twigs. Base V-shaped or rounded; apex often distinctly notched, otherwise broadly obtuse. Shiny and deep green on top, dull and much paler beneath. The short leaf stalk is often channelled.

secondary veins are fine, straight, parallel

leaves often widest towards the apex

FRUIT a yellow, edible berry about the size and shape of an olive or slightly smaller. Sometimes tinged with red.

BARK dark grey to nearly black, very rough with deep, vertical furrows. The underbark is dark crimson and a milky sap exudes from wounds in the bark.

HABITAT An adaptable tree found in dry deciduous and evergreen jungles as well as coastal forests. In very dry, rocky situations it remains stunted and shrubby, but even in regions with low rainfall, can thrive in sandy nalas. On favourable sites it reaches magnificent proportions, with a short, thick bole and great spreading head.

RANGE Gujarat, C India (the Satpuras and slightly further north), Bengal, much of the Deccan and drier parts of Sri Lanka. Widely cultivated as far W as Lahore. Also found in Thailand, Cambodia, Vietnam.

USES The fruit is a useful famine food but is seldom available even in rural markets. The bark is used as a febrifugal medicine in some parts of India. The seeds yield an edible oil. Khirni is often utilized as a rootstock for select varieties of chikoos. The timber is extremely hard, heavy and tough and takes a good finish. The heartwood is reddish brown, close-grained and reputed as an excellent wood for turning. It is used to make hard-wearing wooden rollers for sugar-mills and oil-presses, and in C India walking sticks made from khirni are prized above all others.

DELHI'S OLDEST TREE

We do not, of course, know for sure what Delhi's oldest tree is, but Mandu's khirnis remind us that this species can live for over 500 years. My leading candidates for Delhi's oldest tree are the tall khirnis in Ladha Sarai (Mehrauli). The large khirni opposite the National Museum is not to be sneezed at, either – obviously out of kilter with the row of planted trees, it must antedate the building of New Delhi by some centuries and may once have graced the fields of Raisina village.

MAHUA *Madhuca longifolia* var. *latifolia*

mowra buttertree • moa • honey tree

mahua • mahula • maul

chikoo family

Large tree; deciduous

Bark grey-brown, rough, lightly fissured; sap milky

Leaves firm, 13-25 cm long, broadly oval, pointy-tipped; prominently clustered near the ends of branchlets

Flowers creamy white, in dense clusters; the petals form a fleshy tube with a long, protruding style

Fruit olive-shaped, fleshy, 2-5 cm long; orange when ripe

15 m

A shapely, long-lived tree with a gnarled trunk and wide, spreading crown. In the tribal belt in C India it is valued above all other trees for its many economic products and is never felled. It makes a beautiful avenue tree and it seems a pity that Delhi has only one major mahua avenue. Planted in gardens.

SEASONS - LEAVES start turning yellow in late March; most trees are bare by late April. New leaves, in a lovely tint of pink, appear early in May. **FLOWERS** through most of April. **FRUIT** ripen in July or August.

WHERE TO SEE IT Southend Road, between Claridge's Hotel and Lodi Garden, is very nearly a pure mahua avenue. Planted here and there in large gardens. There are specimens in Safdarjang's Tomb garden and a large tree in NISCOM (IARI campus).

FLOWERS creamy white, in dense clusters near the ends of twigs, on short stalks about 3 cm long. The petals are joined together to make a short, fleshy tube about 15 mm long, with many stamens and a long, prominent style protruding through the mouth of the tube. The sweet, edible flowers have a distinctive nutty-musky smell. In season, the tree sheds its flowers just before dawn.

protruding
• style

petals are joined to
form a fleshy tube that
falls off in one piece

the colour of new leaves

LEAVES clustered near the ends of branchlets, up to 25 cm but more commonly 15 cm long. The base narrows into the leaf stalk and the broadly rounded apex has an abruptly pointy tip. When young the leaves are softly woolly and a delicate shade of pink, becoming dark green, leathery and smooth as they age.

apex nearly always has a small, pointy tip

10-12 pairs of strong lateral nerves

FRUIT 2-5 cm long, fleshy, green at first, turning rusty orange when ripe. *(Watercolour by anonymous Indian artist c. 1845. Courtesy of the Royal Botanic Garden, Edinburgh)*

BARK greyish brown, lightly cracked and fissured. A milky sap oozes from incisions in the bark.

CAN BE CONFUSED WITH

The baheda, whose leaves and bark are very similar. The differences are listed on p151.

HABITAT A tree of stony ground in dry deciduous forests, commonly associated with sal (*Shorea robusta*). Though drought-hardy, mahua prefers annual rainfall in the 500-1500 mm range. It is somewhat sensitive to frost, especially when young.

RANGE An emblematic C Indian tree, also found in Gujarat and in a belt stretching from sub-Himalayan Kangra to N Bihar. Also in Upper Myanmar and Nepal.

USES Arguably the most valuable of Indian trees because its flowers are a nutritive lifeline for millions of poor people. In season, the succulent flowers fall to the ground just before dawn. Deer, monkeys, wild pig, jackals and bears compete to gather them. A large tree bears up to 300 kg of flowers in a season. They are eaten raw or sun-dried and are distilled into a strong country spirit with a smokey, nutty flavour. (The milk of cows fed on mahua flowers acquires the same taste.) The seeds yield 'mahua butter' used in cooking and to adulterate ghee. The 'oil-cake' is used as a detergent and fish poison. The extremely hard, durable timber has a dark reddish-brown heartwood, but is seldom used because the tree is too valuable to be felled.

❧ SAPTAPARNI *Alstonia scholaris*

devil's tree • ditabark tree • white cheesewood • milkwood pine • blackboard tree   *frangipani/oleander family*

saptaparni • satpatia • chatium • satwin • satni • shaitan ka jhad

Medium-sized tree; evergreen

Bark pale grey-brown; exuding a milky latex when wounded

Leaves seem palmately compound but are not; 4-8 leaves arise around a stem at the same height

Flowers small, fragrant, white, in tight clusters

Fruit long and slender, bean-like, in pairs

14 m

FLOWERS small, greenish white, in tightly packed clusters at the ends of branchlets. Strongly scented, especially in the evenings – a fragrance that makes you turn your head, then wonder if you really like it.

A large evergreen tree from moist forests in the submontane Himalaya where it reaches 30 m or more, but stunted in Delhi. Its glossy leaves radiate from a common centre, creating starry symmetries. First planted in Delhi in the late 1940s when Golf Links colony was being laid out, it is now a popular avenue tree.

flowers in dense, flat-topped clusters

SEASONS - LEAVES more or less evergreen; new, paler flushes stand out against dark, old leaves in March-April and again in the rains. **FLOWERS** not synchronized, sometime between mid October and December. **FRUIT** conspicuous from March onwards, beginning to split and give this pert tree a somewhat untidy look in April.

WHERE TO SEE IT The oldest, largest trees line A. Makarios Marg, flanking Delhi Golf Course. Tall trees W of the Sheesh Gumbad in Lodi Garden and outside IIC lounge. Not originally planted in Lutyens' Delhi, commonplace now in Chanakyapuri and along Press Enclave Marg.

left margins of petals overlapping

the tip of the leaf
is notched or
bluntly pointed

the simple leaves
are arranged in a
'whorl' around a
central stem

numerous pale
lateral nerves,
running parallel

HABITAT In its native submontane forests, a grand tree growing on deep, moist soil. Its tolerance of drier conditions allows it to be cultivated in Delhi but it pays a price by losing both height and nobility. It owes much of its popularity in cities to the fact that it is fast-growing and evergreen. On the evidence of the last 50 years in Delhi, it must also be extremely tolerant of pollution.

LEAVES look deceptively like leaflets of a palmately compound leaf. They are actually a collar of 4-8 simple leaves – most often 7 – attached all around a stem like the spokes of a wheel. Each leaf is up to 24 cm long, dark green and somewhat glossy above, matte pale below.

RANGE A broad belt in the sub-Himalayan tract E of the Yamuna. Also in peninsular India, in moist forests in the E and W Ghats up to about 1000 m. Its natural range stretches from Sri Lanka E to Myanmar and S China, and from the Malay Peninsula to Australia.

FRUIT in pairs of slim follicles like spindly beans, up to 40 cm long. The follicles open while still on the tree, releasing flat seeds tufted with long hairs that assist them on their airborne journey.

USES The bark yields a bitter drug (ditabark) used to treat an astonishing range of complaints, from chronic diarrhoea, dysentery and asthma to fevers. It also has a reputation as an aphrodisiac. The milky latex too is much valued for its medicinal properties. The wood is white when first sawn, with no pronounced heartwood. It is soft, light and fine-textured but seasons poorly and is not very durable. It is sometimes used to make minor furniture, writing tablets (hence the specific name 'scholaris'), tea chests, coffins and masks.

BARK pale greyish-brown, studded with a distinctive pattern of raised corky dots. The trunk exudes a milky latex when wounded.

old trees become
ropey and fluted
at their bases

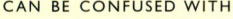

CAN BE CONFUSED WITH

The other *Alstonia* – batino, with somewhat similar leaves. Batino leaves have more distant lateral veins and have pointy tips, unlike saptaparni.

◗ KATTHAL *Artocarpus heterophyllus* *Syn: Artocarpus integrifolius*

jackfruit • jack • jac
katthal • kantthal

mulberry/fig family

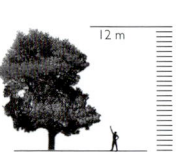

Middle-sized tree; evergreen

Bark thick and dark, deeply cracked, flaky

Leaves broad, deep glossy green on top, paler underneath, up to 20 cm long

Flowers male and female separate, on the same tree; male flowers tiny, in clusters emerging from new branchlets; female flowers densely crowded on old branches or directly from the trunk

Fruit gigantic, lumpy, barrel- or pear-shaped; pollinated by small flies and beetles attracted by its mawkish smell

A handsome evergreen tree with glossy leaves up to 20 m tall in ideal conditions, stunted in Delhi. Cultivated for its misshapen fruits, the largest edible fruit in the world. Native to humid forests in the W Ghats and adapted to moist conditions, which is why katthal is relatively rare in Delhi.

WHERE TO SEE IT Not common. 2 or 3 trees in Sundar Nagar, one tree opposite Jumna Lodge in Qudsia Bagh. Delhi University nursery has a few specimens.

◗ FRESHWATER MANGROVE *Barringtonia acutangula*

freshwater mangrove • red barringtonia • cut nut • kandu almond
neora • jujar

barringtonia family

Middle-sized tree; deciduous

Bark dark brown, rugged, with vertical furrows

Leaves crowded at the ends of branchlets, up to 18 cm long; minutely toothed

Flowers deep scarlet, fragrant, in pendulous clusters up to 40 cm long; petals 4, stamens numerous

Fruit about 3 cm long, smooth, oblong, square in section [see pic below]

A middle-sized tree with a huge natural range stretching from Afghanistan across India and SE Asia to N Australia. In the wild it grows in moist places like the banks of streams but is often cultivated in gardens for the beautiful, pendulous clusters of red flowers that it produces just before the rains.

WHERE TO SEE IT I have found only one small grove in Delhi, in Lodi Garden, close to the entrance leading to the glasshouse.

KANKERA *Maytenus senegalensis*

red spike-thorn • confetti tree

saffron family

kankera • kakra • khatai • baikal

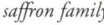
5 m

Bush or small tree; deciduous

Bark grey or yellowish, rough, deeply fissured

Spines long, straight, up to 7 cm long; often bearing leaves and flowers or fruit

Leaves grey-green, 4-7 cm long, with a narrow base, apex rounded or notched; edge of leaf minutely toothed

Flowers white, very small, in loose, branched clusters; 5 thin, spreading petals and 5 little stamens

Fruit in branched clusters, about the size of a pepper-corn, dull red when ripe, gradually turning black

red berries, not quite ripe

A spiny shrub or short, untidy tree with stiff branches, adapted to hot, dry, barren country. Look for leaves and tiny flowers growing out of its long spines. In favourable sites, kankera grows a large, oval crown and, especially in new leaf, can look quite pretty. A native tree found in dry, rocky or sandy sites on the Ridge. Not cultivated anywhere.

BUTCHER BIRDS or shrikes often use the kankera tree as a 'larder', leaving their prey (in this case a skink) impaled on its thorns until they are ready to eat them.

SEASONS - **LEAVES** thin out in January; renewed towards late April and May. **FLOWERS** erratically at various times of the year, chiefly between September and November. **FRUITING** also erratic, seen mostly at end of January.

WHERE TO SEE IT Only on the Ridge and in scrubby outskirts of the city. Parks that were carved out of former Ridge forest may still harbour a few specimens – there are 2 trees in Buddha Jayanti Park and a number of bushes inside JNU campus.

THE LARGEST kankera tree I found was next to a temple in a village on the outskirts of Delhi, in rocky, Ridge-like terrain.

>> *Maytenus senegalensis?* – see p341

GONDI *Cordia gharaf*

Syn: Cordia rothii

narrow-leaved sepistan • grey leaved saucerberry

lasora family

gondi • gundi • gondni • gundani • lasoodi

Small tree; deciduous

Bark grey or ashy brown, with fine vertical fissures

Leaves opposite or nearly so, narrowed at base; rough on both surfaces; usually toothed near the apex

Flowers white or creamish in loose clusters; 4 or 5 petals bent backwards, fused in a short tube at base

Fruit like a large pea, yellow or orange when ripe [see pic below]; seeds embedded in a clear, gelatinous pulp

A slight tree with a crooked trunk and drooping branches, capable of reaching 12 m though usually smaller. It is almost certainly a part of Delhi's native drought-hardy flora but is extremely scarce now. Its natural range extends westwards through Pakistan and the Middle-East into dry parts of Africa.

WHERE TO SEE IT Some on the N Ridge but not the S or C Ridge. One tree in Nicholson Cemetery. Mehrauli has a few trees, including one or 2 inside the Qutb gardens.

CHALTA *Dillenia indica*

elephant apple • large-flowered dillenia • hondapara tree

chalta family

chalta • girnar

Middle-sized tree; nearly evergreen

Bark smooth, cinnamon-brown, peeling

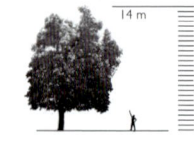

Leaves up to 35 cm long, with a pointy tip and sharply toothed margins; side-nerves many, parallel, ending in serrations; leaf stalk channelled, densely hairy

Flowers white, fragrant, solitary, up to 20 cm wide, with a fleshy flower-cup

Fruit slightly larger than a baseball, pale green [see pic]

A handsome near-evergreen tree with a dense canopy of large, pointy, sharply toothed leaves. Native to moist evergreen forests from Nepal eastwards, the chalta struggles in Delhi's climate and grows straggly and bare in February. It does not flower here, which is a pity because its large, white flowers and green fruit are very striking.

WHERE TO SEE IT 6 small trees planted in Vir Bhumi; some in Rajghat. A short tree near the botany department in Delhi University, and 2 sorry specimens in Buddha Jayanti Park, not far from Nehru's Testament rock.

TORCH TREE *Ixora pavetta*

Syn: Ixora parviflora

torch/torchwood tree

coffee/gardenia family

gandhal • nivari

5 m

Small tree; evergreen

Bark thick, reddish brown

Leaves in opposite pairs, smooth, leathery, up to 15 cm long; leaf stalk short; apex rounded with a tiny point

Flowers white, in large, dense clusters; buds club-shaped; flower has a short tube and 4 petals bent sharply backwards [see pic]

Fruit nearly round, about 10 mm wide, red when ripe

A small evergreen tree or large bush with a dense, much-branched crown of smooth, leathery leaves. It has masses of tiny white scented flowers in mid April. Widely distributed in dry to moist forests throughout the subcontinent but nowhere common. Delhi has only a solitary specimen that seems to do quite well.

WHERE TO SEE IT A solitary tree growing on the northern greensward slope of Gandhiji's samadhi in Rajghat.

COCA TREE *Erythroxylum coca*

coca tree • peru coca • cocaine tree

coca family

no local name

4 m

Small tree; deciduous

Bark pale brown, not very rough or remarkable

Leaves fresh green, about 4 cm long, pointy at both ends, often many leaves growing together from one place

Flowers small, in little clusters on short stalks; 5 yellowish-white petals [see pic at left]

Fruit small, red berries; not seen in Delhi

A small, bushy tree from lower slopes in the Peruvian and Bolivian Andes, whose leaves are the source for the narcotic drug cocaine. Originally chewed by poor peasants simply to relieve hunger and fatigue, the coca plant was considered sacred by Andean tribes for thousands of years. The flowers are tiny.

WHERE TO SEE IT Only a lone tree in the northern part of Sundar Nursery (close to the boundary with the zoo).

KAIM *Mitragyna parviflora*

no english common name

coffee/gardenia family

kaim • kaima • kadamb • kallam • phaldu • mundi

15 m

Large tree; deciduous

Bark pale grey or yellowish, not rough; flaking off

Leaves in opposite pairs, very variable in size and shape; pink leaf-buds protect new leaves at ends of twigs

Flowers tiny, yellowish, clustered in round heads; fragrant

Fruit tiny capsules, also clustered in round heads; green at first, black when ripe

FLOWERS tiny, pale yellow, clustered in spherical heads about 2.5 cm in diameter. The heads are either solitary or in sets of 3 – the middle one on a short stalk, the 2 on either side on much longer stalks. At the base of each flower stalk is a pair of long-stalked leaves.

A hardy tree adapted to growing in sandy beds of seasonal streams. With a short trunk often curiously irregular in shape and a cheerful, spreading crown, it is capable of growing quite large in favourable sites. This is the true 'kadamb' tree associated with Brindavan and Krishna's gopis. Native to Delhi and also cultivated in gardens.

SEASONS - LEAVES start thinning out in January, some trees remain bare through March. New leaf in early May, with another flush in the rains. FLOWERS mid May or June, continuing into the rains. FRUIT start forming in August or a bit later, remaining on the tree for many months.

• long, white protruding styles make the flower-heads look hairy

WHERE TO SEE IT Nehru's samadhi nestles in a wide semi-circle of kaim trees. Teen Murti Bhavan has large specimens. Lodi Garden and Talkatora Garden have closely planted groves. Lots on Bhagwandas Road, near the Supreme Court. On the Ridge too, but rare.

BUDS at far right are green and immature. Buds near right are just beginning to open.

rounded or slightly
heart-shaped at
base ●

LEAVES in opposite pairs, confusingly variable in size and shape. Between 5 and 17 cm long, sometimes oval, at other times inverted oval (so the broadest part is near the top), occasionally almost round. New leaves are protected by a pair of thin, pink leaf-buds which fall off.

● apex broadly
rounded, with a
short point

FRUIT capsules tiny, clustered in round heads, between 100 and 150 in each cluster, mimicking the form of the flower-heads. The fruiting-heads start off green, turn brown and eventually black.

BARK pale grey or yellowish, relatively smooth, pitted by shallow depressions where pieces of old bark have flaked off.

HABITAT A tree of hot, dry forests in the plains, ascending to about 1300 m. It tends to seek out moist places such as the beds of seasonal streams, where it often congregates in pure stands. (It is found in gravelly stream-beds on the C Ridge too.) An unusual tree in that it withstands water-logging but is also remarkably drought-hardy. It grows rapidly and coppices well. It is sometimes found self-sown on abandoned cultivated land.

RANGE Found in the sub-Himalayan tract from the Chenab river eastwards, throughout N, E and peninsular India, Nepal, Bangla-desh, Myanmar, Sri Lanka and also in dry parts of Cambodia and Malaysia.

USES The bark and root are used to treat colic and fevers in traditional medicine. The leaves are a nutri-tious fodder. The flowers are an excellent bee-forage and the wood yields high-quality charcoal and fuel. The pinkish-brown timber lacks any dis-tinct heartwood and is light, moderately heavy, compact and fine-grained. It is suitable for turning and carving, and also finds local use for making small articles such as combs, cups, picture frames, brush-backs and cricket stumps and bails.

THE 'REAL' KRISHNA-KADAMB

Many tree books will tell you that the kadamb associated with Lord Krishna in Brindavan is *Neolamarckia cadamba* (see pages 80-81). This is a case of mistaken identity. *Neolamarckia cadamba* is native to moist forests in NE India and would not survive unaided in the hot, dry Brindavan area. Kaim is not only native to the (remnant) Brindavan forests but is their dominant tree. Clinchingly, everyone in Brindavan calls kaim 'kadamb'. Time to revise some of those old books!

BAHEDA *Terminalia bellirica*

belleric (belliric, beleric) myrobalan • bedda nut tree

baheda • bhaira • bharla • sagona

arjun family

Large tree; deciduous

Bark pale brown or ashy, with shallow fissures

Leaves smooth, broadly oval, tapering at base, blunt or notched at apex

Flowers greenish yellow, in slender, crowded spikes, lacking petals; scent sweet but nauseating

Fruit ovoid or flask-shaped, up to 4 cm long, grey-brown, velvety on the outside

FLOWERS greenish yellow, male and bisexual flowers mixed, crowded together on spikes. There are no petals. The most prominent parts are the long stamens and star-shaped, woolly flower-cups. The flowers have a honey-like but nauseating smell.

• the stamens and flower-cup are most prominent

A tall, handsome tree with a massive dome-shaped crown and broad leaves prominently clustered at the ends of twigs. One of the select few species chosen to line major avenues in Lutyens' Delhi. For a forest tree that can grow to 40 m tall, it does not achieve impressive stature in Delhi.

SEASONS - LEAVES start to yellow and drop either early or late in March (depending on winter rains). New leaves (deep red) in early April, completely renewed by the third week. **FLOWERS** along with the new leaves towards end April. **FRUIT** ripen in winter.

WHERE TO SEE IT Barakhamba, Sikandra and Rajendra Prasad Roads were once pure baheda avenues, but there has been noticeable erosion in the plan. Canning Road has lots of trees and the zoo has 2 prominent groves (one next to the elephant enclosure). Not common in parks, but here and there.

NEW LEAVES emerge a startling shade of deep crimson and at first glance can look like blossoms. New leaves are faintly downy at first.

• leaves may be alternate, opposite or whorled

• arching secondary veins prominent

LEAVES are clustered at the ends of twigs, on stout leaf stalks; up to 24 cm long, broadly oval, tapering at base, blunt or notched at apex. They are paler beneath and smooth on both surfaces.

FRUIT grey-brown, flask-shaped or ovoid, about 4 cm long. The outer skin is covered with a fine velvety down. The stone inside the fleshy fruit is very hard.

the fruit is covered • with a velvety down

BARK pale ashy grey or brown, sometimes with a distinct bluish tinge, covered with numerous shallow interlacing cracks and fissures.

CAN BE CONFUSED WITH

The mahua, whose similar leaves are also bunched together towards the ends of its branchlets. The main difference is that mahua leaves are narrower and more pointy at their apex, with closer, regularly spaced, parallel secondary veins. (See pages 140-41 for mahua.)

HABITAT A fairly common tree of mixed deciduous and moist forests throughout the subcontinent, within a rainfall range of 90-300 cm. Reasonably tolerant of most soils, baheda grows best in well-drained, deep, sandy loams. Fairly resistant to drought and withstands moderate frosts.

RANGE Widely distributed in the humid and subhumid plains and lower hills throughout the subcontinent and Sri Lanka, absent only from arid tracts in the W and NW. Its range extends eastwards through Myanmar into Indonesia.

USES The fruit was once exported as one of the myrobalans, used for dyeing cloth ('snuffy yellow' or brown), as a dyeing mordant and for tanning leather. The astringent fruit is one of the 3 ingredients of Ayurvedic triphala, prescribed for coughs, leprosy, dropsy (and almost everything else). The fruit and leaves are eaten by cattle and sheep. The yellowish-grey wood (with no noticeable heartwood) is hard but not durable. The baheda makes an excellent avenue tree but some people consider it to be the abode of demons and avoid sitting in its shade.

❧ TEAK *Tectona grandis*

teak

teak family

sagwan • sagaun

18 m

Large tree; deciduous

Bark pale brown, peeling in long, thin, shreddy strips

Leaves very large, in opposite pairs; shape variable; apex bluntly pointy, narrowed at base, often escorting the stalk to the bottom like a 'wing'; very rough on upper surface, softly downy beneath

Flowers small, in very large terminal clusters; 6 white petals; stamens topped by yellow, paddle-shaped anthers

Fruit a small, hard stone densely covered with wool enveloped in a loose-fitting, papery jacket [pic below]

A tall, straight tree with huge, dark, rough-textured leaves. Young branchlets are square (in section) and deeply channelled. Native to dry and moist forests in peninsular India S of the Narmada, teak is widely grown outside its range for its timber but is not common in Delhi, and remains stunted.

WHERE TO SEE IT Most large parks have specimens. AIIMS has a row near the gate leading in from Ring Road. Delhi University campus has a relatively large number.

❧ AUSTRALIAN ALMOND *Terminalia muelleri*

australian/west indian almond • mueller's terminalia/almond/damson • beach damson • jam fruit

arjun family

no local name

9 m

Small tree; deciduous

Bark brown, lightly flaking

Leaves up to 12 cm long, blunt or short-pointy at apex, narrowed into short leaf stalk at base; old leaves turn various shades of red before being shed

Flowers tiny, white, clustered in 10-cm-long spikes

Fruit ovoid, up to 15 mm long, pale green at first, ripening purple or dark blue [pic below]

A slender, attractive tree with horizontally layered branches and leaves turning red before dropping. Native to Queensland (Australia), possibly the Andaman Islands too. There are only 2 specimens in Delhi and though they look happy enough, would much prefer a wetter climate than Delhi's.

WHERE TO SEE IT One tree in Sundar Nursery next to the mist-house; another in front of the physics department (new block) in Delhi University.

❧ CHINAR-LIKE LEAVES *Lobed*

leaves broad,
3-5 lobes

leaf stalk
very long

purging nut
29 cm p154

lobes
many,
pointy

**broadleaved
bottle tree**
20 cm p154

lobes
pointy,
irregular

densely
grey, downy
below

leaf stalk
attached
away from
edge

kanak champa
33 cm p156

3-5 long
main lobes

5 nerves
from base

chinar
24 cm p158

apex with
irregular
teeth

tada
16 cm p158

3 pointy
lobes

edges
finely
toothed

formosan sweetgum
18 cm p159

margins
wavy

stalk
densely
woolly

mahoe
26 cm p63

Sometimes lobed, sometimes not

lobes
deeply
incised

toot
15 cm p106

edges
toothed,
softly hairy

3-5 basal
veins

paper mulberry
22 cm p104

serrations
finer than
toot's

small
leaves,
3-4 lobed

badhara bush
5 cm p159

lobes
rounded

margins toothed

7 nerves at base

anjeeri
16 cm p95

leaves opposite;
toothed or
lobed

arni
6 cm p155

2 flat
glands

candlenut
27 cm p155

only lower
canopy leaves
are lobed

lobes
long, very
narrow

desert kurrajong
14 cm p168

*Lobed only
when young*

softly,
densely
downy

empress tree
26 cm p121

coarse
teeth or
lobes

gamhar
22 cm p124

PURGING NUT *Jatropha curcas*

purging nut • (french) physic nut • barbados/poison nut
pahadi/jangli arand

amla/castor family

Bush or small tree; deciduous

Bark grey, smooth, with peeling, papery skin

Leaves broad, with heart-shaped base and 3-5 pointy lobes; leaf stalk very long

Flowers greenish yellow, bell-shaped, in small terminal clusters; male and female separate on the same tree

Fruit a 3-lobed capsule up to 4 cm long, black when ripe

4 m

A soft-wooded shrub that occasionally grows tree-like, with a short trunk and thin, papery skin with green underbark. The broad, angular leaves have 3 to 5 lobes and long leaf stalks. Native to Mexico and the Caribbean region, it is widely grown in hot climates as a hedge and ornamental plant.

WHERE TO SEE IT
In hedgerows and boundaries, common in farmhouses. Lodi Garden has a small grove, not far from the glass house.

BROADLEAVED BOTTLE TREE *Brachychiton australis*

broadleaved bottle tree • broadleaved kurrajong
no local name

cocoa family

A beautiful tree belonging to an unusual Australian genus known as 'kurrajongs' or 'bottle trees', though this species lacks the typical bottle-shaped trunk. It has a light canopy of long-fingered, maple-like leaves. Native to dry hillsides in Northern Australia. Rare in Delhi – only a few specimens have been planted, for curiosity value.

Large tree; deciduous

Bark grey-green, not rough, marked with horizontal lines [see pic below right]

Leaves up to 20 cm long, smooth, with 5-7 lobes tapering to slender points

Flowers just ahead of the new leaves, bell-shaped, white; 5 petals, bent backwards [pic at near left]

Fruit not seen in Delhi

15 m

WHERE TO SEE IT
3 small trees in NISCOM (in the IARI campus, Pusa). There are solitary specimens in Lodi Garden and Sundar Nursery.

✿ ARNI *Clerodendrum phlomidis*

no english common name

teak family

arni • pirun • safed tekar

Tall bush or short tree; deciduous

Bark yellowish or pale brown, with deep, vertical fissures

Leaves in opposite pairs, about 4 cm long; V-shaped at base, coarsely, bluntly toothed or lobed towards the apex; they have a characteristic smell when crushed

Flowers white, fragrant, in dense clusters; petals rounded on a long, greenish tube; 4 very long stamens and a style

Fruit 4-lobed, shiny green when young, turning black

Usually just an untidy shrub, rarely struggling into an ungainly tree. A Delhi native found on the Ridge where it is fairly common. Self-effacing when bare, arni is almost beautiful in new leaf and has one of Delhi's most fragrant native flowers. Widespread in dry parts of the subcontinent but not cultivated anywhere.

WHERE TO SEE IT Only on the Ridge and in semi-wild enclaves carved out of the Ridge. Occasionally in wastelands too.

✿ CANDLENUT *Aleurites moluccana*

candlenut • belgaum/indian walnut • varnish tree

amla/castor family

no local name

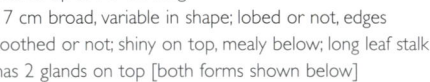

Smallish tree; near-evergreen

Bark grey, fairly smooth, with vertical lines

Leaves up to 20 cm long, 17 cm broad, variable in shape; lobed or not, edges toothed or not; shiny on top, mealy below; long leaf stalk has 2 glands on top [both forms shown below]

Flowers small, dirty white, in terminal clusters; male and female separate, on the same tree

Fruit semi-circular to circular in outline, 4-6 cm long, green to brownish

A tall, spreading tree from moist regions in SE Asia and on both sides of the Pacific. One of the great domesticated trees, chiefly for the oil from its seeds which can be lit like a candle, but also a thousand other uses. Out of place in Delhi; stunted and rare.

WHERE TO SEE IT Rare. Delhi University's nursery has one tree. A few more in Delhi U, not far from the physics block.

❧ KANAK CHAMPA *Pterospermum acerifolium*

bayur • maple-leaved bayur • dinnerplate tree

kanak/katha champa • kaniar • muchkand

cocoa family

Large tree; deciduous

Bark greyish, gradually becoming darker and rough

Twigs densely rusty-hairy when young

Leaves large, very broad, irregularly lobed; glossy green on top, woolly-grey underneath

Flower buds khaki, rusty-hairy, splitting into 5 narrow segments; 5 very long petals, pure white, fragrant

Fruit a 5-angled woody capsule up to 15 cm long

16 m

FLOWERS solitary or 2-3 together, arising from leaf axils. The long, khaki flower buds open by splitting into 5 slender segments, peeling backwards. The 5 pure-white petals are only slightly shorter, tubular at first, opening at night and visited by bats. Each flower lasts only for a single night. They are deliciously fragrant.

A large tree from moist sub-Himalayan tracts with very broad, shallowly lobed leaves, dark green on top and downy pale underneath. Young twigs and flower buds are densely rusty-hairy. The fragrant, pure-white flowers are exposed when the flower-cup peels backwards like a banana skin. A common ornamental tree in large gardens in Delhi.

flower-cup segments

SEASONS - LEAVES shed in late February or early March, followed soon after by new leaves. FLOWERS appear in March, with some trees still in flower at the end of April. FRUIT take nearly a year to develop, releasing their seeds in February-March.

WHERE TO SEE IT The largest tree in Delhi is probably the one outside the VC's office in Old Viceregal Lodge. A short row under the Oberoi Hotel flyover, just off Lodi Road. Specimens in most large gardens such as Lodi Garden, Buddha Jayanti Park and Aliganj Tomb gardens.

young leaves are pale brown and densely furred

Leaves variable in shape and size – up to 40 cm long and nearly as broad. Margins are irregularly, shallowly lobed. The leaves are smooth, dark glossy green on top, pale grey and densely downy underneath.

main nerves spreading, radiating from the point where the leaf stalk is attached

leaf stalk is often attached to the leaf some distance away from the leaf edge

the tip of each lobe is usually pointy

HABITAT A typical 'pioneer' tree tending to regenerate in gaps in the forest or at the fringes. In dry areas, it grows near swamps or along streams, ascending to about 1200 m in the hills. It is normally evergreen in its natural, moist habitat but goes bare for a brief period in dry situations like Delhi. It tolerates frost well and prefers full sunshine.

RANGE Within the subcontinent, it occurs throughout the sub-Himalayan tract E of the Yamuna but is more at home towards the wetter, eastern hills. MP and Orissa have scattered populations. Outside India, its range extends through Myanmar and Thailand into Java.

USES The leaves are used as plates and both bark and leaves were once used as a remedy for small-pox and still find use in folk medicine to treat wounds and itching. The flowers are believed to cure ulcers, tumours, leprosy and diseases of the blood, and to be an insect repellant. The reddish heartwood can be ornamental with a purplish tinge and fine ripple marks. The timber is durable, moderately hard and strong and is used for high-class joinery, panelling, flooring, furniture and toys.

Fruit a woody capsule up to 15 cm long, covered with rough, brown hair. It is distinctly 5-angled and opens in 5 sections to reveal neatly packaged rows of flattened seeds with thin, shiny wings on one side.

surface of capsule is rough and warty

winged seed

Bark grey or grey-brown, becoming progressively rougher and cracked as the tree ages.

❧ CHINAR *Platanus orientalis*

oriental plane • (kashmir) chinar

plane tree family

chinar • buna • boin • bhunj

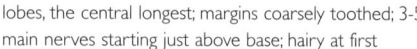

Large tree; deciduous

Bark flaking to expose dull grey or greenish underbark

Leaves broad with 3-5 lobes, the central longest; margins coarsely toothed; 3-5 main nerves starting just above base; hairy at first

Flowers greenish, very tiny, male and female usually separate on the same tree; crowded in ball-like heads

Fruit also spherical, pendant, about 2-3 cm in diameter, dense with bristly hairs

A magnificent tree with a broad, spreading crown and long-fingered, maple-like leaves, popularly associated with the Kashmir Valley. It is not actually native to Kashmir but to a region stretching from Asia Minor to Iran. Delhi has a few stunted specimens that struggle in uncongenial conditions.

WHERE TO SEE IT Stray specimens in the IIC (at the back), the VC's residence at Delhi University and more than one farmhouse in Chhattarpur.

>> The Long-fingered Chinar – see p339

❧ TADA *Pterospermum xylocarpum*

no english common name

cocoa family

no local name (*tada* in telugu)

Middle-sized tree; evergreen

Bark medium brown, smooth

Leaves variable, with heart-shaped base and irregularly toothed apex; smooth on upper surface, downy below

Flowers white, about 5 cm wide, fragrant; petals 5

Fruit a brown, velvety, pear-shaped capsule, up to 6 cm long, pointy at both ends. Not seen in Delhi

An evergreen tree from the E Ghats represented in Delhi only by a solitary specimen. It has variable grey-green leaves up to 15 cm long, coarsely toothed or lobed at their terminal ends. They are smooth on top but grey-felted or rusty-downy underneath. You will notice its affinity with the kanak champa at once.

WHERE TO SEE IT Only one modest-sized specimen in Sundar Nursery, on the left as you drive towards the timber section.

🍂 BADHARA BUSH *Gmelina asiatica*

badhara bush • asiatic beechberry • oval-leafed gmelina

badhara • kalisewan • nagphul

teak family

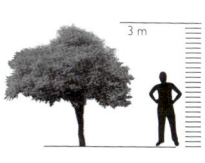

Shrub or small tree; deciduous	
Bark dark brown or yellowish, becoming rough and fissured with age	
Spines short, single, not always present	
Leaves 2-4 cm long, often 3-lobed; smooth, paler below	
Flowers yellow, bell-shaped, with a prominent lower 'lip'	
Fruit small, pear-shaped	

A large, sometimes spiny, shrub that at times attains tree-size, with a dense head of wiry twigs bearing small, dark leaves. It has arresting bright-yellow flowers. Native to S India (especially the E coast), Sri Lanka, SE Asia and S China, but extremely rare in Delhi – only a single specimen seen.

WHERE TO SEE IT
A solitary tree seen in the Qutb compound, on the right as you walk towards the minar.

🍂 FORMOSAN SWEETGUM *Liquidambar formosana*

formosan/chinese sweetgum

no local name

sweetgum family

An unusual tree in Delhi, with dark, maple-like leaves terminating in 3 pointy lobes, turning yellow before they fall. Like other members of the sweetgum genus, the resin oozing from cuts in the stem smells spicy-sweet. Native to Taiwan and S China, it appears to tolerate Delhi's climate and moisture regime well but remains stunted.

Middle-sized tree; deciduous	
Bark dark grey-brown, with prominent dot-lenticels	
Leaves 12-15 cm wide, 3-lobed; margins finely toothed	
Flowers without petals; male and female flowers [see pic below] separate on the same plant	
Fruit like spiky balls, at the ends of long stalks	

WHERE TO SEE IT Only a single specimen in the front lawns of NISCOM, inside the IARI (Pusa) campus.

PINE-LIKE LEAVES *Linear, narrow*

Needle and scale leaves

The leaves on this page are far too small to be depicted on
their own and are shown as they appear on the twig

leaves like
tiny over-
lapping scales

leaves tiny, scale-
like, closely pressed
to the twig

juvenile
needle-like
leaves in
2s or 3s

adult leaves
scale-like,
closely
pressed

twigs
branch in all
directions

leaves in
erect, fan-
like sprays

italian cypress
less than one mm
p163

chinese juniper
needle leaves 8 mm,
scale leaves 1.5 mm
p164

morpankhi
3 mm p165

leaves closely
pressed to twig,
overlapping

leaves flat,
thin, pointy

leaves look
imli-like but
are not

leaves
slightly
curved,
pointy

leaves
crowded,
flat, soft

montezuma cypress
12 mm p166

black tea-tree
2 cm p167

new caledonian pine
juvenile leaves 8 mm
p166

leaves look
imli-like but
are not

pointy tip,
rounded
base, stalk
very short

leaves reduced
to tiny scales
encircling twig-
joints

leaves
reduced to
tiny
sheaths

amla
12 mm p184

leaves like
little
triangular
teeth

apex of leaf
triangular

succulent,
with very
short
stalks

leaves fall
early and may
be absent

whistling pine
less than one mm
p162

farash
3 mm p167

kareel
14 mm p170

Long, thin leaves

softly hairy, esp. when young

weeping bottlebrush
7 cm p172

shiny, smooth

yellow oleander
14 cm p174

stalkless or nearly so

needle-like leaves, leathery, glossy

blue-green with a white bloom

fern pine
10 cm p168

leaves sometimes 3-5 lobed; shiny, smooth

desert kurrajong
14 cm p168

needles long, waxy, in bundles of 3

enclosed at base by a papery sheath

chir pine
32 cm p169

leaves in opposite pairs

new leaves red; later shiny, dark green

nagkesar
12 cm p176

smooth, shiny, firm

stalk short, stout

alii fig
18 cm p176

leaves in opposite pairs; slightly rough

apex blunt

edges often wavy

roheda
12 cm p185

dull grey; somewhat fleshy

veins faintly embossed

khabbar
10 cm p177

leaves in opposite pairs; thick, leathery; silver-white below

olive tree
8 cm p177

glossy, pale green on both sides

sharp lemon-scented when crushed

lemon-scented gum
20 cm p183

dull green; usually curved

forest red gum
20 cm p178

dull grey-blue; often curved

river red gum
25 cm p181

slightly thick, leathery

dull blue-green to greyish; paler below

coolabah
17 cm p180

glossy khaki-green; thick

reid river box
15 cm p180

WHISTLING PINE *Casuarina equisetifolia*

whistling/australian pine • she-oak • red beefwood • casuarina • cassowary tree

jangli saru • vilaiti jhau

casuarina family

Large tree; evergreen	

Large tree; evergreen

Branchlets long, green, jointed

Bark dark brown, flaking off to reveal rusty underbark

Leaves obscure, encircling each joint of the twig; so small they are difficult to see with the naked eye

Flowers male and female usually (not always) on separate trees; male flowers in spikes at ends of twigs; female flowers in axils, with untidy red threads

Fruit woody 'cones', 2 cm long

male flowers are clustered in slender, rusty brown spikes at the ends of drooping branchlets

female flowers

tiny teeth-like leaves at each joint

A graceful evergreen tree with wispy, jointed twigs that could – at a pinch – be mistaken for the needles of a conifer. Female trees even grow small woody 'cones' but whistling pines are not really pines at all. Native to sandy beaches in Asia and Australia, their appearance has everything to do with adapting to heat and drought.

FEMALE FLOWERS growing in axils of side branchlets look like a tangle of red threads. Each pair of threads is the forked style of a single female flower.

LEAVES – Pull a twig apart at a joint, and you will see minute teeth fringing the end of one stem. These are the 'true' leaves – a rosette of tiny scales at each joint of the green twigs.

SEASONS - LEAVES
evergreen. **FLOWERS** from February to April and again briefly in the rains. **FRUIT** cones form quickly, remaining for many months on the tree.

cones about 2 cm long, with tiny winged seeds

WHERE TO SEE IT Most parks and large gardens have stands of whistling pine. (Delhi's municipal gardeners seem to have decided that they must be planted in groves, never individually.) There is a prominent stand of tall specimens under INA flyover.

PROFILE OF A HABITAT SPECIALIST

Tropical beach plants have to negotiate heat, sun, poor soils and must withstand the salt in sea-spray. Casuarinas evolved as specialists to deal with precisely these conditions, with reduced leaves to cut down moisture loss. Their slender, ribbed branchlets are also a clever adaptation – tissues of photosynthesis and respiration are tucked away in grooves between ridges, protected against strong sunlight.

ITALIAN CYPRESS *Cupressus sempervirens*

mediterranean/italian cypress • churchyard/graveyard cypress • pencil pine

cypress family

saru

Tall, thin tree; evergreen

Bark grey-brown, thin, with shallow, vertical fissures

Leaves small, dark green, blunt, like fish-scales, closely pressed to the twigs

Flowers tiny, inconspicuous, male and female separate on the same tree at the ends of branchlets

Fruit a glossy brown cone, almost round, made up of 8 to 14 shield-like scales

8 m

LEAVES scale-like, only 0.5-1 mm long, closely pressed to the twigs. Unlike morpankhi, the twigs branch out in all directions.

Tall and slim with dense, dark-green foliage, this is the classic pencil conifer of Mediterranean scenery. It does not grow as tall in Delhi but was planted for formal effect in Mughal charbaghs. Reputed to live for up to a thousand years but not at all happy in Delhi's heat. It is seldom planted any more.

SEED CONES woody and deep brown, with 8-14 scales. Each fertile scale holds up to 20 narrowly winged seeds.

SEASONS - LEAVES constantly renewed. **FLOWERS** not observed in Delhi; probably February-March. **FRUIT** seen in March and April.

WHERE TO SEE IT In the Mughal Gardens in Rashtrapati Bhavan. Humayun's and Safdarjang's Tombs also use them formally. Large specimens in the French Cultural Centre at 2 Aurangzeb Road, and in 8 Amrita Shergil Marg. 3 small specimens in the parking lot of the IIC.

CAN BE CONFUSED WITH

Chinese juniper and morpankhi, whose scale-leaves are similar. The key differences are:

Chinese juniper always has some juvenile needle-like leaves, absent from the Italian cypress.

Morpankhi holds its branchlets flat, in one plane. Those of the Italian cypress grow in every direction.

CHINESE JUNIPER *Juniperus chinensis*

chinese juniper

no local name

cypress family

Small tree; evergreen

Bark nearly black, rough, peeling

Leaves of 2 kinds - juveniles spiny, in groups of 2 or 3; adult leaves like fish-scales, closely overlapping

Flowers small, yellow, male and female on separate trees; not seen in Delhi

Fruit a small, round cone, bluish white

3 m

LEAVES like other junipers, both adult and juvenile leaves persist on the same twigs. Juvenile leaves are needles 8-12 mm long, in sets of 2 or 3. Adult leaves are flat, rhombic-shaped, only about 1.5 mm long, overlapping closely on the twig.

A dwarf evergreen tree with a narrow conical form, rarely exceeding 3 m. The one grown in Delhi is almost certainly an ornamental cultivar – possibly 'Stricta' – but its horticultural origins are obscure. All trees have both needle-like juvenile leaves and diamond-shaped adult foliage, overlapping on the twigs like tiny fish-scales. It does not flower or fruit in Delhi.

needle-like
juvenile leaves

scale-like adult
leaves, closely
overlapping

SEASONS - LEAVES
evergreen, constantly renewed. Plants always have both juvenile and adult foliage. **FLOWERS** and **FRUIT** not seen in Delhi.

WHERE TO SEE IT
Occasional, in most parks and gardens. Lodi Garden has about 8 trees near the montezuma cypress grove.

BARK greyish brown or darker, conspicuously shreddy and peeling, exposing a slightly ruddy underbark

MORPANKHI *Platycladus orientalis*   *Syn: Thuja orientalis*

chinese/oriental arborvitae • chinese/oriental thuja • (northern) white cedar • biota   *cypress family*
morpankhi

Smallish tree; evergreen

Bark reddish brown, shreddy, flaking in long strips

Leaves scale-like, overlapping, closely arranged on the shoots; 1-3 mm long, blunt-tipped, dark green; grooved at the back

Flowers male and female separate, on the same tree; male cone-flowers yellowish green, near base of shoots; female cone-flowers purplish, at ends of shoots

Fruit from fertilized female cone-flowers, bluish-green, upright fruit-cones, ripening dark brown; 6-8 overlapping scales, each one with a downturned hook

MALE CONE-FLOWERS or pollen cones are brown or dull yellow, only 2-3 mm wide, borne at the tips of branchlets.

A bushy, densely branched, ornamental conifer with foliage always held up in flat, vertical, fan-like sprays. It grows into a small tree but is normally seen in Delhi as a trimmed, teardrop-shaped bush branching close to the ground. Native to W China and N Korea, very widely cultivated worldwide with many recognized garden cultivars.

CULTIVATED VARIETIES of morpankhi. 'Aurea nana' on the left and 'Elegantissima' (right) are the most common.

FRUIT fleshy at first, about 2 cm long, blue-green with a waxy bloom. Each of the 6-8 scales has a curved hook.

SEASONS - LEAVES evergreen, shed after a very long period. **FLOWERING** normally in February-March, but sometimes also in October. **FRUIT** ripen in April-May.

WHERE TO SEE IT Common in most gardens of all sizes and in traffic roundabouts. Safdarjang's Tomb garden and the gardens at Aliganj Tomb have a large number of trimmed bushes.

CAN BE CONFUSED WITH

Other conifers with scale-like leaves such as the Italian cypress and Chinese juniper. Italian cypress stands apart because its twigs grow in all directions, instead of in one vertical plane. Chinese juniper always has juvenile needle-like leaves to distinguish it from morpankhi.

MONTEZUMA CYPRESS *Taxodium mucronatum*

montezuma cypress/baldcypress • mexican swamp cypress • mexican cypress
no local name

redwood family

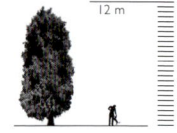

Medium-sized tree; semi-evergreen

Bark ruddy brown, fibrous, with long, shallow fissures

Leaves crowded, narrow, flat, up to 12 mm long on short twigs; larger, more loosely arranged on annual branchlets

Flowers male and female separate on the same tree; males in long, slender, pendant strings; females grey-green, with overlapping scales, few at ends of twigs

Fruit more or less round, with pointy scales; grey-green, about 2 cm wide [pic below]

A slender semi-evergreen conifer with gracefully drooping feathery foliage. Its original habitat is the banks of seasonal streams in the Sonoran Desert in Mexico. One famous giant tree in Santa Maria del Tule has a girth of 52 m and is estimated to be over 4000 years old! Delhi's specimens are modest by comparison.

WHERE TO SEE IT A grove in Lodi Garden. 2 small trees in Artsfac, and in Miranda House, Delhi University. Some trees inside the compound of 32 Aurangzeb Road.

>> Which *Taxodium*? – see p341

NEW CALEDONIAN PINE *Araucaria columnaris*

new caledonian pine • cook's pine • coral reef araucaria
christmas tree (incorrectly)

monkey-puzzle family

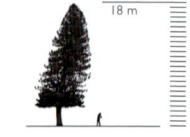

Narrowly tall tree; evergreen

Trunk long, clear; symmetric branches in tiers

Bark grey, peeling in thin flakes

Leaves on young trees needle-like, closely overlapping; adult leaves also overlapping but small and triangular

Flowers male and female separate, on the same tree

Fruit cones large, roundish, ripening in 2-3 years; not seen in Delhi

A distinctive conifer belonging to a very ancient genus, though it is not really a pine at all. It grows to a massive 60 m in its native Pacific Islands but is usually only a potted plant in Delhi. Until it is about 25 years old, it bears only needle-like juvenile foliage, closely overlapping along the twigs.

WHERE TO SEE IT Very few tall specimens in Delhi. NISCOM (Pusa) has a tree 14 m high. Sundar Nursery has a few.

ADULT (above) and juvenile foliage

>> Where *Araucarias* Come From – see p321
Identifying Delhi's 'Christmas Tree' – see p328

BLACK TEA-TREE *Melaleuca bracteata*

black/river tea-tree • prickly-leaved tea-tree   *jamun/eucalyptus family*

no local name

Bush or small tree; evergreen

Bark grey-brown, becoming thick and spongy with age

Leaves small, narrow, sharp-pointed, almost needle-like but flat; without stalks

Flowers white, in dense, cylindrical spikes; long stamens

Fruit small, brown, woody capsules

A large, bushy shrub or small evergreen tree with narrow leaves that are often yellowish green. It produces small, white flowers that are unmistakably related to the bottle-brushes. Wild near creeks and watercourses in large swathes of Australia. A valuable essential oil is distilled from the flowers.

WHERE TO SEE IT 2 tall trees in IIC and Annexe; small groves in Talkatora and most other public gardens. In the centre of the big roundabout near Janpath Hotel. Becoming popular in recent years.

FARASH *Tamarix aphylla*

athel tamarisk   *tamarisk family*

farash • lal jhau • pharwan

With its slender, jointed green twigs and insignificant leaves, the farash is easily mistaken for a casuarina, but the pink flowers in narrow, dense spikes are a giveaway. Adapted for living in inhospitable saline conditions, this is the only one of our tamarisks that grows into a tree, but has become very rare in the city.

Medium-sized tree; evergreen

Bark grey, rough, with deep, vertical furrows

Leaves barely recognizable; reduced to very tiny, triangular teeth about 2 mm long, clasping the twig

Flowers small, mauve or pink, in narrow, dense spikes arranged in drooping clusters at branch ends [below]

Fruit a small pyramidal capsule, 3-4 mm long

WHERE TO SEE IT A small specimen in the botany dept. garden, Delhi Univ. Sundar Nursery had many trees until the area was ploughed up in 2003, but there are a few left. Reported near Okhla barrage and along the Yamuna.

╲ FERN PINE *Afrocarpus gracilior*

Syn: Podocarpus gracilior

(african) fern pine • weeping podocarpus • east african yellowwood

no local name

podocarpus family

Middle-sized tree; evergreen

Bark brown, thin and flaky

Leaves narrow, tapering to a fine point, thick, glossy, 6-10 cm long; young leaves pale green, old ones with a 'bloom'

Flowers male and female on separate trees; male flower-cones in cylindrical clusters; females with only 2-4 scales

Fruit purplish, at the ends of short twigs on female trees; a small nut embedded in fleshy pulp

A beautiful conifer from the highlands of East Africa, with narrow, flat leaves like a bottlebrush's. It is not at all happy in Delhi's climate, but mature specimens (in Dehra Dun, for instance) develop a magnificent, billowing crown. The fruit (technically a 'cone') is a nut embedded in flesh, like a tiny plum.

WHERE TO SEE IT A prominent young tree inside Gandhiji's samadhi; Talkatora Garden has a few specimens.

╲ DESERT KURRAJONG *Brachychiton gregorii*

desert kurrajong

no local name

cocoa family

Middle-sized tree; deciduous

Bark bright green, with horizontal bands of calloused tissue [see pic below]

Leaves very narrow and long; both unlobed and 2-5 lobed leaves are found together [pic at left]

Flowers about 2 cm long, bell-shaped, creamish and brown; not seen in Delhi

Fruit 4-5 cm long, leathery, with a hooked point

An unusual tree with a green trunk and long, narrow leaves that are often 2-5 lobed on the same plant. From arid, inland parts of the Australian bush, it has a reputation for being immensely drought-hardy and adaptable. It is not much cultivated and is a somewhat surprising tree to find planted in Delhi.

WHERE TO SEE IT 2 trees in Lodi Garden, beside a path leading to Joseph Allen Stein Lane.

CHIR PINE *Pinus roxburghii*   *Syn: Pinus longifolia*

chir pine • longleaf/longleaved pine • three-leaved pine • kumaon pine   *pine family*
chir • cheel

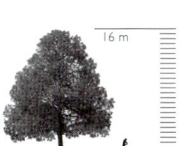

Large tree; semi-deciduous

Bark very thick, deeply furrowed, forming large 'plates'

Leaves needle-like, 20-32 cm long; in bundles of 3 encased by a papery sheath at base; triangular in section

Flowers male and female grow at separate sites on the same tree; males in dense clusters, yellow when mature; female flower-cones upright at the tips of new shoots

Fruit ovoid, woody, 10-20 cm long, with beaked scales; solitary or in clusters of 2-5

FEMALE FLOWER-CONES are fertilized in February and start growing immediately. They slowly turn woody and dark brown, eventually releasing their seed when the scales open 25 months after fertilization.

From hot, dry slopes of the Himalaya up to about 2000 m, chir is the only Himalayan pine that can be grown in the plains. It has an open canopy, a long trunk with symmetrically whorled branches and distinctively thick, reddish-brown bark. The needles always grow (and fall) in bundles of 3s.

SEASONS - NEEDLES are shed in May-June. The average lifespan of a needle is 2-3 years. **MALE FLOWER CATKINS** release their pollen sometime in the first 2 weeks of February. **FRUIT CONES** remain on the tree for upwards of 2 years.

bark thick, made up of thin, crisp, plate-like layers

thousands of minute stamens on the male catkins produce huge quantities of yellow pollen, which is released in 'sulphur showers' by the wind

WHERE TO SEE IT Lots of chir pines were planted in Vijay Chowk in the 1920s. Buddha Jayanti and Nehru Parks have groves; St Stephen's College has many trees. Two prominent trees in front of Ghiyas-ud-din's mosque in the Delhi College.

AT HOME

Chir is the only Himalayan pine to withstand bare rock and is therefore used to afforest bare slopes. It also has the ability to tolerate fire, drought and frost. It is one of the most successful pioneer species in the Himalaya.

KAREEL *Capparis decidua*

bare caper

barna family

kareel • kareer • kari • kair • karu • taint • dela • dhalu

4 m

Small tree or large bush; deciduous

Crown dense, with leafless, green, wiry twigs

Bark corky and deeply furrowed on mature trees

Spines small, orange-yellow, in pairs

Leaves narrow, small, only on young shoots; quickly shed

Flowers brick-red, in showy clusters; with long stamens

Fruit the size of a grape, with a waxy bloom

FLOWERS in showy clusters, brick-red, pink or less often orange-yellow. The four petals are long and narrow, with a prominent bonnet-like flower-cup. The long stamens are deep red and cheerfully tipped with gold. A small, green ovary is borne at the end of a long stalk.

A spiny bush or less commonly a small tree with a dark, furrowed bole topped by a mop of wiry, green branchlets. Native to arid regions, the kareel adopts the severe strategy of being leafless most of the year to cut down on water-loss. It has beautiful flowers and edible fruit. Fairly common on the Ridge and nowhere cultivated.

green ovary

bonnet-like flower-cup

SEASONS - LEAVES mostly absent; new leaves appear briefly in March/April and are shed in less than a month. **FLOWERS** irregular, in two distinct peaks — one between April and June, and again from August to October. **FRUIT** ripen within a few weeks of flowering; I have picked ripe fruit in 5 different months of the year.

WHERE TO SEE IT On the Ridge and in derelict wasteland on the outskirts of habitation. Common in the Jaunapur ravines and Jahanpanah City Forest. One superb specimen in the Qutb compound and a tall tree in the Nicholson Range. Absent from most parks.

• kareel is happy enough to flower with its roots in dry mortar

LEAVES only on young shoots, remaining for a very short time – about a month – before falling off. The narrow, grooved leaves are no more than 14 mm long. Without leaves, the work of photosynthesis is taken over by the wiry, green twigs.

• spines in pairs on slender, green branchlets, about 5 mm long, straight or slightly curved, orange-yellow

FRUIT grey-green at first, pink or dull red when ripe, about the size and shape of a grape, with a grape-like waxy bloom on the thin skin.

BARK smooth and yellowish when young, darkening and becoming thick, corky and deeply furrowed as it grows older. The corky tissue helps the tree to withstand ground fires.

HABITAT Superbly adapted to dry, exposed, rocky or sandy habitats, tolerating heat, drought, fire, frost, and saline or alkaline soils. Kareel requires only 100 mm of annual rainfall to survive. It has a huge root system spreading deep and wide, and reproduces through root-suckers. Writing of remnant forest patches ('rakhs') in the Punjab early last century, Parker noticed that in sites ruined by browsing kareel is the very last species to disappear.

RANGE Punjab, Haryana and W India, extending into dry parts of peninsular India. It extends W through Pakistan and Iran into Saudi Arabia, Egypt, Ethiopia and the Sudan.

USES Its flower buds and fruit are pickled. The tender shoots and fleeting leaves are used widely in indigenous medicine – powdered and used as a poultice on boils and swellings, and also chewed to relieve toothaches. The fruit are said to be useful in treating cardiac ailments and biliousness, and cause 'obstinate constipation'. The bitter bark, on the other hand, is laxative. The light-brown timber is hard, heavy and termite-resistant, and is suitable for making small-sized articles such as oil-mill parts and tool handles. It is not well known or much utilized.

WHY KAREEL LIKES TERMITE MOUNDS

On the Delhi Ridge, I have often noticed kareel growing out of old, abandoned termite mounds, which are like small islands of aerated, better-drained soil on the rocky Ridge. The mounds are made more porous by the tunnels within and are probably high in nutrients because of the fungi and plant seeds deposited there by the termites.

\ WEEPING BOTTLEBRUSH *Callistemon viminalis*

weeping/drooping bottlebrush

jamun/eucalyptus family

botalburoosh

Middle-sized tree, evergreen

Bark dark brown, rough, with deep, vertical furrows

Leaves narrow, tapering at both ends; young leaves softly hairy

Flowers small, crowded on spikes about 8 cm long, bright scarlet with long stamens

Fruit small, woody, cup-shaped capsules

stamens are
joined in a ring
at base

A graceful, willowy tree with slender, drooping branchlets. The largest of all the species of bottlebrush, capable of reaching 18 m but more often only 5-10 m tall. The flower spikes are bright scarlet but a host of ornamental forms have been bred with many different colours. Native to NE Australia, very popular now in Delhi gardens.

petals small,
greenish, dropping
off early

coloured stamens do
the job of attracting
insect pollinators

SEASONS - **LEAVES** more or less ever-green, but noticeable leaf-shedding in January. New leaves in February-March with more flushes in the rains. **FLOWERS** in the last week of February; prime time mid March. More low-key sputterings of flowers from August to October. **FRUIT** ripen in July-August.

WHERE TO SEE IT Very common. Every park and large garden boasts speci-mens. Also in some traffic islands.

FLOWERS crowded in dense spikes, about 8 cm long, commonly scarlet. Petals are a dispensable luxury for a plant growing in arid conditions and they are tiny and fall off early. The scarlet colour is contributed entirely by the long stamens tipped with gold.

veins are not prominent

LEAVES narrow, up to 10 cm long, pointed at both ends. New leaves are pale pink or bronzed and downy soft, eventually turning darker.

new leaves have fine hairs

FRUIT small (about 5 mm wide), woody, cup-shaped, at the ends of twigs. Unlike other bottlebrush species, its seeds are released before the next flowering season, so old fruit are not usually seen on 'old wood' .

BARK dark brown or greyish, thick, corky and deeply furrowed in a vertical axis.

HABITAT In its native range in Australia, the weeping bottlebrush is usually found growing along freshwater streams as they flow down to the sea, sometimes forming a continuous riparian fringe. It can stand some degree of immersion of its roots in water. It is highly adaptable, tolerating drought, wind and a variety of soils. It likes full sun but is decidedly less tolerant of frost than the crimson bottle-brush, for example.

RANGE NE Australia, from N Queensland, stretching halfway down the coast to N New South Wales. There are many regional races and forms and it is the parent of a huge number of popular hybrids. Widely culti-vated now in warm regions of the world.

USES Widely planted as an ornamental tree in tropical and subtropical parts of the world. In Australian cities, the weeping bottlebrush is highly valued for its tolerance of atmos-pheric pollution, a quality that it must also bank on heavily in Delhi. Its timber is reputedly tough and strong but is seldom available in sizes large enough to be used for anything more than tool handles and small objects. No local use of any of its parts has been discerned in Delhi or anywhere else in India.

CAN BE CONFUSED WITH

The **crimson bottlebrush** (*Callistemon citrinus*), which:
• is usually **smaller** (3-4 m) with shorter, arching branches
• has **flower spikes** that are usually less dense but slightly longer
• has the **filaments of its stamens free**, not united, at base
• has **fruit that remain longer**, usually 2-3 years, on the twigs
I have found no specimens of the crimson bottlebrush in Delhi.

YELLOW OLEANDER *Thevetia peruviana*

yellow/bastard oleander • be-still tree • lucky nut/bean • exile tree • tiger apple
peeli kaner

frangipani/oleander family

Shrub or small tree; evergreen

Bark grey, with shallow cracks; exudes milky latex when cut

Leaves up to 14 cm long, very slim, crowded on twigs; narrowed at both ends

Flowers trumpet-shaped with 5 overlapping petals; usually yellow, sometimes pale orange or white

Fruit oddly shaped, smooth, green at first, turning black

5 m

FLOWERS trumpet-shaped, up to 7 cm long, in long-stalked clusters. The 5 overlapping petals are joined into a tube at the bottom. The stamens and stigma lie deep inside the tube. The commonest variety has yellow flowers but white and peach-coloured forms are also cultivated.

• tube, containing the sexual organs

A small evergreen tree from Mexico and the West Indies with narrow, shiny leaves and bright-yellow trumpet-flowers. Not always tree-like and not really an oleander at all, it has become popular with civic agencies in India at least partly because not even goats will touch it owing to the poisonous principle in its milky sap.

the mouth of the flower is • 3-4 cm wide

SEASONS - **LEAVES** evergreen, but a distinct thinning out of leaves in March-April and a new flush in the rains. **FLOWERS** most of the year with a lean period from December to March; prime time from late June to September. **FRUIT** at different times, principally October to February.

WHERE TO SEE IT Common in parks and small gardens and frequent as an understorey 'filler' along avenues. For instance: on one side of Lodi Road between Lodi Garden and Max Mueller Marg; at the foot of Sewa Nagar flyover, near Jawaharlal Nehru Stadium.

leaves glossy on top, dull and paler below

leaves are neither opposite nor alternate, but spirally arranged

LEAVES very slim, 9-14 cm long, narrowed at both ends, with barely any noticeable leaf stalk. Dark green and dully glossy on the upper surface, paler beneath. The midrib is easily visible but the secondary veins are very faint.

FRUIT an oddly shaped, smooth 'apple', somewhat like a rugby ball with a transverse ridge, notched at each end. The 'apples' are green and milky when young, ripening dark brown, eventually black. In its native lands, the fruit are regarded as lucky charms, even though known to be poisonous.

transverse ridge across the rugby-ball-shaped fruit

BARK grey or grey-brown, with a thin outer skin and shallow fissures forming as the tree matures. Studded with lenticels.

HABITAT A shallow-rooted tree that will survive in dry, nutrient-poor conditions but prefers sandy, well-drained, organically rich soils. It thrives in heat and full sun but is distinctly frost-tender.

RANGE Its precise origins in tropical America are somewhat obscure but hot, dry parts of Mexico and the West Indies certainly form part of its native range. Very widely cultivated throughout the tropics worldwide as an ornamental plant.

USES The milky sap contains a highly poisonous narcotic substance that can cause serious cardiac and gastrointestinal problems, leading eventually to death. The seeds yield a bright-yellow oil that is used as a purgative and emetic and the bark is used to treat fevers, but because of the poison-ous principle, all parts of the plant must be used with extreme caution. The seed-oil is reputed to burn well without smoking.

NAGKESAR *Mesua ferrea* var. *ferrea*

(assam/ceylon) ironwood • indian rose chestnut • mesua
nagkesar • nageswar • nagchampa

mangosteen/kokam family

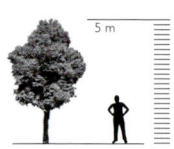

Small tree; evergreen

Bark dull brown to ashy grey, fissured and peeling in white scales on mature trees

Leaves smooth, narrow, 6-12 cm long, tapering at both ends; young leaves bright red; old leaves dark green, shiny on top, with white, powdery undersurface

Flowers fragrant, up to 10 cm wide; petals 4, white, with crisped margins; numerous yellow stamens [see below]

Fruit a pointy, ovoid capsule, about 3.5 cm long; somewhat woody

An elegant tree with a conical, bushy crown that grows quite large in its native moist forests but is stunted in Delhi. New leaves (in early March) emerge astonishingly bright red, turn pink and then pale green before darkening. Flowers with large, white petals and yellow stamens are likened to fried eggs.

WHERE TO SEE IT Only a single specimen seen in Delhi, in Sundar Nursery, but more trees are likely to be hidden away in private gardens.

ALII FIG *Ficus binnendijkii* 'Alii'

alii (weeping) fig • 'alii' • sabre-leaved fig • narrow-leaved fig
no local name

mulberry/fig family

Small tree; evergreen

Bark grey-brown, not rough

Leaves firm and narrow, up to 18 cm long; perfectly smooth, shiny on top, deep olive green

Fruit uncertain; does not seem to produce figs in Delhi

A smallish tree with firm, narrow leaves, not easily recognized as a fig tree until you notice its leaf-buds and milky latex. This is a patented, man-made hybrid, introduced recently into India as an indoor plant, but it does well outside too. Not yet common in Delhi, but it has been bred to become popular.

WHERE TO SEE IT Sundar Nursery has a small, prominent grove of alii figs. Veer Bhumi has a neat specimen. It is beginning to become more common as an indoor decorative potted plant and a hedge, too.

>> The Man-made Fig Tree – see p336

KHABBAR *Salvadora oleoides*

no english common name

peelu family

khabbar • jal • khara jal • bada peelu • diar

5 m

Smallish tree or bush; semi-evergreen

Bark pale grey, moderately rough and warty

Leaves on short stalks, in opposite pairs; narrow, up to 10 cm long; smooth, grey-green

Flowers tiny, greenish white, without stalks; arranged in compact clusters arising from leaf axils

Fruit small, yellowish, one-seeded berries, red-brown when dry; sweet

A gnarled, twisted tree (or only a bush) of dry watercourses and rocky depressions with as much character as the peelu, and easily distinguished by its narrow, olive-like leaves. For reasons not clear, it is found in Delhi almost exclusively in Mehrauli. Its native range is also more restricted than the peelu's.

WHERE TO SEE IT The Qutb has some magnificent old trees; smaller khabbar trees near the neglected walls of Lalkot in Mehrauli. 2 trees in Khusro Park, Nizamuddin.

OLIVE TREE *Olea europaea*

common/black olive • sevillano

olive/jasmine family

no local name

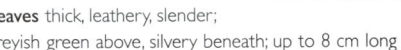

7 m

Smallish tree; evergreen

Bark grey or pale grey-brown, very rough and flaky

Leaves thick, leathery, slender; greyish green above, silvery beneath; up to 8 cm long

Flowers small, cream-coloured, fragrant

Fruit the familiar olive, up to 4 cm long; fleshy in cultivated forms, small and thinly fleshy in wild varieties

Immensely gnarled, single-trunked olive trees in Mediterranean tourist brochures can be misleading. In nature, the olive tends to form a large, bushy shrub – single trunks are achieved only through heavy pruning. Very rare in Delhi. In its native habitat, it enjoys a dry climate with winter rains.

WHERE TO SEE IT Vijay Ghat has the oldest specimen I've found in Delhi. The Italian embassy grows olive trees inside and outside its compound, but these are young trees. Lots inside the compound of the Embassy of the Holy See.

FOREST RED GUM *Eucalyptus tereticornis*

forest red gum • red irongum • queensland blue/mysore gum • eucalyptus hybrid
safeda • yeukali

jamun/eucalyptus family

Tall tree; evergreen

Bark thin, mottled, grey; underbark creamy, smooth

Leaves long, narrow, often curved, with tapering apex; dull green on both sides

Flowers in stalked clusters, usually in 7s; buds have long, conical caps which fall off

Fruit a small woody capsule, with protruding teeth

22 m

long, conical 'pixie-caps' are useful for identification

A familiar eucalyptus with upswept branches and mottled grey bark, planted extensively in India. A variable species that comes in many forms, differing in minor details. One characteristic feature is the long, conical 'pixie-cap' on the flower bud, but even this varies in shape and size. It is not a hybrid, as many people assume.

SEASONS - LEAVES evergreen, but a new flush in March-April is noticeable. FLOWERS erratic; between June-August, and/or a second flush in December-February. FRUIT depend on flowering times; mainly in our winter months.

WHERE TO SEE IT Common in parks and as a gap-filler. Railway cuttings and major stormwater drains often have dense strip plantations. Stretches of Mathura Road, the GT Road to Karnal and Jorbagh Road are lined with this tree.

FLOWERS in clusters of 5-12, usually 7. The buds wear a long, conical cap, longer than any other Delhi gum tree, though it varies somewhat in shape. The caps fall off to reveal long, crowded stamens (usually white, sometimes very pale pink). There are no petals.

LEAVES long and narrow, 10-21 cm. Usually sickle-shaped with a long, tapering, pointy tip. Dull green or bluish green on both sides.

juvenile leaves are broader than adult • leaves

base V-shaped, • slightly asymmetrical

HABITAT A tree of open forests and coastal tablelands. Versatile and adaptable, this species has the widest latitudinal distribution of any eucalypt, ranging from very dry tropical to warm temperate and moist forests. It grows on a variety of soils except strongly acidic ones. It tolerates some waterlogging, is fairly drought-resistant, but is sensitive to severe frosts.

RANGE The entire length of E Australia from the cooler SE to tropical Queensland, mostly within 100 km of the sea. Also in Papua New Guinea. Widely introduced into warm countries, particularly in places with summer rainfall. Adopted on a massive scale for agro-forestry in India in the 1960s and misleadingly called 'Mysore gum' or 'eucalyptus hybrid'.

FRUIT little woody capsules 6-9 mm long, shaped like wine goblets, growing on short stalks. 4-5 triangular teeth project above the rim of the capsule. The minute seeds inside are shiny black to dark brown.

• the 'teeth' are valves which open to release the seeds when they are ready

BARK smooth, grey, shedding in thin flakes to expose pale underbark. The overall effect is mottled. There is often a stocking of dark, rough bark at the base of the trunk.

>> How Eucalypts Are Differentiated – see p330

USES The most important use of this tree in India is for paper pulp. Also extensively planted for fuelwood and small timber needs. It is used as a shelterbelt species and produces an amber honey of distinctive flavour. The wood is hard, heavy and dense but tends to warp in seasoning and is difficult to work when dry. It is not used as extensively in India as it is in Australia, where the wood is known to be durable, especially underground.

CAN BE CONFUSED WITH

Most of Delhi's eucalypt species are easily confused, even by botanists. The two crucial characters to help tell eucalypts apart are their flower buds and fruit (or 'gumnuts') and, to a lesser extent, the colour and texture of their bark. See page 182 for a key to Delhi's eucalypts.

\ COOLABAH *Eucalyptus microtheca*

(black) coolabah • coolibah • flooded box

jamun/eucalyptus family

no local names that distinguish it from other eucalypts

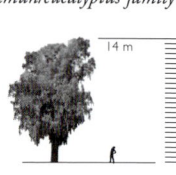

Medium-sized tree; evergreen

Bark very dark and rough, deeply furrowed at base

Leaves blue-green to greyish, narrow, up to 18 cm long; apex pointy

Flower buds usually in 7s, very small, with a short, rounded cap; flowers white, about one cm wide, fragrant

Fruit capsules very small, funnel-shaped or hemispherical

A spreading gum-tree with dark, persistent bark and pale blossoms that smell deliciously like mehndi flowers. Not well known or common in India but distributed widely in Australia along river systems in semi-arid regions. This is the 'coolabah' that figures in the famous Ozzy song *Waltzing Matilda*.

WHERE TO SEE IT
3 prominent trees on K. Ataturk Marg outside the Delhi Gymkhana Club. A long row near the VC's office in Delhi University, and a pretty tree in 5 Aurobindo Marg.

\ REID RIVER BOX *Eucalyptus brownii*

reid river box • brown stringybark • grey box

jamun/eucalyptus family

no local names that distinguish it from other eucalypts

Medium-sized tree; evergreen

Bark grey to grey-brown, fibrous and flaky

Leaves dull grey-green, up to 12 cm long; usually straight, seldom curved; apex pointy

Flower buds in clusters of 7-11, tiny, with a short, rounded cap; flowers white

Fruit capsules small, conical or bell-like, with 4 valves, not protruding beyond the rim

A relatively unknown gum-tree with a very restricted provenance in Australia, which has somehow found its way into the Qutb gardens. It may have once had companions there, but only a solitary specimen survives. It belongs to the 'box' group of eucalypts with characteristically thick, persistent bark.

WHERE TO SEE IT Only a solitary tree in the Qutb compound, towards the back.

RIVER RED GUM *Eucalyptus camaldulensis*

river red gum • murray red gum • river gum
safeda • yeukali

jamun/eucalyptus family

Large tree; evergreen

Trunk usually short, thick, often leaning to one side

Twigs reddish when young

Bark rough at base; smooth, shed in flakes or ribbons higher up, exposing startlingly white or creamy trunk

Leaves long and narrow, curved, tapering to a point, up to 25 cm long; dull green or grey green

Flowers white; shape of the buds and their deciduous 'caps' is used to separate 2 varieties of this species

Fruit small woody capsules with 3-5 (usually 4) projecting 'teeth'

The stately river red gum is the most wide-spread and best-loved of all Australian eucalypts. With their heavy, twisted branches and attractively mottled bark, river red gums stand apart from other eucalypts but scientists use the shape of their flower buds to distinguish between 2 or more varieties. Delhi has specimens of both kinds.

the 'long-beaked' bud of var. *camaldulensis*

BUDS are either round, with a long 'beak', or conical, with barely any 'beak' – and serve to distinguish the 2 varieties.

BARK grey, yellow or pink-grey, shedding in flakes to expose pale underbark. Var. *camaldulensis* has a stocking of darker bark at its base.

the bud of var. *obtusa* is conical, with a much less pronounced beak

SEASONS - LEAVES evergreen, thinning out in February. FLOWERS a little erratic, mostly in October-November. FRUIT ripen about 3 months after flowering.

WHERE TO SEE IT Tolstoy Marg (off Janpath) and the road running past Rajghat to the river. Rash-trapati Bhavan has a woodlot all leaning in one direction. Lodi Garden has specimens of both varieties; Talkatora Garden has a grand specimen.

A KEY TO

DELHI'S EUCALYPTS

The 2 crucial characters you need to examine to differentiate the eucalypts are the flower buds and the little woody fruit or 'gumnuts'. The colour and texture of the bark can sometimes be useful but is often misleading; the flowers and leaves are broadly similar and are seldom useful for identification. (See page 330 – How Eucalypts Are Differentiated.)

RIVER RED GUM *Eucalyptus camaldulensis* (p181)

var. *camaldulensis* – BUDS in clusters of 4-12, usually 7; nearly spherical, with the tip extended into a pointy nipple.

var. *obtusa* – BUDS in clusters of 5-11. Relative to var. *camaldulensis*, the bud is conical, with only the faintest suggestion of a nipple.

GUMNUTS of both varieties are similar and difficult to tell apart. They have a short base topped by a prominent rim 7-10 mm wide. There are 4-5 raised, triangular teeth, making a pattern that looks like the head of a Phillips screw. Difficult to distinguish from forest red gum – one useful clue is that the seeds are yellowish, while those of forest red gum are black and shiny.

raised teeth

var. *camaldulensis*

var. *obtusa*

long caps

FOREST RED GUM *Eucalyptus tereticornis* (pp178-79)

BUDS in clusters of 5-12, most often 7; up to 2 cm long, with noticeably long, conical caps. There is some variation in the length and shape of the bud-caps.

GUMNUTS (like river red gum's) have 4-5 triangular teeth projecting straight upwards from the rim.

LEMON-SCENTED GUM *Corymbia citriodora* (p183)

BUDS in clusters of 2-5; club-shaped, with a big base and hemispherical cap (actually 2 caps, one under the other) with a very tiny point at the apex.

GUMNUTS are shaped like little goblets, up to 1.5 cm long, with a sunken disc and teeth deep inside.

sunken disc and teeth

sunken teeth

REID RIVER BOX *Eucalyptus brownii* (p180)

BUDS in clusters of 7-11, with a short, rounded cap. (Somehow I have missed seeing Delhi's only specimen in flower – so no pictures!)

GUMNUTS very small, with no disc visible and 4 sunken teeth.

COOLABAH *Eucalyptus microtheca* (p180)

BUDS usually in 7s, relatively small; base large, extending beyond the broadest part of the bud; cap short (1-2 mm) and conical, with a little point at the apex.

GUMNUTS are the tiniest of all the eucalypts found in Delhi, with a hemispherical base and very narrow disc. Teeth 3-4, prominent and strongly ascending.

base of the bud

teeth ascending, with a wide 'gape'

╲ LEMON-SCENTED GUM *Corymbia citriodora*

lemon-scented gum • citron-scent gum • spotted gum • safeda • *yeukali*

jamun/eucalyptus family

Large tree; evergreen	

Bark pink or grey, flaking near base; underbark smooth, cream or bluish, often dimpled

Leaves smell sharply of odomos when crushed; adult leaves narrow, smooth; young leaves broad, hairy

Flower buds in groups of 2-5, club-shaped, with a short-pointed hemispherical cap; flowers have long, creamy stamens, no petals

Fruit large, urn-shaped with sunken disc and valves

FLOWER BUDS club-shaped and wear 2 caps, one under the other. The uppermost cap is khaki green and falls off to reveal a rose-coloured cap which falls off only when it is time for the long stamens to unfurl.

A tall, small-crowned gum-tree capable of reaching 40 m in its native coastal NE Australia but never more than 18 m in Delhi. One of the easiest eucalypts to recognize by its ultra smooth bark, large urn-shaped 'gumnuts' and lemon-scented leaves. Depending on the season, the trunk may look mottled with flaking bark or be completely smooth.

reddish cap is the last to fall off •

FRUIT like miniature wine goblets, with their valves or 'teeth' sunk deep inside.

SEASONS - LEAVES evergreen. **FLOWERS** somewhat erratic in Delhi; March-April or mid-winter. **FRUIT** ripen some 3 months after flowering.

WHERE TO SEE IT Many trees fringing the central park in Delhi University, and many more inside St Stephen's College and other colleges in Delhi University. 2 slim trees skulking close to the entrance into Lodi Garden from Joseph Allen Stein Lane. Many parks have them.

BARK perfectly smooth in certain seasons.

>> This tree used to be called *Eucalyptus citriodora*. See p331 – *Corymbia* vs *Eucalyptus*

AMLA *Phyllanthus emblica*

emblic • emblic myrobalan • amla • indian gooseberry • malacca tree
amla • *aonla* • *amlaki* • *aungra* • *aunra*

amla/castor family

Medium-sized tree; deciduous

Bark thin, grey, flaking off to expose yellow-brown underbark

Leaves only 8-12 mm long, narrow, close-set; tiny point at apex

Flowers also small, with 6 pink or greenish petal-like flower-cup segments but no petals; in clusters on naked twigs below the leaves; male and female flowers separate

Fruit nearly round, 2-4 cm in diameter, smooth, yellow-green with thin, translucent skin; 6-8 faint lines from base to apex; flesh crisp, extremely sour

MALE FLOWERS are far more numerous and 'flower-like', and are clustered towards the base of the twig. They have tiny stalks. You can recognize the females by their 3-forked styles, just a few of them towards the apex.

A distinctive tree from dry forests with a fluted trunk, fine, feathery foliage and thin, grey bark peeling in small, irregular patches. The tiny leaves can be mistaken for leaflets of a feather-compound leaf but are really the smallest simple leaves of any Delhi tree. The tart fruit are a familiar ingredient of pickles and sherbets.

• male flower

• female flower

SEASONS - LEAFLESS through January and February; new leaves appear early in March. **FLOWERS** late March to mid April. **FRUIT** ripen in just under a year but remain for long on the tree.

WHERE TO SEE IT Humayun's and Safdarjang's Tomb gardens have large, old specimens. Kamla Nehru Park and Shalimar Bagh in N Delhi have a large number. A tall, prominent tree in Talkatora Garden.

BARK usually distinctive enough to spot an amla tree from a great distance. The smooth outer bark is greyish, flaking off in small patches to reveal yellow underbark. The trunk is fluted and gnarled on old trees.

>> Amla: The One-fruit Pharmacy – see p327

ROHEDA *Tecomella undulata*

wavy-leaved tecomella • barmer/desert teak

roheda • lahura • luar

jacaranda family

Small tree; deciduous

Bark dark grey-brown, rough with shallow furrows; often missing in broad strips

Leaves in opposite or near-opposite pairs, dull greyish-green, 5-12 cm long; margins slightly wavy

Flowers up to 8 cm long, trumpet-shaped, in small clusters; pale to deep orange, with paler throat

Fruit a long, thin, slightly curved capsule up to 20 cm long, with winged seeds

LEAVES in opposite pairs, set at right angles to the pair immediately above and below it. Margins wavy.

A somewhat untidy tree with a loose, open crown and drooping extremities that can delight you in March with its magnificent, bright-orange trumpet-flowers. Native to dry, semi-arid areas, it is sometimes seen as an isolated tree on the outskirts of Delhi and in places where Delhi's native vegetation has not yet been completely cleared.

SEASONS - LEAVES shed in January, renewed in mid February, but also at other times – the tree appears to be highly responsive to rain. FLOWERS begin erratically in the middle of March, usually peaking by March end. FRUIT ripen in June, but not seen anywhere in Delhi, perhaps because of ineffective pollination.

WHERE TO SEE IT Not on the Ridge, which is too rocky, but in Jaunapur's sandy ravines. Lodi Garden, Nehru Park, Mahavir Jayanti Park, JNU campus and the DDA Park in R Block, Greater Kailash I have a few specimens each. There's a big tree close to the director's office in the zoo, and a curious specimen growing out of sheer rock opposite house # N258A in GK I.

ONE TREE in Lodi Garden, credited with curing children's skin diseases, is festooned with the clothes of its young 'patients'.

❧ BAEL-LIKE LEAVES *With only 2 or 3 leaflets*

2 leaflets

downy when young

grey-green when mature

leaflets joined only at base

4-5 arching veins

anjan
7 cm p188

silver-hairy when young

hingot
5 cm p187

tiny sub-stalks

looks like 2 leaflets; actuallly twice-feathered

gainti
15 cm p280

cleft very shallow

broader than long

11-15 nerves at base

kachnar
15 cm p192

mostly smooth

cleft deep; inner edges touching

9-11 nerves at base

kaniar
18 cm p194

longer than broad

largest bauhinia leaf

more or less smooth

9-13 nerves at base

hong kong orchid tree
22 cm p196

underside and stalk densely woolly

smallest bauhinia leaf

jhinjheri
9 cm p190

7-9 nerves at base

3 leaflets

shiny, dark green

tiny teeth on margins

bishopwood
23 cm p197

sometimes faintly toothed

smooth on top, downy below

tiny, rounded teeth on margins

sandan
24 cm p197

broad wing along leaf stalk

central leaflet has long sub-stalk

smooth

bael
18 cm p198

glossy, dark green

gourd tree
15 cm p199

leathery, tips rounded

downy when young, becoming smooth

smooth on both sides

tips pointy

central leaflet has no stalk

central leaflet much longer

more usually a simple leaf; margins toothed

chestnutleaf trumpet-bush
18 cm p199

round glands

dhak
38 cm p200

leaflets broad

barna
23 cm p202

round glands

sometimes prickly

dhaul dhak
36 cm p204

leaflets smooth

smallest leaf of the coral trees

blake's coral tree
14 cm p204

smooth, dull

indian coral tree
38 cm p205

smooth above, downy below

HINGOT *Balanites roxburghii*

desert date

hingot family

hingot • hingua • hingan

Small tree or bush; deciduous

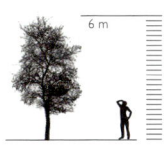
6 m

Bark green at first, turning yellowish or dark, with shallow, vertical furrows

Spines up to 7 cm long, from leaf axils; straight, sharp, green or yellow-grey; often leaf- and flower-bearing

Leaves compound with 2 slim leaflets, up to 4 cm long, tapering at both ends; downy when young

Flowers greenish yellow; flower-cup and 5 spreading petals densely furry; 10 long stamens

Fruit woody, ovoid, about 6 cm long, green turning yellow; faintly grooved; filled with a bitter, edible pulp

LEAVES do not, at first sight, look compound – look closely for a pair of ashy green leaflets springing from a very short common leaf stalk.

A small, stiff, spiny tree or straggly bush, a characteristic plant of Indian dry scrub and thorn forests. Deciduous, with green twigs and stout thorns that are often leaf-bearing. A common native tree on the Ridge and inside JNU campus, but hardly ever seen in cultivation or in manicured spaces.

SEASONS - **LEAVES** shed in February-March, renewed in late April. **FLOWERING** with the new leaves, peaking by late April or early May. **FRUIT** ripen about 6 months after flowering, remaining on the tree till February.

the fruit has 5 faint grooves

WHERE TO SEE IT A native tree now seen only on the Ridge and in relict bits of original scrub forest. There are 2 trees on Africa Avenue outside Navsena Bagh 1, and a small copse next to the Dhaula Kuan flyover. It tends to get weeded out of parks and gardens for its untidy appearance.

TIT FOR TAT

Hingot fruit form part of the diet of neelgai, jackals and porcupines, and may even act as a 'de-wormer', helping to rid them of stomach parasites. In return, the seeds get dispersed and stand a better chance of germination after passing through their tracts.

ANJAN *Hardwickia binata*

indian blackwood

pea family – cassia subfamily

anjan

Large tree; deciduous

Bark very dark, rough, cracked

Leaves compound with only 2 leaflets, joined at base

Flowers very tiny, white, inconspicuous

Fruit a short, flat, brown pod with a single seed

16 m

4 or 5 arching veins in each leaflet

In its natural forests, anjan is an imperiously tall tree 11 storeys high, but it reaches less than half this height in Delhi. With drooping branches and small leaves, this is one of Delhi's most graceful trees especially in new leaf. The tiny, white flowers are inconspicuous and easily overlooked. Planted somewhat tentatively along a few avenues in Lutyens' Delhi.

LEAFLETS have no stalks of their own and are joined at their bases.

SEASONS - LEAVES shed in April; new leaves, tinged red, in early May and trees look loveliest from June to August. FLOWERS August-September. FRUIT appear soon after the flowers, remaining till the following May.

WHERE TO SEE IT Pandara Road and Maulana Azad Road are anjan avenues (though not exclusively), with a concentration near the Udyog Bhavan roundabout. More on the roundabout at the E end of Dalhousie Road. The IIC has a large tree overlooking the parking lot. There is a large anjan grove in the southern part of Buddha Jayanti Park.

there are no petals, but the lobes of the flower-cup are petal-like

FLOWERS very tiny, loosely arranged in clusters. Whitish or greenish yellow, inconspicuous and easy to miss.

LEAVES have only 2 leaflets. Each leaflet is up to 6 cm long with 4 or 5 main veins. Mature foliage is dull greyish-green but young leaves turn through tints of pink to an impossible light green before darkening.

the twin leaflets are likened to a butterfly's wings

FRUIT a short, flat pod about 6 cm long, with a solitary seed near the apex. Chestnut brown when mature.

BARK grey-brown, rough, riven with deep, vertical cracks, becoming even darker as it ages.

CAN BE CONFUSED WITH

One of the kachnars, perhaps, but easily distinguished by its leaflets which are *not* joined along the middle but only at one single point.

Jungle jalebi has leaflets of very similar shape, but its leaves are twice-feathered, with side-stalks containing 4 leaflets in all.

HABITAT A characteristic tree of dry, open forests in C India and the Deccan, where it sometimes forms pure stands. It grows on porous soils – even shallow, gravelly soils – but attains its greatest size on deep, sandy soil with underlying sandstone or quartz. Seedlings throw all their energy into developing long taproots that penetrate fissures in rock to reach underlying moisture. It does not stand waterlogging.

RANGE Restricted to dry forests in C India and the Deccan, with a northerly limit near MP's border with UP.

USES Its bark-fibre yields a strong rope. Cattle are especially fond of its leaves. Anjan is among the hardest and heaviest of all Indian timbers. The sapwood is pale, the heartwood dark reddish-brown, often streaked with purple. It is exceedingly difficult to work but is close-grained and finishes well. It is also exceptionally durable – anjan piles have been dug up from a riverbed after 20 years and found to be completely sound. The wood is used for posts and beams, cartwheels, ploughshares and tool handles. It was once employed in place of brass to make ball-bearings and milling parts. The wood makes excellent charcoal.

❧ JHINJHERI *Bauhinia racemosa*

burmese silk orchid

pea family – cassia subfamily

jhinjheri • jhanjhora • jhinja • ashta • gurial • makuna • maula • ghila • thaur

Small tree; deciduous

Bark very dark, rough, deeply fissured

Leaves with 2 leaflets joined in the middle, broader than long; downy underneath

Flowers small, white, inconspicuous, with 5 narrow petals

Fruit pods thick, woody, dark, slightly curved

5 m

narrow, white
petals

A diminutive tree with a crooked trunk and spreading crown, looking top-heavy and in need of a haircut. It has smaller leaves than other bauhinias and flowers not nearly as showy, but makes up by great ostentation in new leaf. Native to Delhi and the Aravallis, but relatively uncommon on the Ridge.

SEASONS - **LEAVES** begin to drop in late March. New leaf in mid April, canopy completely renewed by May. More flushes in the rains. **FLOWERS** in May, peaking by the middle of the month. **FRUIT** pods ripen in October-November and remain on the tree for many months.

WHERE TO SEE IT A brace of trees outside Santushti, Chanakyapuri. The small charbagh next to the Qutb has some old specimens. 2 pretty trees in Nehru Park. Lodi Garden has a small grove and one outsize tree. Delhi Golf Club has a few. A nice tree outside the Chinese embassy on Shanti Path. Rare on the Ridge.

FLOWERS small and easily overlooked, white or creamish, with 5 narrow petals 8-13 mm long. There are 10 stamens. The flowers are arranged on long, densely downy stalks that emerge close to or at the terminal ends of twigs.

leaves are up to 7 cm long, usually a little broader than long

LEAVES like a characteristic bauhinia, camel's foot-shaped, but smaller than other Delhi bauhinias. The twin leaflets are united in the middle, with a shallow cleft. The lower lobes are not prominent. The leaves have 7-9 main nerves and are densely woolly underneath and along the leaf stalk.

leaf stalk is densely woolly

FRUIT a dark, woody pod, surprisingly large for such a small tree. The curved pod is up to 30 cm long and 2.5 cm broad, and contains 10-20 seeds.

BARK dark, rough, riven by deep, vertical fissures. Inner bark deep pink.

CAN BE CONFUSED WITH

One of the other bauhinias, but only outside its flowering season. Easily distinguished by the smallness and woolliness of its leaves and its insignificant flowers.

HABITAT A tree of dry deciduous forests. Equally at home in hilly tracts, valleys and plateaux, and tolerant of a wide range of soils. Paradoxically, it is more drought-hardy as well as more tolerant of higher rainfall than other bauhinias growing in Delhi. It is seldom seen on the Delhi Ridge but the city has specimens that are clearly old, relict trees from a time before the city's roads were aligned. It is present in numbers in nearby hill tracts in Faridabad district.

RANGE Throughout the sub-Himalayan tract (up to 1300 m in Kumaon) from the Ravi eastwards to Bengal and in peninsular India. Very much a native Aravalli tree. Its natural range extends beyond India to Myanmar, Sri Lanka, the Malay islands and S China.

USES The inner bark yields a strong fibre used for cordage and its bark is useful in dyeing. The gum and leaves are used in traditional medicine. It is sometimes used as a substitute for tendu leaves for wrapping beedis. The seeds can be roasted and eaten. The wood is pale brown and very hard with irregular masses of darker heartwood at its centre. It is not much used only because it is seldom available in large enough sizes. It makes a good fuelwood.

❧ KACHNAR *Bauhinia variegata*

mountain ebony • buddhist/variegated bauhinia • (poor man's) orchid tree

pea family – cassia subfamily

kachnar • koilar • guiral • khwairal • padrian • kaniar

Middle-sized tree; deciduous

Bark dark brown with black, scaly patches

Leaf typical 'camel's hoof' shape, usually slightly broader than long

Flowers showy, variously coloured, with 5 petals, the central one distinct; 3 central petals overlapping

Fruit a flat pod up to 30 cm long

10 m

Var. *candida* has white petals, the central one splashed with lime green ●

3 central petals overlapping; 5 long stamens ●

A smallish tree seldom more than 8 m tall in Delhi, with a short, dark trunk and thin, ascending branches forming a modest crown. Self-effacing most of the year, it is resplendent in flower in mid March, with two distinct varieties of blooms. Cultivated in gardens and occasionally as street trees.

SEASONS - **LEAVES** start to be shed in March, completed by late April. New leaf in May-June. **FLOWERING** may begin as early as end January, but prime time is generally in the first half of March; flowering is over by mid April. **FRUIT** form quickly after the flowers, splitting and releasing their seeds towards late May.

WHERE TO SEE IT Kakanagar has lots of both varieties. Var. *variegata* in Talkatora Garden, Teen Murti Bhavan, Shakti Sthal, #1 A. Shergil Marg, Nehru Park, Kamla Nehru Park. Var. *candida* near Nehru Yuvak Kendra, Chanakyapuri Police Station, in Lodi Garden, Shanti Vana, Shakti Sthal, Nehru Park, Laxmibai Nagar.

FLOWERS appear first on the upper branches as the leaves start to drop. The 2 varieties are distinguished by their colour: var. *variegata* has pink, lavender, white or purplish petals, 4 of a similar colour, the 5th (central) petal broader and darker, with deep-magenta veins. Var. *candida* is nearly pure white.

between 9 and 15 main nerves • in the leaf

inner edges of the lobes are not overlapping

LEAVES about 15 cm long and usually slightly broader, shaped like a camel's hoofprint. The twin leaflets are partly joined in the middle, with a cleft that runs a third (or less) down the middle. The two lobes are well rounded at their apices. Young leaves are downy, becoming smoother with age.

FRUIT a flat pod up to 30 cm long, pale brown or rufous. Like the kaniar, it splits open with explosive force to scatter the seeds when it is ripe.

BUDS smooth, not ribbed.

BARK dark grey with black patches. Fissured, rough, sometimes quite knobbly.

CAN BE CONFUSED WITH

Other bauhinias in Delhi. This species is distinguished by its 3 central overlapping petals, 5 long stamens and a very shallow cleft to its leaf.

HABITAT A scattered tree of dry deciduous forests. It inhabits rocky slopes, plateaux and valleys, preferring southern aspects in hilly terrain. Like other bauhinias naturalized in Delhi, it adapts to a range of soils but does not tolerate waterlogging. It is frost-tender.

RANGE The sub-Himalayan tract up to about 1300 m from the Indus eastwards to Assam and in dry forests in peninsular India. Scattered but nowhere abundant. Outside the subcontinent, it extends into Myanmar, S China and much of SE Asia. Widely cultivated as an ornamental in warm climates or under glass.

USES The astringent bark is useful in tanning and dyeing but is not much used. The leaves are a good fodder and are sometimes used to make beedis. The flowers and especially the buds are eaten as a vegetable. Root, flower and bark are considered useful in traditional medicine – the bark for treating diarrhoea, the flowers as a laxative. The tree yields a gum that swells in water. The pale brown or slightly reddish wood is moderately hard and is used to fashion agricultural implements. It is seldom available in sizes large enough to be put to other uses. It makes an excellent fuelwood.

KANIAR *Bauhinia purpurea*

purple bauhinia • butterfly tree • geranium tree • orchid tree

pea family – cassia subfamily

kaniar • koliar • keelra • khairwal • kandan • sona • kachnar • karar • karalli

Smallish tree; nearly evergreen

Bark ashy, with silvery surface; not very rough

Leaf typical 'camel's hoof' shape, slightly longer than broad

Flowers rose pink or lilac with 5 narrow petals

Fruit a thin, flat pod up to 28 cm long

9 m

3 long, fertile stamens (sometimes 4), and 2 (or more) short ones ●

the long, narrow petals do not overlap ●

Usually only a small tree with a short, crooked trunk supporting a compact, cheerful canopy. Nearly evergreen, with leaves shaped like a camel's hoof and showy pink flowers. Widely distributed throughout India but not strictly native to Delhi. Fairly common in parks and gardens and only occasionally a street tree.

SEASONS - LEAVES nearly evergreen, turning khaki before being shed in April and quickly renewed. Another flush in the rains. FLOWERS October to December, prime time in mid November. FRUIT pods form quickly after the flowers, ripening by March-April when they burst open.

WHERE TO SEE IT In most parks and many small gardens but only rarely as a street tree. Lodi Garden has a grove of kaniar trees along its N edge, flanking Sikander Lodi's tomb. Specimens inside Purana Qila, in Nehru and Buddha Jayanti Parks and Talkatora Garden. Fairly common.

FLOWERS showy, fragrant, with 5 narrow petals, rose pink or lilac. 4 petals are alike, the 5th lighter but with darker markings. The flowers are pollinated by bees.

LEAVES like the outline of a camel's hoof, usually slightly longer than broad. The twin leaflets are partly joined in the middle with a deep cleft. The inner edges of the lobes on top overlap slightly. Young leaflets are faintly downy.

inner edges of lobes overlapping

cleft runs about halfway down the middle

BUDS velvety, distinctly 5-angled, appearing striped.

FRUIT a flat pod up to 28 cm long, pointy at both ends. When ripe, the pod splits open with explosive force, ejecting seeds up to 6 m away.

the pods after splitting open

young pods are green and often stippled with maroon

BARK ashy grey, silvery, fairly smooth in young trees, becoming rougher and forming small, crusty plates as the tree grows older.

CAN BE CONFUSED WITH

Other bauhinias in Delhi. The simplest distinction is that its petals do not overlap and the flower has only 3 long stamens.

HABITAT A characteristic tree of dry deciduous forests, growing on hill slopes, valleys and along streams, often associated with sal (*Shorea robusta*). It is the least drought-hardy of Indian bauhinias and requires 75-500 cm of annual rainfall. It tolerates frost and a wide range of soils, including shallow and rocky sites to rich black cotton soil. It does not withstand waterlogging.

RANGE Native to lower slopes of the Himalaya E of the Indus, up to about 1400 m. It extends eastwards to Assam and NE India and south through peninsular India as a scattered tree. Also found in Myanmar, Sri Lanka, S China. Widely cultivated.

USES The astringent bark is employed for tanning, dyeing and rope-making. The root and flowers are used in traditional medicine as a tonic and laxative. The flowers are pickled or eaten fresh as a pot herb. The leaves are a nutritious fodder. The pale sapwood is no good but the heartwood is hard, strong and easy to saw and work. The heartwood is pinkish when freshly cut and oxidizes to a handsome greyish red or brown. It is mostly used in the countryside, mainly for agricultural implements and light construction.

❧ HONG KONG ORCHID TREE *Bauhinia* x *blakeana*

hong kong orchid tree • red-flowered bauhinia
(loosely) *kachnar*

pea family – cassia subfamily

Middle-sized tree; deciduous

Bark ashy, studded with dark lenticels, similar to kaniar's

Leaves shaped like a camel's hoofprint, larger than other bauhinias; with 9-11 base nerves; upper lobes set apart, pointy or rounded

Flowers large, up to 15 cm across, rich magenta-purple; central petal limned with scarlet; 3 long stamens and 2 short ones

Fruit not produced (because it is sterile)

8 m

>> How *Bauhinia* x *blakeana* Got Its Name – see p328

FLOWERS larger and deeper-coloured than other bauhinias. Petals broad like kachnar's; only 3 long stamens like kaniar.

A medium-sized tree with a spreading crown of characteristic bauhinia leaves shaped like a camel's hoofprint. This natural hybrid, first discovered in S China, produces the most beautiful and the largest blooms of all the bauhinias. It is only occasionally cultivated in parks and gardens in Delhi as an ornamental, but deserves more notice.

central petal has deep-scarlet markings •

SEASONS - LEAVES bare or thin for a short while in March-April; renewed towards late April. **FLOWER** buds appear early in January; flowering usually in late January, peaking in February and petering out by early March. **FRUIT** not produced.

lobes not over-lapping
• near cleft

WHERE TO SEE IT Most large parks have specimens. Sundar Nursery has a large tree near its central gumbad. IIC has a row of 4 trees near its central court; there is a small grove in Mahavir Vanasthali. Greater Kailash and Maharani Bagh have a few short avenues devoted exclusively to this beautiful tree.

CAN BE CONFUSED WITH

Either or both of its parents, the kaniar and kachnar, especially when not in flower.

BISHOPWOOD *Bischofia javanica*

bishopwood • bischofia • tiger tree • toog
kain • pankain • bhillar • paniala

amla/castor family

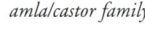

Middle-sized tree; deciduous

Bark soft, with angular scales

Leaves shiny, compound with 3 leaflets, up to 15 cm long; margins toothed, apex long-pointy; new leaves bronzed, old leaves turn a startling red

Flowers greenish yellow, in large clusters; male and female on separate trees; petals lacking

Fruit a pea-sized berry, blue-black or reddish, in bunches

A fairly large tree in its natural habitat, with a dense, spreading canopy that is particularly attractive in bronzy new leaf. Easy to recognize by its compound leaves with 3 bluntly toothed leaflets. Native to moist places, widely dispersed in India, ranging eastwards to the Pacific Islands. Rare in Delhi.

WHERE TO SEE IT
One solitary female tree in Sundar Nursery. Another in the Delhi University nursery.

WHY 'TIGER TREE'?

Because the soft bark of bishopwood trees are often preferred 'scratch-pads' on which resident tigers clean and sharpen their claws and mark their territory as well.

SANDAN *Desmodium oojeinense*

Syn: Ougeinia oojeinensis

no english common name
sandan • asainda • tinsa • tiwas

pea family and subfamily

Small tree; deciduous

Trunk usually crooked

Bark ashy, with vertical cracks

Leaves compound, with 3 leathery leaflets; middle leaflet largest, broadly oval; side leaflets unequal at base [see pic below]

Flowers pea-like, pale pink or rose, in short clusters

Pod flat, brown, veined, about 8 cm long

A tree with a crooked trunk and compact crown of compound leaves with 3 broad, leathery leaflets. It produces dense clusters of pink blossoms in March before its new leaves appear, a spectacular sight. Native to moist and dry forests in the sub-Himalayan region and C India. Undeservedly rare in Delhi.

WHERE TO SEE IT
Only a single specimen in the timber section of Sundar Nursery.

BAEL *Aegle marmelos*

golden apple • bengal/indian quince • stone apple

bael • bel • bil • beel • bila • sirphal

orange family

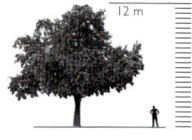

Middle-sized tree; deciduous

Spines strong, straight, solitary, about 2.5 cm long

Bark pale, somewhat corky, with shallow furrows

Leaves compound with 3 leaflets, the central one largest with a long stalk; side leaflets on very short stalks; margins have minute, rounded teeth

Flowers fragrant, about 3 cm wide, with 4 or 5 thick petals bent backwards; numerous spreading stamens

Fruit large, globose, with a hard shell; orange, glutinous pulp inside

FLOWERS in clusters of 4-7, petals green on the outside, creamy white inside. In the centre of the flower is a strong, green style. The flowers are wonderfully fragrant.

A middle-sized, thorny tree with a narrow, oval crown. Bare for many months when its large, round fruit become conspicuous, it turns strikingly beautiful in new leaf. Native to monsoon forests throughout India, the bael is only an occasional tree in Delhi's parks and gardens and deserves more notice.

stamens

SEASONS - LEAVES begin to be shed in March, bare or straggly in April; new leaf in late April, tinged pink at first. FLOWERS in late May. FRUIT form quickly, still green in April of the year after flowering, ripening June or July.

FRUIT woody, 12-14 cm in diameter, turning yellow when ripe. The seeds are encased in a strong-smelling pulp.

WHERE TO SEE IT Here and there in gardens and temple compounds. Specimens in the Sri Lankan embassy on Kautilya Marg; Satya Marg, Sundar Nursery, Humayun's Tomb garden, Modern School (Barakhamba Road).

BAEL PHARMA

'No drug has been longer and better known nor more appreciated by the inhabitants of India than bel,' wrote George Watt in 1889. The fruit (ripe, unripe and sun-dried), leaf and root bark are all used to treat an astonishing range of maladies. See p325 for more on bael cures.

🦋 GOURD TREE *Crescentia alata*

gourd tree • winged calabash • jicaro • music tree • mexican calabash

jacaranda family

no local name

6 m

Small tree; deciduous

Bark greyish, not very rough

Leaves crowded, both simple and compound (3 leaflets); leaf stalks long, with prominent, broad 'wings'

Flowers 6 cm long, bell-shaped, greenish yellow veined with brown; growing from 'old wood'; opening at night

Fruit large, up to 10 cm in diameter, growing straight from the trunk and main limbs, with a smooth, hard, thin shell; green at first, brown when ripe [see pic below]

A small but vividly unusual tree with hard, gourd-like fruit and dingy, greenish-yellow flowers growing straight out of the trunk. The leaves, too, are distinctive, both simple and compound leaves being found on the same tree. Native to dry forests in Mexico and Guatemala. Cultivated for its oddity value. It does very well in Delhi but is rare.

WHERE TO SEE IT One tree near the Talkatora swimming pool; another in the NISCOM garden (IARI). The zoo has 2 specimens opposite the emus.

>> The Puzzle of the Gourd Tree – see p321, *Crescentia alata* and *Crescentia cujete* – see p332

🦋 CHESTNUTLEAF TRUMPET-BUSH *Tecoma castanifolia*

chestnutleaf trumpet-bush

jacaranda family

gaudichaudi

6 m

Bush or small tree; deciduous

Bark medium brown, lightly fissured when old

Leaves in opposite pairs, mostly simple but sometimes with 3 leaflets; edges coarsely toothed, undersides pale and hairy; apex tapering [see pic below]

Flowers bright-yellow trumpets up to 5 cm long, in clusters at ends of branchlets; mouth of trumpet 5-lobed

Fruit pod-like, up to 12 cm long, thin and flattish

A large bush or smallish tree with a dense, dark-green canopy and a brilliant display of bright-yellow trumpet-flowers at most times of the year. Native to dry regions of tropical S America (Ecuador, Colombia), it does exceptionally well in Delhi but is not as popular as it deserves to be.

WHERE TO SEE IT The IIC and Sundar Nursery have specimens. There is a prominent tree in the DDA colony opposite JMC in Chanakyapuri.

✣ DHAK *Butea monosperma*

flame of the forest • bengal kino • bastard teak

dhak • palash • tesu • kesu • chhichra

pea family and subfamily

Middle-sized tree, deciduous

Bark pale brown, flaky

Leaves compound with 3 large, leathery leaflets

Flowers showy, bright orange; insides of petals smooth, densely downy outside

Fruit pods up to 20 cm long, velvety, with a single seed

9 m

the stamens lie hidden inside the boat-shaped 'keel' petals

the 'standard' petal is the largest

'wing' petal

A crooked, unarmed native Delhi tree capable of reaching 14 m but usually much smaller. The compound leaves with 3 large, leathery leaflets form a patchy, open crown. Clusters of fiery orange blossoms on leafless branches in March are unmistakable. Found in Delhi as a scattered tree on the Ridge and in some large parks.

SEASONS - LEAVES shed in February-March, starting near the top of the tree. New leaf in late April. **FLOWER** buds appear in January but do not open till early to mid March; flowering sputters on into April. **FRUIT** form very quickly after flowering, ripening just before the rains.

WHERE TO SEE IT Throughout the Ridge. Groves or specimens in large gardens like Nehru Park, Buddha Jayanti Park and Mahavir Vanasthali. Teen Murti Bhavan has a large tree near its entrance. Dhak is nowhere planted as a street tree, but there is a solitary relict tree on Nauroji Nagar Marg in Safdarjang Enclave.

FLOWERS in clusters near the top of the tree. The velvety buds appear black but are actually deeply bronzed. The flower is typically pea-like – a large 'standard' petal dominates two narrower 'wings' on either side. Two more petals join together to form a claw-like 'keel'. The petals are fiery orange and smooth on the inside and are covered with fine, silky hairs outside.

LEAVES compound, with 3 large leaflets at the end of a long common stalk. Starting pale green and densely grey-silky on their under-surface, the leaflets become darker and coarser, losing their silk altogether. The middle leaflet, growing from a longer stalk, widens gradually, becoming as broad as it is long. The side leaflets widen asymmetrically from their bases.

the middle leaflet often faces in a different direction in order to optimize the surface area presented to sunlight

a rare but beautiful natural golden form is known as 'var. *aurea*'

FRUIT a flat pod. For a structure designed to house only a single seed, the pods are unusually large. Pale grey-green at first, velvety and strongly marked with nerves, they grow to about 20 cm, gradually turning straw coloured and papery, when they are scattered by summer breezes.

BARK light brown or ashy, fibrous, more or less rough with shallow cracks. When cut or bruised, a ruby-red latex oozes from the trunk and hardens into a gum.

HABITAT A tree of open country, not dense forests. Dhak is a 'pioneer' species, the first to regenerate where gaps appear or a forest has been cleared. It withstands heat, frost, waterlogging, drought and poor soils, including heavy clays and salinity. These qualities enable it to colonize sites where most plants falter and to form nearly pure forests.

RANGE On the sub-continent, its range is bounded by the river Jhelum in the NW. It extends eastwards through Myanmar and most of Indo-China.

USES Dhak is the host tree most used to rear lac-insects, producing a quality shellac known as 'rangini'. The ruby-red gum – called 'Bengal kino' – along with the seed oil and flowers, has medicinal uses. The inner bark is used to make rope. The flowers yield an orange dye used at Holi. Young leaves are eaten by buffaloes and elephants but not by goats. An extensive rural cottage industry is based on the stitching together of dhak leaves as plates. The timber is not durable except under-water and is used for well-curbs and scoops. It is also burnt to make gunpowder-grade charcoal. Dhak is some-times planted to reclaim saline lands where little else will grow.

❧ BARNA *Crataeva adansonii* subsp. *odora*

sacred barna • garlic pear • bengal quince   *barna family*

barna • barun • bila • bilasi • biliana • narnohi

Smallish tree; deciduous

Bark pale brown, not very rough, becoming scabby

Leaves compound with only 3 leaflets; all leaflets smooth, with short, pointy tips

Flowers in dense clusters, with 4 white petals; stamens long, purple; ovary at the end of a very long stalk

Fruit spherical, on a thick stalk, red-brown when ripe, with pale spots

6 m

FLOWERS in dense terminal clusters, just before or along with the new leaves. There are 4 white petals (not all of equal length) that fade gradually to yellow. The stamens have long, electric-purple filaments. The solitary round ovary is held at the end of a long stalk, even longer than the stamens.

Usually a small, crooked tree, though Delhi has a few leggy specimens over 10 m tall. Bare for a very long period in the dry season but arrestingly beautiful in full bloom in late April. The smooth compound leaves with 3 leaflets are a useful diganostic clue. Wild on the Ridge and only occasionally cultivated for ornament in parks and gardens.

small, green ovary, at the end of a long stalk ●

SEASONS - LEAVES straggly or shed by November. New leaves in April, canopy renewed by May. **FLOWERS** with the new leaves, peaking by late April. **FRUIT** appear in May, turn red in September.

WHERE TO SEE IT Lots on the N Ridge. Groves in Vir Bhumi and Buddha Jayanti Park. Inside Qudsia mosque compound, Talkatora Garden, St Stephen's College. Some outsize trees on Delhi Golf Course; a big relict tree on Aurobindo Marg near Ansari Nagar W; one small tree growing outside Lal Bangla Maqbara on Z. Hussain Marg is especially lovely in flower.

side leaflets
have unequal
bases

the common stalk
is about 8 cm long

LEAVES compound
with 3 thin, smooth
leaflets growing on a long
common stalk. The
2 leaflets on either side are
markedly asymmetric at their
bases. The central one is
symmetrical, 8-12 cm long,
narrowed at both ends, with a
short, pointy tip.

BEING LEAFLESS for many
months is a tactic to survive
drought. This tree is on the 9th
fairway at the Delhi Golf Club.

FRUIT about the size of a golf
ball (though not perfectly round),
growing at the end of a thick
stalk. Green at first, turning red
and woody, and eventually a rich
leathery brown. The yellow pulp
inside smells of garlic and
eventually turns black.

BARK pale grey or brown, with a
silvery sheen and studded with
small, white lenticel dots. Not very
rough, becoming crusty with age.

HABITAT Undulating
land in open forest and
scrub jungle, usually in
relatively shady sites
near water sources. It
prefers deep alluvial
soil, but puzzlingly is
also found in dry,
bouldery formations in
a low, stunted avatar. It
is drought-hardy and
tolerates frost well.

RANGE Open forests
from sea level ascending
to about 750 m, from
the river Ravi eastwards
and practically through-
out the Indian subcon-
tinent and Myanmar.
Absent from the high-
rainfall regions of NE
India. Its natural range
extends into S China,
the Malay Peninsula
and Archipelago and
tropical Africa.

USES Ancient Hindu
medicine makes exten-
sive use of most parts of
the barna tree – the
bark for treating
disorders of the gastric
and urinary system and
for its action as an
antipyretic, sedative and
tonic. The fresh leaves
are applied externally to
swellings, bruises and
rheumatic joints. The
fruit are edible when
cooked and the leaves
are lopped for fodder.
The moderately hard
and even-grained wood
is white when first
exposed, turning pale
brown, without any
distinctive grain. It is
used for making drums,
writing tablets and for
turnery, but is not
widely utilized.

❧ BLAKE'S CORAL TREE *Erythrina blakei*

blake's coral tree

no local name

pea family and subfamily

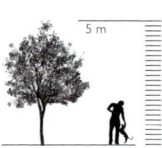

Small tree; deciduous

Bark grey, not rough

Spines few or absent

Leaves compound with 3 oval, long-pointed leaflets; up to 10 cm long

Flowers in elongated terminal clusters, deep scarlet

Fruit not seen in Delhi

A delicate-limbed, ornamental tree of uncertain botanical standing. It is probably a hybrid of garden origin whose parentage was not properly documented and is thereby prevented from gaining scientific recognition. It is widely sold in nurseries and seems to be gaining popularity as a pretty tree suitable for small gardens.

WHERE TO SEE IT IIC has 2 little trees just outside the library. Not yet common in Delhi, but becoming a farmhouse favourite.

❧ DHAUL DHAK *Erythrina suberosa*

corky coral tree

dhaul dhak • pangra • gulnashtar

pea family and subfamily

Middle-sized tree; deciduous

Bark corky, orange-tinged with deep, vertical cracks

Spines conical, pale, scattered

Leaves compound with 3 broad leaflets, the terminal largest; sometimes prickly along the main leaf stalk

Flowers bright scarlet, in dense clusters near ends of branchlets; petals 5, of unequal length; stamens 10

Fruit pods narrow, cylindrical, tapering at both ends; pinched between the seeds

A middle-sized, prickly tree with distinctly orange, corky bark and an irregular crown. It is an arresting sight in flower, with clusters of bright-scarlet flowers presented at the ends of its branchlets. Native to dry, mixed forests throughout India, it also ranges eastwards into SE Asia. Not very common in Delhi.

WHERE TO SEE IT Good specimens in and around Tughlak Crescent. Roshanara Bagh and Sundar Nursery have some big trees. Not otherwise common at all.

INDIAN CORAL TREE *Erythrina variegata*

indian/variegated coral tree • tiger's claw tree

mandara • pangra • tota • gadha-palash

pea family and subfamily

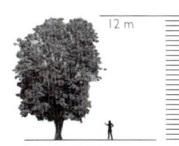

Middle-sized tree; deciduous

Bark thin, smooth, greenish grey, streaked with vertical lines of green or buff

Spines black, conical, on stem and branches

Leaves compound with 3 broad leaflets; main leaf stalk very long; leaflets pointy-tipped, smooth, often variegated

Flowers in dense clusters; bright scarlet or white; petals 5, unequal, with long stamens

Fruit up to 30 cm long, cylindrical, pointy at both ends; black when ripe; indented between the seeds

the white-flowered variety is called 'var. *alba*'

A soft-wooded, spiny, ornamental tree with brilliant scarlet blossoms. There is also a white-flowered variety. The tree often has multiple stems ascending steeply upwards, and compound leaves with 3 diamond-shaped leaflets that are sometimes variegated with white or cream. Primarily a coastal species with a very wide distribution throughout tropical Asia.

FLOWERS 4-5 cm long, in dense, long-stalked clusters. 'Standard' petal nearly 3 cm long, dwarfing the other petals, and longer than those of other coral trees.

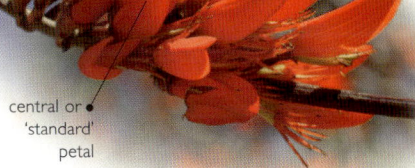

central or 'standard' petal

SEASONS - LEAVES shed in February; trees bare till after the flowers in April. **FLOWERS** in late March or early April; over before the end of April. **FRUIT** ripen between May and July.

bark greenish white or grey, smooth or with shallow fissures

WHERE TO SEE IT Not uncommon – lots in Shakti Sthal. Roshanara Bagh, Najaf Khan's Tomb in Aliganj and the Oberoi Hotel have many trees. A prominent specimen in 32 Aurangzeb Road.

CAN BE CONFUSED WITH

The closely related dhaul dhak. The simplest way to tell them apart is that dhaul dhak flowers are smaller and appear while the tree is still leafy; the Indian coral tree flowers when it is completely leafless.

❀ SEMAL-LIKE LEAVES

Palmately compound

coppery
when young

edges
often
scalloped

leaflets have
no stalks

baobab
22 cm p207

edges
wavy

leaf stalk
channelled

araranut tree
24 cm p208

leaflets
broad,
edges
wavy

shaving brush tree
42 cm p208

leaves of
these 2 trees
very hard to
distinguish

forward
pointing,
sharp
teeth

white floss-silk tree
22 cm p209

floss-silk tree
26 cm p210

leaflets
leathery, downy
when young

leaf stalk
channelled

semal
40 cm p212

5-9 leaflets,
commonly 7

leaflets
smooth, dull

leaflet
stalks
very long

grey-green
colour

kapok
35 cm p214

caribbean trumpet tree
26 cm p215

leaflets
broad,
downy

sometimes
toothed
near apex

pink trumpet tree
28 cm p216

leaflets
leathery,
without
stalks

wild almond
36 cm p217

Leaves that look palmately
compound but are not

this is actually
a rosette of
simple leaves

saptaparni
40 cm p142

this is
really a
lobed leaf

desert kurrajong
10 cm p168

BAOBAB *Adansonia digitata*

baobab • african calabash • monkey-bread tree • judas' bag • cream of tartar tree *semal family*

gorakh amli/imli • gorakh chinch • khorasani imli

Large tree; deciduous

Bark grey or silvery, tinged with purple; dimpled

Leaves palmately compound on a long leaf stalk; leaflets 5-7, smooth, up to 14 cm long, without any stalks of their own

Flowers large, hanging downwards; 5 white petals, flower-cup bent backwards; anthers numerous, forming a ball

Fruit large, oval to round, gourd-like, furry

Uniquely engineered with the fattest trunks of any tree, tapering into absurdly thin branchlets on top. Baobabs were first brought from sub-Saharan Africa to the west coast of India by Arab traders more than a millennium ago. They are superbly adapted to withstand drought by storing water in the spongy, fibrous tissue of their outsize trunks.

FLOWERS white, upside down, opening as the sun sets. They have a musky odour that attracts fruit bats which arrive soon after dark to drink the nectar and in the process pollinate the flowers. The flower wilts within 24 hours.

stamens with golden anthers

SEASONS - **LEAVES** start drying in December; bare for many months from mid January. New leaves in April. **FLOWERS** begin in June and peak in the rains; August is prime time. **FRUIT** not seen in Delhi; no cross-pollination happens here.

WHERE TO SEE IT Delhi's largest baobab, in Buddha Jayanti Park, was decapitated in a windstorm in 2004, but should recover and resprout. One young specimen in the Indian Institute of Immunology, near JNU. Lodi Garden lost a 9-year-old tree to a fire in 2000.

leaflets without stalks

GREYBEARD

Known to reach a great age, the baobab has been called 'the oldest organic monument of our planet'. This is not quite true – the bristlecone pine is longer-lived – but at something like 3000 years, the baobab is definitely one of the venerable greybeards of the natural world.

❋ ARARANUT TREE *Joannesia princeps*

araranut tree • boleiro • anda-assu

amla/castor family

no local name

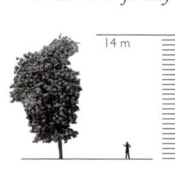

14 m

Medium-sized tree; deciduous

Bark grey-brown, not rough

Leaves palmately compound with 5-7 broad, pointy-tipped leaflets; they turn red before dropping

Flowers small, inconspicuous, yellowish

Fruit a large woody nut, with 4 prominent ridges [see pic below right]

WHERE TO SEE IT
Only one tree in the main timber section of Sundar Nursery.

A fairly large tree from coastal Brazil with a dense crown of palmately compound leaves. The leaflets emerge waxy pink, turn deep green and then red again before falling. Look for two tiny, raised knobs, like spiders' eyes, at the top of the common leaf stalk [see pic]. Flowers but no fruit seen in Delhi.

❋ SHAVING BRUSH TREE *Pseudobombax ellipticum*

shaving brush tree • cotton tree • pink bombax

semal family

no local name

12 m

Middle-sized tree; deciduous

Bark more or less smooth, grey, with shallow, vertical fissures

Leaves palmately compound with 3-6 shortly stalked leaflets with wavy margins; leaflets coppery when young, undersides softly hairy

Flowers with 5 long, silky petals, deep pink or purple outside, paler inside; long stamens in a thick brush, shiny purple with golden anthers

Fruit a woody capsule up to 15 cm long, yellowish brown; seeds embedded in cottony fibres

An ornamental tree from Mexico and Guatemala that produces long-stamened, pink flowers in spring, when still leafless. The buds are said to open at night with an audible 'pop'. The leaves are clustered at the ends of twigs. This species is consistently misidentified in India as *Pachira rosea*.

WHERE TO SEE IT The IIC, Nehru Park, Sundar Nursery, Delhi University office, and reported from inside Rashtrapati Bhavan gardens.

WHITE FLOSS-SILK TREE *Ceiba insignis*

white floss-silk tree • chorry • white dragon
no local name

semal family

Middle-sized tree, deciduous

Trunk studded with large, conical prickles

Bark greenish when young, becoming grey and corky

Leaves palmately compound with 5-7 smooth, toothed leaflets with long, pointy tips

Flowers with 5 long, white petals with a golden blush at base; ivory corona at centre of flower, smooth, hairless; stamens and stigma on a long column

Fruit an oblong capsule up to 15 cm long

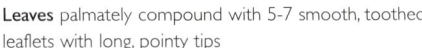

FLOWERS large, lily-like with petals up to 12 cm long. The stamens are fused into a column; the style extends even further, ending in a round, rose-coloured stigma.

A close relative of the pink-flowered floss-silk tree, distinguished by its striking ivory flowers with gold in the throat. It is hard to tell the two species apart when they are not in flower. Native to dry forests in Peru and Argentina, it tends to develop a bottle-shaped trunk studded with conical prickles.

stigma •

big anthers •
of 5 fused
stamens

SEASONS - LEAVES start to fall in December, trees bare by mid January. New leaves in April, canopy renewed by May. **FLOWERS** late in the rains, peaking by early October. Flowers persist on leafless trees till February or so. **FRUIT** not seen in Delhi.

conical •
prickles on
trunk

>> *Ceiba* or *Chorisia*?
– see p332

CAN BE CONFUSED WITH

The pink-flowered floss-silk tree. In flower, the differences are plain to see, but outside the flowering season, you would need special powers to divine the differences. See page 211 for the difference in their flowers.

WHERE TO SEE IT A few trees inside Asian Games Village, another inside # 25 SP Marg. It is easy to mistake pale-flowered variants of the pink floss-silk tree for this one.

✳ FLOSS-SILK TREE *Ceiba speciosa* Syn: *Chorisia speciosa*

(pink) floss-silk tree • mexican silk cotton

no local name. malis call it *'kurayjia'*

semal family

Middle-sized tree, deciduous

Bark bright green in young trees, turning grey

Trunk studded with conical prickles when young

Leaves palmately compound on a long leaf stalk; leaflets 5-7, toothed, on short stalks of their own

Flowers have 5 long petals with rippled edges; pink with ivory throat, flecked with brown

Fruit ovoid, up to 20 cm long, packed with white floss

12 m

Showy pink, orchid-like blossoms make this Delhi's most conspicuous flowering tree immediately after the rains. Like the kapok, it has palmately compound leaves and a bright-green, prickly trunk when it is young. Native to dry forests in S America, the floss-silk tree was introduced to Delhi and planted en masse in the 1950s.

FLOWERS large, 5-petalled, appearing when the tree is leafless. Seen from below, the long, ripple-edged petals are downy and uniformly pink. From above, the pink shades into an ivory throat flecked with brown dashes. The shade of pink can vary. The stamens and style rise imperiously out of the centre of the flower in a long, pink column.

at the base of the staminal column, notice the 'corona' covered with fuzzy white hairs ●

long staminal ● column

SEASONS - LEAVES renewed late in February. It sheds again in the rains, has a brief, stuttering second flush in October, then is bare again till the following spring. **FLOWERS** in September, peaking in late October. Straggling blooms may persist till January. **FRUITING** is inconsistent in Delhi. I have seen 'cotton' only in April-May.

WHERE TO SEE IT It was 'discovered' by Delhi's civic agencies in the 1950s and quickly became a favourite tree for round-abouts. Delhi has no pure avenues of floss-silk trees but it has been planted in every park and inviting patch of ground – squandering to some degree its potential to surprise and delight you.

HABITAT The floss-silk tree prefers a tropical climate with a distinct, long dry season, followed by heavy rain. It thrives on most kinds of soil, provided it is well-drained. Fairly drought-tolerant.

RANGE Native to relatively dry regions in S Brazil, Argentina and Paraguay. Widely cultivated in tropical and subtropical climates around the world.

LEAVES palmately compound, from a long common leaf stalk. Leaflets 5-7, on short stalks of their own. They are usually about 13 cm long, smooth and narrowed at both ends, with pointy tips. The edges have small, forward-pointing teeth.

• edges of leaflets are toothed

USES Mainly as an ornamental tree, on account of its lavish flowering when it is completely leafless. The floss in the fruit capsule is inferior to kapok and is not much valued. The wood is soft and fibrous and has little use, except perhaps for cordage.

SPINES broad-based, conical, grey, but only on young stems. They are shed as the tree grows older.

BARK a startling grass-green at first. As it stretches over the widening trunk, the green patches become furrows, separated by ridges of newer grey bark.

FRUIT a large capsule, green at first, ripening grey-brown. The pod splits open to reveal silky fibres like the semal's. When fully open, the 'cotton' blows away in a strong wind, helping to disperse the seeds.

CAN BE CONFUSED WITH

The **white floss-silk tree**, to which it is closely related. The differences are:

• **white floss-silk tree** – has petals with a white base and yellow throat; corona is ivory-white and without hairs

• **floss-silk tree** – has petals with a pink base and ivory throat; corona is fuzzy with white hairs

Outside flowering time, it can perhaps be mistaken for any one of its cousins in the semal family with palmately compound leaves – the baobab, semal, and kapok. In this crowd, the 2 floss-silk trees are the only ones with toothed leaflets. (*Ceiba* or *Chorisia*? see page 332)

• flower of white floss-silk tree

❧ SEMAL *Bombax ceiba*

(red) silk cotton • bombax • indian kapok   *semal family*

semal • shembal • semur

Large tree; deciduous

Bark ashy, not rough; lower trunk with conical prickles

Leaves palmately compound with 5-7 pointy leaflets

Flowers large, deep red, coral or yellow with 5 waxy petals; stamens many, in separate bundles

Fruit a capsule up to 18 cm long; white silk cotton inside

20 m

petals in bud are softly downy •

65-80 stamens in all – one bundle in front of each of the 5 petals; another bundle in the centre •

A towering deciduous tree capable of reaching 60 m, but seldom more than 20 m in Delhi. Large trees are supported at base by thin, spreading flanges. Its branches grow in tiers radiating from the trunk like the ribs of an umbrella. Cultivated on Delhi avenues mainly for its voluptuous, waxy blooms in March.

5-forked • stigma

SEASONS - **LEAVES** thin out in January; most trees are bare by mid February. New leaves in late March, early April. **FLOWER** buds appear long before the first flowers wink on in February; prime time in Delhi is early to mid March. **FRUIT** ripen and split open in May, releasing microfibres into the air (asthmatics beware).

WHERE TO SEE IT Semal did not make the cut for Imperial Delhi but has more than made up since 1947. Trees in flower arrest attention all over the city. Neeti Marg is nearly pure semal. Two huge trees dominate the front lawns of Teen Murti Bhavan. Most parks (Hauz Khas District Park in particular) have specimens.

FLOWERS large, showy, usually scarlet but can be coral, turmeric, pale yellow or even white, with 5 fleshy petals bent backwards. The long stamens are grouped in 6 separate bundles and the style in the centre terminates in a dainty 5-forked stigma. Pollinated mostly by bats.

LEAVES palmately compound with 5 (sometimes 6 or 7) leaflets on short stalks of their own, radiating from the end of a long common leaf stalk. The smooth leaflets feel like rexine.

leaflets are faintly downy at first but not for long

leaflets up to 25 cm long, tapering at both ends, with pointy tips

FRUIT a woody capsule up to 18 cm long, covered outside with velvety down. The capsule splits open along 5 sutures, releasing masses of silky fibres along with the seeds, which drift out on the wind.

BARK ashy or old silver, relatively smooth when young. The lower trunk is covered with broad-based, conical prickles. With age, the bark develops vertical fissures and the prickles become blunt and finally drop off.

prickles on a young stem

CAN BE CONFUSED WITH

Other Delhi trees with palmate leaves, the baobab, wild almond and kapok in particular. The waxy red flowers in February-March are distinctive.

HABITAT A scattered tree of dry deciduous and moist forests throughout India and the dominant tree of grassy savannahs in the terai. Often found near streams and rivulets but it avoids heavy clay soils and does not withstand waterlogging. Reasonably drought-hardy.

RANGE Widespread in India (avoiding the most arid areas), in the sub-Himalayan tract, in dry teak and mixed deciduous forests in peninsular India and in moist forests on the W coast. Beyond India it extends from Myanmar to S China and throughout tropical SE Asia to N Australia.

USES Semal bark and roots are a tonic and stimulant. A gummy exudation from the stem is used in traditional medicine to prepare an aphrodisiac and to treat stomach disorders. The leaves and twigs are lopped for fodder, and squirrels, deer and other wild animals feast on the fallen flowers. The silk cotton is collected to stuff pillows and quilts. (Collecting rights to individual trees are auctioned in Delhi.) The light wood is white when first exposed, gradually turning dark, but is weak and used only for planking, tea-boxes, fishing-floats and for making shoe heels. Much planted for ornament in Indian cities.

❋ KAPOK *Ceiba pentandra*

kapok • true/singapore kapok • white silk cotton
hattian • katan • safed semal

semal family

25 m

Very tall tree; deciduous

Bark smooth, green when young, turning greyish; conical prickles fall off as the tree ages

Leaves palmately compound, usually with 5-7 leaflets on short stalks; pointy at both ends; smooth but not glossy

Flowers about 3 cm long, with 5 creamy white or pale-pink petals, in clusters; opening at night

Fruit capsules green at first, up to 15 cm long, shaped like slim cucumbers; seeds embedded in white floss when capsule ripens

FRUIT ripen and split open into 5 sections, releasing the white floss (along with the seeds). The floss is produced from the inside wall of the capsule.

The tallest tree on the African and South American continents at 60 m, but much shorter in Delhi. Like the semal, it has immensely cantilevered, whorled branches, three or more starting from the same height on the trunk. Semal-like too are the conical prickles and flanges at the base of its trunk.

SEASONS - LEAVES shed in January; trees bare till early March when new leaves appear with the flowers. **FLOWERS** in March, lasting through the first half of April. **FRUIT** green in early May; splitting to release its seeds in June.

BARK can show traces of green and bronze when it is young, but eventually it turns a dull grey.

WHERE TO SEE IT On Ring Road near the entrance to Vir Bhumi and near Salimgarh Railway overbridge; in front of Krishi Bhavan and in the parking lot of Siri Fort Auditorium. Tall specimens in Sundar Nursery, Humayun's Tomb garden and Vijay Ghat.

THE STUFF OF LIFE JACKETS

Kapok fibre has too short a staple to be spun into thread, but being elastic and buoyant it makes excellent stuffing for pillows, mattresses and life jackets. It was also quite widely used for thermal and acoustic insulation but has mostly been replaced now by synthetic fibres.

❋ CARIBBEAN TRUMPET TREE *Tabebuia aurea*

caribbean/paraguayan/silver trumpet tree • yellow poui/tabebuia • tree of gold   *jacaranda family*
no local name

Smallish tree; deciduous

Bark pale grey, with thick, vertical ridges of cork

Leaves palmately compound, with 5-7 narrow leaflets on long stalks of their own; smooth, sometimes covered with minute silvery scales

Flowers showy, bright-yellow trumpets growing in dense clusters at the ends of branches

Fruit a pale-brown capsule, narrowed at both ends, about 10 cm long, splitting open to release winged seeds

FLOWERS in dense clusters. The insides of the trumpets are pencilled with rust-red lines. One of our showiest flowering trees because it is completely leafless when it flowers.

A smallish, crooked tree that remains self-effacing most of the year but bursts into traffic-stopping bright-yellow blossoms in March. A characteristic tree of the dry forests of the Brazilian Cerrado. Also found in Paraguay, Bolivia and Argentina, and widely cultivated pantropically. It seems to have been introduced to Delhi in the 1970s.

SEASONS - LEAVES start to thin out in February; trees are quite bare by mid March. New leaf early in April. **FLOWERS** in the second week of March, reaching a spectacular crescendo in early April. Brief bursts of flowering also seen between July and December. **FRUIT** ripen in May.

WHERE TO SEE IT Fairly common in large parks in the city. Safdarjang's Tomb has some of the oldest trees. Nehru Memorial Museum has a prominent specimen. There are lots in the samadhi gardens along the Yamuna and in the premium car park at the IG International airport.

BARK has thick, corky tissue, a sign that it is adapted to ground fires in its habitat.

LEAFLETS have very long stalks, not a very common character in palmate leaves.

✱ PINK TRUMPET TREE *Tabebuia impetiginosa*

pink trumpet tree • palmer trumpet tree • pau d'arco

no local name

jacaranda family

Small tree; deciduous

Bark grey or darkly silver, not very rough but scaly

7 m

Leaves palmately compound, usually with 5 broad leaflets, faintly to densely hairy especially underneath; sometimes toothed near apex

Flowers lavender-pink or pale-purple trumpets in dense clusters at the ends of branches

Fruit a pale-brown capsule, narrowed at both ends; not often seen in Delhi

FLOWERS in dense clusters, usually in 3s, but not all opening together. Varying from pale pink to purple, with a yellow throat that turns deep pink as it ages.

A smallish tree with a light canopy and beautiful pink trumpet-shaped blossoms appearing when the branches are bare. This is only one of a showy genus – the *Tabebuias* – from tropical America in which the pink-flowered species, in particular, are very difficult to tell apart. In Delhi this species is often erroneously called *Tabebuia rosea*.

SEASONS - LEAVES start to thin out in January; new leaves appear in April just after the flowers. **FLOWERS** from mid February to late March, some-times with short bursts of 'mistaken' flowering during warm weather in mid-winter. **FRUIT** in May, but rare.

WHERE TO SEE IT A row in front of the Talkatora swimming pool, particularly lovely in flower against the grey stone backdrop. Most large parks have specimens; Nehru Park and Pragati Maidan probably have the best.

LEAVES dark or olive green, minutely downy especially underneath. The long leaf stalk is usually channelled.

>> Not *Tabebuia rosea*? – see p340

❋ WILD ALMOND *Sterculia foetida*

wild/indian almond • java olive • great sterculia • skunk tree • bastard poon tree   *cocoa family*
jangli badam

Large tree; deciduous

Bark pale grey-brown, flaky

Leaves palmately compound, on long stalks, clustered at the ends of branchlets; leaflets 5-9, up to 20 cm long, tapering at both ends, shortly stalked

Flowers without petals, smelling of dung; flower-cup fleshy, purply brown, bell-shaped; male and female flowers separate but on the same tree

Fruit large, woody, boat-shaped; green at first, turning bright scarlet, eventually dark brown; seeds large, edible

16 m

FRUIT grow in clusters, radiating from a common centre. Each woody capsule grows to about 12 cm long. The seeds inside are roasted and eaten and are likened to almonds.

A tall tree with a spreading canopy whose general habit and leaf form are easily mistaken for a semal's. It is native to coastal monsoon forests in W and S India, extending eastwards to N Australia. The common name is misleading because this is not the source of the common edible almond.

SEASONS - LEAVES shed in early February; new leaves in late March or early April. **FLOWERS** mid to late March just before the new leaves. **FRUIT** begin to form in May; they ripen and split open about February or March of the following year.

FLOWERS have no petals. The flower-cup is deeply divided into 5 velvety lobes, beautifully mottled on their insides.

WHERE TO SEE IT 8 lovely trees used to stand inside the traffic island at Dhaula Kuan – all but one were felled for the flyover. Sundar Nursery has a short avenue; Shanti Vana and Vijay Ghat have a few; # 4 Aurangzeb Road has a particularly large specimen. There are some trees next to Moolchand flyover, inviting comparison with their semal neighbours.

CAN BE CONFUSED WITH

The semal and kapok, which also have palmately compound leaves and branches in tiers. Unlike the other two, the wild almond has no prickles on its trunk. Its leaflets and common leaf stalks are also longer than the others'.

IMLI-LIKE LEAVES *Feather-compound*

Without terminals, smooth

imli
12 cm p220

apices blunt or notched

many pairs of leaflets

usually has terminal

carrotwood
22 cm p247

reettha
40 cm p222

leaflets roughly same size

leaflets without stalks

few pairs of leaflets

leaf stalk winged

fern leaf tree
30 cm p236

kosam
35 cm p224

sita-ashok
28 cm p227

tun
40 cm p223

kakkar
20 cm p222

largest leaflets below

leaflets curved; unequal at base

spanish mahogany
18 cm p226

large-leaved mahogany
30 cm p226

apices long, pointy

apices long, pointy

archibald's cassia
33 cm p237

apices abruptly pointy

african mahogany
35 cm p236

Without terminals, hairy

blunt or pointy

light silver-hairy when young

leaflets large

java cassia
30 cm p234

amaltas
38 cm p228

apices blunt

apices notched

apices rounded with tiny point

kassod
28 cm p230

red cassia
28 cm p235

burmese pink cassia
30 cm p237

terminals reddish

glands at lower junctions

chikrassy
40 cm p233

glaucous cassia
20 cm p232

bronzy when young

brazilian cassia
25 cm p232

Leaves that look feather-compound but are not

actually simple leaves

montezuma cypress
8 cm p166

actually simple leaves

amla
15 cm p184

With terminals, toothed

up to one m long

leaflets curved, teeth coarse

neem
35 cm p242

rhodesian wistaria
10 cm p244

leaflets curved, teeth tiny

stalk very narrowly winged

yellow bells
19 cm p245

leaves usually simple

chestnutleaf trumpet-bush
22 cm p199

maharukh
60 cm p240

apices blunt, teeth tiny

kaith
10 cm p246

may have large stipules at base

siala
30 cm p244

teeth tiny, rounded

kadi patta
22 cm p246

edges toothed or not

indian red pear
25 cm p245

With terminals, not toothed

apices blunt, no teeth

natal laburnum
7 cm p247

apices notched; leaflets leathery

carrotwood
22 cm p247

apices notched

takoli
22 cm p255

unequal at base

amda
45 cm p254

fern-like

silky oak
25 cm p250

apices blunt

moulmein rosewood
20 cm p252

unequal bases

sausage tree
30 cm p248

largest leaflet at apex

kamrakh
16 cm p255

largest leaflet at apex

quickstick
20 cm p261

usually without terminal

tun
40 cm p223

apices pointy, many leaflets

african tulip tree
44 cm p254

apices pointy

karanj
25 cm p256

apices long, pointy

kamini
16 cm p260

shiny; apices blunt

usually without terminal

kakkar
20 cm p222

shiny, long leaflets

black bean
48 cm p261

shisham
12 cm p258

leafy stipules at base

katsagon
45 cm p262

🌿 IMLI *Tamarindus indica*

tamarind

imli • amli

pea family – cassia subfamily

Large tree; deciduous

Bark dark grey, rough, with shallow fissures

Leaves feather-compound with up to 20 pairs of small leaflets, rounded at both ends

Flowers small, with 3 unequal-sized yellow petals veined with red; flower-cup has 4 creamy segments

Fruit a beanlike pod bulging over the seeds, up to 20 cm long; green at first, ripening cinnamon-brown

A large, handsome, long-lived tree with a squat trunk, spreading limbs and a high, shady crown of feathery foliage. Introduced into India from tropical E Africa so long ago that it is virtually indigenous. The imli is frost-prone and Delhi lies close to the limits of its natural range on the subcontinent.

SEASONS - LEAVES shed early in February; new leaves early to mid March, light green at first, darkening later. FLOWERS in June or early July, lasting into August or later. FRUIT ripen in winter but do not set luxuriously in Delhi.

WHERE TO SEE IT Widely used in the sahiblog's bungalows and as an avenue tree in Lutyens' Delhi – on Akbar Road, Tilak Marg and (mixed) on Mother Teresa Marg. The largest specimens are probably those in Humayun's Tomb gardens, but it is not very common in public gardens, possibly because it is slow-growing.

FLOWERS about 15 mm wide, pale yellow veined with red, arranged in short, loose clusters. Only the upper 3 petals are visible, the central one narrow and hooded, the lateral ones thrown back like wings ready for flight. 2 more petals are reduced to bristles. The flower-cup is made up of 4 pointy segments, deep pink on the outside (so the buds are pink) and creamy yellow inside.

yellow petal with delicate red veins

pink buds

3 perfect stamens and style

FRUIT POD up to 20 cm long, like a large, flattened peanut, bulging over its seeds and pinched in between. Often slightly curved. Green at first, the pods develop a dun-coloured felting that eventually becomes a thin, brittle shell. Inside, the seeds are embedded in a tart pulp that dries into a sticky brown paste, enclosed by coarse fibres as the pods mature.

the young pod is covered with a downy felt

LEAVES 7-15 cm long, feather-compound, starting out pale green before darkening. Each leaf has 10-20 pairs of opposite leaflets growing on barely visible stalks. The leaflets are up to 25 mm long, more or less rounded at each end. They tend to 'close' at night.

the leaflets have hardly any stalks

BARK dark grey, grey-brown or sometimes ashy, lightly fissured and flaking off in small patches.

HABITAT A scattered tree in dry deciduous forests, sometimes growing to a great size and age. Deep-rooted, windfirm and reasonably drought-resistant, but sensitive to frost. Does not do well N or W of Delhi.

RANGE Introduced into India from tropical Africa, but so long ago that the Arab traders who came here in the 2nd century named it 'tamar-i-hind' (Indian date). Its exact origins within Africa are not known. It is sometimes found self-sown in forests in C and S India but is doubtfully truly wild anywhere in India. A common tree in warm, frost-free areas throughout the subcontinent.

USES Its tart fruit is used in curries, chut-neys, jams and sauces. High in vitamin C, tartaric, malic and citric acids, the fruit pulp is used to treat fevers, digestive disorders and certain kinds of poison-ing. Various parts are used in tanning and dyeing and the seeds yield an oil-varnish and illuminant. The pale timber is extremely hard and heavy but is not liked by carpenters because it quickly blunts their tools. There is a superstition that it is harmful to sleep under an imli tree. Surprisingly, the imli is not venerated in prop-ortion to its many uses.

REETTHA *Sapindus mukorossi*

soapnut tree • chinese soapberry

reettha/litchi family

reettha • dodan • dodani • thali

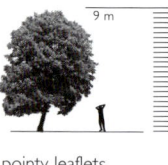

9 m

Smallish tree; deciduous

Bark grey, smooth at first, becoming dark and scaly

Leaves feather-compound with up to 10 pairs of thin, smooth, pointy leaflets

Flowers tiny, greenish white, numerous, in large, pyramidal clusters; mostly bisexual, male flowers few

Fruit round, fleshy, cherry-sized, yellow-brown

A pretty, dense-canopied tree originally from China, naturalized and commonly cultivated in the lower Himalaya for the natural soapy substance in its fruit. It reaches 20 m in ideal conditions, but Delhi's young trees will struggle to attain 10 m. The leaves turn deep yellow before being shed in December.

WHERE TO SEE IT Many young trees planted in Hauz Rani City Forest; 3 trees behind the bonnet macaques in the zoo; a lone specimen in Sundar Nursery.

KAKKAR *Pistacia chinensis* subsp. *integerrima*

pistachio wood • east indian mastiche

mango/cashew family

kakkar • kakroi • kakra • kakrasingi

16 m

Large tree; deciduous

Bark dark grey, very rough

Leaves feather-compound with 3-6 pairs of smooth leaflets with or without a terminal; base of leaflets asymmetrical, apex long, pointy

Flowers male and female on separate trees; male flowers in short, red, compact clusters; female flowers longer, looser, with style divided in 3

Fruit small, in loose clusters, 6 mm diameter, pink at first, wrinkled and grey-green when ripe

A magnificent tree with a huge, shady crown, found in Delhi only at Talkatora Garden. Particularly lovely in mid March when the new leaves and flower clusters appear in tints of pink and cerise. Native to hot, dry sub-Himalayan slopes from Afghanistan to Kumaon, but it does well enough in Delhi.

WHERE TO SEE IT Talkatora Garden has 3 large trees at its far end, on either side of the water-channel (one male, 2 female trees).

TUN *Toona ciliata*

red cedar • (indian) toon • indian mahogany

neem/mahogany family

tun • tuni • mahaneem

Middle-sized tree; deciduous

Bark grey to ruddy brown, flaking off in rectangular, woody scales

Leaves up to 50 cm long, feather-compound, with 5-10 pairs of smooth, pointy leaflets with or without a terminal leaflet; margins smooth or wavy

Flowers white, scented, in large, drooping clusters at the ends of branchlets; male and female flowers are separate on the same tree

Fruit like a slim olive, green at first, drying and splitting open to release winged seeds

A large, handsome tree with a dense, shady crown found in moist valleys in the sub-Himalayan tract and ranging widely across India and SE Asia into Australia. It does not reach full stature in Delhi but is particularly attractive in new leaf, which emerges pink at first, then becomes bronze-tipped before turning deep green.

FLOWERS appear in pendulous, branching clusters soon after the new leaves, and are honey-scented.

5 petals, with long hairs on their edges ●

SEASONS - **LEAVES** start to fall in December; completely bare by mid January. New leaves in early February, loveliest in March. **FLOWERS** by mid March, lasting till early April. **FRUIT** in May-June.

leaflets ● unequal at base

>> Will the Real Tun Please Stand Up! – see p341

WHERE TO SEE IT Malcha Marg was clearly intended to be a tun avenue but only a few relict trees survive. Qudsia Bagh has some old trees and there are good specimens on Red Cross Marg, in the Nehru Memorial office and along the Sundar Nursery boundary wall, facing Humayun's Tomb.

CAN BE CONFUSED WITH

Kakkar, perhaps, because of the general similarity of their leaf-forms. Tun leaves are however much longer, with many more pairs of leaflets.

KOSAM *Schleichera oleosa*

lac tree • gum lac tree • ceylon oak • macassar oil tree

chikoo family

kosam • kussumb • kusum • kasma

Large tree; deciduous

Bark grey or pale brown, more or less smooth

Leaves feather-compound with 2-4 (normally 3) pairs of opposite, stalkless leaflets, becoming larger towards the apex

Flowers tiny, yellowish, in dense clusters; no petals

Fruit grape- or olive-shaped with a pointy beak, up to 3 cm long; smooth or slightly prickly

LEAVES feather-compound, on a common stalk up to 13 cm long. Each leaf has 2-4 pairs of opposite leaflets – usually 3 pairs – that are attached directly to the leaf stalk without little stalks of their own. The terminal pair of leaflets is the largest.

A lovely tree with a broad, shady crown, found scattered in mixed deciduous forests throughout the subcontinent. Its most distinctive character is its new leaves which emerge bright scarlet (in March in Delhi). The inconspicuous flowers and fruit are easily overlooked. It is becoming popular as an avenue tree in Delhi, but only recently.

SEASONS - **LEAVES** start to yellow and fall by late February. New bright-red leaves in mid March, but individual trees can be noticeably out of synch. The red phase ends by mid April and is triggered afresh by the rains. **FLOWERS** appear with the young leaves or just before. **FRUIT** ripen between late June and August.

WHERE TO SEE IT Shanti Vana has an extensive grove. Outer Ring Road near the IIT is planted with kosam trees. Satya Marg and one end of Vinay Marg in Chanakyapuri have a few. Most large parks like Lodi and Talkatora Gardens have specimens.

the leaflets lack little stalks of their own

the terminal pair of leaflets may be 2 or 3 times longer than the lowest pair

YOUNG LEAVES
emerge a startling
shade of red and
are faintly downy at
first, turning light
green before
darkening. Old
leaves turn bright
yellow before
dropping.

FLOWERS tiny, yellowish, in short,
dense clusters. The flowers are
mostly bisexual but on some trees
may be only male. They have 6-8
stamens which protrude far
beyond the flower-cup in male
flowers, but scarcely so in bisexual
ones. There are no petals.

each fruit has one
or 2 seeds ●

FRUIT about the size of a small plum but
with a pointy beak, smooth or sometimes
with small, blunt prickles. The seeds are
encased in an edible, pleasantly acid pulp.

BARK grey or pale
brown, not very rough,
pocked by small
hollows where old bark
has flaked off. The inner
bark is reddish.

HABITAT Monsoon
forests. It prefers light,
well-drained soils and
is well adapted to
gravelly, bouldery or
sandy loam. It is a
drought-hardy tree and
tolerates shade and
moderate frost, but
seldom ascends above
1000 m altitude.

RANGE From the
Himalayan foothills to
Sri Lanka. Particularly
common in the dry
forests of C and S India
and the Shivaliks.
Beyond the Indian
subcontinent it extends
eastwards through
Myanmar, Malaysia
and Indo-China to
Indonesia and Timor.

USES One of the
primary host trees of
the lac insect and said
to yield the finest
quality of shellac
('kosumi laakh'). Oil
expressed from the
seeds is used for
treating rheumatism,
headaches and skin
diseases; also for
cooking, soaps and
illumination. In earlier
times, it was used to
make a hairdressing
called 'macassar oil'
(hence 'anti-macassars'
on Victorian sofas).
The leaves are lopped
for fodder. The reddish-
brown timber is
difficult to season but
is one of the hardest
and heaviest of Indian
woods. It is used to
make mineshaft props,
oil and sugar mills, tool
handles, bullock-carts
and ploughs. It also
makes good charcoal.

🌿 SPANISH MAHOGANY *Swietenia mahagoni*

spanish/west indian mahogany • jamaican/cuban/small-leaved mahogany • madeira redwood *neem/mahogany family*
no local name

Large tree; deciduous

Bark grey-brown, flaky, rough

Leaves feather-compound with 2-5 pairs of leaflets, the smallest pair at base; leaflets narrow, smooth, glossy, markedly asymmetrical at base

Flowers inconspicuous, unisexual, greenish yellow, in branched clusters, scented; petals (usually) 5, spreading; stamens united in a tube

Fruit a woody capsule up to 10 cm long, seeds winged

A handsome tree which produces the most famous cabinet-grade timber in the world. Native to the Caribbean islands and with a small foothold in the Florida Keys, it was first brought to Calcutta in 1795 and to northern India in 1818. It does fairly well in Delhi's climate but is not at all common.

WHERE TO SEE IT A large tree inside RM Lohia Hospital. Delhi Golf Club has some at the edge of the fairway. Delhi Univ. nursery and Talkatora Garden have small trees.

🌿 LARGE-LEAVED MAHOGANY *Swietenia macrophylla*

large-/big-/broad-leaved mahogany • honduras/bastard mahogany *neem/mahogany family*
no local name

Medium-sized tree; deciduous

Bark dark brown, shallowly grooved

Leaves feather-compound, with 3-8 pairs of dark-green, glossy leaflets with pointy tips and asymmetrical bases

Flowers greenish white, only about 8 mm wide, arranged in branched clusters; 5 petals, spreading, with stamens bundled together in a column

Fruit a woody capsule shaped like an inverted club, up to 20 cm long [see pic below]

A large tree, much taller than the related Spanish mahogany, with a long, clean bole. Native to tropical America from Mexico to Brazil, it was first brought to India from British Honduras in 1872 and planted in high-rainfall areas of S India. It remains stunted and struggles in Delhi's dry climate.

WHERE TO SEE IT I have seen only 2 specimens in Delhi – one in the nursery at Delhi University, the other near the white tiger enclosure in the zoo.

SITA-ASHOK *Saraca asoca*

sorrowless tree • ashoka tree
sita-ashok • ashok

pea family – cassia subfamily

Small tree; nearly evergreen

Bark brown, rough, with horizontal, raised lenticels

Leaves feather-compound, with 3-6 pairs of narrow, pointy leaflets; glossy above, dull beneath; new leaves hang in limp tassels, pinkish at first

Flowers orange-red, faintly fragrant, in clusters often borne directly from the main branches; flower-cup orange, bracts leafy and coloured; stamens scarlet, very long, conspicuous; true petals absent

Fruit a slightly curved pod up to 25 cm long, tapering at both ends; reddish when young, black when mature

FLOWERS do not have true petals. The colour is provided by red leafy bracts and orange flower-cups. The long stamens too are brightly coloured.

Rated by some as India's most beautiful tree for its exquisite pale-apricot flowers which turn bright red. In its native moist forests in E India and SE Asia, it is an evergreen tree with a dense, spreading crown. It struggles in Delhi's climate, but is still worth travelling miles to see in full flower.

SEASONS - LEAVES never completely shed, but thin in March. New leaves appear towards late March. **FLOWERS** in the last week of March, peaking early in April. **FRUIT** not seen in Delhi; elsewhere, August-September.

WHERE TO SEE IT Roshanara Bagh has a row of 12 trees; Buddha Jayanti Park and Sundar Nursery have 2 trees each. Not common in Delhi, though there are a few hidden away inside private houses, such as D409 Defence Colony and 4 Rajaji Marg.

NEW LEAVES OF THE SITA-ASHOK

If you see a sita-ashok in new leaf, you will notice that the youngest leaves hang down in limp tassels and are a peculiar colour, pinkish at first, slowly turning a translucent tan and then pale purple. See page 326 if you want to know more about this trait.

🌿 AMALTAS *Cassia fistula*

indian laburnum • golden shower • purging fistula • pudding-pipe tree
pea family – cassia subfamily

amaltas • girmala • rajbrikh • alash • kiar • kirwara • ali

Middle-sized tree; deciduous

Bark yellowish, more or less smooth; crusty when old

Leaves feather-compound, up to 45 cm long with 4-8 pairs of large leaflets

Flowers bright yellow in long, drooping clusters; 5 petals

Fruit long, cylindrical pipes, green at first, turning black

10 m

leaflets larger than other Delhi cassias

A medium-sized, ornamental tree with a spreading, irregular canopy. Widely cultivated for its arrestingly beautiful, drooping sprays of bright-yellow flowers. Surprisingly, the amaltas was not among the trees originally chosen to line avenues in Lutyens' Delhi. Thinly scattered on the Ridge, qualifying, but only just, as a native Delhi tree.

SEASONS - LEAVES shed early in April, renewed in May. **FLOWERS** in late April, peaking by mid May. The rains always induce more flushes of flowering that can last (weakly) into October. **FRUIT** mature around March-April of the year following flowering.

WHERE TO SEE IT In danger of becoming (like the peacock) so common that we stop noticing it. Amrita Shergil Marg, Shanti Path and Akbar Road are lined with it; Shakti Sthal has many trees. Common as crows in every park and large garden and thinly scattered throughout the Ridge and in JNU's untended areas.

terminal pair of leaflets is the largest

leaflets are arranged opposite each other or very nearly so

LEAVES feather-compound, up to 45 cm long with 4-8 pairs of large leaflets. Young leaflets are silvered by faint down, becoming smooth and without gloss as they mature.

new leaflets emerge a lovely coppery brown

3 shortest stamens are straight

the petals overlap slightly and are not all the same size

4 shorter stamens are bent the other way

3 longest stamens are bent into an S-shape

FLOWERS fragrant, bright yellow, in drooping sprays up to 60 cm long with the oldest flowers at the base. The intensity of yellow varies. A flower has 10 stamens of unequal length, grouped 3-4-3. Only the 3 longer ones are fertile.

FRUIT long, cylindrical pipes ('fistula' in Latin) up to 60 cm long. The seeds inside are stored in little compartments encased in a strong-smelling, sweetish pulp. Ripe pods are black and fall whole to the ground.

BARK smooth, yellowish when young, coarsening with age and becoming ruddy or dark grey with crusty plates that fall off like scabs.

HABITAT A scattered tree of both dry and moist deciduous forests in India, avoiding only the most arid tracts. It tolerates poor, shallow and rocky soils, and requires 75-190 cm of rainfall. It withstands drought but young plants are sensitive to frost. It has a superficial root system which porcupines love to gnaw on. Many forest animals feed on the sweetish pulp in the fruit.

RANGE One of the most widespread forest trees of India. It is found all along the base of the Himalaya from the Indus eastwards and throughout C and peninsular India. Its natural range extends to Myanmar and further E to Indo-China and the Philippines.

USES The bark (called 'sumari') is used as a tan and yields a red dye. The sweetish fruit pulp is an effective purgative, safe even for pregnant women. A paste made from the roots is used to cure skin diseases and leprosy. The leaves are reputed to heal ulcers. The twigs and leaves are lopped for fodder. The sapwood is useless but the brick-red heartwood is hard, heavy and can be beautifully mottled and streaked. It is durable but tends to crack and warp. It is used for posts, tool handles and rice-pounders. It makes good fuelwood and excellent charcoal.

WHY THE AMALTAS NEEDS JACKALS

Foresters are always intrigued by fruit that do not split open to release their seeds for germination. In a famous experiment early last century, Robert Troup tried to find out how amaltas seeds are freed from their pods and he discovered that jackals, bears and pigs play an important part by eating the pods. See page 327 for more about how the amaltas depends on these animals for assisting with natural regeneration.

KASSOD *Senna siamea*

Syn: *Cassia siamea*

siamese/thai/yellow cassia • ironwood tree • bombay blackwood • thailand shower • kassod

pea family – cassia subfamily

Middle-sized tree, deciduous

Bark light grey, becoming cracked and rough

Leaves feather-compound, with up to 14 pairs of dark-green leaflets with blunt tips

Flowers pale yellow in large clusters at branch ends; 5 unequal petals; 10 stamens of different sizes

Fruit a flattish, narrow pod up to 30 cm long

14 m

>> *Cassias* and ex-*Cassias* – see p330

LEAVES feather-compound with 6-14 pairs of leaflets. Common leaf stalk up to 30 cm long. Each leaflet is 6-7 cm long, broadest in the middle, with the midrib prolonged into a tiny bristle beyond the blunt tip.

An unarmed tree with a dense, spreading crown of near-glossy leaves. Twice a year it bears clusters of (not particularly showy) pale-yellow flowers at the ends of its branchlets, peaking towards the end of the rains. Cultivated in Delhi's parks and along some roads, mostly in residential areas newly developed since Independence.

SEASONS - LEAVES start to fall towards late January; most trees straggle through February, most of March. New leaf in late March or early April. **FLOWERS** in two distinct peaks, the major one after the rains lasting into December, a shorter one in May. **FRUIT** ripen towards late February.

WHERE TO SEE IT A relatively recent introduction but becoming common in newer parts of the city. The main road through Greater Kailash1 and a stretch of Ring Road near Defence Colony are dominated by kassod. Hauz Khas District park has a pure avenue. Most parks have trees, but completely absent from the Ridge.

the common leaf stalk is reddish and channelled on top

leaflets are glossy on top, duller and paler beneath

FLOWERS in large, branching clusters at ends of branchlets. Each flower has 5 concave petals, 2 of them larger than the others. There are 10 yellow stamens – 7 are 'developed' (2 long and 5 short ones) and 3 are tiny, vestigial ones.

unlike Cassia flowers, the stamens are straight and thick

flowers are borne in very large, branching clusters

HABITAT Lowland dry forests with more than 65 cm rain. Normally evergreen, it goes straggly for a short time in very dry conditions. Drought-hardy once established and not too exacting about soil conditions, it grows best in light, well-drained soils but does not tolerate frost and fire. It is very fast-growing.

RANGE Native to Myanmar and SE Asia. There is less agreement about whether it is found naturally in Sri Lanka and S Tamil Nadu. Extensively planted in recent years.

FRUIT pods up to 30 cm long, more or less flat except where the seeds make them ripple and bulge. The pods feel minutely furry, but you can only see the fur with a hand lens. Young pods are often 'tanned' deep magenta on the side facing the sun and pale green on the side facing away.

USES The leaves and seeds are eaten by cattle and sheep but are toxic to non-ruminants (such as pigs and poultry). The roots are used to treat intestinal worms. The bark contains tannin. Cultivated as a 'nurse' shade tree in coffee/tea plantations. Useful for afforesting degraded tracts and as a windbreak. The pale sapwood is useless, but the dark heartwood – known as 'Bombay blackwood' – is hard and heavy with beautiful partridge-feather mottling. It is exceedingly durable, and is used for cabinet-work and for making helves, mallets and walking sticks. In 19th-century Ceylon, it was considered the best fuel for steam locomotives. It makes excellent charcoal.

BARK grey, often marked with dark, parallel streaks. Relatively smooth, becoming cracked and rougher as the tree ages.

CAN BE CONFUSED WITH

Archibald's cassia (also a yellow-flowered senna) but this has pointy leaflets instead of kassod's blunt leaflets. When not in flower, the kassod could be mistaken for one of the pink cassias, but all the pink cassias in Delhi have large, creset-shaped stipules at the base of their leaves (absent in the kassod). See key on pages 238-39.

🌿 BRAZILIAN CASSIA *Cassia grandis*

brazilian/horse cassia • coral/pink shower • liquorice tree • stinking toe   *pea family – cassia subfamily*
no local name

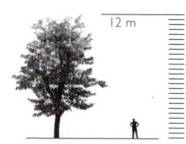

Middle-sized tree; deciduous

Bark grey, relatively smooth

Young shoots and leaves densely woolly

Leaves feather-compound with up to 20 pairs of close leaflets, rounded at both ends with a minute point at apex; new leaflets conspicuously bronzed or coppery

Flowers pink or salmon, in clusters; one petal with yellow spots

Fruit pod dark, cylindric, up to 60 cm long

A slender deciduous tree with deep-green, velvety leaves, easily spotted by a coppery tone to its newest leaflets. It is the first of Delhi's pink cassias to flower, with pink petals limned with yellow spots. Native to tropical America and widely cultivated in tropical climates, but not at all common in Delhi.

WHERE TO SEE IT Nehru Park, Buddha Jayanti Park, Mahavir Vanasthali and Sundar Nursery have specimens but it is not nearly as common as other pink cassias.

🌿 GLAUCOUS CASSIA *Senna surattensis*

glaucous cassia • kalamona • scrambled eggs • sunshine tree   *pea family – cassia subfamily*
no local name

Small tree; deciduous

Bark rough, dark, with lenticels running in vertical lines

Leaves feather-compound with up to 10 pairs of leaflets, rounded or notched at apex; prominent glands between lowest pairs of leaflets

Flowers in axillary clusters, bright yellow, up to 3 cm wide, with 5 not-quite-equal petals; 10 unequal stamens

Fruit a thin, flattish pod up to 20 cm long, dark brown

pods marked with thin, horizontal lines between the seeds

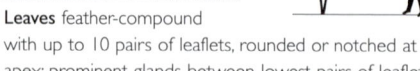

A tall shrub or a small, ornamental tree that flowers after the rains and retains its bright-yellow blossoms well into December. The origins of this garden plant are uncertain – some authorities say S India, but Malaysia, Indonesia or N Australia are more likely sites. Surprisingly uncommon in Delhi.

WHERE TO SEE IT Some large parks have specimens, but not common. A row of plants on Outer Ring Road beyond Vasant Vihar leading to Gurgaon. Mathura Road has a row planted on the opposite side of Pragati Maidan.

CHIKRASSY *Chukrasia tabularis*

chikrassy • chittagong wood • indian redwood • bastard cedar • east indian mahogany *neem/mahogany family*
chikrassi

Large tree; deciduous

Bark rusty brown, becoming cracked, rougher with age

Leaves up to 50 cm long, feather-compound with about 12 pairs of leaflets, hairy or not; asymmetrical at base; newest leaflets are red

Flowers in loose clusters, male and female on separate trees; petals 4-5, yellowy white, narrow, spreading; stamens fused in a column, like the neem

Fruit a dark, woody capsule, about 5 cm long

A large, handsome tree with a generous crown, capable of reaching 40 m but not in Delhi. The newest leaflets towards the tips of the long, feather-compound leaves are a fulvous red. Native to moist forests in India and SE Asia, and cultivated as an occasional park and roundabout tree in Delhi.

SEASONS - **LEAVES** begin to thin out sometime between February and March (depending on winter rains); new leaf follows quickly, in early to late March. **FLOWERS** in late April or May (var. *velutina* somewhat later, in the rains). **FRUIT** ripen in winter; not seen in Delhi.

PETALS 12-15 mm long. The tube in the centre is stout and you can just see the tips of the anthers peeping over the rim. The flowers are wonderfully fragrant.

• pointy leaflets are up to 15 cm long, with noticeably unequal bases

• more furry underneath than on top

WHERE TO SEE IT Mandi House and Kamaraj roundabouts. Shanti Vana has an extensive grove. 4 big trees in Green Park Market; beautiful specimens in Talkatora Garden. (All these are var. *tabularis*.) Var. *velutina* is represented by 3 trees on Dharam Marg and some more planted inside C crescent, Malcha Marg.

TWO VARIETIES OF THE CHIKRASSY

Delhi has both varieties of the chikrassy, var. *tabularis* and var. *velutina*. They differ mainly in the degree of velvetiness of their leaflets and the character of their bark. See page 333 for details.

JAVA CASSIA *Cassia javanica*

java cassia • pink mohur/lady • pink and white shower
no local name

pea family – cassia subfamily

Middle-sized tree; deciduous

Bark grey-brown, becoming darker, rougher on older trees

Leaves feather-compound with up to 14 pairs of leaflets, glossy or silky, pointy or blunt

Flowers in clusters on long, slender stalks; 5 pink petals, fading to white; 3 of the 10 stamens much longer than the others, with round swellings on their filaments

Fruit a cylindrical pod up to 60 cm long

LEAFLETS of var. *javanica* are dull, silky-hairy, rounded at both ends, with a tiny point at the tip; the crescent-shaped leafy stipules tend to be noticeably large.

A small to medium-sized tree with a large, spreading crown. Very beautiful in flower, with clusters of pink blossoms that fade quickly to white. Native to SE Asia and one variety possibly to NE India. The two varieties found in Delhi share many traits but also differ in particular details. Precise identification is hazardous because of their well-known ability to hybridize. (See pages 238-39 for distinguishing features.)

LEAFLETS of var. *indochinensis* are more or less smooth with rounded base and pointy apex; the crescent-shaped leafy stipules are usually pointed at each end.

SEASONS - LEAVES thin out in January; renewed in late April or May. **FLOWERS** appear with the new leaves and are spent by June (slightly later for var. *indochinensis*). **FRUIT** pods ripen February or March.

WHERE TO SEE IT Var. *javanica* in Nehru, Buddha Jayanti and Mahavir Jayanti Parks; var. *indochinensis* in IIC, Teen Murti Bhavan, Lodi Garden.

var. *indochinensis* is said to have smaller stipules than var. *javanica*, but clearly not in this picture

VARIETIES OF THE JAVA CASSIA

The Java cassia is a difficult species with many different varieties and hybrids that are hard to tell apart, even by experts. This page treats 2 of the varieties found in Delhi: var. *javanica* and var. *indochinensis* (known as var. *nodosa* until recently) or the appleblossom shower. See page 329 for 'Name Changes in the Pink-flowering Cassias'.

RED CASSIA *Cassia roxburghii*

red cassia • ceylon senna • red indian laburnum • roxburgh's cassia
no local name

pea family – cassia subfamily

5 m

Small tree; deciduous

Branchlets downy, distinctly zigzag

Bark fissured, dark brown

Leaves feather-compound with up to 20 pairs of velvety leaflets, unequal at base, notched or blunt, with a minute point at apex

Flower clusters from leaf axils, on long, woolly stalks; flowers brick-red, 5-petalled, with 10 stamens (without swellings on their filaments); anthers red

Fruit cylindrical, up to 25 cm long, black when ripe

FLOWER petals are finely veined. Like other pink cassias, there are 10 stamens but they lack the round swellings. The pink filaments and dark-red anthers are useful clues.

A diminutive tree rarely exceeding 5 m, with a compact canopy and downward-sweeping, densely velvety branchlets. Viewed head on, the rows of feathery leaflets form a neat, inverted 'V'. This is the longest blooming of the pink cassias, lasting through the rains and beyond. Native to Sri Lanka and parts of S India.

SEASONS - **LEAVES** shed in February, renewed in early May. **FLOWERS** from June to October; prime time is mid August. **FRUIT** ripen January or February.

WHERE TO SEE IT Most large parks have specimens: Buddha Jayanti, Nehru, Kamla Nehru, Talkatora Garden, Shakti Sthal.

• flowers are distinctly more brick-red than other Delhi cassias

FRUIT reddish at first, darkening later. There are thin, papery partitions between the seeds.

CAN BE CONFUSED WITH

Other pink-flowered cassias. See page 239 for a key to Delhi's pink cassias.

🌿 FERN LEAF TREE *Filicium decipiens*

fern leaf tree • fern tree • japanese fern tree

no local name

reettha/litchi family

12 m

Middle-sized tree; evergreen

Bark rusty grey, becoming scaly and cracked with age

Leaves feather-compound with 6-8 pairs of fern-like leaflets; conspicuous leafy wing runs down the length of main leaf stalk

Flowers small, white, in branching clusters from leaf axils

Fruit smooth, olive-like, purple when ripe

An attractive evergreen tree with a dense crown of unusual foliage with prominent 'wings' all along the main leaf stalk. Native to moist forests in the southern W Ghats, yet (on the evidence of a single specimen in Delhi) able to adapt well to much drier conditions. A slow-growing, long-lived tree.

WHERE TO SEE IT 2 specimens in Sundar Nursery, near the mist house.

leafy wing ● on leaf stalk

🌿 AFRICAN MAHOGANY *Khaya senegalensis*

african/gambia/senegal mahogany • dryzone mahogany • bisselon

no local name

neem/mahogany family

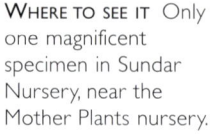

22 m

Large tree; deciduous

Bark ashy, scaly, pink-tinged

Leaves feather-compound, very long, in tufts at the ends of twigs; up to 7 pairs of near-opposite leaflets

Flowers small, in loose sprays; 4 white petals; male and female flowers on separate trees

Fruit an upright woody capsule; not seen in Delhi

A strikingly tall, handsome tree found near streams or in moist depressions in C African tropical savannah. It furnishes the best quality African mahogany and is widely grown in the tropics as a street tree but is little known in India. Delhi has only a lone specimen which seems much too big for its surroundings.

WHERE TO SEE IT Only one magnificent specimen in Sundar Nursery, near the Mother Plants nursery.

ARCHIBALD'S CASSIA *Senna spectabilis*

archibald's cassia • calceolaria cassia • golden shower
no local name

pea family – cassia subfamily

Smallish tree; nearly but not quite evergreen

Bark brown, smooth, with wavy vertical patterns of lenticels

Leaves feather-compound with up to 16 pairs of slim, glossy leaflets with pointy tips; a pair of thin, curved stipules at base of leaf stalk

Flowers in small terminal clusters, bright yellow; 7 fertile stamens, 3 undeveloped ones, all yellow

Fruit pods cylindrical, smooth, up to 25 cm long

A modest tree with a loose, spreading crown of glossy leaves and terminal bunches of bright-yellow flowers. Pointy leaflets and thread-like stipules at the base of the leaf stalk are diagnostic. Native to C America, introduced into India as an ornamental tree. Uncommon in Delhi, though it does well.

WHERE TO SEE IT Not common. One biggish tree in Nehru Park, close to Vinay Marg; 2 more near Lenin's statue. One multi-stemmed tree in Arab Sarai (near Humayun's Tomb).

BURMESE PINK CASSIA *Cassia renigera*

burmese pink cassia • burmese cassia
no local name

pea family – cassia subfamily

Small tree; deciduous

Bark brown, cracked but not very rough

Leaves feather-compound with up to 20 pairs of soft, velvety leaflets, rounded at both ends; kidney-shaped leafy stipules at base of stalk

Flowers rose-pink fading to white, in clusters up to 14 cm long; 5 pink petals and 10 stamens of unequal length

Fruit pods smooth, cylindric, up to 60 cm long

A small, unremarkable tree from dry forests in Upper Myanmar that turns sublimely beautiful when it bursts into flower early in May. Easily mistaken for one of the other pink-flowering cassias and distinguished by its densely velvety young shoots and leaves. Not at all common in Delhi.

WHERE TO SEE IT A small tree in the IIC parking lot that flowers profusely. At least 3 specimens in different parks are mislabelled as this tree. Not common.

• the only one of Delhi's pink cassias with leafy bracts at the base of its flowers

DELHI'S CASSIA AND SENNA TREES

Cassia and *Senna* are closely related and until quite recently were united under *Cassia*. The easiest way of telling a *Cassia* from a *Senna* is to look closely at their stamens. A *Cassia* flower has 10 stamens: 3 of them are long, fertile and curved in an elaborate S-shape; the smaller stamens are all infertile.

Cassia flower with 3 long, curving, fertile stamens

Senna flowers too have 10 stamens (rarely 12 or 13), but though they vary in size, most or sometimes all of them are fertile. They are also more or less straight, not curved. Another characteristic is that all the *Senna* have yellow flowers. (Don't be misled by the word 'cassia' in their common names! It is a relic of the past.) (See page 330 – 'Cassias and ex-Cassias')

Senna flower with straight, thick stamens; 7 are fertile

YELLOW FLOWERS

WITH 3 LONG, S-SHAPED STAMENS

AMALTAS *Cassia fistula* (pp228-29)

The only *Cassia* in the yellow-flowering group, therefore the only one with long, S-shaped stamens.
Flowers in long, loose, pendulous clusters.
The long, cylindrical, pipe-like pods are also diagnostic (*Senna* pods are usually flatter or strap-shaped).

WITH SHORT, STRAIGHT STAMENS

The 3 *Senna* species can be separated by their leaves alone

KASSOD *Senna siamea* (pp230-31)

Up to 15 pairs of leaflets, blunt or notched at apex; the midrib ends in a tiny, stiff bristle; stipules minute, not prominent; main leaf stalk is distinctly grooved

ARCHIBALD'S CASSIA *Senna spectabilis* (p237)

Has the largest leaves of the 3 *Senna* species (up to 35 cm or more); 8-15 pairs of leaflets, long-pointy at apex; a pair of thin, thread-like, curved stipules at base of main leaf stalk

GLAUCOUS CASSIA *Senna surattensis* (p232)

Has few pairs of leaflets (4-10); prominent glands between first 3 pairs of leaflets; apex of leaflets blunt; stipules fall early, not very prominent

PINK FLOWERS

The pink-flowering *Cassia* are more difficult to separate because they are more closely allied (and often hybridize). All 3 trees in the top row have prominent round swellings on their long, S-shaped stamens. The red and Brazilian cassia, in the lower row, have no swellings.

The scientific names of some *Cassia* are unstable. See 'Name Changes in the Pink-flowering *Cassias*' page 329.

WITH ROUND SWELLINGS ON 3 LONG STAMENS

JAVA CASSIA
Cassia javanica var. *javanica* (p234)

Usually has spiny remains of old branches on its trunk
Leaflets silky below, dull
Tips of leaflets rounded or blunt
Stipules large, kidney-shaped
Petals pink, turning dark red, fading to white
Flower-cup red or red-brown

APPLEBLOSSOM SHOWER
Cassia javanica var. *indochinensis* (p234)

No spiny remnants on trunk
Leaflets more or less smooth
Tips of leaflets usually pointy
Stipules crescent-shaped
Petals pink, fading to yellow-pink or white
Flower-cup greenish

BURMESE PINK CASSIA
Cassia renigera (p237)

Leaflets densely velvety
Tips of leaflets rounded, with a very tiny point
Broad leafy bracts at base of each flower (diagnostic)
Stipules large, kidney-shaped
Petals rose-pink, fading white
Soft, silky hairs on flower-cup and petals

WITH NO SWELLINGS ON 3 LONG STAMENS

RED CASSIA *Cassia roxburghii* (p235)

Branchlets zigzag
Leaves and branchlets woolly
Leaf stalk grooved
Leaflets notched at apex, with a tiny point
Starts flowering just before the rains
Flower clusters erect from leaf axils; flowers terracotta red; stamens pink; petals veined in green

BRAZILIAN CASSIA *Cassia grandis* (p232)

Branchlets not zigzag
Leaves, all parts, densely woolly
Leaf stalk not grooved
Leaflets rounded at apex, with a tiny point
Young leaves coppery or bronzed
The first Delhi *Cassia* to bloom
Flowers red, fading to pink, finally orange, upper petal with yellow spots

MAHARUKH *Ailanthus excelsa*

tree of heaven • coromandel ailanto
maharukh • mahaneem • pirneem • ulloo • ardu • arua

maharukh family

Large tree; deciduous

Bark grey, corky, thick, with intense vertical fissures

Leaves very large, feather-compound, with 8-14 pairs of toothed leaflets

Flowers small, greenish yellow, in large clusters; male and female flowers usually on separate trees

Fruit a thin, papery pod, pointy at both ends

18 m

female flowers have green, wormy styles

A large deciduous tree with a neat, dome-shaped crown. The main branches typically emerge at right angles to the massive trunk before sweeping upwards. Its unevenly serrated leaves are like a giant version of the neem's. Common in Delhi but not native. It is naturalized on the Ridge, self-sown in wastelands and only occasionally cultivated.

male flowers have saffron-yellow anthers

SEASONS - **LEAVES** start falling in mid April; new leaves in late May or early June. The canopy fills out only in the rains. **FLOWER BUDS** form early in January but do not open till March. Flowering is over before the end of March. **FRUIT** form quickly (on trees with female flowers), dropping by July.

WHERE TO SEE IT Copernicus Marg is predominantly a maharukh avenue. Many trees outside Maitreyi College and in Delhi Golf Club. Self-sown and scattered on the Ridge and tending to colonize waste urban spaces. Most parks and public gardens have specimens.

FLOWERS small, yellowish, in large, drooping clusters. Male and female flowers are separate, usually on different trees – though sometimes male, female and bisexual flowers can all be together on the same tree. Flowers of all kinds have 5 narrow, spreading petals.

LEAVES feather-compound, strikingly similar to neem leaves but on a much bigger scale (hence 'mahaneem'). They can grow to a metre or more in length. Leaflets 8-14 pairs sometimes with a solitary leaflet at the apex, all coarsely toothed and softly downy. The leaflets are nearly but not quite opposite each other, and have asymmetrical bases. Crushed leaves smell of marmite or peanuts (well, sort of).

FRUIT thin, papery, single-seeded pods, hanging in large bunches. Pale green at first, turning yellow and eventually brown. Purely male trees, of course, do not fruit.

BARK dark grey with close, deep, vertical fissures in mature trees. The texture is a bit like the wrinkly skin on an elephant's legs.

HABITAT Mixed deciduous forests but rare or absent in heavy rainfall areas. Fast-growing and adaptable, maharukh grows on a variety of soils but does not tolerate waterlogging. It has a talent for springing up unaided in wastelands even in cities. It is a somewhat brittle tree, needing to be sheltered from high winds. Municipal authorities love the tree because all it seems to need is plenty of sunshine.

RANGE Native to drier parts of C, E and peninsular India south of the Ganga, ascending no more than about 1000 m. Absent in the heavy-rainfall belt along the W coast and in the NW. Increasingly cultivated in cities for the sheer ease of its cultivation.

USES Its leaves and bitter bark have a reputation in folk medicine as a tonic and cure for fever, bronchitis and dyspepsia. It is a good fodder tree, though sheep and goats need to first overcome their distaste of the strong nutty smell of its leaves. A useful shade and shelterbelt tree. The wood is soft and light, easy to saw and work but is not attractive or durable in the open. It is used mainly for packing cases, toys, fishing floats and for carving Rajasthani marionettes.

🌿 NEEM *Azadirachta indica*

margosa • neem • indian lilac

neem • nimb • balnimb

neem/mahogany family

Middle-sized tree; semi-evergreen

Bark dark grey-brown, rough, vertically furrowed

Leaves feather-compound with 4-8 pairs of curved, toothed leaflets plus one terminal leaflet

Flowers with 5 spreading, white petals; stamens fused in a central column

Fruit up to 2 cm long; yellow when ripe

petals broader towards their tips and faintly downy on the outside ●

the top of the staminal column has ● tiny teeth

A familiar, middle-sized tree with a billowing cumulus crown, almost but not quite evergreen in Delhi. A short trunk and dense canopy make it wind-firm and an excellent shade tree. One of the 13 exalted species chosen to line avenues in Imperial Delhi. Not native to Delhi but naturalized now even on the Ridge.

SEASONS - LEAVES begin to fall in mid March, starting from the tops of trees; new pink leaves emerge quickly afterwards. Canopy renewed by early April. **FLOWERS** in second week of April, peaking in the fourth week. **FRUIT** follow quickly, ripening and dropping in July.

WHERE TO SEE IT Akbar Road, Lodi Road, Prithviraj Road, Aurangzeb Road are lined exclusively or predominantly with neem. The IARI campus, Pusa, also has neem avenues. Common in parks and on the Ridge, notably in untended ravines inside JNU and Jaunapur.

FLOWERS white, in short, branching clusters emerging from leaf axils. Bisexual and purely male flowers are usually found on the same tree. The flowers open in the afternoon, with a delicate honey scent that is strongest at night. A flower has 5 slender, spreading petals and 10 stamens fused into a central column.

LEAVES feather-compound, up to 40 cm long, crowded at the ends of twigs. A leaf has 4-8 pairs of pointy leaflets with a solitary terminal leaflet (sometimes missing). The leaflets are slightly curved, with toothed margins. New leaves start out a subtle tint of pink, darkening to a shiny green.

leaflets attached to the main stalk with short stalks of their own

base of leaflets very asymmetrical

FRUIT up to 2 cm long, with a thin pulp enclosing a hard stone. Green at first, bright yellow when ripe.

BARK thick, rough. Outer bark dark greyish-brown, scabby and riven with vertical furrows. It grows more flaky with age. Rufous brown on the inside.

HABITAT Tolerates drought and most soils but avoids sites prone to frost and waterlogging. Ideal conditions for neem are well-drained, deep, sandy soils and annual rainfall between 450 and 1000 mm. Trees can live up to 200 years or more.

RANGE Its precise wild origins are obscure – most likely a region in N Myanmar near the Assam-Bangladesh border. It is now thoroughly naturalized in most of India, even appearing wild as an escape from cultivation. Neem was carried to Fiji, Guyana and Mauritius by Indian immigrants in the 19th century and to sub-Saharan Africa by British colonists.

USES Most parts of the tree are credited with medicinal value, even the watery exudation from the trunk known as 'neem toddy'. The seeds yield a yellow bitter oil used to treat leprosy, skin diseases, ulcers, rheumatism and has many other uses that no summary can do justice to. The principal active compound in the leaves – 'azadirachtin' – repels insects. A 19th-century treatise says the leaves are 'much used by holy men to help them resist the allurements of beauty'. Neem wood is handsome, hard and durable and is much used in the countryside.

CAN BE CONFUSED WITH

Bakain, which also has toothed leaflets and is superficially alike. The simple distinction is that:
Neem leaves are 1-pinnate; its fruit are oblong
Bakain leaves are 2- and 3-pinnate; its fruit are shaped like miniature apples (see pages 302-03)

❧ RHODESIAN WISTARIA *Bolusanthus speciosus*

rhodesian wistaria • tree/wild wistaria

pea family and subfamily

no local name

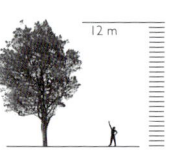

Middle-sized tree; deciduous

Bark medium brown, rough and deeply fissured

Leaves feather-compound with 3-7 pairs of sickle-shaped leaflets plus a terminal one; base of leaflets unequal; margins minutely toothed

Flowers deep blue or violet in loose sprays up to 24 cm long; petals like the pea-flower; 10 stamens [pic below]

Fruit a flat, narrow, greyish pod up to 8 cm long

A modest tree that at most times of the year you might walk past without a second glance, but impossible to ignore when it produces clusters of deep-blue pea-flowers in Delhi's spring. Native to relatively dry parts of southern tropical Africa and valued for its timber and as an outstanding landscape tree.

WHERE TO SEE IT Only one solitary specimen near the 9th green at the Delhi Golf Club.

❧ SIALA *Markhamia lutea*

Syn: Markhamia platycalyx

siala (ugandan name)

jacaranda family

no local name

Small tree; evergreen

Bark greyish brown, cracking and flaking in small patches

Leaves feather-compound with 3-5 pairs of large leaflets plus an odd terminal one; margins toothed; young leaves have 2 large, roundish, leafy stipules at base of main leaf stalk [see below]

Flowers handsome, trumpet-shaped; bright yellow stippled with red inside the throat; mouth of flower 5-lobed, not all quite equal

Fruit long, thin, brown capsules; sometimes spiral

A middle-sized evergreen tree from tropical Africa with a narrow, light crown. It has bright-yellow trumpet-shaped flowers with throats stippled and misted in red. New leaves carry a pair of round, leaf-like stipules at the base of their leaf stalks. Stunted in Delhi's dry climate and not at all common.

WHERE TO SEE IT 3 small trees near the lake in Shakti Sthal. Nehru Park has 3 trees at the extremity closest to Yashwant Place.

🌿 YELLOW BELLS *Tecoma stans*

yellow bells/elder • yellow trumpet bush • ginger thomas
no local name

jacaranda family

4 m

Small tree or lanky shrub; semi-evergreen

Bark pale brown or greyish, unremarkable

Leaves feather-compound usually with 5-7 leaflets; side leaflets almost without stalks; margins toothed, apex long-pointy, base tapered and asymmetrical; main leaf stalk often narrowly winged

Flowers bright-yellow trumpets in short clusters at ends or forks of branches; mouth 5-lobed with faint rust lines pencilling the throat

A somewhat unruly shrub with bright-yellow trumpet-flowers, not uncommon in hedgerows. It seldom becomes tree-sized, and this happens more by neglect than design. Native to warm parts of tropical America, widely cultivated in hot, dry climates. Many different garden varieties and hybrids exist.

Fruit pod-like, up to 20 cm long, narrow, flattish, ruddy brown speckled with white; apex sharp-pointy

WHERE TO SEE IT Fairly common in hedgerows as a straggly bush. Tree-sized specimens in Mahavir Vanasthali and Talkatora Garden.

🌿 INDIAN RED PEAR *Protium serratum*

indian red pear
no local name

salai/frankincense family

11 m

Middle-sized tree; semi-evergreen

Bark brown, scaly

Leaves feather-compound with 5-9 pointy leaflets with unequal bases; margins (not always) sharply toothed; turning red before falling

Flowers tiny, greenish, inconspicuous, arranged in short, branching clusters; petals 4-5, stamens 8-10 [see below]

Fruit on thick stalks, almost round, 2-3 cm across, red or bright pink when ripe; edible, sour-sweet

A fairly large, handsome evergreen tree usually found near streams in moist forests in NE India and SE Asia. It is noticeably stunted and goes bare for a brief while in Delhi's dry climate. It has edible fruit and attractive compound leaves with toothed leaflets. Found in Delhi only at a single site.

WHERE TO SEE IT Only 2 specimens, inside the timber section of Sundar Nursery.

🌿 KADI PATTA *Bergera koenigii*

Syn: Murraya koenigii

curry-leaf tree • curry bush

orange family

kadi patta • meettha neem • kathneem • gandhela • gandi • bowala • barsanga

Small tree or bush; deciduous

Bark thin, purplish brown; old bark shallowly fissured

Leaves feather-compound with 9-25 thin, pointy leaflets; base asymmetric, apex notched; edges often with minute, rounded teeth

Flowers small, white, fragrant, in sprays at the ends of twigs; 5 petals

Fruit a berry, pink at first, turning purple, then shiny black; skin rough with glands [see pic below]

A bush whose strongly scented leaves are a familiar ingredient of many Indian cuisines. In the right conditions it grows into a small, pretty tree with a shady crown of bright-green foliage and dense sprays of white flowers. It is native to dry and moist deciduous forests throughout India and SE Asia.

WHERE TO SEE IT A commonly cultivated bush, less common as a tree. Sundar Nursery has some large specimens. JNU has some kadi patta hedgerows.

🌿 KAITH *Limonia acidissima*

Syn: Limonia elephantum

(indian) wood-apple

orange family

kaith • katbel • bilin • keiri

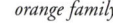

Medium-sized tree; deciduous

Bark grey, scaly, with shallow ridges and furrows

Spines stout, straight, up to 5 cm long

Leaves feather-compound with 2-3 pairs and an odd terminal leaflet, all blunt or notched at apex; leaf stalk narrowly winged

Flowers 12 mm wide, yellowish or green, tinged red, in small clusters; 5 petals [see pic below]

Fruit grey, woody, round, very hard; pulp brown, sticky

A thorny tree with an oval head of glossy foliage. Easily recognized by its grey, woody fruit, the size of tennis balls. The narrowly winged compound leaves smell of aniseed (*saunf*). Wild in dry and moist deciduous forests and widely cultivated but not native to Delhi and disappointingly rare in the city.

WHERE TO SEE IT One old tree on SP Marg, near Railway Colony. 2 small trees in Buddha Jayanti Park. Moolchand Hospital has a tree in its garden.

🌿 NATAL LABURNUM *Calpurnia aurea* subsp. *aurea*

natal/cape laburnum • east african/wild laburnum   *pea family and subfamily*

no local name

Smallish tree; deciduous

Bark dark, cracked, almost shaggy [see pic below]

Leaves feather-compound with 3-6 pairs and a terminal leaflet; tips of leaflets blunt or notched

Flowers bright yellow, pea-like, in short, dense clusters

Fruit a thin, flat pod up to 8 cm, not seen in Delhi

4 m

A small, rough-barked tree that puts up a stunning display of bright-yellow pea-flowers on bare branchlets in early March. Native to warm, dry regions from Ethiopia to S Africa, it is not really a true laburnum at all. A subspecies of the Natal laburnum is endemic to the Nilgiris. Undeservedly rare in Delhi.

WHERE TO SEE IT A prominent tree next to Indira Gandhi's bust in Pragati Maidan. A dense plantation in a triangular plot close to the Delhi University nursery.

🌿 CARROTWOOD *Cupaniopsis anacardioides*

carrotwood • tuckeroo   *reettha/litchi family*

no local name

Small tree; evergreen

Bark grey, not rough

Leaves feather-compound with up to 6 pairs of glossy leaflets, sometimes with a terminal; leaflets blunt or notched; prominent round pegs at base of leaflet stalks

Flowers greenish white, not showy, in small clusters [see pic below]

Fruit yellow or orange, like miniature pumpkins; not seen in Delhi

5 m

A compact evergreen tree with a dense head of shiny, feather-compound leaves, a little like a sausage tree's but on a smaller scale. Native to seashore forests and heathlands in N and E Australia. Delhi's solitary specimen is dramatically out of place. It is regarded in some countries as an invasive pest.

WHERE TO SEE IT Only one specimen in Sundar Nursery (close to the row of wild almond trees).

SAUSAGE TREE *Kigelia africana* Syn: *Kigelia pinnata*

sausage tree

balam kheera • jhad fanoos

jacaranda family

Large tree; deciduous

Bark grey-brown, not very rough; flaking in small plates

Leaves feather-compound with 3-4 pairs of large, leathery leaflets + a terminal

Flowers large, fleshy, funnel-shaped, maroon or liverish

Fruit large, woody, cucumber-shaped, up to 60 cm long

FLOWERS in loose clusters on very long, dangling stalks up to 6 m in length. The funnel-shaped flowers are about 15 cm long, with gaping mouths. Dull maroon on the outside, streaked with yellow or green. Inside the throat, dark glossy crimson with a wrinkled, embossed texture like seersucker. The buds open at night and fall off before dawn.

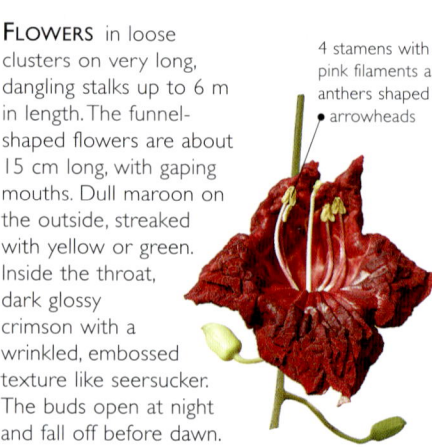

4 stamens with pink filaments and anthers shaped like arrowheads

A large tree from tropical Africa with a short, thick trunk and spreading crown. At most times of the year it either has large, waxy, liver-coloured flowers or grey sausage-shaped fruit dangling at the ends of very long, ropelike stalks. It is the only exotic tree among the 13 species selected to line avenues in Lutyens' Delhi.

SEASONS - LEAVES straggly or shed in January-February; new leaves in March-April, individual trees differing widely. FLOWERS April to August. FRUIT form in the rains and remain for very long on the tree.

WHERE TO SEE IT Gol Dak Khana area and Laxmibai Nagar (near Dilli Haat). All along Copernicus Marg (with maharukh) and S. Bharti Marg in front of Khan Market. A large specimen in Roshanara Bagh. A few (very few) remnant trees along Chandni Chowk and Khari Baoli, possibly quite old.

flower bud about to unfurl, showing the strong green veins

pale green flower-cup

lower leaflets have short stalks, upper ones have none

side leaflets have asymmetrical bases; not so in the terminal leaflet

margins are often wavy

LEAVES feather-compound, with 3 or 4 (sometimes 5) pairs of leaflets plus a single terminal one. Leaflets up to 15 cm long, leathery and rough. New leaves emerge bright green, becoming sombre green above, pale underneath.

FRUIT cucumber-shaped, 50 cm or more in length. (Self-pollinated flowers produce shorter fruit.) Inside the grey woody shell is a fibrous pulp full of seeds, like orange pips. The fruit are inedible and the seeds poisonous.

Fruit bats are the main pollinators of the sausage tree in Africa and the flowers have a peculiar sweet-mousey smell that bats must like. The long stalks probably evolved to hold the flowers exposed, away from the dense canopy where bats would have difficulty navigating with their sonar.

BARK grey-brown or ashy. Fairly smooth on young trees, flaking off in small, roundish plates as the tree ages.

CAN BE CONFUSED WITH

The carrotwood (an Australian tree, of which there is only a solitary specimen in Delhi) with similar leaves. Carrotwood leaflets are smaller and notched at their tips; those of the sausage tree end in a short, blunt point.

HABITAT In its native African habitat, a tree of open woodlands and not-too-dry savannahs, needing a warm climate and deep, well-drained soil and plenty of water, especially when young. It prefers areas of high humidity and often forms 'gallery forests' that follow the course of a river. Seedlings are sensitive to frost.

RANGE Mozambique, Zimbabwe and large swathes of tropical Africa, avoiding only the most arid areas.

USES African elephants and kudus relish its leaves, but most other browsers on the African savannah do not. The tree has a long history of medicinal use in Africa. Various parts are used, mostly for treating skin ailments but also for gastric complaints. A number of cosmetics companies produce skin creams and shampoos derived from the fruit. The boiled fruit also yields a reddish dye. The timber is pale brown to yellowish with no distinct heartwood. It is not especially hard or heavy but is known to be very troublesome to work and bring to a finish. Its firewood is also of poor quality. A Botswana superstition holds that hanging the fruit inside the house protects it from whirlwinds.

SILKY OAK *Grevillea robusta*

silky/silk/silver oak • river/southern silky oak • golden pine
no local name

silky oak family

Tall tree; semi-evergreen

Crown conical with branches ascending at 45°

Bark very dark, nearly black, with vertical furrows

Leaves feather-compound, with deeply divided leaflets; smooth above, silvery-mealy beneath

Flowers orange-yellow, in pairs on long brush-like 'spikes'

Fruit follicles like little black tadpoles

16 m

LEAVES feather-compound, 15-35 cm long, with each leaflet deeply dissected like a fern leaf. Deep green and almost smooth above, greyish white or silvery and lightly downy beneath. Young shoots are densely hairy.

A slim, symmetrical tree reaching 30 m in its native Australian forests but considerably less in Delhi. Not really an oak at all. Recognized by its deep-green fern-like foliage with silvery undersides, and bright-orange brush-like blossoms in late March. Very popular as a fast-growing ornamental and fairly common now in parks and gardens.

deeply dissected leaflets make the leaves look twice-feathered. They are only one-pinnate

SEASONS - LEAVES seldom completely shed, renewed in March-April. FLOWERS towards end March, lasting for about a month. FRUIT ripen in June-July.

WHERE TO SEE IT On Lodi Road along the perimeter of Lodi Garden and the round-about in front of 1 Safdarjang Road. Most large parks have silky oaks, but they tend to dry out on top and become 'stag-headed' in Delhi, a sign that they are not happy in this climate.

FLOWERS – Between 60-80 of the cadmium-yellow flowers are clustered together (in pairs) on a 'spike', the whole assembly looking like a wire brush. The most conspicuous feature of each flower is the stigma mounted on a long stalk which at first is bent over like a hairpin, then straightens out to 'present' itself to receive pollen. There are no petals.

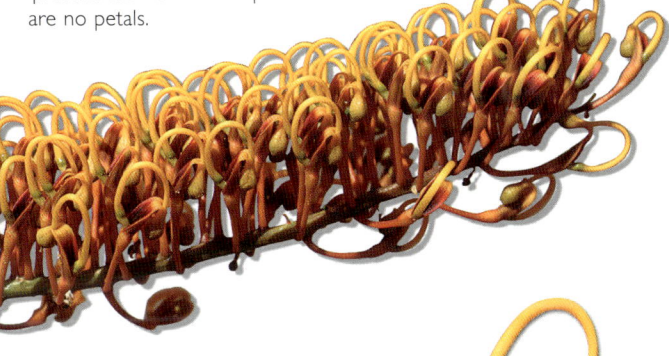

close view of the stigma bent over

FRUIT like little tadpoles, eventually splitting open to release one or 2 seeds. The tiny seeds float out on the wind with the help of thin wings and travel surprising distances.

BARK dark grey or brown, deeply fissured, with an outer corky layer.

HABITAT Silky oak occurs naturally along coastal river banks in well-drained soils. It is reasonably drought-tolerant. The roots produce a chemical substance that inhibits and kills off seedlings growing nearby – including its own – which is why it does not form dense stands. It is highly intolerant of shade and frost.

RANGE Its native habitat is a restricted swathe of brush forest in coastal E Australia, not extending very far inland from the sea. Silky oak is highly vulnerable to fire and is therefore absent from neighbouring eucalyptus forests and grasslands. Widely cultivated in warm parts of the world.

USES First introduced into India as a shade tree in tea plantations and still used mainly for windbreaks, alley cropping and as an ornamental tree. Birds, bats and insects visit its nectar-laden flowers. Its medicinal uses are not well documented. The timber, known in the trade as 'southern silky oak', is attractively figured and easy to work. The heartwood – pale pink darkening to a handsome red-brown – is of medium strength and is employed for a wide range of purposes. These properties are little known in India and the wood is not put to any use here.

❧ MOULMEIN ROSEWOOD *Millettia peguensis*

moulmein rosewood • jewels on a string
no local name

pea family and subfamily

Medium-sized tree; deciduous

Bark ashy or pale brown, smooth except in patches

Leaves feather-compound, with 2-3 pairs of opposite leaflets and a terminal leaflet

Flowers purple-mauve, tiny versions of the pea-flower, in long, drooping clusters

Fruit a flat woody pod, 5-10 cm long

12 m

FLOWERS small, typically pea-like in structure, arranged in long, drooping sprays. With purplish-mauve petals and rusty-red flower-cups, in full bloom the massed, tiny flowers look like a diaphanous mauve mist.

A striking, ornamental tree with a somewhat irregular but dense crown. Native to dry parts of Myanmar and Thailand, it is cultivated for its exquisitely beautiful mauve flowers produced when it is leafless in April. The tree is bare only for a very brief period and many people count it among Delhi's most beautiful flowering trees.

SEASONS - LEAVES shed in mid March; bare briefly until new leaf begins in April. **FLOWERS** sometimes late in March but prime time usually in the second week of April. **FRUIT** appear in May and remain for a long time.

WHERE TO SEE IT Along Maharshi Ramana Marg between Lodi Road and Khan Market; on the roundabout where Jantar Mantar Road and Ashok Road converge. A large grove inside Shanti Vana and Buddha Jayanti Park. Most large parks, such as Nehru Park and Talkatora Garden, have specimens.

the flower-cup is a rusty-red collar

sub-stalks of the
leaflets are noticeably
thickened

LEAVES feather-compound, with 3 (sometimes
just 2) pairs of opposed leaflets and one
solitary terminal leaflet. The smooth leaflets
taper at both ends, with a short, blunt tip.

• solitary
terminal leaflet is
always the largest

HABITAT A tree of dry
or only slightly humid
forests, in secondary
jungle or open
savannah, often near
streams. It is somewhat
sensitive to frost but
does impressively in
Delhi's dry climate.
Very easy to cultivate
from seed, to the point
where it can become
weedy and invasive.

RANGE Native to dry
forests and savannahs in
Myanmar, Thailand,
and possibly Cambodia
and Vietnam too. One
author claims it is
found in W peninsular
India but this is
doubtful – it is unlikely
to be truly wild
anywhere in India.
Cultivated today in hot,
dry climates mainly
for its spectacular
flowers. It has been
grown in Lahore (which
has a similar climate
to Delhi's) for at least
a century.

FRUIT a hard, flat, almost woody pod,
green at first, turning pale brown. Up
to 10 cm long, slightly indented
between the seeds and narrowed at
both base and apex.

USES No medicinal or
other uses reported, but
the common name
'Moulmein rosewood'
suggests that its timber
is probably hard, heavy
and as useful as some of
our own rosewoods.
Of course, it makes a
beautiful ornamental
and avenue tree, and its
success in Delhi and the
ease with which it can
be propagated have led
to it being widely
planted, but it does not
appear to be well
known in other tropical
countries.

BARK pale grey or brown, more or
less smooth, very like the barna's in
general effect. Older trees develop
small, rough plates that flake off.

CAN BE CONFUSED WITH

The karanj, perhaps, because of the
similarity in the form of their flowers and
compound leaves. The flowers of moulmein
rosewood are a deeper mauve and its leaves
not nearly as broad as that of the karanj.

🌿 AFRICAN TULIP TREE *Spathodea campanulata*

african tulip/flame tree • fountain tree • scarlet bell • squirt tree
no local name

jacaranda family

Middle-sized tree; deciduous

Bark pale greyish-brown, relatively smooth

Leaves large, feather-compound with 4-9 pairs of leaflets plus an odd terminal; leaflets oval, furry when young, later smooth and glossy

Flowers large, cup-shaped, orange-scarlet, in dense, terminal clusters; upper rim limned in yellow

Fruit a woody pod, pointy at both ends, up to 25 cm long [pic below]

A conspicuous, wide-crowned, ornamental tree from equatorial Africa with masses of brilliant orange-red flowers. Introduced into India towards the end of the 19th century, it does especially well in Bangalore and Pune but struggles in Delhi where it goes through a bare phase and remains relatively stunted.

WHERE TO SEE IT Not common. Planted in Shanti Vana and Shakti Sthal. Another in front of the Physics Block in Delhi University. Not at all suited to Delhi's climate.

🌿 AMDA *Spondias pinnata*

hog plum • bile tree • indian mombin • traveller's delight
amda • ambada • bahamb

Syn: Spondias mangifera

mango/cashew family

Smallish tree; deciduous

Bark pale ashy brown, smooth, soft and thick; shallowly fissured when old

Leaves large, up to 45 cm long, feather-compound with 7-13 leaflets; leaflets smooth, shiny, pointy at apex, rounded and asymmetrical at base; mango-scented

Flowers tiny, white, both male and bisexual flowers together in branched clusters up to 30 cm long; 5 white or greenish petals, about 6 mm wide [pic below]

Fruit 3-5 cm long, ovoid, fleshy, with a single stone inside; skin smooth, ripening yellow, edible (taste acid, astringent)

A monsoon forest tree that is only middle-sized in N India but can reach 35 m in S India and Myanmar. Bare for many months in winter. Amda is widespread in the wild but is nowhere common. It is cultivated mainly for its acid fruit which are pickled and much sought after. Rare in Delhi.

WHERE TO SEE IT Shalimar Bagh in N Delhi has many cultivated trees. Lots more in Jagdish Nursery, near Roshanara Bagh.

KAMRAKH *Averrhoa carambola*

carambola • star fruit • coromandel gooseberry • coolie tamarind

kamrakh • kamaranga

wood-sorrel family

Middle-sized tree; semi-evergreen

Leaves feather-compound, with 5-11 pointy leaflets, becoming progressively larger towards the apex

Flowers small, white with lilac on pink stalks; 5 petals [pic below]

Fruit up to 15 cm long, with 5-6 prominent angles; skin waxy, orange-yellow

A slender near-evergreen tree with a short trunk and ample crown. It has pretty, glossy foliage and attractive tiny pink flowers. The sour, yellow fruit – star-shaped in cross-section (hence the name) – are a familiar street food. Its precise origins are obscure – possibly SE Asia, Sri Lanka or S China.

WHERE TO SEE IT Lots of trees in Shalimar Bagh. The largest tree in Delhi is probably the one next to Jumna Lodge in Qudsia Bagh. Safdarjang's Tomb garden has a lone tree.

TAKOLI *Dalbergia lanceolaria* subsp. *lanceolaria*

no english common name

takoli • sirsa • bithua • hardi

pea family and subfamily

Smallish tree; deciduous

Bark pale grey, often tinged greenish yellow

Leaves feather-compound with up to 17 oval leaflets arranged alternately; leaflets rounded or notched at apex

Flowers pea-like in panicles, white tinged with lilac [see below]

Pods thin, flat, tapering at both ends, up to 10 cm long

A little-known tree in Delhi, somewhat like a puny version of the siris except that its leaves are feather-compound. The flowers emerge just before the new leaves, dull-white sprays laced with mauve or lilac. Widely distributed in India without being common anywhere – possibly native to the Delhi region.

WHERE TO SEE IT Bhagwandas Road has 3 trees, 2 near the main gate of Mandi House – possibly relicts of an earlier planting scheme. One tree on Dharam Marg, popping out of a corner of the Community Centre.

KARANJ *Pongamia pinnata*

indian beech • poonga-oil tree • karum tree

pea family and subfamily

karanj • papdi • sukhchain • kanji

Medium-sized tree; deciduous

Bark medium grey, not rough

Leaves feather-compound, with 2 or 3 pairs of broad leaflets and one solitary terminal leaflet

Flowers in short clusters, pea-like, white or pinkish

Fruit flattened, oval, woody pods, beaked at both ends; yellowish grey when ripe

12 m

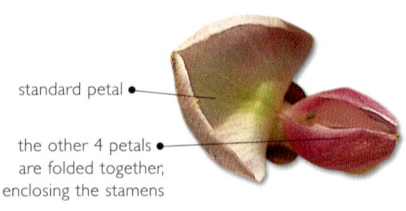

standard petal •

the other 4 petals • are folded together, enclosing the stamens

>> *Pongamia* or *Millettia*? – see p340

A familiar tree with a short, crooked bole and broad, shady head. It grows wild along rivers and tidal beaches but is remarkably adaptable and has become a popular city tree in India because it is not nibbled by goats. The karanj is particularly beautiful in pale-green new leaf, but mature leaves are terribly disfigured by leaf-mining worms.

FLOWERS in short, drooping sprays. The small, fragrant flowers are white or tinged pale pink or lilac. The 5 petals are reminiscent of the pea-flower, with the large 'standard' petal hooded like a bonnet over the other four which are folded together. The stamens are clustered toothbrush-style inside the inner pair of petals.

SEASONS - **LEAVES** shed between mid March and early April. New leaves soon after, with a second flush in the rains. The leaf-mining worms start their work in December. **FLOWERS** from the third week of April to late May; often a second flush in the rains. **FRUIT** ripen in the spring of the year after flowering – usually April or May.

the flower-cup is a • rusty-maroon collar

WHERE TO SEE IT A fairly common bungalow tree in Lutyens' Delhi, but not chosen to line any of its avenues. Hauz Khas District Park has a karanj avenue. Lots planted along roads in the Qutb Institutional Area and a row of trees along a strip park on Rajdoot Marg that was once a stormwater drain.

LEAVES feather-compound, with 2 or 3 (rarely 4) pairs of opposite leaflets and a single larger terminal leaflet. The leaflets are all broadly oval and pointy tipped, shiny on top, dull below. New leaves emerge a beautiful waxy pale green, darkening later.

curved stipules at the base of new leaves. They fall off early ●

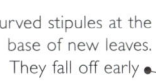

leaf-mining worms disfigure the leaves from December onwards ●

FRUIT woody pods about 5 cm long, almost oval but flattened, with a pointy beak at the apex. A pod contains only one or rarely 2 seeds. The pods are green at first, ripening straw-yellow or grey-brown. They do not open to release the seeds but decay slowly after falling to the ground.

BARK medium grey with a somewhat mealy texture, not cracked or fissured. Apt to come up in weals when scored, hence often disfigured with names and love-hearts.

HABITAT Karanj grows wild along streams and in tidal mudflats on the coast, surviving even in salt water. Mature trees are highly adaptable, tolerating drought, wind, fire and to a lesser extent frost.

RANGE Along the foot of the Himalaya E of the Ravi and on river banks and tidal flats throughout India especially in the Sundarbans. It extends eastwards into the Andamans and across Indo-China into the SW Pacific islands and Northern Australia.

USES A veritable one-stop pharmacy credited with an astonishing range of remedies in folk medicine: oil pressed from the seeds is used to treat scabies, herpes and rheumatism; the root and bark for piles, beriberi, tumours, ulcers and diseases of the eye, skin and vagina. Powdered seeds, crushed leaves, flowers and even the ash are medicinal. Red-brown 'pongam' or 'karanja' oil (from the seeds) is used as a lubricant, lamp-oil, pesticide and in soap-making and there is recent interest in its potential as a bio-fuel. The pale-yellow timber is not durable but is strong and easy to saw, turn and finish. It is used locally for making implements and tool handles but is used chiefly as a fuelwood.

CAN BE CONFUSED WITH

The moulmein rosewood (at a pinch) whose leaves and flowers have a similar structure, though its flowers are a much deeper mauve and its leaves are not nearly as broad. (Moulmein rosewood – pages 252-53)

🌿 SHISHAM *Dalbergia sissoo*

indian rosewood • indian dalbergia • bombay blackwood • sisu
shisham • tali • sissoo • shewa • sissai

pea family and subfamily

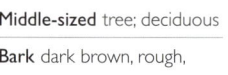

Middle-sized tree; deciduous

Bark dark brown, rough, with vertical furrows

Leaves feather-compound, with 3 or 5 broadly oval leaflets with long, pointy tips

Flowers inconspicuous, creamy yellow, in short clusters

Fruit pods 3-7 cm long, thin, flat, pale brown

WATERCOLOUR by unknown Indian artist c. 1800.
Courtesy of the Royal Botanic Garden, Edinburgh

A large tree from river banks in the sub-Himalayan tract, with stout branches supporting an extensive crown. Often crooked in Delhi, where it is only medium-sized. Once a favourite street tree, less popular today. Beautiful in pale-green new leaf in March. Seen in parks and in some parts of the Ridge where it is naturalized.

small, white flowers are 5-8 mm long

SEASONS - LEAVES start falling in January; trees bare or straggly by mid February. New leaves in late February, completely renewed by late March. FLOWERS in mid March, lasting only a short time. FRUIT form very soon after the flowers, persisting till the following February.

WHERE TO SEE IT Stretches of Ring Road, Rao Tula Ram and Aurobindo Marg have been planted with shisham, but they are still young. Chomsky spoke (in 2001) beneath a large tree behind Delhi School of Economics. Most large parks have specimens; lots of regenerating trees on the Ridge near Jaunapur and in JNU. The big tank at Hauz Khas is invaded by shisham.

FLOWERS small, white or pale yellow, faintly fragrant, in short clusters arising from leaf axils. Each flower has 5 petals of the same irregular form as the pea-flower (though this is hard to make out on such a small scale) and 9 stamens.

HABITAT It grows naturally along sub-Himalayan river banks on freshly exposed alluvium. It likes a lot of moisture but adapts to fairly dry conditions. It is frost-tolerant.

RANGE The sub-Himalayan tract and outer valleys from the Indus eastwards to Assam, ascending to about 1500 m. In some parts of Afghanistan as well. Extensively planted in N India.

young leaflets are faintly downy at first; mature ones are smooth

LEAVES easy to mistake as 'simple', but are actually feather-compound with 3 or 5 leaflets (always an unequal number) set alternately on the common leaf stalk. The leaf stalk tends to zigzag between the leaflets.

leaflets are broadly oval, ending in a long, pointy tip

USES One of the finest all-round timbers of India – the nut-brown heartwood is hard, heavy, strong, elastic and very handsome. It was used extensively for boat-building, carts and carriages, implements, construction and quality cabinet-making, and by the mid 19th century this led to the logging of all large shisham trees in Nepal's terai jungles. A favourite roadside tree in the Punjab in the 19th century. It is less well known for its medicinal uses – 'raspings' of the wood are used in treating leprosy, boils and vomiting and the bark for curing diseases of the blood, dysentery, leucoderma and skin ailments. The leaves make a good fodder. Shisham is planted to reclaim eroding sites and as a windbreak. The flowers are visited by bees and produce a dark, strongly flavoured honey.

FRUIT thin, flat pods, 3-7 cm long, green at first, turning pale brown, hanging together in bunches. Each pod contains one to 4 seeds.

BARK dark brown, rough, becoming more cracked and vertically furrowed as the tree ages.

CAN BE CONFUSED WITH

The Chinese tallow tree, whose leaves are a lot like shisham leaflets in outline. The former, however, are not only slightly broader and larger, but, crucially, are simple leaves, not parts of a compound leaf.

KAMINI *Murraya paniculata*

Syn: Murraya exotica

orange jessamine • mock orange • chinese/sumatran box • satinwood

orange family

kamini • marchula • juti

Small tree or shrub; evergreen

Bark yellowish, becoming fissured and corky with age

Leaves feather-compound with 3-9 shiny leaflets, the terminal leaflet usually the largest; leaflets are narrowed at base, bluntly pointed at apex, often notched

Flowers pure white, fragrant, in dense terminal clusters; petals 5 (rarely 6), overlapping; buds pale green

Fruit a shiny berry up to 18 mm long, red when ripe, narrowed at both ends

LEAVES up to 18 cm long, with 3-9 dark, shiny leaflets arranged alternately on the main leaf stalk, on short stalks of their own.

Delhi's favourite hedge-plant on account of its evergreen, dark, glossy foliage and fragrant white flowers. When not kept down, it grows into a small, crooked tree with pale, corky bark and an untidy crown. Native to dry deciduous forests throughout India but, surprisingly, not seen as a wild understorey tree anywhere on the Ridge.

leaflets arranged alternately •

SEASONS - LEAVES evergreen, with conspicuous new flushes in March and again early in the rains. **FLOWERS** March to May and again in the rains, occasionally at other times too. **FRUIT** mostly in April and again in June-July.

WHERE TO SEE IT Very common as a glossy hedge-plant but not so easy to locate as a tree. Lodi Garden has a few and the gate to the Ford Foundation (near the IIC) has a tall sentinel tree that flowers profusely. Humayun's Tomb gardens probably has the largest number of tree-like kaminis.

FRUIT oblong berries with a bitter, watery pulp inside. They contain one or 2 teardrop-shaped seeds.

🌿 QUICKSTICK *Gliricidia sepium*

quickstick • nicaraguan shade tree • cocoa shade • spotted gliricidia • mexican lilac
no local name

pea family and subfamily

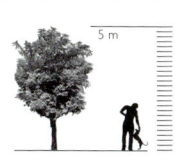

Small tree; deciduous

Bark pale brown, not very rough, becoming wrinkled

Leaves feather-compound with up to 8 pairs of leaflets and a terminal one, increasing in size towards the apex; spotted underneath

Flowers pea-like, pale pink, in dense clusters [pic at left]

Fruit a flattish pod up to 15 cm long [see pic below]

A small deciduous tree that leaps out of obscurity in March with masses of pale-pink blossoms along its bare, drooping branches. Native to tropical America and widely cultivated in the tropics to provide light shade in cocoa plantations but also for ornament. Unaccountably rare in Delhi.

WHERE TO SEE IT Rare. JNU campus has some young trees. A few more on the outskirts of Lado Sarai and an odd tree or two among the government flats in Vinay Nagar.

🌿 BLACK BEAN *Castanospermum australe*

black bean • moreton bay chestnut • australian chestnut
no local name

pea family and subfamily

Large tree; evergreen

Bark grey or brown, rough

Leaves feather-compound with 4-8 pairs of leaflets and a solitary terminal; leaflets long, dark, glossy with rounded base and pointy apex

Flowers attractive, in large clusters; yellow at first, turning red, up to 4 cm long [pic at left]

Fruit a fat, glossy pod up to 20 cm long; not seen in Delhi

A majestic evergreen shade-tree up to 35 m tall in its native Australian rainforests, but considerably shorter when cultivated. Delhi's dry season is much too long for the black bean and the city's solitary specimen is stunted and unhappy. It does not flower or fruit here but thrives in Dehra Dun.

WHERE TO SEE IT Only a solitary specimen, in Humayun's Tomb gardens.

KATSAGON *Fernandoa adenophyllum*   Syn: *Haplophragma adenophyllum*

no english common name

jacaranda family

katsagon • marodphali

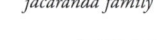

Large tree; deciduous

Bark smooth, greyish, often with deep, vertical splits

Leaves up to 45 cm long, feather-compound, with 5-7 leaflets; terminal leaflet largest; side ones are without stalks

Flowers bell-shaped, pale yellow; outside of petals and flower-cup densely downy

Fruit up to 90 cm long, cylindrical, twisted, ribbed

FLOWERS in short, erect clusters at the ends of branchlets. Similar to those of the sausage tree, with 5 large, crinkly lobes forming a gaping mouth. The pale-yellow petals are densely woolly on the outside and on the flower-cup. The flowers open at night and are pollinated by small bats.

Tall, somewhat untidy trees with a raggedy crown of coarse, feather-compound leaves. Pale-yellow bell-shaped flowers in the rains and long, curly, cylindrical fruit make it easy to recognize. Adapted to relatively dry conditions in its native forests in NE India, it is becoming more common in parks and streets in Delhi.

SEASONS - LEAVES turn purple, then yellow before being shed in late March or early April. New leaves follow quickly; canopy renewed by early May. FLOWERS in the rains, peaking in the third week of July. FRUIT form soon after the flowers, then remain on the tree for many months.

WHERE TO SEE IT Jaswant Singh Road, near Andhra Bhavan; Laxmibai Nagar. Interspersed with arjun trees along Avenue #1 inside IARI campus, Pusa. Quite a few trees near the central nala in Defence Colony and in JNU campus.

buds and flower-cup are both densely brown-felted outside

LEAVES up to 45 cm or more, feather-compound, with 2-3 pairs of opposite leaflets (without stalks) and a single stalked, terminal leaflet that is the largest. The leaflets are variable in size – on average the terminal leaflet would be 18 cm long, the side leaflets about 13 cm. All the leaflets are rusty-hairy underneath.

HABITAT In its native forests in India and SE Asia, this tree is found both in evergreen and mixed deciduous forests, and seems to adapt to relatively dry conditions quite well. It shows a marked preference for soils derived from limestone. It does not tolerate frost well. Extremely fast-growing.

RANGE Evergreen and deciduous forests in NE India and the Andaman Islands, and to a limited extent, in the W Ghats. Beyond the Indian subcontinent, it is found in Bangladesh, Myanmar and is widely distributed through SE Asia.

USES First cultivated at the Indian Botanic Garden, Calcutta, in the 1830s, it is only in recent times becoming popular as an avenue tree throughout India, partly because it is so fast-growing and does not seem to be browsed by cattle or goats. Its timber is orange-yellow streaked with brown and has the reputation of being hard and resistant to termites. It is suitable for cabinet work, mouldings, and for house building. It is also used to make fishing rods, billiard cues and carriage shafts.

look for a pair of small, ear-like leafy stipules near the base of the main leaf stalk

the rusty flower-cup persists at the base of the fruit

FRUIT CAPSULES green cylinders usually about 60 cm long but can grow to 90 cm, twisting and curling as they mature. If you look closely, you can see that they are ribbed and densely woolly, with an underlying texture of small, white dots.

the capsules split open to release their seeds

BARK ashy grey or pale brown, not very rough. Often riven by long, deep, vertical fisuures, as if raked by a giant claw.

GULMOHUR-LIKE LEAVES

Twice-feathered, without spines

leaflets numerous, crowded, hairy, rounded at apex

side-stalks 2-4 pairs

side-stalks 3-5 pairs

leaflets 5-12 pairs; stalked; unequal at base

leaflets 5-10 pairs; stalked; unequal at base; rounded at apex

leaflets rounded at apex

krishna siris
15 cm p288

gland

siris
32 cm p286

large gland

side-stalks 1-3 pairs

leaflets 2-3 pairs, shiny

side-stalks 4-8 pairs

doon siris
55 cm p289

prominent glands

leaflets 10-20 pairs; lacking stalks; pointy at apex

side-stalks 6-12 pairs

potka siris
24 cm p290

oval glands

leaflets 15-20 pairs; lacking stalks; curving

side-stalks 6-20 pairs

subabool
30 cm p291

molucca albizia
30 cm p290

leaflets 8-22 pairs; notched at apex; dark green, shiny on top

side-stalks 2-5 pairs

leaflets many, curving, pointy at apex

side-stalks 3-4 pairs + one terminal pinna

leaflets 4-8 pairs; stalked

brazilian ironwood
10 cm p298

stalk rusty-hairy

copperpod
50 cm p292

stalk channelled

gland

earpod tree
20 cm p295

leaflets alternate, stalked, blunt at both ends

side-stalks 3-6 pairs

side-stalks 4-9 pairs

leaflets up to 23 pairs; pale green; apex has a minute, pointy tip

up to 40 pairs of side-stalks

african wattle
42 cm p294

branching stipules at base of new leaves

leaflets small, crowded, very numerous

badminton ball tree
35 cm p298

red sandalwood
50 cm p295

side-stalks 20-30 pairs, widely spaced

side-stalks 10-20 pairs, close together

leaflets 20-30 pairs; more than 10 mm long; on short stalks; smooth; apex obtuse

side-stalks 9-22 pairs

leaflets 14-24 pairs with one terminal; apex pointy

leaflets up to 28 pairs; 3-4 mm long, on short stalks

stalk hairy, channelled

jacaranda
35 cm p300

colville's glory
60 cm p299

stalk smooth, channelled

gulmohur
60 cm p296

side-stalks 4-5 pairs

leaflets 3-9 pairs with terminal; apex rounded

side-stalks 4-6 pairs

side-stalks 3-7 pairs

leaflets 3-7 pairs with terminal; toothed, pointy

leaflets 5-10 pairs; alternate; toothed

side-stalks 3-5 pairs

bakain
60 cm p302

flamegold
55 cm p304

terminal leaflet

sonjna
75 cm p301

leaflets 5-7 pairs with terminal; bluntly toothed

akash neem
45 cm p304

leaflets 4-9 pairs, pointy; hairy when young

terminal pinna

side-stalks 3-4 pairs

leaflets 3-5 pairs, with terminal

arlu
160 cm p305

pink cedar
80 cm p305

side-stalks 3-5 pairs with one terminal

GULMOHUR-LIKE LEAVES

Twice-feathered, with spines

leaflets small, smooth

sweet acacia
5 cm p267

side-stalks widely spaced

israeli babool
4 cm p267

leaflets with rounded tips

leaf stalk downy

babool
5 cm p268

back of leaf stalk prickly

leaflets tiny, crowded, numerous

khair
14 cm p274

leaflets tiny, numerous, without stalks

sickle bush
6 cm p275

leaflets with rounded tips, almost no stalks

ronjh
7 cm p270

leaflets rounded, widest at apex

phulai
6 cm p272

2 pairs side-stalks; leaflets kidney-shaped

gainti
18 cm p280

side-stalks very long; leaflets tiny

leaflets with rounded ends

only 1 pair of side-stalks and leaflets

kumttha
4 cm p273

jungle jalebi
8 cm p282

main leaf stalk very short

leaflets grey-green, 3-nerved

jerusalem thorn
40 cm p281

jhand
6 cm p276

leaflets thin, widely spaced

honey mesquite
17 cm p280

main stalk ends in a tiny bristle

leaflets crowded, pointy

vilaiti keekar
14 cm p278

SWEET ACACIA *Acacia farnesiana*

sweet acacia • popinac • opoponax • cassie flower • fragrant acacia • huisache   *pea family – mimosa subfamily*
gandh babool • passi babool • dei babool

3 m

Bush or small tree; deciduous

Bark dark brown or greyish, smooth in young trees

Spines in pairs, brown, straight, short, up to 18 mm

Leaves twice-feathered, with 2-8 pairs of side-stalks and small, smooth leaflets, 10-20 pairs

Flowers tiny, clustered in round heads, bright to deep yellow, deliciously fragrant

Fruit pods thick, black, up to 7.5 cm long

A thorny bush or straggly tree with slender zigzag branches, reaching only 3 m in Delhi. Its spherical flower clusters are bright yellow like the babool's but much more strongly scented. Originally from tropical America, long cultivated in the Mediterranean and dry tropics. It is quite rare in Delhi.

WHERE TO SEE IT Sundar Nursery has a small plantation that announces its presence by the fragrance of its flowers in February-March. I came across a lone specimen in the Jaunapur ravines, probably an 'escape' from cultivation in a nearby farm.

ISRAELI BABOOL *Acacia tortilis*

umbrella thorn/acacia   *pea family – mimosa subfamily*
israeli babool

6 m

Smallish tree; deciduous

Bark reddish brown to very dark, fissured, rough

Spines paired, of 2 kinds: long, straight and white; also short, brown and curved

Leaves twice-feathered with up to 10 pairs of side-stalks; leaflets very small and delicate, up to 15 pairs

Flowers tiny, white, tightly clustered in balled heads

Fruit pods flat, spirally twisted and coiled

A small acacia with an uncanny resemblance to our desi babool except that its flowers are white. Introduced into N India from N Africa because of its remarkable resilience to drought and poor soils. Forest departments of Haryana and Rajasthan have planted this tree en masse, but it is not yet common in Delhi.

WHERE TO SEE IT Many trees planted in the Jaunapur ravines. One prominent tree outside Springdales School. Roadside plantations on the outskirts of Delhi and beyond.

SPINES of 2 kinds. The short, curved ones seen here.

BABOOL *Acacia nilotica* subsp. *indica*

egyptian mimosa • egyptian thorn

(telia/teli) babool • keekar • desi babool

pea family – mimosa subfamily

Middle-sized tree; deciduous

Bark nearly black, thick, deeply ridged and fissured

Spines in pairs, very long, straight, white

Leaves twice-feathered, with 3-6 pairs of side-stalks and numerous tiny leaflets

Flowers tiny, clustered in bright-yellow, round heads

Fruit pods greyish, beaded like a necklace

10 m

SPINES in pairs, up to 5 cm long, straight, slender, ivory white. A pair of spines makes a wide angle, something like 100° or so.

A middle-sized, thorny tree with nearly black bark and a spreading, open, feathery crown. Bright-yellow pom-pom flowers in the rainy season are distinctive. Naturalized in Delhi – Connaught Place was built in a cleared babool forest – but becoming rare and now found only in localized patches in the former floodplain of the Yamuna.

SEASONS - LEAVES shed in March or early April; renewed fairly quickly. FLOWERS from June into the rains, peaking in August; straggling flowers persist till November. FRUIT in September, ripening between April and June.

WHERE TO SEE IT It was the most common tree in Khairpur, where Lodi Garden was created, in 1936. (There is no babool anywhere in Lodi Garden today.) Now only an occasional tree in parks that still bear remnants of Delhi's original flora, such as Hauz Khas District Park and low-lying areas of JNU. Also in Jaunapur ravines. Rare on the Ridge (too dry, too rocky).

bright-yellow stamens give the heads their colour

the round heads are 8-15 mm in diameter

FLOWERS tiny, bright yellow, clustered tightly together to form round heads. Like all other acacias, the petals are insignificant. The slender flower stalks arise from leaf axils and are densely downy. The flowers are fragrant.

LEAVES twice-feathered, 2.5-5 cm long, dividing into 3 to 6 (rarely more) pairs of side-stalks. There are small glands at the base of the lowest and uppermost pairs of side-stalks. Each side-stalk bears up to 25 pairs of tiny leaflets. The leaf stalk, flower stalk and twigs are all lightly downy but the leaflets are smooth.

cup-shaped gland at junction of side-stalks

FRUIT a greyish, velvety pod up to 20 cm long, deeply pinched between the seeds like a bead necklace. Ripe pods do not split open on their own but are adapted for dispersal by browsing animals that eat the fruit.

8-14 seeds arranged in a single row

the only Indian acacia with such a markedly beaded pod

BARK dark brown to almost black, thick and rough, with deep, vertical fissures joined by short crisscross cracks. The inner bark is fulvous red-brown.

>> Varieties of the Baboool – see p334

HABITAT A 'pioneer' tree of hot, dry lowlands. Baboool tolerates a wide range of soils and mild salinity. It thrives in dry conditions but must have sufficient moisture in the subsoil. In the right conditions, it forms pure stands.

RANGE Widespread in dry regions throughout Africa and from Arabia through Afghanistan to the Indian subcontinent. Indigenous in Sindh, Gujarat and the N Deccan, cultivated and naturalized everywhere else in India.

USES One of the most important Indian trees, much planted on field-crop boundaries. For centuries its bark and pods have provided the most valuable tanning materials of N India. They also yield a rich, black dye known as 'siyah-bhoora' and beautiful shades of grey and khaki (the word comes from 'akhakhiya', the Arabic word for 'acacia'). Baboool gum is used in calico-printing and dyeing, in the manufacture of paper, matches, inks, paints and confectionary. Most parts of the tree are used in folk medicine, especially in Africa. The fruit is lopped and collected as fodder. The sapwood is not durable but the dark-rufous heartwood is nearly twice as hard and much heavier than teak and is widely used. It makes excellent charcoal.

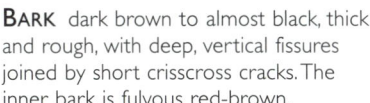

CAN BE CONFUSED WITH

Other spiny mimosas. The baboool is hard to mistake when it is in flower, because it is one of the only 2 species of spiny mimosas with flowers massed in bright-yellow spheres. Its beaded fruit is also diagnostic. Outside the flowering and fruiting season, you have to learn to recognize distinctive aspects of its leaves, bark and spines. See pages 284-85 for a 'Key to Delhi's Spiny Mimosas'.

RONJH *Acacia leucophloea*

white-barked acacia • panicled/distiller's acacia

pea family – mimosa subfamily

ronjh • rinj • reru • riya • rini • safed keekar • sharab ki keekar • kareer • nimbar

Middle-sized tree; deciduous

Bark yellowish, with dark blotches

Spines paired, straight, brown

Leaves twice-feathered, with 6-13 pairs of side-stalks, each one with up to 30 pairs of tiny, crowded leaflets

Flowers tiny, creamy, clustered in round heads

Fruit a velvety, khaki pod 8-20 cm long, curved or curly

12 m

SPINES 1-4 cm long, straight, in pairs arising from leaf axils. They are usually dusty brown to dark red, rarely white. Trees become less thorny with age.

A characteristic, thorny native tree of the Delhi region, with a crooked trunk and spreading, feathery crown. Its most distinctive feature is its creamy yellow bark with black blotches. Not normally considered attractive, ronjh can be surprisingly lovely in new leaf and late in the rains when its canopy is studded with small, spherical clusters of flowers.

SEASONS - **LEAVES** shed in January; bare through February and March. Most trees begin new leaf early in April. **FLOWERS** in the rains from late August till October. **FRUIT** turn khaki by January. Fallen fruit are crunchy underfoot in April.

WHERE TO SEE IT Very common in Delhi's rocky, hilly tracts and wherever Delhi's native flora has not been exchanged for an exotic one – on the Ridge, and as remnant trees in Lodi Garden, Hauz Khas District Park, etc. JNU campus is particularly well endowed with old ronjh trees.

flowers fragrant at dusk

long stamens conspicuous

FLOWERS tiny, creamy white to pale yellow, clustered in round heads. The large flower-bearing stalks are produced at the terminal ends of twigs. Because all its flowers are on the 'outside', a ronjh looks fuzzy from a distance.

leaflets small,
hairless, with
rounded ends

main leaf stalk
minutely downy

LEAVES twice-feathered, forking into
5-15 pairs of side-stalks which bear up
to 30 pairs of small, crowded leaflets.
Look for tiny cup-shaped glands at the
junctions of each pair of side-stalks.

FRUIT a flattish pod, slightly
curved, covered in khaki velvet
when ripe. If you hold a pod up
to the sun, you will be able to
see 8-12 seeds lodged in
separate compartments.

pods 8-20 cm long,
5-10 mm wide

like most acacias,
the leaflets 'close' at
night, conserving
scarce moisture

BARK yellowish, becoming rougher and
darker as the tree ages. Mature trees are
piebald with patches of dark, rough bark on
a lighter ground, yellowish grey to dull
yellow. Old trees can be nearly black but
traces of lighter colour are a giveaway.

CAN BE CONFUSED WITH

Other acacias, but the terminal flower clusters
and patchy, yellowish bark are unmistakable
distinguishing features. See pages 284-85 for a
'Key to Delhi's Spiny Mimosas'.

HABITAT A character-
istic tree of dry, open
scrub forest and
savannahs up to about
800 m. It prefers poor,
rocky, sandy or chalky
soils but will grow in
richer soils and clay. It
tolerates drought well
but remains stunted and
shrubby in highly arid
conditions. Annual
rainfall in its natural
range is 40-150 cm.
Mature trees are both
fire- and frost-hardy.

RANGE Widespread in
dry tracts from the
Punjab and Shivalik
hills across N India into
Bangladesh, Myanmar,
and Sri Lanka. Extends
into dry parts of
Thailand, Indonesia,
Vietnam and Malaysia
with Timor as its
easternmost extremity.

USES Ronjh provides
invaluable dry-season
fodder and pasture for
herdsmen in the desert.
Its (smelly) inner bark
furnishes a red-brown
dye and fibre for cord-
age and fishing nets.
The leaves yield a black
dye. The bark is used to
distil liquor from palm-
sap. The astringent bark
and gum are used in
traditional medicine to
treat bronchitis and
biliousness and are
regarded as 'cooling'.
The sapwood is useless
but the brick-red heart-
wood is strong, hard
and heavy. It is not easy
to work but is valued
for strength in making
rural furniture, tools,
cartwheels, oil-presses,
posts and beams.

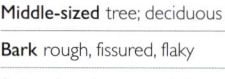

PHULAI *Acacia modesta*

black sally • amritsar gum

pea family – mimosa subfamily

phulai • phulahi • phala

Middle-sized tree; deciduous	
Bark rough, fissured, flaky	9 m
Spines in pairs, curved, deep maroon, shiny	

Leaves twice-feathered, with only 2-3 pairs of side-stalks and 3-6 pairs of broadly oval, greyish leaflets

Flowers tiny, white, clustered in short spikes

Fruit pods thin, flat, 5-8 cm long

LEAVES distinguished from other acacias by the broadly rounded ends of the leaflets. There are only 3-5 pairs of leaflets per side-stalk.

ends of leaflets rounded, widest near apex

A characteristic, thorny tree of hot, dry, stony hills in the Punjab and Afghanistan. The Yamuna marks the eastern edge of its range. Easily distinguished from other acacias by its pretty, rounded leaflets. It was once used to make the best armed hedges in the Punjab, but has nearly disappeared from Delhi.

spines in leaf axils, short and shiny

FLOWERS pale creamy-white, clustered in spikes 2-6 cm long. They appear when the tree is leafless and are faintly scented.

SEASONS - LEAVES shed in January, renewed in March. **FLOWERS** conspicuous in the first three weeks of April. **FRUIT** pods remain on the tree for very long, falling in December or January.

WHERE TO SEE IT Quite a few trees in Kamla Nehru Park on the N Ridge and a stand of about 10 trees in the C Ridge; one large tree in Buddha Jayanti Park. Becoming rare in Delhi.

KUMTTHA *Acacia senegal*

gum arabic tree • senegal/sudan gum (arabic) • three-hook acacia
kumttha • kumatth • khor

pea family – mimosa subfamily

Small tree; deciduous

Bark pale, peeling thinly to reveal yellow underbark

Spines curved, usually in 3s; outer 2 spines straight or only slightly curved upwards, the middle one strongly hooked downwards

Leaves twice-feathered, small; main leaf stalk downy, dividing into 3-5 pairs of side-stalks; leaflets tiny, 8-15 pairs, with rounded ends, pale green

Flowers creamy white, tiny, clustered in spikes

Fruit pods broad, flat, dark brown, up to 7.5 cm long

LEAVES relatively small, even for an acacia. Only 3-5 pairs of side-stalks, with up to 15 pairs of leaflets.

A small, crooked, thorny tree 3-5 m tall, with an open crown and smooth, yellowish bark. It is the only acacia in Delhi with spines in 3s. Superbly adapted to dry, stony hills, kumttha is becoming very scarce in Delhi. It is confined today to the Mehrauli-Asola part of the Ridge.

BARK greenish grey, peeling in characteristic papery flakes to reveal new yellow bark.

the only acacia in Delhi with spines arranged in 3s

SEASONS - LEAVES shed in December, trees bare till new leaf in May. **FLOWERS** in late May or early June; fresh pulses in the rains. **FRUIT** pods remain for many months, dropping in March-April in the year following flowering.

WHERE TO SEE IT Most abundant on the N Ridge. Occasional on S-C Ridge – in undisturbed parts of Mehrauli, the JNU campus and Asola-Bhatti Sanctuary. Completely absent from the C Ridge.

'TRUE' GUM ARABIC

Kumttha yields 'gum arabic', a tasteless gum that was once a major article of commerce. Tapped by the Egyptians 4000 years ago, gum arabic found extensive use in the printing trade, as an adhesive, in inks and paints, for giving lustre to silk and crepe, and in pharmaceuticals. It is still a major ingredient in processed foods.

KHAIR *Acacia catechu*

black cutch tree • catechu • black catechu

khair • khair babool

pea family – mimosa subfamily

5 m

Smallish tree; deciduous

Bark deeply cracked and flaky, lifting off the trunk in narrow, rectangular plates

Spines curved, with a long base; always in pairs; young spines reddish and shiny

Leaves twice-feathered; leaflets tiny, 30-50 pairs, minutely hairy. Conspicuous gland near base of leaf stalk, several more further up, between side-stalks

Flowers tiny, clustered on long 'pipe-cleaner' spikes, cream or the palest yellow; stamens prominent

Fruit small, flat pods, pointy at ends, with an irregular outline; in clusters

PODS 4-9 cm long. Young pods are magenta at first, go through a green phase, then turn buff or dark golden-brown.

A thorny deciduous tree with a thin, feathery crown and flaky, rough bark. Mature trees are invariably crooked and seldom attain more than 6 m in Delhi. A native Delhi tree, adapted to harsh conditions on the Ridge where it sometimes forms dense stands. Nowhere cultivated in parks or as an avenue tree.

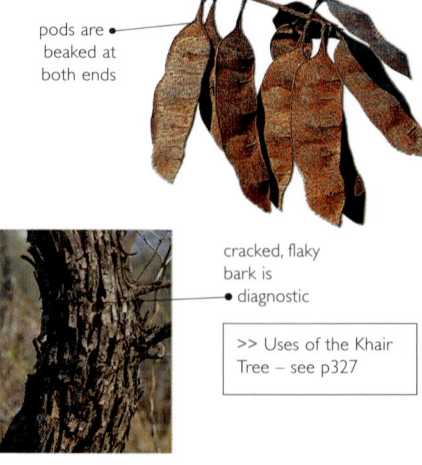

pods are beaked at both ends

• spines hooked, with a broad base

cracked, flaky bark is • diagnostic

>> Uses of the Khair Tree – see p327

SEASONS - LEAVES shed in January; trees bare till new leaves appear late in May. **FLOWERS** soon after the new leaves, lasting till July or a little later. **FRUIT** pods form by August-September and last through winter till March.

WHERE TO SEE IT Scattered on the C and S Ridge, but nearly eliminated from the N Ridge. There are no khair trees in any of Delhi's parks or avenues, so far as I can tell.

CAN BE CONFUSED WITH

Jhand, which also has cracked, flaky bark. But jhand has only 1-3 side-stalks and far fewer leaflets. The spines are also reliable clues: khair spines are more curved, with broader bases and a greater flared angle between the pair than any other Delhi acacia. (See pages 284-85 for key.)

SICKLE BUSH *Dichrostachys cinerea*

sickle bush • chinese lantern tree • kalahari christmas tree • marabou thorn

pea family – mimosa subfamily

bilatri • bartuli • goya-khair • khairi • kolai • kunlai

Bush or small tree; deciduous

Bark thin, ashy grey or pale brown, vertically fissured

Spines at branch ends, of varying lengths; longer spines are often leaf-bearing

Leaves twice-feathered, 6 or 7 cm long with up to 15 pairs of side-stalks and numerous pairs of tiny, crowded, stalkless leaflets

Flowers tiny, tightly packed together in spikes 6-9 cm long; those at base are fluffy pink; terminal end of spike has bright-yellow flowers

Fruit pods thin, tightly coiled and twisted

FLOWERS of 2 kinds - the pink flowers with long filaments, closest to the stalk, are all sterile. Their role is probably to attract insect pollinators. The yellow flowers towards the apex are fertile, with shorter stamens.

A small, multi-stemmed tree up to 3 m – often just a bush – with feathery acacia-like foliage. Its striking pink and yellow flower spikes, appearing early in the rains, serve to identify it immediately. A native deciduous tree, found only in dry, rocky parts of the Ridge. Not cultivated anywhere in the city.

FRUIT PODS russet brown, coiled and often intertwined. They do not split open on the tree.

fluffy pink flowers, all sterile. They will fade to white

yellow flowers with shorter stamens are bisexual, fertile

SEASONS - LEAVES very thin or lost by January; a weak flush of new leaves in March, quickly subsiding. Fresh leaves in early June. **FLOWERS** June to September, sometimes triggered by early rains. **FRUIT** pods remain for very long, eventually falling between January and March.

WHERE TO SEE IT Only on the C Ridge and certain parts of the S Ridge, where it is localized in small patches. The only plant I have seen outside the Ridge is near Gate no.8 of the Chinese embassy on Shanti Path.

CAN BE CONFUSED WITH

The ronjh, when not in flower, but the absence of paired spines in the sickle bush is a way of telling them apart.

JHAND *Prosopis cineraria*

Syn: Prosopis spicigera

no english common name

pea family – mimosa subfamily

Jhand • jat • chaunkra • sangri • khar • sheh • shami • kanda • khejdi

Medium-sized tree; deciduous

Bark ashy, deeply fissured

Twigs reddish when young

Spines solitary, with a conical base; scattered on twigs

Leaves twice-feathered, with 1-3 pairs of side-stalks; leaflets 7-12 pairs, small, pointy

Flowers tiny, yellow, densely clustered on spikes

Fruit pods long and slender, cylindrical

SPINES short, solitary, straight or only slightly hooked. Large ones have a conical base. The prickles are scattered sparsely along the twigs.

unlike other species of *Prosopis*, spines are solitary, not paired

A thorny desert tree with deeply fissured bark and feathery, grey-green foliage that droops delicately from the ends of branches. Superbly adapted to Delhi's ecology, this is a characteristic native tree of the region, though it struggles in the thin soil of the Ridge. It is not cultivated anywhere in the city and is in real danger of disappearing.

SEASONS - LEAVES shed in January; new leaves by late February or early March, bright green at first, turning grey-green. **FLOWERS** late March to early May. Often a second flush after the rains. **FRUIT** ripen sometime between May and August (depending on when it flowered).

WHERE TO SEE IT Scarce on the Ridge except in the Jaunapur ravines. Fairly common in places where remnants of Delhi's original flora persist: Hauz Khas District Park, Lodi Garden, Delhi Golf Club, the area behind Santushti in Chanakyapuri. Max Mueller Marg has 4 prominent relict trees near the crossing with Lodi Road.

LEAVES twice-feathered, dividing into only 1-3 pairs of side-stalks, 7-12 pairs of small, oblong leaflets on each side-stalk. Leaflets have a minuscule point at their tips and are faintly marked with 2-3 main nerves. Compared to thin acacia leaflets, these ones appear almost fleshy.

the leaves start out salad green, then turn grey-green

FLOWERS yellow to creamy, very small, clustered in 'pipe-cleaner' spikes up to 13 cm long. If you look at the tiny flowers with a hand lens, you can just make out the 10 stamens and miniature petals. Eagerly visited by bees.

tips of the petals curl backwards as they age

HABITAT A quintessential tree of arid regions that receive less than 75 cm of annual rain. Remarkably adaptable, tolerating alkaline soil and salt concentrations up to half that of the sea. The tree finds water with the help of an enormous taproot penetrating vertically to 30 m or more.

RANGE Follows the desert from Arabia into NW and W India; also in dry tracts in C and S India. Once the principal tree of remnant forests in the Punjab, but has retreated with the spread of irrigation.

GALLS – curious misshapen growths on long stalks easily mistaken for fruit. Galls are produced by insect infestation and appear to do no harm to the tree.

FRUIT a slender, stalked pod 8-20 cm long, more or less cylindrical, smooth, green at first, turning dull brown. The pods curl lazily as they elongate but can sometimes grow fairly straight.

the pods are filled with a dry, mealy pulp

USES A vital resource in arid regions. The sweetish bark can be ground into flour and saved lives in the Great Rajputana Famine of 1868-69. It forms part of an ancient agro-forestry system (with millets) in the desert. It provides nutritious fodder and the pods are cooked and eaten in Rajasthan. The pale timber is threaded with beautiful wavy lines and is used to make boats, houses, carts and furniture. The bark is used medicinally to treat a range of maladies from asthma, leucoderma, leprosy, muscular tremors, even 'wandering of the mind'. Jhand is deeply revered in the desert.

BARK ashy grey or brown, extremely rough, with deep, vertical fissures and cracks, becoming even more pronounced in older trees.

CAN BE CONFUSED WITH

The exotic mesquites (vilaiti keekar and honey mesquite), which belong to the same genus (*Prosopis*). Easily separated from them by the spines, which are short, solitary and randomly scattered in jhand; the spines are long, paired and always grow from leaf axils in the mesquites. (See pages 284-85 for key.)

VILAITI KEEKAR *Prosopis juliflora*

mesquite • algarroba (or algarrobo) • southwest thorn

pea family – mimosa subfamily

vilaiti keekar/babool • *angrezi/kabuli keekar* • (misleadingly) *keekar*

Bush or medium-sized tree; deciduous

Young branchlets zigzag

Bark ruddy brown with long, vertical fissures and ridges

Spines in pairs, straight, arising from leaf axils

Leaves twice-feathered, with only 1-2 pairs of side-stalks and numerous crowded, blunt leaflets

Flowers tiny, greenish yellow, crowded on narrow spikes

Fruit pods flattish, straw-coloured, slightly curved

A medium-sized, thorny tree or straggling bush with crooked main branches and a spreading, feathery canopy. First introduced from S America on to the Ridge around 1915, it is superbly adapted to Delhi's ecology and has become the city's most common tree by edging out many native species. It is now a serious pest.

LEAVES twice-feathered, the main leaf stalk branching only once or twice (rarely three times). If you look closely, the main leaf stalk is prolonged beyond the last pair of side-stalks into a minute bristle. The leaflets are small (6-19 mm), rounded at both ends, up to 26 pairs crowded on each side-stalk.

zigzag branchlets

SEASONS - **LEAVES** shed early in January, renewed between late January and early March. New leaves pale green, darkening gradually. Another less dramatic flush of new leaves in the rains. **FLOWERING** from mid March to late April; another cycle of flowering just after the rains. **FRUIT** ripen April-May, also in late October, November.

WHERE TO SEE IT Almost everywhere in the city and its surroundings. Mehrauli, for example, is now a sea of vilaiti keekar when seen from above. By far the dominant tree in all parts of Delhi Ridge and in many parks – even though it is no longer cultivated.

tiny bristle at end of leaf stalk

the leaflets have no stalks of their own

FLOWERS pale to greenish yellow, very small, clustered in long spikes like 'pipe-cleaners' 4-10 cm long, arising from leaf axils. The spikes may be solitary or in groups of 2-4. They are mildly fragrant and are visited by bees.

unopened green flower buds

FRUIT a flattish pod 12-25 cm long, variable in shape, usually curved to some degree. Pale green when young, ripening straw-yellow. Parakeets love them.

SPINES strong, straight, arising from leaf axils. Usually in pairs (sometimes of unequal length), occasionally solitary, 1-4 cm long, more prominent on young branchlets. Rarely, spines may be completely absent.

> >> 'Keekar' or 'Vilaiti Keekar'? – see p327
> American Species of *Prosopis* in Delhi – see p333

BARK rich brown, rufous when chipped, ridged and fissured in very long, vertical strips. The bark sometimes appears to twist up the tree in a lazy spiral.

CAN BE CONFUSED WITH

The other 2 species of *Prosopis* in Delhi – jhand and honey mesquite.

Vilaiti keekar is easily separated from jhand by the difference in their spines – paired and axillary in the former, solitary and randomly scattered along twigs in jhand.

Honey mesquite has its leaflets spaced conspicuously further apart than those of vilaiti keekar.

(See pages 284-85 for a key to the different species of spiny mimosas in Delhi.)

HABITAT Superbly adapted to drought, heat and poor soils, vilaiti keekar is an aggressive colonizer. It obliterated Asia's biggest grassland in the Rann of Kutch. Planted on the Delhi Ridge early last century, it edged out most native trees. It does not tolerate high rainfall or waterlogging.

RANGE Native to dry, coastal parts of Mexico, Columbia, Venezuela and the Caribbean. Introduced widely in Africa, Asia and Australia, it has become the most widespread tree of all in hot, arid regions. It is rampant in dry tracts in India.

USES Mesquite flour is among the earliest known foods of prehistoric man in the Americas. Foliage and pods make good animal fodder. Valued for firewood and fodder in ecologically poor tracts, thus a vital resource for poor desert-dwelling people. Various parts are used in folk medicine to cure a range of ailments including 'superfluous flesh'. Its pale sapwood is useless but the heavy, strong heart-wood is used for tools, crushers, fence posts and cheap furniture. It also makes high-quality charcoal and is prized as a barbecue fuel, imparting a subtle flavour to meats and fish.

GAINTI *Indopiptadenia oudhensis*

Syn: Piptadenia oudhensis

no english common name

gainti (in eastern UP); no local name

pea family – mimosa subfamily

An unusual tree from Nepal, Kumaon and eastern UP, not often cultivated, with a short trunk dividing early and young shoots bearing large, conical prickles. New leaves are blood red and very attractive. The flowers are clustered in 'pipe-cleaner' spikes. Only a single cultivated specimen found in Delhi.

Middle-sized tree; deciduous

Bark dark brown or dusky red, scaly, very rough

Leaves twice-feathered, with only 2 pairs of side-stalks; leaflets broad, in pairs, kidney-shaped, ends rounded

Flowers greenish yellow, in dense spikes up to 7 cm long [see pic below]

Fruit a long, flat pod up to 30 cm long

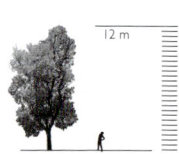

WHERE TO SEE IT Only a solitary specimen in the south-eastern periphery of Gandhiji's samadhi at Rajghat.

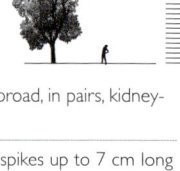

HONEY MESQUITE *Prosopis glandulosa*

honey mesquite

(loosely) *vilaiti keekar*

pea family – mimosa subfamily

A small, crooked tree easy to mistake for the other vilaiti keekar, but with longer leaflets spaced much more widely apart. The two species have hybridized and in-between forms are common. The honey mesquite itself is now very rare in Delhi. It is native to dry subtropical N America.

Smallish tree; deciduous

Bark reddish brown; thick, rough and deeply furrowed

Spines yellowish, stout, more commonly solitary, sometimes in pairs

Leaves twice-feathered, usually with just a single pair of side-stalks; leaflets spaced widely apart [see pic below]

Flowers tiny, clustered on long pipe-cleaner spikes

Fruit pods straw-yellow, curved, somewhat constricted between the seeds

WHERE TO SEE IT Qudsia Bagh has a lovely old specimen. I have found only one tree on the C Ridge that is unmistakenly a honey mesquite but there are many intermediate forms.

JERUSALEM THORN *Parkinsonia aculeata*

jerusalem thorn • horse-bean • mexican/blue palo verde • barbados flower fence   *pea family – cassia subfamily*
vilaiti babool • ram babool

Bush or small tree; deciduous

Bark green and smooth when young, becoming dark brown and fissured with age

Spines usually 3 at the base of the leaf, the central one long and stout, flanked by two smaller, weaker spines

Leaves twice-feathered; a very short main stalk (3-4 mm long) divides into 1-3 pairs of flat side-stalks up to 40 cm long; leaflets on either side numerous, tiny, 3-5 mm long

Flowers yellow, in loose clusters; 5 roundish petals - 4 petals alike, one larger, flecked with red dots at base

Fruit a slender, pointy pod 5-10 cm long, slightly narrowed between the seeds

FLOWERS bright yellow with a crinkly texture. Each flower has 4 petals that are roughly similar and a 5th that is conspicuously larger.

A large bush or small, thorny tree from dry subtropical America, with an irregular, sparse crown that casts little shade. Usually multi-stemmed from near its base, with slender, green limbs rising vertically but ultimately drooping at their extremities. An arresting sight early in April, when it is studded with masses of yellow flowers.

• the larger petal with red dots turns deep orange and folds forward after pollination

SEASONS - LEAVES shed in January; new leaves in March-April.
FLOWERS in late March, peaking by mid April and declining suddenly early in May. Flowers sporadically at odd times of the year, too.
FRUIT appear by mid May and ripen rapidly.

central • spine long and straight

only when you • look closely at the base of the leaf do you notice that it is twice-feathered

side-stalks very • long; leaflets tiny

WHERE TO SEE IT Sundar Nursery has a tree that flowers more profusely than most. Buddha Jayanti Park and the PBG grounds on the C Ridge have specimens. Planted on the outskirts of Delhi by forest departments.

COPING WITH DROUGHT

This tree shows a rare ability to deal with drought by shedding its tiny leaflets (to shut down water-loss) and even its twigs if severe drought persists. Its green bark continues the job of photosynthesis after every leaf has fallen.

JUNGLE JALEBI *Pithecellobium dulce*

madras thorn • manila tamarind • monkeypod • sweet inga • blackbead

pea family – mimosa subfamily

jungle jalebi • vilaiti imli • dakhani babool

Large tree; deciduous

Bark greyish, smooth on young trees, becoming rough and fissured

Spines short, paired, spreading, arising from leaf bases

Leaves twice-feathered, with only one pair of side-stalks, each with one pair of curving, blunt leaflets

Flowers in round, woolly clusters, with long, dirty white stamens

Fruit a slightly flattened pod, becoming tightly coiled as it matures; green tinged with red

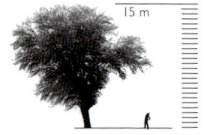

A spiny tree with a broad, spreading crown, commonly clipped down to form a dense, beautiful hedge. Its jalebi-like coiled fruit pods and grey bark with horizontal weals are diagnostic. Native to dry regions of tropical America, it was first brought by Spanish galleons to Asia long ago and has run wild in some parts of India.

FLOWERS appear in dense, woolly clusters of 7-25, forming a round 'head' at the end of a common flower stalk about 10 cm long. The tiny petals are green, but the most obvious feature of the flower is its long, untidy, soiled white stamens, about 40-50 per flower. The flowers have a faint aroma.

long, dirty white stamens

SEASONS - LEAVES begin to fall by late February when trees look conspicuously twiggy. New leaves coppery around late February to early March. FLOWERS from mid March to mid April. FRUIT ripen in June.

WHERE TO SEE IT Extremely common as a hedge, especially in Lutyens' Delhi where it was one of 3 prescribed hedgerow plants in official bunga-lows. You can see a fine, tall hedge around the park in front of 25 Sardar Patel Marg. Qudsia Bagh has large, old trees; so does Jorbagh Market, near the tennis courts. Planted along vil-lage roads near the Yamuna, south of Delhi.

SPINES in pairs, short, straight, spreading, at the base of each leaf. Sometimes absent.

small, lumpy glands at the base of the side-stalks and the junction of the leaflets

MAIN LEAF STALK divides only once, and each side-stalk bears only a single pair of leaflets. There are thus always 4 leaflets in a leaf. The leaflets are a bit like the anjan's, slightly curved with an unequal-sided base and virtually no stalks. They are dull green, paler beneath, but attractively coppery when new. The main leaf stalk as well as the side-stalks end in tiny bristles.

HABITAT Jungle jalebi tolerates a wide range of soil conditions, including shallow, rocky soils. It generally grows on lowlands but also succeeds in hilly terrain up to an elevation of 900 m. It prefers full sun and up to 1500 mm rainfall, with a distinct dry season. It is drought-tolerant but frost-tender.

RANGE Native to seasonally dry tropical forests in America, from Mexico to Colombia and Venezuela. It was first introduced into the Philippines where it ran wild, and later to warmer and drier parts of India and Africa where it has also become naturalised and is sometimes a pest.

FRUIT pods about one cm wide, slightly flattened, straight at first, becoming tightly coiled as they elongate. The pods are noticeably pinched between the seeds. Starting green, they are gradually tinged red or pink until they dry to a reddish brown. After splitting open, the shiny black seeds hang from red threads (the stalks of the ovules) before falling.

large gland at base of side-stalks

fruit in red phase, nearly ripe

USES In C America, the pods are harvested for their sweetish pulp which is either eaten raw or roasted or made into a lemonade-like drink. The leaves and pods are an excellent animal fodder. Various uses in folk medicine are reported but are not known in India. It makes an excellent 'living fence' that can withstand any amount of coppicing. The wood – a little stinky when freshly cut – has yellowish sapwood and red-brown heartwood. It is hard, heavy and strong but not all that easy to work. It is mostly used for agricultural implements, crates and cheap furniture.

BARK slate grey and relatively smooth on young trees, becoming cracked and fissured when old. The horizontal weals on the trunk are distinctive.

CAN BE CONFUSED WITH

The anjan, whose leaflets have a similar shape. The difference is that the anjan leaf is only 1-pinnate, with 2 leaflets, while jungle jalebi is 2-pinnate and has 4 leaflets.

A KEY TO
DELHI'S SPINY MIMOSAS

Delhi has 12 spiny trees in the subfamily of mimosas, which can be difficult to tell apart. It takes a little practice, but here is a handy guide to separating them by the size and shape of their spines alone. Other defining characters are summarized on the following page.

SPINES IN PAIRS

LONG, STRAIGHT SPINES

BABOOL spines are brown or ivory white, up to 5 cm long, wide apart.

ISRAELI BABOOL has BOTH long, white spines and short, brown, curved spines.

SHORT, STRAIGHT SPINES

RONJH spines are long and reddish on young stems; more usually, short and brown.

SWEET ACACIA spines are short, dark brown; occasionally also long and white.

JUNGLE JALEBI has small spines with flared bases.

VILAITI KEEKAR spines are pale or dark brown, short and stout.

CURVED SPINES

KHAIR spines are hooked, with broad bases. Red and shiny on young twigs.

PHULAI spines are short, shiny, maroon, and hooked.

SPINES SINGLE

SICKLE BUSH spines are modified twigs, up to 10 cm long.

HONEY MESQUITE spines are very long. Rarely, in pairs.

JHAND spines are short, with broad conical bases.

SPINES IN THREES

KUMTTHA has a central curved spine; 2 outer ones less so.

Defining characters

* Flowers in round heads, yellow

BABOOL *Acacia nilotica* pp268-69 **DARK BARK**, deeply fissured. Flower heads bright yellow, about 12 mm in diameter (July-September). Pods **VELVETY**, more **PROMINENTLY BEADED** than any other Delhi mimosa, 7-15 cm long.

SWEET ACACIA *Acacia farnesiana* p267 Bark brown, **STUDDED WITH LITTLE LENTICELS**. Flower heads **GOLDEN** yellow, more orange than babool's, about 15 mm in diameter (February-March). Pods black, thick, nearly **CYLINDRICAL**, 4-8 cm long.

* Flowers in round heads, white or creamy

RONJH *Acacia leucophloea* pp270-71 **BARK YELLOWISH WHITE**, blotched with black, darkening with age. Flowers in **CREAMY WHITE HEADS**, 8-9 mm in diameter, at **ENDS OF TWIGS** (August-October). Pods **FLAT, VELVETY, KHAKI**, not beaded; sometimes curly; 10-20 cm long.

ISRAELI BABOOL *Acacia tortilis* p267 Bark dark, reddish brown. Flower **HEADS WHITE**, about 10 mm in diameter (July-August). Pods **CURLED**, **TWISTED**, 8-12 cm long.

JUNGLE JALEBI *Pithecellobium dulce* pp282-83 Bark grey, with **HORIZONTAL WEALS**. Leaves have only a **SINGLE PAIR OF SIDE-STALKS**, each with **2 LEAFLETS**. Flowers pale whitish-green, with **LONG, UNTIDY STAMENS** (March-April). Pods narrow, flattened and **CURLED**; **PINK** or greenish.

* Flowers in spikes; leaves with only 2 or 3 pairs of side-stalks

VILAITI KEEKAR *Prosopis juliflora* pp278-79 **TWIGS ZIGZAG**. Bark **RUFOUS BROWN, IN LONG, FISSURED STRIPS**. Flowers greenish yellow, spikes 4-10 cm long (March-April; September). Pods **FLATTISH**, straight or slightly curved, **WEAKLY BEADED**, pale yellow when ripe, 12-25 cm long.

JHAND *Prosopis cinerarea* pp276-77 Bark thick, **ASHY, DEEPLY CRACKED**. Foliage greyish when mature. Flowers **YELLOW**, spikes longer than vilaiti keekar's (April-May). Pods **CYLINDRICAL, SLENDER**, pale yellow; often **SLIGHTLY CURLED**; up to 25 cm long.

HONEY MESQUITE *Prosopis glandulosa* p280 Bark rough, pale or dark brown. Flowers yellow, in narrow spikes up to 8 cm long (April-May). Pods **STRAIGHT**, straw-yellow when ripe; very **SLIGHTLY BEADED** towards the apex; 8-20 cm long.

PHULAI *Acacia modesta* p272 Bark dark brown, rough. Leaves with **SMALL, BROADLY OVAL** leaflets. Flowers creamy white, in **SHORT SPIKES** up to 6 cm long (April). Pods flat, smooth, biscuit-brown, with a triangular apex; up to 7 cm long.

* Flowers in spikes; leaves with many pairs of side-stalks

KHAIR *Acacia catechu* p274 Bark brown, deeply cracked, **LIFTING OFF IN SMALL RECTANGULAR FLAKES**. Leaves with **NUMEROUS SIDE-STALKS AND LEAFLETS**; main **LEAF STALK HAIRY, OFTEN PRICKLY**. Flowers white, in slender spikes up to 12 cm long (May-June). Pods flat, brown, with wavy margins.

SICKLE BUSH *Dichrostachys cinerea* p275 Bark pale brown, with shallow grooves. Leaflets very **SMALL, CROWDED**, leaf stalks hairy. **FLOWER SPIKES OF 2 COLOURS** – fluffy pink filaments at base, shorter yellow filaments at tip (June-September). Pods **RUSTY BROWN, NARROW, TWISTED, COILED**.

KUMTTHA *Acacia senegal* p273 Bark **GREENISH GREY**, peeling thinly to expose **YELLOW UNDERBARK**. Foliage greyish green. Flower spikes white, **NOT VERY CROWDED**, up to 12 cm long (May-June). Pods thin, flat, pale brown, with pointy apex; broader than khair pods; 5-8 cm long.

SIRIS *Albizia lebbeck*

koko • east indian walnut • frywood • shack shack • rattlepod • lebbeck
siris • siras • sirish • sirin • sirar • kalshish • tantia

pea family – mimosa subfamily

Middle-sized tree; deciduous

Bark rough but not deeply fissured, biscuit-brown

Leaves twice-feathered with only a few pairs of side-stalks; each side-stalk has 3-10 pairs of leaflets

Flowers fragrant with long, greenish-yellow stamens

Fruit pods up to 30 cm long, flat, straw-coloured when ripe

12 m

FLOWERS grouped in 2-4 long-stalked 'heads', each one with up to 40 hemispheric 'powder-puff' flowers. The most prominent part of a flower is its long, silken stamens, whitish or yellow tipped with green. The petals are insignificant.

An unarmed mimosa with a shortish bole and thin, spreading crown. It bears fragrant 'powder-puff' flowers with long, greenish-yellow stamens and is festooned for many months with straw-coloured pods that clatter noisily in the slightest breeze. A common street tree, especially in newer areas of Delhi, and naturalized now on the Ridge.

'powder-puffs' are formed by the stamens of lots of little flowers tightly clustered together

the central flower in each cluster is slightly larger than the others

SEASONS - LEAVES start dropping in January; bare till late March, when new leaf begins. **FLOWERS** early in April, spent by May; new flushes are triggered by showers in June and July. **FRUIT** pods start turning yellow in November, and remain through winter till March or even later.

WHERE TO SEE IT A common avenue tree in newer areas of Delhi but conspicuously absent in Lutyens' Delhi – probably due to a stated bias against deciduous trees. Moti Bagh has many trees. So do most parks and gardens and it is now more or less naturalized on the Ridge and in JNU campus as a scattered tree.

LEAVES twice-feathered, up to 25 cm long, forking into 2-4 pairs of side-stalks. Each side-stalk bears 3-10 pairs of leaflets, about 5 cm long and distinctly asymmetrical. Look for a small, circular gland near the base of the leaf stalk – there is usually another gland between the topmost pair of side-stalks.

the midrib lies closer to one edge, creating an asymmetrical base

leaflets are very shortly stalked

prominent circular gland at base of stalk

FRUIT flat, straw-coloured pods 20-30 cm long. Most common names of the tree (shack shack, frywood…) allude to the sound of the dry pods rustling in the breeze. The way in which the papery pod ripples over the seeds is characteristic.

BARK varies from pale biscuity-brown to dark brown or grey. Rough and textured with short, irregular cracks, looking patchy. The inner bark is startlingly red.

pattern of lenticels shows up on young bark

CAN BE CONFUSED WITH

The doon siris because of the similarity of their leaves, but the smooth, creamy-yellow bark of the doon siris is a reliable means of telling them apart.

HABITAT Reaching up for sunlight in a dense stand, siris can grow to 30 m. In open situations it branches early, spreads out and remains moderate-sized. It likes 60-250 cm of annual rain but tolerates drier conditions. It has a shallow root system and is liable to be blown down in a high wind. Quick-growing but relatively short-lived.

RANGE Moist and dry forests in India, Myanmar and the Andamans, extending into SE Asia and N Australia. The Indus forms the western limit of its range.

USES Widely planted as an avenue tree and to provide shade to coffee, tea and cardamom. The seeds have a reputation in folk medicine as a remedy for leprosy. The leaves make an excellent fodder and the flowers are a rich source of nectar. The white sapwood is useless but the rich, dark heartwood is beautifully mottled and streaked. It is tough, heavy, takes a good polish and in the early 1900s was exported in considerable quantity to Europe as 'East Indian walnut' or 'koko'. Its value as a fine cabinet wood has largely been forgotten but it is still used for sugarcane crushers, oil mills and well curbs. Carpenters dislike working the wood because its peppery sawdust causes uncontrollable sneezing.

KRISHNA SIRIS *Albizia amara* subsp. *amara*

bitter albizia • wheel tree

krishna siris

pea family – mimosa subfamily

11 m

Middle-sized tree; deciduous

Bark grey, scaly, grainy

Twigs densely furry when young

Leaves twice-feathered, up to 15 pairs of side-stalks; leaflets tiny, crowded, 15-35 pairs

Flowers whitish-yellow powder puffs; stamens long

Fruit flat pods, brown, up to 20 cm long

A middle-sized tree with a feathery canopy, easily mistaken for an acacia except that it is unarmed. Its leaflets and powder-puff flowers are the smallest of any Delhi albizia. Native to drier parts of S India, where it is a common tree on low hills, and to parts of Africa. Uncommon in Delhi.

FLOWERS faintly fragrant, closely packed into spherical heads 1.5-3 cm in diameter. The long, white stamens are the most prominent part of the flower.

long stamens tipped with golden pollen

SEASONS - **LEAVES** thin out in February-March; renewed in early April, with another flush in the rains. **FLOWERS** last through most of May. **FRUIT** ripen in October-November.

WHERE TO SEE IT Nehru Park and Talkatora Garden (in the open-air stage) have some large, old trees. 4 or 5 trees line the road near Ber Sarai, relicts of earlier planting. Some trees near the office of the deputy conservator of forests on Mandir Lane.

FRUIT PODS greyish brown with slightly wavy margins. You can clearly see the seeds as little bumps in the flat pods.

DOON SIRIS *Albizia procera*

white siris • tall albizia

pea family – mimosa subfamily

doon siris • safed siris • karra • karak • karo

Middle-sized tree; deciduous

Bark creamy yellow, often tinged green; scored with horizontal ridges or wavy lines

Leaves twice-feathered, about 40 cm long, forking into 2-6 pairs of side-stalks; 6-16 pairs of large, blunt leaflets on each side-stalk

Flowers small, yellowish-white powder-puffs, 12-20 clustered together to form a 'head'; threadlike stamens conspicuous, shorter than most albizias

Fruit pods thin, flat, 10-18 cm long, ripening rich rufous-brown

A slender albizia with distinctively pale-yellow bark and a light, open crown. It does not grow very tall in Delhi but still manages to look leggy. Few large parks in the city are without a doon siris. Native to moist, swampy places in the sub-Himalayan terai, it is uncomfortable in Delhi's dry climate.

LEAFLETS relatively large, on tiny stalklets of their own. The midrib runs closer to the lower margin, making the base asymmetrical. There is usually a prominent, circular gland near the base of the leaf stalk, and one or 2 oval glands between the uppermost pair of side-stalks.

SEASONS - LEAVES shed in January; trees remain bare for many months, till April. **FLOWERS** sometime between July and early September. **FRUIT** pods form quickly, turn reddish in December and are shed between March and April.

distinctive bark of the doon siris

large, oval gland near junction of side-stalks

WHERE TO SEE IT Shanti Vana has a dense grove of doon siris. Most parks such as Lodi Garden and Kamla Nehru Park have specimens. Not seen in Delhi as a street tree, except inside JNU campus and on André Malraux Marg in Chanakyapuri.

CAN BE CONFUSED WITH

The siris, but only if you shut your eyes to the pale-yellow bark of the doon siris. Another useful clue: the midrib in the siris leaflet runs closer to the upper margin. In the doon siris, the midrib lies closer to the lower margin.

POTKA SIRIS *Albizia lucidior*

no english common name

no local name. *potka siris* (assamese)

pea family – mimosa subfamily

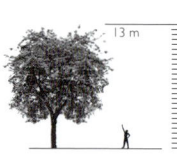

Medium-sized tree; deciduous

Bark grey, not very rough, with faint horizontal wrinkles

Leaves twice-feathered with only one pair of side-stalks, rarely 2; leaflets 2-3 pairs, the terminal pair largest; cup-shaped gland at base of leaf stalk

Flowers small, white 'powder-puffs', clustered in heads

Fruit pods flat, deep brown, up to 25 cm long [see pic below]

A good-looking albizia with small powder-puff flowers that are unmistakably siris-like. Its large compound leaves are distinctive, forking into 1-2 pairs of side-stalks, with very few leaflets. Native to moist forests in NE India, Nepal and parts of SE Asia, it struggles in Delhi's climate.

WHERE TO SEE IT Not at all common – one tree in Nehru Park; 2 more specimens inside Sundar Nursery.

MOLUCCA ALBIZIA *Paraserianthes falcataria*

molucca albizia • indonesia albizia • white albizia

no local name

pea family – mimosa subfamily

Large tree; deciduous

Bark light grey, silvery or yellowish, somewhat warty

Leaves twice-feathered, up to 30 cm long, with 4-6 pairs of side-stalks, each with 15-20 pairs of small, stalkless leaflets, blunt at both ends

Flowers small, white, siris-like, with long, untidy, threadlike stamens; clustered in heads

Fruit a flat, red-brown pod, about 10 cm long

A tall, unarmed tree with feathery foliage with the reputation of being one of the fastest-growing trees in the world. In general appearance similar to the siris but it has been hived off from genus *Albizia*. Native to Papua New Guinea, the Moluccas and some Pacific islands. Rare in Delhi.

WHERE TO SEE IT Only one tree just inside the perimeter fence of Humayun's Tomb, seen from the new parking lot.

SUBABOOL *Leucaena leucocephala*

white popinac • lead tree • horse/wild tamarind • jumbie bean • ipil ipil
subabool

pea family – mimosa subfamily

Medium-sized tree; deciduous

Bark smooth, brown, with vertical lines of orange lenticels; rough on older stems

Leaves twice-feathered, side-stalks 4-9 pairs; leaflets smooth, opposite, 10-26 pairs, without stalks; grey-green, paler beneath, dull; rounded and unequal at base, pointy

Flowers white or creamy; very tiny, about 150 massed together in spherical clusters 2 cm wide; each cluster borne at the end of a long stalk

Fruit a flat pod, up to 18 cm long; glossy reddish-brown; in clusters

PODS hold roughly 20 seeds in separate cells. About 4 months after the flowers are fertilized, the pods dry out and split open to disgorge ripe seeds.

A thornless, drought-hardy mimosa native to C America with a thin, airy canopy, variable in height and form. Once touted as a miracle green manure and fodder tree, its reputation has slipped somewhat. Often planted in waste places where it self-seeds and grows densely. The clusters of white flowers sometimes appear twice a year.

● seed com-partments

SEASONS - LEAVES thin out in January; new leaves in early March. **FLOWERS** in late March; sometimes a second flush after the rains. **FRUIT** ripen between January and February, splitting open on the tree.

WHERE TO SEE IT 2 fairly large trees inside the Sabz Burj roundabout; many planted along Ring Road in front of Ferozeshah Kotla and on Aurobindo Marg near Hauz Khas flyover. Hauz Rani City Forest has many trees.

vertical lines of ● orange lenticels

CAN BE CONFUSED WITH

The ronjh, whose leaves and leaflets are deceptively similar. Subabool, of course, has no spines.

COPPERPOD *Peltophorum pterocarpum* <small>Syn: *P. ferrugineum*</small>

copperpod • rusty shield bearer • yellow gulmohur/poinciana/flamboyant
peeli gulmohar • arjunjyoti

pea family – cassia subfamily

Middle-sized tree; deciduous

Bark silvery grey, studded with raised dots

Leaves twice-feathered, with 12-15 pairs of side-stalks; 10-30 pairs of leaflets on each side-stalk; apex of leaflets notched

Flowers bright yellow, fragrant, in dense, upright clusters; 5 petals, with crinkly texture

Fruit pods in conspicuous clusters, coppery or rusty

14 m

FLOWERS faintly scented, on long, upright stalks growing at the ends of branchlets. The buds are bronzy green on the outside, starting to open from the base upwards. Each flower is about 5 cm wide with 5 bright-yellow petals like crumpled tissue paper. The flowers last only a short time, carpeting the ground richly with gold.

An umbrella-shaped tree with a dark, dense canopy that grows regally large in moist coastal forests but is noticeably spindly in Delhi. Native to E Asia and the Andamans, it is cultivated chiefly for its abundant crinkly yellow flowers. The common name derives from the flat, coppery pods which remain on the tree for many months.

10 orange-tipped stamens

texture of petals like crumpled tissue paper

base of petals furred with dark, rusty hairs

SEASONS - LEAVES shed by mid February. New leaves towards late March. FLOWERS in two distinct flushes: in May-June, then again after the rains, from early September to October. FRUIT appear soon after the flowers, remaining for a long time.

WHERE TO SEE IT A fairly long stretch of Ring Road from the SPA towards Rajghat is planted with copperpods. Most large parks, gardens and a few traffic roundabouts have specimens.

leaflets notched at apex

unequal at base

HABITAT A tree of open lowland forests with a marked preference for coastal beaches and the inner margins of mangrove forests. Delhi is too dry to be an ideal habitat for this tree, but provided there is adequate moisture, the copperpod prefers a pronounced dry season and a monsoon climate.

RANGE Within India, it is truly native only in the Andamans. Its range extends eastwards from Sri Lanka through the Malay Peninsula, Vietnam, Indonesia and the Philippines into Northern Australia.

USES A dye extracted from the bark is used in Java to colour batik yellow-brown. The bark is high in tannins and is used for tanning leather and in preserving and dyeing fishing nets. In E Asian folk medicine, the bark is employed for curing intestinal disorders and externally as a lotion to treat sprains, muscular aches and as eye lotion, gargle and tooth powder. The leaves make a nutritious fodder. The tree is a host of the lac insect. The pale sapwood is not useful but the light reddish-brown heartwood is moderately heavy and fine-textured and is used in SE Asia for making quality furniture. It is also resistant to insect attack but the timber does not appear to be used in India at all.

LEAVES twice-feathered, 25 cm or more long. The main stalk divides into 6-20 pairs of side-stalks, commonly 12-15. Each side-stalk has 10-30 pairs of small leaflets, attached without any stalks of their own. Light green at first, darkening gradually on top, while the undersides remain pale. They are dull, with little or no shine.

FRUIT pods ripen the colour of old copper or rufous brown, in large, conspicuous clusters. The pods are pointy at both ends with a short 'wing' along the edges. They are slightly sticky to the touch and are studded with tiny raised dots, like braille.

look for a short, stiff 'wing' along both margins

BARK silvery in general effect, studded with little round black lenticels. Not very rough when young, becoming increasingly cracked with age.

CAN BE CONFUSED WITH

The closely related African wattle (page 294). The main differences are:

Copperpod	African wattle
Leaves dark green on top; leaflets notched at apices; stipules (at base of main leaf stalk) unbranched. **Flowers** deep yellow; petals with rusty hairs at base; petals wide, overlapping.	**Leaves** paler green on top; leaflets end in a tiny, sharp point, not notched; stipules branched, like tiny antlers. **Flowers** pale yellow; white hairs at base of petals, which are narrow, not overlapping.

AFRICAN WATTLE *Peltophorum africanum*

african/weeping wattle • rhodesian wattle • huilboom

pea family – cassia subfamily

peeli gulmohur

Medium-sized tree; deciduous

Bark smooth at first; grey-brown, with shallow, vertical fissures on older trees

Leaves twice-feathered, dividing into 4-14 pairs of side-stalks; leaflets up to 23 pairs, ending in a tiny point; stipules delicate, branching antler-like, falling early

Flowers pale yellow, scented, in upright clusters at ends of branchlets; 5 petals with a crinkly crepe texture

Fruit pods flat, in clusters; pointy at both ends, about 10 cm long; yellowish tan; margins with thin wings

FLOWERS are paler and have narrower petals than the copperpod. If you look closely, you can also see that these lack the rusty hairs at the base of the petals.

A striking, feathery-leaved tree with beautiful pale-yellow flowers, easily mistaken for Delhi's other *Peltophorum*, the copperpod. It takes a little practice to tell the two species apart but details of the leaflets and the paler colour of the flowers are reliable giveaways. This one is native to a large territory in west-central and southern Africa.

crinkly petals

SEASONS - LEAFLESS from late January to late March; leaves lovely in early May. FLOWERS in the rains, lasting till October. FRUIT mature by June of the year following flowering.

STIPULES (below left) at the base of the leaf are like delicate antlers. The leaflets (below right) end in a tiny point. (The copperpod has unbranched stipules and notched leaflets.)

WHERE TO SEE IT Interplanted among copperpods on Ring Road near the Ferozeshah Kotla; the IIC has a large tree near the parking gate; a good specimen on the slope up to Gandhiji's samadhi, and a few more in Shakti Sthal and Vir Bhumi. A large tree near the Moti Bagh rail flyover.

EARPOD TREE *Enterolobium contortisiliquum*

earpod tree • elephant ear • monkeysoap • timbo   *pea family – mimosa subfamily*

no local name

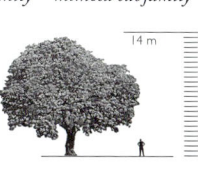

Middle-sized tree; deciduous

Bark brown, very rough, with vertical fissures

Leaves twice-feathered with many pairs of side-stalks; 10 or more pairs of small, pointy leaflets on each side-stalk; glands at junction of lowest and topmost side-stalks

Flowers white, in dense clusters; stamens long, numerous

Fruit an ear-shaped pod forming two-thirds of a circle, woody and black when ripe [pic below]

A spreading tree much broader than it is high, with a huge, squat trunk and fine, feathery foliage almost geometric in silhouette. An unmistakable relative of the raintree but with much smaller leaflets and more woolly, untidy flowers. Native to tropical S America and planted occasionally in Delhi for ornament.

WHERE TO SEE IT Lodi Garden has a magnificent specimen; Man Singh Road has a few relict trees on one side of Rajpath. Planted in Panchsheel Enclave, Najaf Khan's Tomb and outside Dilli Haat.

RED SANDALWOOD *Adenanthera microsperma*

red sandalwood • red bead tree • bead tree • coralwood • peacock tree   *pea family – mimosa subfamily*

raktakambal • ranjana • raktachandan

Middle-sized tree; deciduous

Bark brown or greyish, flaky

Leaves twice-feathered, about 30 cm long with 3-6 pairs of side-stalks; leaflets smooth, arranged alternately on the side-stalks, blunt at both ends

Flowers small, white to yellow, clustered in spikes

Fruit pods twisted when open, proudly displaying red seeds [pic below]

A large, unarmed tree that reaches only about 12 m in Delhi, with attractive twice-feathered leaves. It is particularly handsome in bloom, with small white and yellow flowers arranged on short spikes. Its bright-red, shiny seeds are unmistakable. Native to the sub-Himalayan tract and SE Asia. Not at all happy in Delhi.

WHERE TO SEE IT I have only seen 3 young trees in Buddha Jayanti Park and a few more trees near the Delhi Univ. nursery. Delhi is much too dry for this beautiful species.

GULMOHUR *Delonix regia*

flame tree • flamboyant • royal poinciana • gold mohr • firetree

gulmohur • gul mohr

pea family – cassia subfamily

Middle-sized tree; deciduous

Bark light brown; not rough

Leaves twice-feathered with 10-20 pairs of side-stalks; each one with up to 30 pairs of small, blunt leaflets

Flowers in loose clusters; 5 petals – 4 scarlet, one white splashed with scarlet and yellow

Fruit pods flat, woody, dark, up to 60 cm long

10 m

FLOWERS large and showy, up to 12 cm across, in loose, terminal clusters. A flower has 5 spoon-shaped petals, 4 of them vivid scarlet (of varying intensity), the 5th and largest white splashed with scarlet and yellow. The edges of the petals are delicately crinkled. The flower-cup too has 5 segments, lime green on the outside, looking lined with scarlet inside.

A familiar, ornamental tree with a spreading, sometimes flat-topped crown of thin, feathery foliage. Rated by some as one of the most beautiful of all flowering trees. It has all but disappeared from the wild in its original home in Madagascar but is one of the most extensively cultivated trees in tropical and subtropical climates worldwide.

SEASONS - LEAVES start to yellow in November. Trees are bare through February, most of March. New leaves in late March, early April. FLOWERS begin in late April, peaking in early May. Flowering is over by June but weaker flushes ripple through the rains. FRUIT pods persist for many months, often till March or April.

WHERE TO SEE IT Exceedingly common in all parts of Delhi except the Ridge. Gulmohur Park (surprise!) and Shanti Path have lots. Most parks and large gardens have specimens. Nehru Park has some trees that flower especially brilliantly.

10 stamens with red filaments

long, pointy segments of the flower-cup

the largest petal is white, streaked with red and yellow

HABITAT It prefers a warm climate with a pronounced dry season, especially near the sea. It flowers more profusely when watered regularly in the growing season but requires little or no water while it is dormant and leafless. It is not fussy about soils but will not withstand frost. It has a shallow root system and is not wind-firm. The ground beneath a gulmohur often becomes bare because its surface roots monopolize all nutrients and water.

LEAVES twice-feathered, up to 60 cm long, forming an airy canopy. A single leaf forks into 10 to 20 pairs of side-stalks. Each side-stalk bears up to 30 pairs of small, oblong, blunt-tipped leaflets.

leaflets attached directly, without little stalks of their own

feathery stipules at base of leaf stalk

FRUIT a flat pod up to 60 cm long, with a short beak. It starts out soft and green, turning dark and woody as it matures. A bit like a Ramleela scabbard.

RANGE First discovered as a lone specimen on the east coast of Madagascar around 1828, though its true home lay many miles inland in drier parts of the island. Cultivated initially in Mauritius, spreading from there to tropical and subtropical lands far and wide. Often mistaken as a West Indian tree because it does so well in the Caribbean. The earliest records of its cultivation in India are from Sewree, near Bombay, around 1840.

BARK light brown, not very rough, with prominent patterns of lenticels. Often creased at branch forks, like linen trousers rumpled behind the knee.

USES Primarily as a decorative tree. A water-soluble gum issues from wounds in the trunk but no one has thought of a good use for it! The seeds are sometimes strung together as ornamental beads. The yellowish wood is soft, brittle and coarse-grained, but takes a reasonably good polish.

CAN BE CONFUSED WITH

Colville's glory, whose thin, feathery leaves are deceptively similar. The two trees are easy to tell apart by their flowers, of course, but outside the flowering season, note that the bark of Colville's glory has a rusty or coppery tinge. Also, its tiny leaflets are distinctly stalked, unlike those of the gulmohur.

BRAZILIAN IRONWOOD *Caesalpinia ferrea*

brazilian ironwood • leopard tree • pau-ferro
no local name

pea family – cassia subfamily

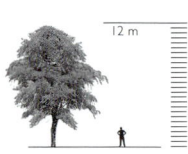

Middle-sized tree; deciduous

Bark smooth, dark, peeling to reveal white beneath

Branchlets very long, drooping

Leaves twice-feathered, with 2-4 pairs of side-stalks plus a terminal one; 4-5 pairs of broadly oval leaflets

Flowers small, fragrant, yellow, mostly near the top; standard petal is spotted with red

Fruit a thick, short pod; not seen in Delhi

A strikingly graceful, slender tree from E Brazil with delicate, feathery foliage on long, drooping branchlets. Easily recognized by its smooth, dark-brown bark that peels off in long scrolls, exposing pale underbark. Small, yellow flowers appear near the top of the tree in August-September. Extremely rare in Delhi but deserves more attention.

WHERE TO SEE IT
I have only come across 2 trees in Sundar Nursery.

BADMINTON BALL TREE *Parkia biglandulosa*

badminton ball tree
no local name

pea family – mimosa subfamily

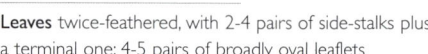

Large tree; deciduous

Bark grey-brown, not particularly rough

Leaves twice-feathered with up to 40 pairs of side-stalks and up to 100 pairs of very small, crowded leaflets on each side-stalk

Flowers tiny, clustered in dense heads about 4 cm in diameter; on stalks up to 25 cm long; bisexual flowers above, purely male flowers below

Fruit a long, flat pod on a very long stalk

A large, spreading tree from Malaysia with a huge bole and numerous tiny leaflets in its compound leaves. It earns its English common name by the peculiar shape of its flower-heads, which have evolved as landing stages for pollinating bats. Extremely rare in Delhi, though it appears to do well here.

WHERE TO SEE IT
Only one specimen inside the entrance gate to the German embassy on Shanti Path. Sundar Nursery lost a large, old tree in 2004.

CAN BE CONFUSED WITH

The gulmohur, at first glance, but the leaflets of the badminton ball tree are a lot tinier and much more numerous.

COLVILLE'S GLORY *Colvillea racemosa*

colville's glory • glory colvillea

no local name

pea family – cassia subfamily

Middle-sized tree; deciduous

Bark with thin, peeling coppery skin; studded with raised, corky dots

Leaves twice-feathered, about 60 cm long, downy; 16-30 pairs of side-stalks, each with up to 30 pairs of leaflets on tiny stalks

Flowers in large, drooping clusters, fiery orange-red

Fruit a cylindrical pod, not seen in Delhi

LEAVES deceptively gulmohur-like. This one has more numerous side-stalks that are more widely spaced apart, with fewer distinctly larger leaflets.

A slender tree with a thin, feathery canopy easily mistaken (when not in flower) for a gulmohur. Like the gulmohur, it was 'discovered' on the coast of Madagascar and first cultivated in Mauritius, mainly for its fiery, drooping, orange blossoms.

THE BOLE is a favourite nesting site for parakeets in Delhi.

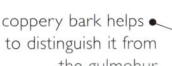

coppery bark helps to distinguish it from the gulmohur

SEASONS - LEAVES shed in January; new leaf towards late April. **FLOWERS** July-August. **FRUIT** not seen in Delhi.

WHERE TO SEE IT Shakti Sthal has a large grove; Nehru Park has a copse of 6 trees close to Vinay Marg. Lodi Garden, Buddha Jayanti Park and Sundar Nursery have a few specimens.

CAN BE CONFUSED WITH

The gulmohur, but only when neither tree is in flower! In its general habit, Colville's glory has the same airy, feathery-leaved aspect of the gulmohur but has less spreading branches. The leaves are not very easy to tell apart unless you hold specimens of both in your hand. The coppery bark is the best diagnostic character.

JACARANDA *Jacaranda mimosifolia*

jacaranda • black poui • green ebony • brazilian rosewood
neeli gulmohur • neelmohur

jacaranda family

Moderate-sized tree; deciduous

Bark pale or dark brown, shallowly cracked and fissured

Leaves twice-feathered, finely cut and fern-like; 9-16 pairs of side-stalks with numerous pairs of tiny, pointy leaflets plus one terminal leaflet

Flowers bell-shaped, lavender- or purply-blue, in open clusters; inside of the bell white and softly downy

Fruit a flat woody capsule, almost round, 3-6 cm in diameter; brown when ripe

MOUTH OF FLOWER TUBE has 2 distinct 'lips', the upper 2-lobed, the lower with 3 lobes. There are 4 fertile stamens and a long, barren one. The flowers open around 4 a.m.

tube is always slightly bent

3-lobed lower lip

woody pods separate into halves when ripe, releasing the winged seeds

A delicate-leaved, ornamental tree – somewhat stunted in Delhi – with an open crown and low-branching habit. First introduced to India in the Calcutta Botanical Garden from Brazil in 1841, the 'jac' is widely planted for its showy clusters of purply-blue flowers that appear along with the wispy, pale-green new foliage.

SEASONS - LEAVES shed in January; renewed in early April. **FLOWERS** with the new leaves, early April to mid May; occasional short flushes in the rains. **FRUIT** appear by June, remaining till the following February or even later.

LARGEST LEAFLET is the solitary one at the end of each side-stalk, a useful diagnostic character.

WHERE TO SEE IT Most parks like Nehru Park and Lodi Garden have jacarandas; a fine grove near the old entranceway to Qudsia Bagh. A large tree in the big roundabout in front of 10 Janpath.

CAN BE CONFUSED WITH
The gulmohur because of the similarity of their feathery leaves. But while the gulmohur's leaflets are rounded, the jacaranda's are pointy. Also, unlike the gulmohur, there is always an odd leaflet at the terminal end of each jacaranda side-stalk.

SONJNA *Moringa oleifera*

drumstick tree • horseradish tree • ben/benzolive/benoil/ben nut tree   *sonjna family*

sonjna • sainjhna • shajna • munga

Medium-sized tree; deciduous

Bark pale brown or silvery-white; corky, furrowed

Leaves twice-feathered (partly 3-times-feathered), very large; main leaf stalk branches into 4-6 pairs of widely spaced side-stalks; leaflets bluntly oval, about 2 cm long

---

Flowers white, in large clusters; somewhat pea-like in form with 5 long, unequal petals, hard to distinguish from 5 lobes of the flower-cup; stamens 5, anthers orange

---

Fruit bean-like, up to 50 cm long with 9 faint ribs; pale green and tender at first, becoming dark green and firm

FLOWERS look as if they have 10 petals. There are actually 5 petals, one of which stands upright, the others bent back. The other petal-like structures are lobes of the flower-cup.

A graceful, softwooded tree with an airy crown of fern-like foliage and generous clusters of creamy flowers. Its fruit are the edible 'drumsticks' used in sambhar curry. Native to the southern foothills of the Himalaya, now widely cultivated as one of the world's most useful plants and its reputation is still growing.

SEASONS - **LEAVES** start to fall in December or January; new foliage in late March. **FLOWERS** in February-March, sometimes twice a year. **FRUIT** ripen in April-May.

dry 'drumsticks' on a tree – a rare sight

LEAVES have a complex compound structure - they are mostly twice-feathered but the lowest side-stalks are themselves feathered, thus becoming 3-times-feathered.

WHERE TO SEE IT Sundar Nursery has a number of trees close together, which look lovely in flower. Fairly common even in small private gardens and farmhouses.

THE MIRACLE TREE

Sonjna leaves and fruit are an astonishingly rich source of calcium, iron, vitamins B, A and C (when raw) and of protein. (See page 326.)

BAKAIN *Melia azedarach*

persian lilac • chinaberry • bead tree • bastard cedar • indian/barbados/cape lilac
bakain • drek • deikna

neem/mahogany family

Middle-sized tree; deciduous

Bark dark brown with long, flat ridges and furrows

Leaves large, twice-feathered, forking into 3-7 pairs of side-stalks; 3, 5 or 7 coarsely toothed leaflets on each side-stalk

Flowers in loose clusters; petals white tipped with lilac; stamens fused into a purple central column

Fruit shaped like miniature apples, in pendant clusters; green at first, turning creamy yellow and wrinkled

14 m

FLOWERS in loose, arching clusters up to 20 cm long, usually quite high up on the tree. The lilac buds open into 5 (sometimes 6) thin, long, spreading petals. The stamens are bundled into a deep-purple central column.

petals mostly white, the tips touched with lilac

the top of the staminal column is fringed with tiny teeth

A long-limbed tree with a dense, spreading crown, superficially resembling the neem (to which it is related). Bakain is quick-growing but short-lived and is prized above all for its talcum-scented white and lilac flowers in spring. Planted here and there in gardens and often self-sown, but nowhere as a pure avenue tree in Delhi.

SEASONS - LEAVES shed in January, renewed in late January or February (reddish, at first). **FLOWERS** in March, reaching a peak around the 20th; mostly over by 1st April. **FRUIT** ripen by October, remaining till the following February or even later.

WHERE TO SEE IT A sizeable grove between Shanti Vana and Shakti Sthal; Rouse Avenue has many trees, and common in most parts of Delhi where it appears often to be self-sown.

most parts of the flower cluster are covered with a mealy down

LEAVES 50 cm long or more, with a complex structure: there are 3-7 pairs of side-stalks, each one bearing 3, 5, 7 or 9 leaflets. The lowest leaflets tend to break up into sub-leaflets, so here the leaf may be 3-pinnate. Most of the rest of the leaf is 2-pinnate, and at the very top there is often just one division, where it is 1-pinnate. The leaflets are coarsely toothed, more or less oval with a long, pointy tip.

largest leaflet at the apex of each side-stalk

the base of each leaflet is asymmetric

the lowest leaflets may be 3-pinnate

lobes at the base of the leaf stalk make it look like a human nose

FRUIT small, nearly round berries, about 1.5 cm in diameter, in clusters. Plump and fleshy when young, they develop a wrinkled, creamy or yellowish skin as they ripen. Inside the fruit, the stone is hard and ridged, with a natural aperture that you can pass a pin through.

BARK dark brown, with long, vertical ridges and shallow furrows, with short, horizontal criss-cross ridges as well. The underbark is brownish red.

CAN BE CONFUSED WITH

The neem, which it resembles in a general way. The key difference is that neem leaves are feather-compound, i.e. only once divided, while those of bakain are mostly twice divided (2-pinnate) but often also 3-pinnate near the base. Another clue is that neem flowers are purely white, with none of the lilac or purple that you see in bakain flowers.

HABITAT Hardy and adaptable, bakain does best on deep, sandy loams in dry, open habitats. It withstands frost and is reasonably drought-hardy but can be somewhat invasive, regenerating without assistance along road-sides and in disturbed land. It grows rapidly at first, but lives only for 20 years or so.

RANGE There is little agreement about its natural range. Wild specimens are reported from Baluchistan and less certainly, from the Shivaliks. Some regard the tree as W Asian, others as purely S Asian, and yet others as being widely distributed from NW India through Sumatra, Java and the Philippines.

USES Many parts of the tree, especially the fruit, are dangerously narcotic, except perhaps to birds (bulbuls seem to be immune). Insect repellants and flea-powder are made from the fruit. Extracts from the bark, leaves or roots help to expel intestinal worms and to treat fevers, rheumatism and inflammations. The leaves and bruised bark are used to stupefy fish. The light-brown timber is of surprisingly good quality for such a fast-growing tree – it is handsome, light but strong, is easily worked, finishes beautifully and is reputedly resitant to termites.

AKASH NEEM *Millingtonia hortensis*

(indian) cork tree • tree jasmine

jacaranda family

akash neem • neem chameli • vilaiti neem

Medium-sized tree; deciduous

Bark thick, corky, yellowish grey, cracked and furrowed [left]

Leaves twice- and three-times-feathered, 25-40 cm long; 3 to 5 pairs of side-stalks, the lowest pair often forking into more sub-stalks; leaflets 2-3 pairs plus a terminal; 2.5-5 cm long, smooth, pointy

Flowers fragrant, in terminal clusters; flower 5-8 cm long, with a pure-white, long, slender tube widening into a short funnel-shaped mouth [see pic below]

Fruit a narrow capsule, about 35 cm long, flattened

A narrow-crowned evergreen tree from Myanmar and the Malay Archipelago that can grow to 24 m in ideal conditions but is stunted and deciduous in Delhi. Recognized by its yellowish, corky bark and valued for its white, scented flowers. It prospers in moist locations but barely flowers in Delhi.

WHERE TO SEE IT The road leading up to Sewa Nagar flyover in front of J. Nehru Stadium has leftovers of earlier planting. There's a short, sad row in Nehru Park.

FLAMEGOLD *Koelreuteria elegans*

flamegold

reettha/litchi family

no local name

Smallish tree; deciduous

Bark grey, becoming cracked and furrowed with age

Leaves twice-feathered, with 4-5 pairs of side-stalks, each with up to 9 pairs plus a terminal leaflet; leaflets toothed, pointy, unequal at base

Flowers tiny, yellow, showy, in large, branched clusters at the ends of branchlets; petals bent sharply backwards

Fruit like little papery bladders, pink at first, drying paperbag brown [see pic below]

A smallish tree often branching close to the ground, with a dense, spreading crown that comes alive when it flowers after the rains. One of a small genus of three species from China, Taiwan and Korea, distinguished by papery, bladder-like fruits which remain on the tree for many months after the flowers.

WHERE TO SEE IT Nehru Park has 2 trees near the swaying wooden bridge; one near Arab ki Serai. Purana Qila has a small grove. One tree in GK I on the central road through the colony.

>> Which *Koelreuteria*? – see p339

ARLU *Oroxylum indicum*

indian trumpet flower • midnight horror • tree of damocles

arlu • ullu • pharri • saona

jacaranda family

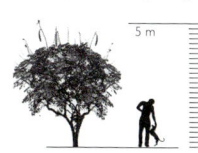

Small tree; deciduous

Bark pale brown, corky

Leaves 60-180 cm long; large leaves are twice-feathered near the top and middle, three-times-feathered towards the bottom; leaflets broadly oval with a short, pointy tip

Flowers trumpet-shaped, purplish pink, fleshy; mouth 12 cm wide; flowers open about 10 p.m., pollinated by bats

Fruit a flat woody capsule up to one m long, like a scabbard; deep purple; surface mottled with tiny dots [pic below]

A small tree with a spare crown that is called some unflattering names because of the foxy stink of its night-blooming flowers. The compound leaves, nearly 2 m long, are the largest of any Delhi tree and its scabbard-like fruit are arresting. The Ridge is too dry to support the arlu and it is not cultivated.

WHERE TO SEE IT Someone has planted 5 trees around the periphery of the pump-house in Anand Niketan; one tree in the main park in Delhi University, in front of the department of anthropology.

PINK CEDAR *Acrocarpus fraxinifolius*

pink cedar • shingle tree • indian ash

no local name

pea family – cassia subfamily

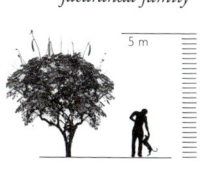

Large tree; deciduous

Bark thin, pale grey-brown, fairly smooth

Leaves twice-feathered, very large with 3-5 pairs of side-stalks; 5-9 pairs of leaflets on each side-stalk, each leaflet up to 10 cm long

Flowers dull red or orange, about 3 cm long, in dense, upstanding clusters

Fruit pods thin, flat, smooth, on a long stalk

A quick-growing, stately tree that can reach 60 m in its native moist forests in the W Ghats and NE India. New foliage is attractive and limned with pink, but Delhi is far from an ideal habitat. It is sometimes planted as a shade tree in tea and coffee plantations in the lower hills. Rare in Delhi.

there is usually a • solitary pinna at the terminal end of the large leaf

WHERE TO SEE IT One young tree growing in Sundar Nursery.

✳ PALM-LIKE LEAVES

Fan-leaved palms

threads
from leaf
margins

leaflets
divided about
halfway

leaflets
split
almost to
base

leaf segments
stiff, rigid,
folded

strong, hooked,
orange teeth
on leaf stalk

leaf stalk
stout, spiny

leaf stalk
smooth,
with no
spines

california fan palm
2.5 m p318

palmyra palm
2 m p318

savannah palm
4 m p319

segments
shallowly
divided

leaves nearly
circular in
outline

leaf-tips
strongly
drooping

leaflets
deeply
divided

leaf stalk
has evenly
spaced
spines

leaf arching
along
prolonged
leaf stalk

leaf stalk
prolonged
through leaf,
strongly arching

leaf stalk
long, no
spines

leaf stalk
spiny at base

cabbage palm
3.75 m p320

footstool palm
3.5 m p319

chinese fan palm
3.25 m p316

Feather-leaved palms

twice-feathered compound leaf, very large

slim leaflets evenly spaced

leaf stalk yellow if grown in sun; no spines

golden cane palm
2 m p315

leaflets triangular with jagged end

large sheath at base of leaf (not shown)

massive arching leaf stalk

leaflets thin, in many planes

jaggery palm
6 m p308

royal palm
3 m p310

leaflets narrow, closely spaced

leaflets in different planes, criss-cross

leaflets slender, evenly spaced

leaflets glossy, in one plane

green spines at base, not woody

strong, woody spines at base

dwarf date palm
1.65 m p314

wild date palm
3 m p312

spines at base not stiff

spines at base of stout leaf stalk

cliff date palm
3 m p314

canary island date palm
5 m p315

✴ JAGGERY PALM *Caryota urens*

jaggery/wine palm • toddy palm • fishtail/horsetail palm • (bastard/indian) sago palm
mari • bankhajur

palm family

Tall palm; evergreen

Trunk cylindrical, grey, with clear rings spaced well apart

Leaves about 6 m long, twice-feathered; leaflets shiny green with ragged ends

Flowers small, massed on long tassels; male and female flowers separate but on the same tassels

Fruit the size of a peepal fig, dark red when ripe

This interesting palm belongs to the only genus of palms with twice-feathered leaves. Also called the 'fishtail-palm' because of the resemblance of the ragged ends of its leaflets with a fish's derriere. It bears flowers and fruit in huge, drooping tassels. Native to relatively moist forests in India, but a fairly common ornamental palm in Delhi.

SEASONS - FLOWERS and **FRUITING** more or less throughout the year or, at any rate, at no particular time of year.

WHERE TO SEE IT In most large gardens, parks and some roundabouts. A row of old palms in front of the Met office on Lodi Road. Humayun's Tomb gardens has a grove of 12 palms originally planted to discourage badminton-playing in one area. The forecourt of the India Habitat Centre has lots. Najaf Khan's Tomb in Aliganj has some.

FLOWERS massed in huge, ponytail-like tassels up to 4 m long. The flowers are arranged in groups of 3, one female flanked by a male on each side. It is not hard to tell them apart – the males develop first and unfurl long stamens when they open. The female flower, opening later, is always at the bottom of the triad and has no stamens.

male flower buds lie on either side and are a little larger

the female bud is in the middle of the triad

LEAVES twice-feathered, up to 6 m long. The strong main leaf stalk emerges from a mass of fibrous leaf sheaths at the top of the stem. Individual leaflets are shiny and triangular, with one ragged edge as if someone has taken a chomp out of it. It is this chewed-up edge that earns it the name 'fishtail'. (They are actually more like the lower fin of a fish than its tail – it just sounds better to say 'fishtail'!)

• triangular leaflets with ragged edge

FRUIT about the size and colour of a peepal fig. Under their skin, the fruit contain sharp crystals that can cause severe irritation and chemical burns. (The word 'urens' in the scientific name means 'burning'.)

WHY NOT 'FISHTAIL PALM'?

All species of *Caryota* and a few other palms too have 'chewed-off' leaflets, so it is not very precise to call any one of them a 'fishtail palm'. It would be very confusing if more than one of these species was found in Delhi.

TRUNK grey, marked with regularly spaced rings (one for every shed leaf) and minutely scored, as if etched in close cuneiform characters.

FROM TOP TO BOTTOM

All species of *Caryota* produce distinctive large, drooping tassels of flowers, starting near the top of the tree. It can take a few years for each of these flowering branches to fruit and become exhausted, but subsequent 'ponytails' are produced lower and lower down the trunk. When the lowest ponytail blooms and its fruit ripen, the palm dies.

HABITAT A lowland palm found in evergreen or moist deciduous forests. It likes deep, rich, well-drained soil with plenty of water and suffers in very dry conditions. It takes full sun but must be protected from frost.

RANGE Indigenous to India, Myanmar, Sri Lanka and possibly Malaysia. Within the subcontinent, it extends all along the sub-Himalayan tract into the foothills of the NE. Also in wetter parts of the peninsula, especially on the SW coast.

USES In 'season' the flowering branch is tapped and yields up to 30 or 40 buckets of sap in a day. The sap is unusually rich in simple sugars and when boiled yields a treacle or a coarse granular sugar called 'jaggery'. The sap is 'toddy' when it is fresh and 'arrack' (palm wine or 'Indian gin') after it has fermented. All products from its toddy are credited with medicinal properties. The leaves provide kittul fibre, used for rope, basketry, brooms and fishing lines. (Wild elephants are tethered with kittul rope in Sri Lanka.) The starchy pith from the central part of the trunk is said to be equal to the best sago. The outer part of the stem provides a durable timber used in house-building and for agricultural implements.

✳ ROYAL PALM *Roystonea regia*

(cuban) royal palm • bottle palm • mountain glory
no local name

palm family

Tall feather-leaved palm; evergreen

Trunk pale grey, smooth, faintly ringed, often with a slight bulge

Leaves about 3 m long, feather-compound, arching; leaflets long, narrow, folded at base; smooth, green crownshaft above stem formed by leaf bases

Flowers tiny, in branched clusters, creamy yellow

Fruit small, more or less round, dark red when ripe

Tall, stately palms from Cuba with smooth, grey trunks that look like they are made of concrete, topped by prominent green crown-shafts. They have large, spreading crowns of feathery leaves and inconspicuous flowers and fruit. Frequently planted in formal arrangements around historical monuments and in danger of becoming a bit of a cliché.

SEASONS - **LEAVES** are evergreen and fall (with a resounding crash) and are renewed throughout the year. **FLOWERS** appear in May-June or just after the rains in late September or October. **FRUIT** in October or December (depending on when it has flowered).

WHERE TO SEE IT Often planted in straight lines around historical monuments and formal walkways. Prime examples are in Azad Park (formerly Queen's Garden, near Old Delhi railway station), Jantar Mantar, Muhammad Shah's tomb in Lodi Garden, Teen Murti roundabout, and Safdarjang's Tomb.

FLOWERS in dense clusters growing from the base of the green crownshaft, enclosed at first in tubular sheaths. The sheaths grow erect, then tilt over when it is time to burst open to let the flower sprays emerge. Flowers are either male or female, the males slightly larger but still only 5 mm long, both sexes white or straw-yellow.

the sheath when it first bursts open. The flowers are still in bud

base of tubular sheath

LEAVES large, feather-compound, only 15-20 in a crown, arising from a green crownshaft made up of the polished, overlapping sheaths or bases of the leaves. A mature leaf is about 3 m long, with narrow leaflets pleated at their base and arranged in slightly different planes.

this is the only palm in Delhi with a smooth, green • crownshaft

leaflets in slightly • different planes

leaf stalk • sharply ridged

TRUNK cement-grey, smooth, with faint horizontal rings marking the places where old leaves have fallen off.

FRUIT in branching clusters like the flowers and about the size of a pea, slightly longer than wide. Green at first, turning dark red to purple when ripe.

❋ WILD DATE PALM *Phoenix sylvestris*

wild/sugar date palm • indian/silver date

khajoor • khajoori • khaji • salma • sendhi

palm family

Tall feather-leaved palm; evergreen

Trunk grey-brown, 'stepped' from the stumps of fallen leaves

Spines on lower leaf-stem sharp, woody

Leaves coconut-like, with long, feathery, greyish green leaves; leaflets thin, folded at base

Flowers tiny, creamy yellow, in tight clusters; male and female flowers on separate trees

Fruit olive-like, orange-yellow when ripe, in large clusters

12 m

SPINES sharp, stiff, triangular in cross-section, but only along the lower part of the main leaf-stem.

With its slender, curving stem and plumose crown, this is the quintessential palm that invariably features in old lithographs of Delhi's antiquity. Hardy and adaptable, it is closely related to the true date palm from N African oases. It nearly always has a mass of exposed air-roots extending up to a metre or so above ground.

● these are immature green fruit. They will ripen orange-yellow

SEASONS - LEAVES evergreen, constantly renewed. **FLOWERS** in March-April. **FRUIT** ripen late June-August, sometimes a little later.

unlike 'true' dates, ● the fruit are dry and astringent

WHERE TO SEE IT A lovely grove by the lake at Roshanara Bagh. Qudsia Bagh, Humayun's Tomb garden and the zoo have good specimens but the wild date palm is becoming conspicuously rare in the city. Some outlying villages still have extensive wild groves.

FRUIT in large clusters (only on female trees, of course). The fruit are about the size and shape of an olive, green at first, ripening orange-yellow and finally turning deep red-brown. Each fruit contains a small quantity of sweetish pulp and a large, grooved seed.

LEAVES long, arching, greyish green, feather-compound with a terminal leaflet. The thin, pointy leaflets are folded neatly into a V where they are attached to the main leaf-stem. They emerge at slightly different planes from the leaf-stem. A leaflet can be up to 45 cm long.

FLOWERS fragrant, 3-petalled, with male and female flowers on separate trees. The stalk of each flowering cluster is flat and thick like a camel's tail. The flower buds are enclosed at first in large, almost woody sheaths which split into two halves as the flowers develop. Male flowers are slightly larger, more closely spaced and creamy yellow. Female flowers grow in more open bunches on longer stalks.

male flowers

● sheath enclosing the flower cluster

exposed rootlets at the base of the trunk ●

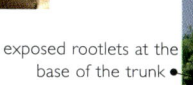

BARK greyish, sometimes nearly black, rough and uneven from the stumps of fallen leaf-bases. The base of the trunk is usually covered with dense rootlets.

HABITAT It regenerates best in moist, sandy depressions where sub-soil water lies not too deep. Extremely adaptable, tolerating full sun, fairly severe drought and frost. On suitable sites, it can form pure forests.

RANGE Native to relatively dry parts of the Indian subcontinent and Sri Lanka. Often seen growing gregariously along streams and watercourses, ascending to about 1300 m.

USES The leaves are woven into floor-mats, baskets, fans and brooms, and the leaf stalks yield paper and rope. The fruit and seeds are used in folk medicine as a tonic and for treating heart ailments, abdominal cramps, fevers and vomiting. Chiefly valued for its sugary sap which exudes (in winter) from incisions made just below the leaves. The ancient industry of making sugar from the sap follows time-honoured methods of intense tapping (at night) with intervening periods of rest for the tree. Freshly tapped juice is rich in sugars and ferments quickly unless boiled. When boiled the juice condenses into palm jaggery (*goodh*). Some of the juice is allowed to ferment to make *taadi* (toddy), akin to but distinct from palmyra or coconut toddy.

DWARF DATE PALM *Phoenix roebelinii*

dwarf/pygmy/miniature date palm • roebelin palm

palm family

no local name

Small feather-leaved palm; evergreen

Trunk slim, dark grey, with peg-like leaf scars from fallen leaves

Spines at base of leaf stalks; sharp, flexible, dark green, about 5 cm long; not woody

Leaves arching, about one m long; leaflets glossy, not quite opposite; base of leaflets folded

Flowers small, in insignificant clusters 30 cm long; male and female flowers on separate plants

Fruit small, ovoid dates; redddish brown when ripe

A diminutive palm with a crown of delicate fronds and distinctive pegs along its slender stem – the remnants of old leaf-bases. Like other *Phoenix* palms, its lowest leaves are modified into sharp spines. Native to Laos, Thailand, possibly Myanmar. Cultivated in India as an ornamental, but not common.

WHERE TO SEE IT
4 specimens close together in the palme-tum in Lodi Garden. Many nurseries sell it.

 # CLIFF DATE PALM *Phoenix rupicola*

cliff date palm • east indian wine palm

palm family

no local name

Middle-sized feather-leaved palm; evergreen

Trunk dark grey, slender, without persistent leaf-bases

Spines at base of leaf-stem soft, sharp

Leaves about 3 m long; leaflets glossy, bright green, about 50 cm long, arranged in one plane [see pic below]

Flowers small, creamy yellow, in large clusters; male and female flowers on separate trees

Fruit about 18 mm long, purplish red, in clusters

The most attractive of the *Phoenix* palms on account of its glossy, elegantly arching fronds. Distinguished from other *Phoenix* palms by its slender leaflets being arranged on the leaf-stem in a single plane. Native to steep, rocky hillsides in the NE Himalaya and not very happy in Delhi.

WHERE TO SEE IT A prominent specimen in Humayun's Tomb garden. Talkatora Garden has a few. One tree next to the white tiger enclosure in the zoo.

CANARY ISLAND DATE PALM *Phoenix canariensis*

canary island date palm

no local name

palm family

A tall relative of the date palm, from the Canary Islands (off the west coast of Africa), with a massive trunk and long, spiny leaves. Too imposing for most gardens, it is planted in formal avenues in Mediterranean towns like Cannes. It was a big surprise to find one planted in a government bungalow in Delhi.

Tall feather-leaved palm; evergreen

Trunk massive, with diamond-shaped pattern of leaf scars

Spines towards base of leaf stalks, long, sharp

Leaves arching, up to 5 m long; leaflets folded in valleys near the base, where they join the leaf stalk

Flowers small, in clusters among the leaves; male and female flowers on separate plants

Fruit up to 5 cm long; orange when ripe, inedible

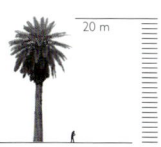

WHERE TO SEE IT
A solitary specimen in the Women's Press Corp office at 5 Windsor Place. Pic [right] shows an avenue at Cannes.

GOLDEN CANE PALM *Dypsis lutescens*

Syn: Chrysalidocarpus lutescens

golden cane palm • yellow/golden butterfly palm • areca/bamboo palm

no local name

palm family

A graceful, clump-forming palm that could be the most widely sold palm in the world. Its slender, bamboo-like stems are topped by curving feather leaves, with yellow stalks if grown in the sun, otherwise green. Native to Madagascar's rainforest, it is an adaptable palm, equally at home indoors as it is in small gardens.

Middle-sized feather-leaved clustering palm; evergreen

Trunk ringed, slim, gently arching, each with 6-8 leaves

Leaves up to 2.6 m long, yellow-green, arching, usually with a slight twist; long, ribbony leaflets are evenly spaced; leaf stalk is not spiny

Flowers small, white, on stalks from among the leaves

Fruit yellow to purple, about 2 cm long

WHERE TO SEE IT
Extremely common, even in small gardens.

✴ CHINESE FAN PALM *Livistona chinensis*

chinese fan palm • chinese livistona • fountain palm

no local name

palm family

5 m

Smallish fan-palm; evergreen

Bark grey-brown, rough, with horizontal ridges

Top of trunk and base of leaves densely matted with fibres

Leaves large, fan-shaped, with 50-60 pleated segments; undivided at the centre, forked at the tips; ends drooping

Flowers in much-branched clusters; tiny, yellowish green

Fruit olive-shaped, bluish green, glossy, in large clusters

Delhi's commonest ornamental palm, widely cultivated in gardens and as decorative tub-specimens. Its most distinctive feature is the splayed tips of its large, fan-shaped leaves which droop suddenly downwards. The base of the very long leaf stalk usually has short, curved spines. The olive-shaped fruit is an unusual glossy bluish-green.

LEAVES fan-shaped, up to 3 m long and nearly as wide. Typically, about 20 leaves in a crown, emerging from a dense mat of fibres. At its centre the leafblade is undivided and consists of 50-60 pleated segments. At their ends, the segments are deeply forked and hang prettily downwards (hence 'fountain palm'). The stalk is prolonged into the leafblade for a short distance.

● the base of the leaf stalk is usually armed with short, curved teeth

SEASONS - **LEAVES** evergreen. **FLOWERS** in March-April and sometimes in January. **FRUIT** form very quickly after the flowers and ripen by August-September.

ends of the leaf-segments are forked and drooping ●

WHERE TO SEE IT Fairly common in gardens big and small in Delhi. Small groves near Arab ki Serai (Humayun's Tomb), Buddha Jay-anti Park, Lodi Garden, Qudsia Bagh, Talkatora Garden.

the leaf stalks can be up to 3 m long, their length varying with the amount of sun the plant receives

HABITAT In its native habitat it grows in open subtropical forests. It develops a long taproot, enabling it to withstand extended periods of drought. Young plants need to be shaded and mature plants prefer semi-shade but will survive full sun. It grows in a wide range of soils, but does not tolerate frost well.

RANGE Native to Japan, the Ryukyu Islands and Taiwan, but now widely cultivated ornamentally in warm climates.

USES Widely grown for ornamental purposes.

FLOWERS in large, branching clusters arising from among the leaves. The small, creamy flowers are only about 2 mm long. If you use a hand lens, you can just make out the deeply 3-lobed petals and 6 stamens.

in this close-up of a flowering stalk, you can see the stamens

THATCH of densely matted fibres at the base of the leaf stalks.

FRUIT in large, hanging bunches, shiny bluish-green or very dark green, more or less olive-shaped. A berry is about 2.5 cm long.

BARK pale grey-brown, with faint horizontal ridges which are the scars of old, fallen leaves. The stem has prominent, vertical fissures.

CAN BE CONFUSED WITH

The closely related footstool palm (page 319). The simple distinction is that the footstool palm's leaves are rounder in outline and the tips of its leaflets do not droop like the Chinese fan palm's.

✳ CALIFORNIA FAN PALM *Washingtonia filifera*

california/desert fan palm • petticoat palm • cotton palm

no local name

palm family

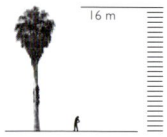

Tall fan-leaved palm; evergreen

Bark grey, closely ringed; often obscured by a 'petticoat' of dead leaves hanging down

Leaves over 2 m wide; leaf stalk with curved, orange prickles [see pic below]; leaf segments narrow, folded, with split ends; cottony threads from leaf margins

Flowers tiny, whitish, in very large, branching clusters

Fruit a small, spherical berry about one cm in diameter, with thin flesh; black when ripe

An imposing palm with massive, fan-shaped leaves that hang down and clothe the trunk in a giant 'petticoat' long after the leaves die. Found in a very limited range – only about 70 oases in the deserts of S California and Baja California – it has become hugely popular worldwide in hot, dry landscapes.

WHERE TO SEE IT Delhi's largest specimens are in Lodi Garden. Sundar Nursery has an avenue of youngish palms; a pair of them in the garden at NISCOM (Pusa).

✳ PALMYRA PALM *Borassus flabellifer*

palmyra palm • toddy palm • wine palm • brab tree

tad • tadi • tal

palm family

Tall fan-leaved palm; evergreen

Trunk dark, with broad rings

Leaves blue-green, broad, stiff, up to 1.5 m long; a leaf has 60-80 leaf segments, folded, divided about half their length; leaf stalks are stout, spiny

Flowers yellow, male and female on separate trees; flower clusters are shorter than the leaves

Fruit large, broadly ovoid, up to 20 cm in diameter; yellow-brown when young, nearly black when ripe; pulp yellow, fleshy

A tall, fan-leaved palm with a thin, ringed trunk whose sap is fermented to make the country liquor known as 'toddy'. Its rigid leaves form a nearly spherical crown and young trees wear a skirt of dead leaves. Native to coastal areas in India and Malaysia, and often cultivated far inland.

WHERE TO SEE IT 14 old palms in Qudsia Bagh; more in the principal's residence, Hindu College, Roshanara Bagh, the forest dept. nursery near Kamla Nehru Park.

✳ SAVANNAH PALM *Sabal mauritiiformis*

savannah palm • bay palmetto • green botan

no local name

palm family

9 m

Middle-sized fan-palm; evergreen

Trunk slender, grey-green, with distinct rings; often retaining the split bases of old leaves

Leaves very large, up to 6 m long, floppy; deeply divided nearly to the base; leaf stalks long, smooth, not armed

Flowers white, fragrant, in long, arching, branched clusters extending beyond the leaves

Fruit small, black, almost round

A distinctive palm native to tropical central America with a slender, ringed stem and large, floppy leaves that are split nearly to their bases. It grows somewhat untidily in Delhi and, though uncommon, is easy to recognize by its outsize, deeply divided leaves which may be deep or bluish green.

WHERE TO SEE IT Nehru Park and Lodi Garden have small groves of savannah palms, planted close together. Roshanara Bagh has 2 old specimens. Not at all common.

✳ FOOTSTOOL PALM *Livistona rotundifolia*

footstool palm • roundleaf/anahaw palm • java fan palm

no local name

palm family

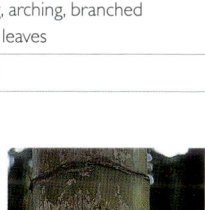

5 m

Smallish fan-palm; evergreen

Trunk thin, prominently marked with brown rings

Leaves large, circular in outline, shallowly divided at the margins; leaf stalk has nasty-looking, curved spines

Flowers small, yellow, in much-branched clusters

Fruit almost round, about 2 cm in diameter; red at first, turning black when ripe

A tall, thin-stemmed palm from SE Asia that does not grow much higher than 5 m in Delhi. Much of its charm has to do with the distinctive circular shape of its large, glossy leaves, though this perfect form is lost when the palm grows older and the leaves get tattered in the wind.

WHERE TO SEE IT The palmetum in Lodi Garden has a few. Sundar Nursery and Karbala Nursery stock them. Not very uncommon.

CABBAGE PALM *Sabal palmetto*

cabbage palm • palmetto palm • carolina/blue palmetto
no local name

palm family

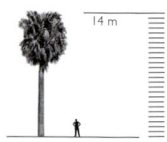

Tall fan-leaved palm; evergreen

Trunk pale brown or grey; 'stepped' with growth rings; often with V-shaped split bases of old leaves

Leaves up to 2 m long and nearly as broad, strongly arched; leaf stalk stout, long, extending all the way through to the apex; leaf divided into long, narrow segments with curling threads at edges

Flowers small, white, fragrant, in much-branched clusters arising from leaf bases

Fruit small, black, shiny, nearly round

arching leaf stalk extends to end of leaf, creating a deep 'valley'

A highly variable palm from south-eastern USA and the Bahamas, with a characteristic criss-cross pattern of split leaf bases (called 'boots') on its trunk. Its large fan-leaves arch strongly along the extended leaf stalk and appear to be folded in the middle. Tiny, scented white flowers in dense clusters are an excellent bee forage.

FLOWERS tiny, in large, branching clusters that are as long as or sometimes a little longer than the leaves. They are bisexual, with a bell-shaped flower-cup and tubular petals.

SEASONS - LEAVES evergreen. **FLOWERS** appear towards late April or early May and fill the air with scent. **FRUIT** in June-July.

flowers are about 4 mm long and highly fragrant

WHERE TO SEE IT Cabbage palms were once planted as formal elements in government bungalows in New Delhi, as sentinels near entrance gates. You can still see a few in Jantar Mantar Road and Ashok Road. Roshanara Bagh has some pretty specimens on a mound, and a small garden in Greater Kailash I has a neat row.

BACK OF THE BOOK

WHERE ARAUCARIAS COME FROM

Scientists recognize 19 species of *Araucaria* worldwide but it is revealing to see how widely scattered their distribution is: 3 species are found in New Guinea and eastern Australia. Thousands of kilometres to the east, the South Pacific islands of New Caledonia are home to 13 species, and Norfolk Island nearby is famous for one species that bears its name. The 2 remaining species are found in Chile and southern Brazil.

The explanation for their scattered occurrence is that the *Araucarias* are an ancient form of plant life and were present on the supercontinent Gondwanaland before it broke up. Their present distribution is related to what happened when the continents drifted free.

The oldest fossil find of an *Araucaria* dates back 190 million years, and comes – surprisingly – from southern India, suggesting that the genus was once much more widely distributed than it is now. The present range of these unusual conifers probably represents only a small fraction of a once extensive distribution, especially over the southern hemisphere.

THE PUZZLE OF THE GOURD TREE

The large, green fruit of *Crescentia* remain on the gourd tree for up to 7 months, then start turning yellow and fall to the ground. Knock on a fruit, even when it is still green, and you will find that the shell is thin and hard – so hard, in fact, that in the dry forests of meso-America where it originates no native herbivores are equipped to crack them open. So how are its seeds dispersed? Not easily.

The most common natural method is for a large herbivore to eat the fruit, softening the hard seed coats with its digestive juices and eventually scattering them in its dung. Many large grazing animals on the African veldt are able to tackle hard fruit and play a crucial role in dispersing seeds. But South America does not have any such animals, so how does the gourd tree get by?

This remained a puzzle for some years, but scientists have found plenty of evidence of the extinction (from the native range of the tree) of a number of large herbivores, including elephant-like creatures called 'gomphotheres'. It is likely that some or all of them once played an important role in aiding this tree to colonize dry, lowland forests. This is an example of a tree that lost its partnership with animals that enabled it to extend its range through neighbouring forests.

EVER SEEN THE FLOWERS OF A PEEPAL TREE?

Have you ever wondered why you don't see flowers on a peepal tree or a banyan?

In certain seasons, both trees grow little, roundish, squishy things that ripen and change colour, eventually dropping to the ground. But surely these are their *fruit*! So where are their flowers?

Peepals and banyans belong to an enormous and very successful plant genus called *Ficus* containing upwards of 1000 species. They are commonly called 'figs' or 'fig trees' after the little fleshy 'containers' that are peculiar to this genus.

'*Containers*'? That's exactly what figs are: hollow containers that house masses of little flowers, which mature into fruit. Fig plants carry their flowers *inside* their figs.

Try and think of the fig not like a pear or an apple, but as a hollow pouch. Inside this pouch are masses of minute flowers densely lining its inner wall. Instead of the usual compact cluster or 'head' of flowers (like that of the babool, for instance), the fig has a head of flowers *turned outside in*. The true fruit are very tiny and develop from these flowers, maturing inside the fig. So when we eat a fig – technically – we are not biting into a *fruit*, but into a *container that holds the flowers and the true fruit*.

There are 3 separate kinds of fig flowers:
- male flowers with male equipment (stamens) to provide pollen
- female flowers with female equipment (ovules and style) to receive the pollen and set seed
- sterile 'gall-flowers', which look much like female flowers, but with much shorter styles

Roughly half the species of *Ficus* hold all 3 kinds of flowers inside each one of their figs. The rest bear 2 separate kinds of figs – one containing only male and gall-flowers, the other only female flowers. Both kinds of fig are never found on the same tree.

The mass of flowers inside a fig are easy to see, but it is not so easy to tell the different kinds of flowers apart because they are so small. However, it is usually possible to recognize male flowers, simply because they tend to be clustered near the 'mouth' of the fig.

Now what exactly are gall-flowers? Their role is to receive the eggs of tiny fig-wasps.

And why should the fig plant be so hospitable?

Because fig-wasps play the all-important role of pollinating its flowers. Without fig-wasps, the female flowers would not receive any pollen and the figs would not set seed.

Here lies one of nature's most amazing symbiotic relationships between a tree and an insect – a clockwork mechanism of such delicate precision that its story deserves to be told properly.

• • •

How Figs Are Pollinated

Fig-Fact 1: Fig flowers can *only* be pollinated by fig-wasps.

Fig-Fact 2: Practically every one of the 1000 or so species of fig plants has its own unique species of 'in-house' wasp pollinator.

So if you took a peepal tree to a suitably warm place in, say, South America – where the peepal's own special kind of fig-wasp is *not* present – the peepal tree might thrive, but its flowers would not be fertilized and its figs would therefore produce no seed.

Fig-fact 3: Fig-wasps, in turn, are absolutely dependent on the fig plants they specialize in, because their larvae develop and their adults breed only *inside* the figs.

Let's follow a fig-wasp from cradle to grave, because then it is a little easier to understand their complex, fascinating mutuality.

Fig-wasps are not at all like the yellow hornets we dread. They are only distantly related to true wasps and do not sting. They are also much smaller, only about a millimetre or so in length.

Fig-wasps are born inside the gall-flowers in a fig.

(I'm going to use the example of a fig in which all 3 kinds of flowers – male, female and gall-flowers – are found within the *same* fig, because Delhi's fig trees are all of that kind.)

The male fig-wasp, blind and wingless, has a somewhat limited outlook. His sole purpose is to bite his way out of the gall-flower in which he was born, and search for and mate with a female fig-wasp (biting, once again, into the gall-flower in which she lies). Then he dies, without ever leaving the comfort zone of his little fig.

The inseminated female crawls out of her gall-flower and prepares to leave the fig. The 'mouth' of the fig (opposite the stem-end) may appear tightly closed but is actually crowded with the scaly bracts of male flowers. It also so happens – though it is no accident – that the female wasp starts leaving the fig at precisely the time when the male flowers have reached maturity and are shedding pollen. As she scrambles out of the narrow mouth of the fig, she brushes past male flowers and emerges covered with pollen.

Now she flies to another tree of the same species, searching for one that is laden with a new crop of young figs – probably guided by her sense of smell. She must now re-enter a young fig through its mouth, though this is not as easy as it was when she exited a swollen, mature fig, and she may even lose a leg or a wing trying to work her way in.

Once inside, she lays her eggs by pushing her ovipositor (a thin tube from the lower part of her body) down the style (pollen tube) of a flower.

Not just any flower.

She ignores the male flowers, because they have no styles.

And there is one important difference between female and gall-flowers that influences her choice of where to lay: female flowers have long, narrow styles, and gall-flowers have very short, funnel-shaped styles. This difference in style length is precisely adapted to the egg-laying habits of the fig-wasp. Her ovipositor is too short to reach the ovary of the long-styled female flower. So she lays her eggs, one by one, *only* in gall-flowers. In the process, however, whenever she brushes past a female flower, she deposits some pollen on its stigma from her pollen load.

Finally, her stock of eggs finished, she dies, exhausted, without having eaten anything since she hatched.

From the egg will hatch a little larva which will live inside the gall-flower by eating the inside of it. Finally, it will become a wingless male or an adult winged female, according to its karma, and will emerge one day to repeat the whole cycle.

THE BIGGEST BANYANS

A massive, ancient banyan known as the 'kabirbadh' grew on an island in the Narmada, 16 km upstream of Bharuch. It once had 320 large trunks and over 3000 prop-roots, and could shelter 7000 men under its 'pillared shade'. Part of the island was washed away by floods towards the end of the 19th century, and with it, portions of this great tree were lost.

The famous banyan tree in the Botanical Garden in Calcutta began life on a wild date palm in 1782. Today, roughly 230 years later, it occupies 1.6 hectares, and has 100 subsidiary trunks and 1775 prop-roots.

The biggest banyan in the world is in the village of Gotte Bayalu in Anantapur district, Andhra Pradesh. It occupies an area in excess of 2 hectares, appearing from a distance like a closed forest. 20,000 people can stand in its shade. It is estimated to be 700 years old.

BANYANS AND BANIAS

Although the banyan tree has been known to the western world at least since Alexander's expedition to India in the 4th century BC, it was known by a series of not-particularly-memorable names. We owe an account of how it came to be called the 'banyan' to Thomas Herbert, who travelled through Persia in 1627-29. One such tree grew close to the present-day port city of Bandar Abbas, where 'banians' (banias or traders) from western India had decorated it with ribbons and built a temple in its shade. Therefore, says Herbert, it has been 'named by us the Bannyan Tree'.

Half a century later, writing of the same place, Tavernier said, 'The usual amusement of Bandar is to walk under the tree of the Banians and have little collations there.'

It is interesting that many botanists use the word 'banyan' today in a different sense – as a generic descriptive term for the tree's characteristic strangling habit. In SE Asian floras, for example, various species of fig trees with aerial roots and of epiphytic habit are described as being 'banyans'.

SACRED PEEPALS

Gautam Buddha, it is believed, achieved enlightenment meditating under a peepal tree growing in Bodh Gaya (Bihar), and this particular tree came to be known as the 'bodhi tree'. The original tree is no longer there, but a sprig of the bodhi tree was taken to the Sinhala capital city of Anuradhapura (in the hills of N Sri Lanka) in 288 BC and was planted in a temple. Here the sprig grew into a tree and was venerated as the Sri Maha Bodhi because of its association with the Buddha. There also grew a superstition that Ceylon's ruling dynasty would be preserved as long as the Sri Maha Bodhi remained alive and so the tree was looked after and guarded day and night.

116 successive Sinhala kings ruled here for nearly 1300 years, but after invasion in the 9th century AD, the city was abandoned for another site. The dynasty did not last much longer. Hidden in thick jungles, the city became inaccessible for many centuries, and so too the Sri Maha Bodhi tree. It was only in the 20th century that Anuradhapura was 'rescued' from the jungle and became accessible once more to pilgrims and visitors. Amazingly, the Sri Maha Bodhi tree was still alive, making it well over 2000 years old! It is still there today, a major focus of pilgrimage in Sri Lanka.

The peepal is also sacred to Hindus, who venerate it as the female to the banyan. Vows are made to it, and spoons are fashioned from its wood for ladling ghee on the sacred fire. A peepal leaf is an essential part of the sacred thread ceremony, and at the laying of the foundation of a building – so sacred that Hindus are averse to destroy a peepal seedling, even when it lodges in the crevices of buildings, threatening to pull them down.

A POTTED HISTORY OF INDIA RUBBER

In 1810, the eminent botanist and physician Dr William Roxburgh (1751-1815) was sent a present of wild honey that had been collected by tribals from the Pundua hills north of Sylhet (now in Bangladesh). The vessel containing the honey had been made out of split cane and then smeared with the juice of some tree, so as to make a perfectly lined 'bottle' for the honey. Roxburgh was far more interested in the lining of the container than in the wild honey. On enquiring, he learnt that it was made of the milky juice or 'caoutchouc' of *Ficus elastica*, and this probably marked the beginning of the East India Company's interest in the substance which later came to be called 'Assam' or 'India rubber'.

Ficus elastica is only one of many plants yielding caoutchouc. All the figs, when bled, yield a milky latex, and caoutchouc is also produced by some other species that belong to a few unrelated plant families. In all of them, caoutchouc is secreted in tiny vessels found in the cortical tissue between the outer bark and the wood, and sometimes also in the leaves. Caoutchouc is sap-like, but should not be confused with sap. It is also gum-like in its properties of sealing incisions and preventing infection, but its exact function is still imperfectly understood. Some of its uses, however, have been known for centuries.

During Columbus's second voyage to the Americas more than 600 years ago, he saw Amerindians playing a game with bouncy balls made from the coagulated juice of a tree. Later travellers reported that Mexican Indians used a plant juice to make their cloaks waterproof, and even fashioned bottles and shoes of it. The source of their caoutchouc was undoubtedly the Amazonian rubber tree and some of its relatives, but it wasn't until 1736 that the trees which yielded caoutchouc were identified. In that year, a French scientific expedition to Peru brought back details of the many Amerindian uses of native rubber. The French word for rubber – *caoutchouc* – is a modification of a Peruvian Indian name for the latex – *cahutchu*. We owe the English word

'rubber' to Joseph Priestley (the chemist who discovered oxygen), who found the material useful for rubbing out pencil marks. Priestley's name stuck. The date – about 1770.

What of the name 'India rubber'? Did the 'India' denote East India, or the American Indians who had first been reported using caoutchouc? It is not quite clear. In the early decades of the 19th century, the name 'India rubber' seems to have been used indiscriminately for all sorts of natural rubber, irrespective of where it came from. By about mid-century, however, the rubber from the Brazilian tree *Hevea brasiliensis* began to be called 'Para rubber', after the name of the Amazonian province where it grew. 'India rubber' began to be applied more strictly to the produce of the Indian tree *Ficus elastica*. The term 'Assam rubber' was sometimes preferred, to avoid confusion, but for most people 'India rubber' and 'Assam rubber' were synonymous.

•   •   •

The trouble with untreated natural rubber is that it tends to become gummy and sticky when it's hot, and hard and inflexible in the cold. Towards the close of the 18th century, European inventors and patent-seekers were looking for ways of combining natural rubber with some other substance which would make it 'behave' better. In 1790, a Frenchman succeeded in making the first rubber tube. The following year an Englishman was granted the first patent for the use of rubber for waterproofing. In 1823, Charles Mackintosh, an industrial chemist in Glasgow, found a way of sandwiching a thin sheet of rubber between cloth to make the first effective raincoat – the 'mackintosh'. But the full utilization of natural rubber did not begin till the invention of 'vulcanizing' in 1839, when it was discovered that dipping natural rubber in a bath of molten sulphur prevents it from softening or hardening in extreme temperatures.

By the 1850s, ever-widening discoveries had made rubber an extremely versatile substance – it could now be hardened and cut like ivory, moulded and engraved, coloured, stetched or pressed. Rubber 'galoshes' or waterproof overshoes made their first appearance about this time. The first solid rubber tyres were tried on a carriage wheel in 1846, and became universal on bicycles by the 1870s. Rubber now became all the rage as inventors and manufacturers sought to find new, untried uses for it.

Back in Assam, the East India Company began to think of ways of collecting caoutchouc for export to England, but *Ficus elastica* was not an automatic first choice. Various kinds of other forest trees were tapped experimentally for their latex. The jackfruit and even the peepal were tried – no good. An African vine (*Crysptostegia grandiflora*) – whose caoutchouc was reputed to be whiter and more elastic than that of *Ficus elastica* – was brought to India and planted in quantities. Its reputation was found to be 'overrated'. (Abandoned, it ran wild and is *still* found in dry forests in India, even on the Ridge in Delhi; the local name *rabad ki bel* persists.) Only sometime around the 1850s was it determined that the best caoutchouc among Indian trees was furnished by *Ficus elastica*, which grew abundantly in the hilly tracts of Assam and Burma. All that remained was to find a means of bringing its produce to Calcutta for export.

For the next 20 years or so, rights to tap rubber in government forests were auctioned to private contractors. With short monopolistic leases and the price of Assam rubber climbing in London, there was immense pressure on the rubber contractors to deliver as much raw rubber as they could possibly collect in the shortest time. The result, to quote a Forest Report for 1868, was 'the most outrageous wholesale destruction of these valuable trees'. Many were tapped so mercilessly that they were killed outright. Others were simply pole-axed. In its native forests, *Ficus elastica* can grow as tall as a 16-storey building. Such a giant would have to be climbed twice – once to make the incisions and then once more to collect the latex. To save themselves the trouble, the tappers simply cut them down and collected all the latex they could from the supine carcass of the tree.

After much destruction had already taken place, the government decided to stop leasing rights and to establish instead plantations managed by the forest department. The first rubber plantation was set up in 1874 in Darang district, Assam.

Ironically, in the previous year, the first seeds of the Brazilian Para rubber tree, *Hevea brasiliensis*, were sent to the Royal Botanic Garden, Calcutta. There was mounting evidence that its caoutchouc was of better quality, and yielded in more copious quantities than the latex of *Ficus elastica*. It also fetched a better price in European markets. Besides, the Brazilian tree had the reputation of very rapid growth, attaining some 8 metres in 3 years in its native Amazonian forests.

The first experiments with Para rubber trees in India, however, were not a success. Very few of the seeds germinated – some plants were raised, but died in the winter, and it was decided that Bengal was too cold to grow Para rubber successfully. Perhaps Ceylon, warmer and frost-free, would be better? After another 10 years of trials, Ceylon too was abandoned, and attention shifted to Burma, where the first successful plantations of Para rubber were established. (The rubber plantations in Malabar lay well in the future.)

Meanwhile, it was becoming clear that Assam rubber was slipping badly in the face of its Brazilian competitor. Annual figures for the export of Assam rubber reached a peak in 1882-83, then showed a steady decline. The future clearly lay with Para rubber. The decline of an industry is seldom documented as well as its rise to prominence, and we know little of what happened to the plantations in Assam. Perhaps they were simply abandoned and allowed to 'return to the jungle'. Did some of them, perhaps, make way for other kinds of plantation, like tea?

Today, some 120 years on, Para rubber too is struggling on world markets, threatened by synthetic substances and the stressed economics of plantations. India rubber, for all intents and purposes, went kaput a very long time ago.

But wait a minute! What's that potted plant sitting there in the corner?

Did you know that something like 30 per cent of indoor potted plant sales in the United States are of some cultivar of the India rubber tree? Now that's called staging a comeback by the back door. Could we say then that India rubber has somehow 'bounced back'?

BAEL PHARMA

Various parts of the bael tree have proven tonic, antibiotic and anti-inflammatory properties and are employed in the treatment of snake bite and maladies of the digestive system, heart, eye, skin and liver. The fruit pulp is most valued for its ability to halt diarrhoea and dysentery.

The mucous obtained from unripe fruit is used as a strong cement, either on its own (by jewellers) or mixed with lime, to form a strong mortar used by masons. The yellowish wood is not handsome and has no evident heartwood but is hard and useful, with a pleasant smell when freshly cut.

Bael is one of the most sacred trees for Hindus, and it is often planted near temples because its leaves are an essential ingredient in offerings to Shiva. It is also an excellent bee-forage.

CULTIVATED MANGOES

The wild mango is small, with fibrous, stringy flesh, and the main purpose in creating cultivated varieties was to select for a large, fleshy, non-fibrous pulp, allied to flavour and, to some extent, colour and aroma. Some authorities think that the cultivated mango originally derived from a hybrid of *Mangifera indica* and a very tall, closely allied species, *Mangifera sylvatica*, found in moist forests of NE India.

In South Asia, the cultivation of select varieties of mango has been going on for at least 4000 years, perhaps even longer. At least 500 named varieties (some say 1000) have been described in India, with some 150 cultivars in the state of Uttar Pradesh alone. Some of them, perhaps, are too closely allied to qualify as distinct varieties, but it is nevertheless an astonishing statistic, testifying to the commercial importance of the mango in India.

HOW BIG CAN A MANGO GROW?

Wild or semi-wild mango trees growing in the right conditions and facing no competition (for light, water, soil nutrients, etc.) can grow to enormous sizes and individual trees towering 45 m into the sky have been reported.

One of the largest in India is in Chandigarh, with a massive trunk measuring 9.6 m in circumference and a crown spreading over 2250 sq. m. In an average year, it produces 10,000 to 15,000 fruit and in a good year, 25,000 mangoes, weighing 17 metric tonnes! Wild mangoes are reported to live up to 300 years, but cultivated forms no more than 80 years.

NEW LEAVES OF THE SITA-ASHOK

When you see a sita-ashok tree in new leaf, you cannot help but notice that the new leaves stand out dramatically against the backdrop of the dark-green canopy. When they first appear, the leaves hang down in limp tassels and stay like this until they reach full size, when they slowly begin to stiffen and grow more erect. They are also a peculiar colour – pinkish at first, slowly turning a translucent tan and then pale purple. This is because the young leaves emerge without any chlorophyll (with a green pigment), and it is only as they begin to stiffen that you can see the chlorophyll leaching into the leaves.

This behaviour of the young leaves is strange but by no means unique. A number of other evergreen trees from relatively dry habitats share this characteristic – notably the mango, nagkesar and Amherstia (*Amherstia nobilis*). There is little agreement among botanists about why exactly it helps to put out new leaves without chlorophyll. But it does make it easy to recognize one of these trees from a great distance.

SONJNA: THE MIRACLE TREE

Both the leaves and fruit of the sonjna are an astonishingly rich source of calcium, iron, vitamins B, A and C (when raw) and of protein. One scientist calculated that ounce for ounce, sonjna contains the calcium contained in 4 glasses of milk, the vitamin C equivalent of 7 oranges, the potassium of 3 bananas and more than 3 times the iron found in spinach.

And that is by no means all: sonjna pods are used to treat diabetes in W Africa and high blood pressure in India. Its glucoside compounds are being studied with great interest because of known antibiotic properties. The oil expressed from its seeds is used to soothe rheumatoid and gout pains. The oil does not go rancid or congeal in the cold, and is therefore used for lubricating small mechanisms like clocks. The oil is also used for salad dressing and in illumination and, because it absorbs and retains odours particularly well, in cosmetics and soaps. Parts of the tree have been used as a domestic cleaning agent, as a perfume, dye, fertilizer, for making rope and as an agent for tanning hides. The wood provides pulp suitable for making paper and the dried, crushed seeds act as a coagulant – similar to alum – used as an effective, low-cost means to purify muddy water and reduce bacterial contamination. The edible roots taste of horseradish, and the flowers are a rich source of nectar for honeybees.

Not bad, for a single tree!

USES OF THE KHAIR TREE

The khair tree is best known for 'catechu' obtained from its red heartwood by a procedure that is thousands of years old. It essentially involves boiling chips of the heartwood in water till a thick paste is formed, which hardens into liver-coloured blocks.

In pure form, this yields dark catechu or 'cutch', a strong astringent with medicinal uses and a dull-red dye. In less pure form, it yields *kathha*, the rusty substance used in paan. A third product, *kheersal*, is a crystalline powder found in wood cavities of some old trees. It is highly valued in traditional medicine as a cough medicine.

AMLA: THE ONE-FRUIT PHARMACY

The amla grows wild in dry and (slightly) moist forests throughout the Indian subcontinent – avoiding only the most arid and frost-prone tracts – and its natural range extends eastwards through tropical SE Asia. Many parts of the tree are highly esteemed in traditional Indian medicine, and here is only a starter-kit of the astonishing properties of its fruit: anyone who has eaten it knows that its extreme sourness is followed by a sweet and refreshing aftertaste, produced when saliva breaks down glycosides in the juice. It contains 20 times as much vitamin C as (an equivalent quantity of) orange juice. It is used to treat jaundice, gastrointestinal disorders, dyspepsia and coughs and is considered diuretic and laxative. In combination with the fruit of harra and baheda in Ayurvedic *triphala*, it is employed in treating chronic dysentery, biliousness, haemorrhoids, enlarged liver, quite apart from a range of digestive disorders. The juice from freshly picked fruit is employed as an eyewash. It is also cooked, baked, boiled, preserved and pickled in various ways as a general purpose tonic. Amla juice is also used in

hair dyes and dried amlas as a detergent and shampoo, where it is believed to cure 'confusion of thoughts' and loss of hair.

THE AMALTAS DEPENDS ON JACKALS AND BEARS

When a hard, whole fruit falls to the ground without splitting open, curiosity sometimes drives foresters to try and find out how its seeds are freed and brought to germination. In a famous experiment in Dehra Dun early last century, Robert Troup probed the reproductive strategy of the amaltas.

He collected a clutch of ripe pods and placed them in a specially marked plot in the Forest Research Institute. Within a week, jackals discovered the cache and cracked open the pods to get at the sweet pulp. From seeds that passed through their digestive tracts, 24 seedlings germinated in the first year, and another 12 in 2 subsequent years.

In another plot of the same size – this one protected from wild creatures by heavy netting – Troup placed the same number of ripe pods taken from the same trees. He observed this plot for 4 seasons – the pods gradually rotted and grew mouldy, freeing the seeds from the pod, but not one seed germinated.

Troup concluded that the amaltas can only reproduce with the assistance of animals that eat its fruit pulp. In forests where it grows naturally, bears, jackals, pigs and monkeys are all unwitting agents in propagating one of our most beautiful trees. On the Ridge in Delhi, this role is probably undertaken by jackals and civets. Porcupines too, though they are perilously close to being exterminated from most parts of the Ridge.

'KEEKAR' OR 'VILAITI KEEKAR'?

Many people in Delhi use the term 'keekar' to refer to *Prosopis juliflora*, though 'keekar' is more properly one of the desi names for the babool (*Acacia nilotica*). It may seem churlish to resist popular usage, except that (a) it is confusing and (b) it is founded on ignorance.

Prosopis juliflora is called 'keekar' by people who haven't learned to distinguish it from the babool. The 2 species do bear a superficial resemblance to each other, mainly in the feathery character of their foliage. In every other respect – the colour and character of their bark, the colour and length of their spines, the number of side-stalks in their leaves, the form and colour of their flower-clusters, the shape of their pods – they are completely distinct. *Prosopis juliflora* is not even an acacia.

For this reason, pedantic though it may seem, I usually stop and correct people who call *Prosopis juliflora* 'keekar'. 'Vilaiti keekar' and 'kabuli keekar' or even 'angrezi babool' are perfectly acceptable appellations for this exotic species which is now so widespread in Delhi and its surrounding areas.

Section 2:
Relating to the Identity, Taxonomy or Name of a Tree

Identifying Delhi's 'Christmas Tree'

The conifer commonly sold as the indoor 'Christmas tree' in Delhi is the New Caledonian pine or *Araucaria columnaris*. In Europe and America, a closely allied species, the Norfolk Island pine (*Araucaria heterophylla*), is widely sold and it is easy to confuse these 2 species.

Adult forms of both these araucarias are not hard to distinguish, but when they are young – and especially as potted specimens – both species have overlapping, needle-like juvenile foliage that is difficult to tell apart. (It does not help that for many decades, the scientific name *Araucaria excelsa* was misapplied to the Norfolk Island pine, and it is only more recent gardening books that set the record right by listing *Araucaria excelsa* as a discarded synonym of the New Caledonian pine.)

Older trees of both these species exchange their juvenile foliage for adult foliage, which has small, overlapping, triangular leaves, and it is only at this stage that it becomes easier to tell the 2 species apart. The leaves of *Araucaria columnaris* have a clear midrib which is missing or obscure in *Araucaria heterophylla* leaves. In general, it can be said that the leaf system of *Araucaria columnaris* is more compact, less 'coarse' and a darker green than that of *Araucaria heterophylla*.

As far as I can tell, *Araucaria heterophylla* is hardly, if ever, grown in India. The only other species of *Araucaria* that you might encounter in botanical gardens in northern India (such as the FRI in Dehra Dun) are *Araucaria cunninghamia* (with stiffer, more sharp-pointed juvenile leaves) and *Araucaria bidwillii* (whose leaves are much broader).

Naming the Almond

The almond has a long history of confusing name changes.

Because it lacks the thick, succulent flesh of peaches, plums and cherries, the almond was at first kept distinct from genus *Prunus* and was named *Amygdalus communis*. The name didn't last – in 1768 it was reunited with the other stone fruits in the Rose family as *Prunus dulcis*, and then in 1801 was renamed again *Prunus amygdalus*. This name remained until 1964, when – in order to clear up some confusion – the name *Prunus dulcis* was revived. There is still a school of botanists today who cling to the name *Prunus amygdalus* in preference to *Prunus dulcis*, and it is useful to remember that there isn't always a clear-cut 'right' and 'wrong' in botanical nomenclature.

Most botanists agree, however, that there are 2 varieties of the species – var. *dulcis* or the sweet almond and var. *amara* or the bitter almond. The bitter almond is quite a lot broader and a mite shorter than the sweet almond and, of course, is bitter tasting. In most cases, the 2 varieties can be told apart by the fact that the sweet almond has pink flowers and the bitter almond white or very pale pink flowers. As you would expect, it is the sweet almond that is extensively cultivated. The bitter almond contains a fixed oil that has some medicinal uses but is toxic if eaten in quantity, and is not commonly grown.

How Bauhinia x blakeana Got Its Name

The Hong Kong orchid tree was first discovered in 1908 as a single specimen growing on the seashore in Canton, southern China. It is thought to be an accidental hybrid between 2 closely related bauhinias – kaniar and kachnar – and in the way that accidents can be brilliantly fortuitous, produces orchid-like blooms of incomparable size and beauty. It was promptly named after the Governor of Hong Kong, Sir Henry Blake, and became, in time, the island's floral emblem.

You may come across the tree as '*Bauhinia blakeana*', but by the rules of botanical names, this is strictly incorrect because the name should reflect its hybrid origin – hence, the 'x' after '*Bauhinia*', denoting that it is a cross, and not a natural species.

Like many hybrids (mules, for instance), *Bauhinia* x *blakeana* is sterile, and produces hardly any fruit, if any, and sets no seed. This means that it can only be propagated through cuttings or by some other method of vegetative cloning. It also means that *every single tree* in cultivation – from California to Calcutta – is a direct descendant of that single tree discovered by accident in Canton early last century.

THE CORRECT NAME OF BISTENDU

Many modern authors merge the identity of *Diospyros cordifolia* and *Diospyros montana* and treat them as synonyms. This is a relatively recent development, because all the great 19th-century botanists took great pains to point out small but crucial differences between the 2 species.

My own experience with both species in the wild leads me to stick with the 19th-century distinction – *Diospyros montana*, with which I am familiar from lower slopes in Garhwal, is so clearly different from the *Diospyros* that we call 'bistendu' in Delhi that it seems hard to believe that anyone should conflate the two. Does it, perhaps, have to do with the perils of working with dried herbarium specimens, instead of real trees in the field?

NAME CHANGES IN THE PINK-FLOWERING CASSIAS

If you find yourself struggling to tell the pink cassias apart, don't worry, because you are in good company – even experts have a hard time. There's a schematic key on page 239 to help you

distinguish between the 4 forms found in Delhi. But quite apart from the differences *between* species, what do you make of the fact that all of the following names are synonyms of the *same* species?

Cathartocarpus nodosus
Cassia nodosa
Cassia javanica var. *nodosa*
Cassia javanica subsp. *nodosa*
Cassia javanica subsp. *agnes*
Cassia javanica var. *agnes*
Cassia agnes
Cassia indochinensis
Cassia javanica var. *indochinensis*

If you follow the sequence of name changes, you will see that this species has had a particularly choppy time. Once regarded as a species in its own right (*Cassia nodosa*), it was reduced to the status of a subspecies by some authors, and to a mere variety by others. And then, as if to cap the confusion, a completely different variety (*agnes*) was raised to the status of a species, and was subsequently recognized as being identical with *Cassia nodosa*. Soon afterwards, it was 'demoted' back to subspecies rank, and then down another step to a variety. Finally, it was given a new name.

Confusing? It's as though the experts couldn't make up their minds – in actual fact, it's partly a result of the old game of snakes and ladders between the 'joiners' and the 'splitters' in the world of taxonomy. In this particular case, it is compounded (and justified) by the inherent variability of some of the pink cassias, and their ability to hybridize and exchange minor characters.

Much of this name confusion first arose when it was argued that *Cassia javanica* was a variable, composite species and that many of the pink cassias were just mere varieties of this 'boss' species. Thus *Cassia javanica*, *Cassia nodosa* and *Cassia renigera* (to mention only those that we encounter in Delhi) were renamed *Cassia javanica* var. *javanica*, *Cassia javanica* var. *nodosa* and *Cassia javanica* var. *renigera*, respectively. (The only one of Delhi's species that was not included as a variety of *Cassia javanica* was *Cassia roxburghii*, and its name has remained unchanged. Thus far, at least.) Subsequently, there has been some minor quibbling about whether these forms are properly 'varieties' or 'subspecies', and in the case of *Cassia renigera*, some authorities have restored it to its old status as a separate species.

As a ready checklist, here is a chart of the name changes for Delhi's pink cassias. The latest accepted name is the last one in each list, and is underlined. Remember that not every authority agrees with 'accepted' nomenclature, and taxonomists will sometimes remind you that '…it's a matter of opinion.' So if you run into someone who disputes your name for a pink cassia, you know what to say!

It is actually more accurate to trace the lineage of *Cassia nodosa* in 2 converging lists, because that is more like what actually happened:

Cassia nodosa

Cassia javanica var. *nodosa*

Cassia javanica subsp. *nodosa*

Cassia javanica var. *indochinensis*

Cassia javanica var. *agnes*

Cassia agnes

Cassia javanica subsp. *agnes*

Cassia indochinensis
<u>*Cassia javanica* var. *indochinensis*</u>

Cassia javanica
Cassia javanica subsp. *javanica*
<u>*Cassia javanica* var. *javanica*</u>

Cassia renigera
Cassia javanica subsp. *renigera*
Cassia javanica var. *renigera*
<u>*Cassia renigera*</u>

<u>*Cassia roxburghii*</u> [no recent change in name]

CASSIAS AND EX-CASSIAS

Not so long ago, *Cassia* was a very large genus of more than 500 species. For convenience, cassias with similar features and characters were sorted into 'tribes' and 'subtribes', for everyone recognized that the genus included a diversity of forms that was difficult to contain in a single ragbag category. In the early 1980s, the genus was formally split into 3 separate genera – *Cassia*, *Senna* and *Chamaecrista*. After the reorganization, only about 30 species were regarded as belonging to genus *Cassia* in the newer, stricter sense of the term. Most of the other species crossed over to *Senna* (270 species) and *Chamaecrista* (250 species).

Unfortunately, the separation of the genera is not based on large, easy-to-figure features that would enable a gardener, for instance, to easily tell a member of one genus from the other. Beware of false claims! I've heard it said that *Cassia* and *Senna* are easily distinguished because the former have cylindrical pods, the latter flat pods. This is often, but by no means always, true and can easily lead you astray. The details and minutiae of the differences are perhaps too technical to be of much interest – one of the key differences, for example, is the shape, number and structure of the stamens. Another is the shape and type of pores (stomata) on the surface of the leaf.

THE IDENTITY OF THE RAMDHAN CHAMPA

You may find that most gardening books list this plant as *Ochna squarrosa* or, in more recent publications, as *Ochna jabotapita*, which is the accepted new name for *Ochna squarrosa*. Both the Botanical Survey of India and Bailey (in 'Hortus'), however, say that the large flowered species commonly cultivated is *Ochna obtusata* and is quite distinct from *Ochna jabotapita*. I have followed their lead, even though it is, perhaps, a little confusing.

HOW EUCALYPTS ARE DIFFERENTIATED

Like the remarkable marsupials – kangaroos and their relatives – that are such a striking feature of the Australian landscape, genus *Eucalyptus* is quintessentially Australian. There are a whole lot of them, for one – something like 700 species – and their range and diversity is mind-boggling. So dominant are the eucalypts that they make up over 90 per cent of the forest trees of this huge continent. There are separate species adapted to growing in sand and in boggy marshes; in hot, dry, rocky sites and on snowy mountain tops; in steaming, wet tropical forests and parched deserts. Some of the tallest trees in the world, as well as little shrubby 'mallees', are eucalypts. Like Australia's array of marsupials that evolved in the absence of (or because of the absence of) any mammals, adapting and radiating to fill every conceivable niche on land, the eucalypts too are a textbook case of adaptive evolution on an isolated island-continent.

Many people use the word 'eucalyptus' and 'eucalypt' to mean the same thing, or as a scientific name and its non-scientific derivative, respectively. This may once have been true, but strictly speaking, this is no longer the case. (I like to think that the word 'eucalypt' probably has a very prosaic origin – someone must have coined it so as not to have to say 'eucalyptusses' – ugh – in the plural.) *Eucalyptus*, of course, denotes any plant belonging to the genus of that name. 'Eucalypt' is a looser, more sweeping term, used to refer to any eucalyptus-like plant, and includes members of at least 2 genera that were once called *'eucalyptus'* but are now regarded as being completely separate (*Angophora* and *Corymbia*). Including them under the general term 'eucalypt' makes sense because it acknowledges their similarity and evolutionary links. So it is useful to remember that 'eucalypt' is a more inclusive term than 'eucalyptus'. It is possible to be a eucalypt without being a eucalyptus, but not vice versa.

The scientific name 'eucalyptus' was coined from 2 Greek words: *eu*, meaning 'well', and *kalypto*, which means 'I cover', referring to the little cap ('calyptra' or 'operculum') which is typical of the genus. The cap hides the flower in bud, and is thrown off when it is time for the flower to bloom and the stamens to expand. The precise shape of this bud-cap is somewhat different for each species – it can be long and pointy, or squat and dome-shaped, or round with a tiny nipple, and so on – and is one key diagnostic tool by which scientists tell one species of *eucalyptus* from another.

The other key diagnostic feature is the woody fruit or seedpod, called a 'gumnut' (in Ozzy speak, all eucalypts are 'gum-trees' or just 'gums'). Here again, each species tends to have a distinctive gumnut, unique not just in size and general shape, but in the particular character of its teeth or valves, the rim, and so on.

There are other obvious diagnostic features as well, such as the colour and texture of the bark. In Australia, this is the commonest way in which people refer to different gum-trees – as 'ironbarks', 'peppermints', 'stringybarks' and so on. But this only differentiates between 5 or 6 broad categories of eucalypts. Leaves and flowers can be helpful too, but not as much as is usual with other kinds of trees, and scientists usually take foliage and flowers into account only as additional features to help confirm an identification.

CORYMBIA VS EUCALYPTUS

Long ago, in simpler times, there was a very large genus of about 700 species called *Eucalyptus*, and a very small genus (with only 7 species) called *Angophora*, and together they were called 'gum-trees' by Australians. The reason they shared this common name is that they *look* very similar. The reason they were differentiated scientifically is that they differ in one fundamental character – unlike *all* species of *Eucalyptus* (whose flower buds are initially covered by a little cap – or 2), the buds of *Angophora* are naked and uncapped. That's pretty fundamental, especially if you remember that the name 'eu-calyptus' means 'well-covered', pointedly referring to the bud-cap. What's more, unlike *Eucalyptus*, the flowers of *Angophora* have petals – tiny little ones, but petals nevertheless – and it wasn't easy to gloss over these differences.

This was the situation until 1995, when 2 Australian botanists called Hill and Johnson published a paper formally recognizing a new genus called *Corymbia*, comprising 113 species that had been scooped out from genus *Eucalyptus*. To understand this story, you need to know that in botany a large genus like *Eucalyptus* tends to be too unwieldy to subsist without being subdivided into smaller groups, which may be known as tribes, sects, sections, or some such term denoting a sub-generic grouping of plants. *Eucalyptus* was divided into 7 to 12 sub-generic groups (depending on which author you relied on), and *Corymbia* was one of them. Hill and Johnson's paper argued that all the species in subgroup *Corymbia* (plus a few others) differed *enough* from the rest of the species in *Eucalyptus* to merit becoming a genus on their own.

'*Eucalyptus*' is such a characteristic Ozzy name that it wasn't surprising that the proposal to split it up aroused some dismay. Many scientists resisted the change and continued to use the old name for *Corymbia*, implicitly disagreeing with Hill and Johnson's proposition. At the same time, studies in DNA sequencing were beginning to show that the *Corymbia* were in fact more closely allied to *Angophora* than to *Eucalyptus*, lending some support to Hill and Johnson.

It was some consolation that all the reclassified species hung on to their second (specific) names as well as their common names. Thus *Eucalyptus ficifolia* (red flowering gum) and *Eucalyptus gummifera* (red bloodwood) became *Corymbia ficifolia* and *Corymbia gummifera*, respectively, and continued to be known as the 'red flowering gum' and 'red bloodwood'. Yet, resistance to the name change continued. One of the fears was that by the same logic, taxonomists might seek to promote *all* the separate sub-genera of *Eucalyptus* into new genera. What probably rankled most of all was that – unlike the separation of *Eucalyptus* from *Angophora*, which was based on easily visible differences – the differences between *Eucalyptus* and *Corymbia* are at a subtle level, not easily recognized. There are no obvious characters of bark or bud or foliage to mark the separation.

Hill and Johnson went to some length to explain to Australians that species of *Corymbia* continued to be 'gums', and that the common name 'eucalypt' could still be used to denote members of all 3 genera. Acceptance of the new genus will probably be a long, slow process, but while the dust settles, what should one do in the meantime?

For the moment, you are free to make your choice. Whether you call a tree *Corymbia citriodora* or *Eucalyptus citriodora*, you are clearly referring to the same plant and both names are valid. Either way, you are referring unambiguously to the lemon-scented gum.

CEIBA OR CHORISIA?

Genus *Chorisia* has been pushed around a bit in recent years. Most authors now agree that it has too many essential characters in common with *Ceiba* (kapok) to be kept separate, and treat them both as belonging to the genus *Ceiba*.

There is less agreement about the names and number of species that made up the old genus *Chorisia* in the first place. The territory is disputed by the usual adversaries, the 'joiners' and the 'splitters'. The joiners gloss over the differences and say that all 5 or 6 putative species are really only variations of a single, composite species. The splitters insist that the differences are consistent and matter enough to recognize separate species.

It's uncertain ground, because most species of floss-silk trees are capable of hybridizing among themselves and, to confound matters even more, there are hybrid forms in cultivation as well. Clearly, appearances are deceptive. How then do we take stock of the species? How many species of floss-silk tree does Delhi actually have?

Most nurseries in Delhi differentiate between the pink and white floss-silk trees, *Chorisia speciosa* and *Chorisia insignis* respectively – this was before they were reclassified and, logically, they should now be known as *Ceiba speciosa* and *Ceiba insignis*. (Try telling a nursery this!)

Here's where you have to make a choice: you can either join the Joiners and treat them both as different forms of a *single* species: *Ceiba insignis*. In botanical language, you would say that both forms are members of the *Ceiba insignis* 'type', or if you want to show off a bit, as 'aff. *Ceiba insignis*' (in botanical jargon, aff. = affinity for).

On the other hand, you may be persuaded – like I am – by the obvious differences between the 2 trees to think of them as separate species. Look carefully at the flowers of the white and pink floss-silk trees – other than the difference in colour, you will notice that there are some features that clearly set them apart. For example, the 'corona' surrounding the staminal tube at the very centre of the flower is ivory-white and completely hairless in the white-flowered form – and dark and fuzzy-hairy in the pink form. Once seen, such differences are impossible to gloss over, and lend weight to the traditional distinction between *Ceiba insignis* (the white-flowered floss-silk tree) and *Ceiba speciosa* (the pink-flowered one).

Beware the liminal categories, though – there's one tree on the Rajaji Marg roundabout with flowers so pale that it's easily mistaken for *Ceiba insignis*. Look inside the flower, however, and its dark, woolly corona at once announces its identity as *Ceiba speciosa*.

In short, all white-flowered ex-*Chorisias* are not necessarily *Ceiba insignis*. And depending on which authority you follow, even the pink-flowered ex-*Chorisia* could be *Ceiba insignis*. Confusing? Treat it as a licence to use whichever name you please. Botany isn't always this accommodating!

CRESCENTIA ALATA AND CRESCENTIA CUJETE

The scientific literature tells us that the closely related *Crescentia cujete* differs from *Crescentia alata* by having simple leaves and noticeably larger fruit. I have been a little puzzled by 3 specimens in Delhi that have both kinds of leaves!

It is possible that I am wrong in treating them all as *Crescentia alata* – in which case the specimens in the zoo and in NISCOM belong to *Crescentia cujete*.

VARIETIES OF THE CHIKRASSY

Chukrasia tabularis is the only species in the *Chukrasia* genus, but some authors distinguish between 2 varieties of the species based primarily on differences in the degree of velvetiness of their leaflets. They are called *Chukrasia tabularis* var. *tabularis* and *Chukrasia tabularis* var. *velutina*. Even though Delhi does not have many chikrassy trees, both varieties are represented here. Var. *tabularis* is more numerous, and can be seen inside the Mandi House and Kamaraj roundabouts. There are only 3 or 4 trees of var. *velutina*, on Dharam Marg, near Malcha Marg market.

The essential differences are:

var. *tabularis* – its leaflets do not feel velvety at all, though with a hand lens you can see that some of the nerve junctions on the undersurface are furry. I have also noticed that its leaflets are more droopy than the other variety. The ends of its leaflets are also more drawn out into longer, pointy tips.

var. *velutina* – its leaflets feel unmistakably velvety, somewhat like the feel of billiards-beige. Generally, this variety feels velvety-hairy in all departments – twigs, leaf stalks, leaflet-stalks, etc. Its leaflets also tend to be more rumpled – i.e. they do not lie flat – compared to var. *tabularis*. They are also broader, and are held out less droopily, more or less on the same plane as the main leaf stalk.

VARIETIES OF THE ASHOK

In the wild, *Polyalthia longifolia* is typically a spreading tree with outstretched branches.

The ashok trees that we see in cultivation are all, to greater or lesser degree, a 'weeping' form of *Polyalthia longifolia* with short, drooping branches hugged close to the main stem, so that the tree looks like a narrow pillar of foliage. The gardening trade tends to call this form *Polyalthia longifolia*

var. *pendula* though, apparently, this name has never been validly published and has no botanical standing. It is probably therefore preferable to call it *Polyalthia longifolia* 'Pendula', the name in single inverted commas denoting that it is a cultivar and not a distinct, recognized variety.

There is yet another cultivar of the ashok with miniaturized leaves (and flowers) which goes by the name *Polyalthia longifolia* 'Angustifolia'. You can see 2 large trees fitting this description inside the Supreme Court, but it is relatively rare in Delhi.

AMERICAN SPECIES OF PROSOPIS IN DELHI

Many different species of *Prosopis* go loosely by the name 'mesquite' (in North America) or 'algarrobo' in (South America), and are extremely difficult to buttonhole because there are so many closely allied species and forms.

Mesquites are aggressive, invasive plants, and their spread is assisted greatly by livestock that graze on their sweetish pods and disperse their seeds. There was probably a time when all the American species were geographically separated and quite distinct. But with the arrival of white colonists and their livestock, the various mesquites spread far beyond their native ranges and hybridized. Gradually there arose intermediate forms, blurring the distinctions between what were once separate species. Not surprisingly, when botanists started classifying the mesquites, they found it difficult to assign them undisputable status as species or varieties. Like all good botanists, they argued and acidly disagreed, and the result was a multiplicity of competing names.

The earliest mesquite seeds were sent out to India in 1877, but the origin of the seed was not clearly specified. Subsequent batches of seed suffered from the same defect, and it is likely that they represented mesquites from very different places in the Americas. Ever since that time, Indian botanists have grappled with a central question: Was the introduced mesquite a single variable species (*Prosopis juliflora*) with a multiplicity of forms or a collection of closely related but separate species?

We don't need to follow the controversy in detail, but gene-mapping has helped to clear away some of the cobwebs, and here is the latest accepted position with regard to the mesquites brought into India:

Basically, most of the forms of *Prosopis juliflora* that were once thought to be mere 'varieties' are now regarded as separate species. Thus *Prosopis chilensis* (Chilean mesquite), *Prosopis velutina* (velvet mesquite) and *Prosopis glandulosa* (honey mesquite) are recognized as species in their own right. Strictly, *Prosopis juliflora* is now treated as a plant originating in coastal tropical America from Mexico south to Columbia, Venezuela and the Caribbean, but is not indigenous to southwestern USA at all. *Prosopis juliflora* has 2 recognized varieties: var. *juliflora* and var. *horrida*.

The bulk of the mesquites brought into India was made up by *Prosopis juliflora* and *Prosopis glandulosa*, with a sprinkling of other species that were given field trials from time to time. These 2 mainline species can be distinguished mainly by differences in the size and shape of their leaflets, which are longer and more spaced apart in *Prosopis glandulosa*. It is also claimed that *Prosopis glandulosa* is deciduous, while *Prosopis juliflora* is evergreen or at least semi-evergreen, but I have not found this to be a reliable distinguishing character in Delhi.

It is worth emphasizing, however, that the exotic mesquites have all hybridized to such an extent that it is now increasingly difficult to tell them apart in the field.

VARIETIES OF THE BABOOL

Acacia nilotica is only one of about 135 thorny African species of acacia. Within the species, however, experts differentiate between 9 separate subspecies, separated mainly by the shape and velvetiness of their fruit pods and the form or 'habit' of the mature tree.

3 of these subspecies are Indian, the other 6 from various places in Africa.

The standard type that we find in Delhi, with a tall, open crown, is known locally as the godi, teli or telia babool. Scientifically, it is more accurate to speak of this subspecies as *Acacia nilotica* subsp. *indica*.

2 other subspecies were until recently regarded as varieties but have now been 'promoted' – one is the kauria or vedi babool (scientifically: *Acacia nilotica* subsp. *vediana*) which is short and crooked, with a more spreading crown of interlacing branches. Its bark is also rougher and more fissured. It is found mostly in the Deccan.

The second is the tall, distinctive ramkanta babool (*Acacia nilotica* subsp. *cupressiformis*) with steeply ascending branches like a cypress or Kashmir poplar. This is the most ornamental (but aptly, somehow!) least useful of the 3 varieties, and is seen in W India, Haryana and the southern Punjab. You can see quite a lot of them in fields on either side of NH8, the Delhi-Jaipur Highway.

WHICH CELTIS?

There is some confusion about the identity of the *Celtis* cultivated in Delhi. Most nurseries, if they know the name at all, call it *Celtis australis* – which is the Mediterranean or southern nettle tree – but even a little acquaintance with the species is enough to tell you that this is most unlikely. The specialist literature is not very helpful. Some authors take a broad view of *Celtis australis*, ignoring small differences and forms and clubbing them all together into one composite, variable species. Others, more alert to the differences, prefer to recognize 3 or 4 separate species of *Celtis* in northern India alone.

In this unresolved tug of war, I find myself leaning towards the 'splitters' rather than the 'joiners'. My reasons have more to do with climate and ecology than any differences in minor characters. *Celtis australis* is widely planted as a street tree in southern France and Italy, where it is perfectly at home in mild Mediterranean summers and moderate winters. From there, its range extends eastwards into Iran, Afghanistan and the Suleiman Range and Salt Ranges in Pakistan, climbing higher and higher up the western Himalaya as it edges towards subtropical heat. Everything I have read about *Celtis australis* suggests that it is most unlikely to tolerate Delhi's scorching summers.

Celtis tetrandra, on the other hand, is found at lower altitudes in the Himalaya and seems much more likely to be the species that we see in Delhi. The writings of R.N. Parker and U.N. Kanjilal in the 1930s support this view. But the clinching evidence, for me, was actually seeing *Celtis australis* in the south of France. It would take a lot of arm-twisting to convince me that I was looking at the same tree that I know so well in Delhi.

IN WHICH THE KRISHNA FIG IS IDENTIFIED

The Krishna fig is not even mentioned in older Indian Floras – certainly not before 1910 – and I became curious about when it was first described and assigned a botanical identity. This, briefly, is its story.

The director of the Royal Botanic Garden at Howrah, David Prain, was brought a branch of the tree by a resident of Calcutta in 1896 who would not say where it came from or how old the tree was. All he revealed was that it grew somewhere close to Calcutta, and recounted the legend that the tree is an ordinary banyan tree whose leaves were miraculously transformed into little jars by Lord Rama (or Lord Krishna, according to a competing legend). It is easy to imagine Prain's excitement at seeing the unusual pocket-forming leaves, but it must have been equally frustrating not to be able to examine the parent tree.

By 1901, Prain had succeeded in growing 2 specimens in the Botanic Garden from cuttings. (He must somehow have won over 'the resident of Calcutta', for how else could he have obtained the cuttings?) One specimen was planted out in the main collection of the Garden; the other he sent to Kew Gardens in London to be grown under glass. And while he was waiting for the plants to grow older and develop their first figs, he sent specimens of the strange leaves to be examined by expert botanists. One such expert was Dr C. de Candolle in Geneva.

de Candolle studied the pocket-leaves closely, and likened them to those of 'pitcher plants', which are modified to trap insects or nutrients. He noticed, however, that this was the only kind of pitcher-leaf whose 'outside' is made up of the upper surface of the leaf. (In all other cases, it is the underside of the leaf that forms the 'outside' of the pocket.) But de Candolle was unable to say what function, if any, the 'pitchers' of the fig tree actually performed, except that they might perhaps help the tree to retain small quantities of rainwater.

de Candolle was faced with a basic question – did these leaves come from a new species of plant? Or were they just strange, anatomical 'freaks', a chance mutation perhaps, of an ordinary banyan tree? de Candolle decided that it was a true natural species in its own right. He would need to examine the figs to confirm this fact, and that might take a few years... In the meantime, he named the plant *Ficus krishnae*, and published his findings.

I have not been able to discover if de Candolle lived to discover his error. Probably not, because it took an awfully long time for botanists to begin to doubt the specific status of *Ficus krishnae*. Sometime in the 1930s, perhaps even later, it slowly became clear that the tree was not really a separate species, but a freakish variety of the banyan. The basis of their discovery was this: if you grow the Krishna fig from a *cutting*, it will produce pocket-leaves identical with its mother-plant, as you would expect. But when raised from *seed*, 90 per cent of the seedlings revert to the true banyan form, with only 10 per cent retaining the unusual pocket-leaves. Botanists call such trees 'bud-sports', and they are indeed merely horticultural varieties of some stable species. That's why and how *Ficus krishnae* became *Ficus benghalensis* var. *krishnae*.

VARIETIES OF THE WEEPING FIG

The taxonomy of weeping figs is something of a minefield not just because there is little accord about its varieties and subspecies, but also because there is a bewildering amount of hybrids and cultivars around, competing for a share in the flourishing market for indoor plants.

Most 19th-century authorities distinguished between 3 varieties of *Ficus benjamina*:

1 *Ficus benjamina* var. *benjamina*: the typical or 'normal' weeping fig, a large strangler with aerial roots and bright-red figs

2 *Ficus benjamina* var. *comosa*: resembling #1 in habit, but with larger leaves clustered towards the ends of its branches, and yellowish figs

3 *Ficus benjamina* var. *nuda*: with distinctly smaller, narrower leaves and pale-green to reddish-brown figs

Much of the modern confusion turns on whether or not a particular form should be regarded as a variety, subspecies or a full-fledged species in its own right. Var. *comosa*, for example, has been treated by some authors as a separate species (*Ficus comosa*). A recent publication of the BSI pokes the ashes of this debate by elevating it from a 'variety' to a 'subspecies' of *Ficus benjamina*. Var. *nuda*, on the other hand, was reduced by some authors to a synonym of var. *comosa*.

The thicket of discarded names testifies to the problems of trying to find an agreed list of the various forms of *Ficus benjamina*. Even big-time botanists don't seem to agree among themselves. How on earth does a layman make sense of this drizzle of fine differentiation? Actually (come to think of it), does it really *matter*?

Luckily – only because it makes life simpler – Delhi doesn't seem to have any specimens of var. *benjamina* at all. And it's relatively easy to tell var. *comosa* apart from var. *nuda* because var. *nuda* is much smaller, both in stature and in its leaves.

In Delhi, it's more useful and interesting to learn how to tell a weeping fig from a laurel fig (*Ficus microcarpa*), because that's a more likely area of confusion. Learn to spot the various kinds of benjamina leaves – the ones with short apical 'tails'. The ones with a little twist. Smaller, thinner ones. Bigger, broader ones. With a little practice, you will find that the weeping figs will snap into your recognition template and announce their identity even before you've begun to look closely at their details.

Now is when you can begin to bone up on the small differences, the various cultivars, their names, the controversies. Now is when you can take sides. If you like. Or if no like, just leave the squabbling to professional taxonomists.

THE MAN-MADE FIG TREE

I had a hard time identifying the Alii fig, and the story is worth telling if only to point to some of the difficulties of trying to identify man-made varieties or 'cultivars'.

When I first noticed this tree in Delhi – as recently as the year 2001 – and started to make enquiries, nurserymen told me (with complete

confidence) that it is a 'new variety' (the term 'variety' is used quite loosely here) called '*Ficus longifolia*'. While the term 'longifolia' is a perfectly adequate description of the shape of its leaves, it is not a valid or recognized botanical name.

I then searched through botanical sources, but failed to find it. Perhaps it had been 'discovered' or brought in from the wild too recently to have made it into the books I was consulting…?

Next, I tried to track it down through the Web, and finally found photographs and descriptions that matched, but much of the information proved to be misleading. Some websites referred to it as *Ficus maclellandii* – or *F. macleilandii* – followed by names like 'Alii', 'Amstel King', and 'Amstel Queen'. I made another search through the botanical literature – and *Ficus maclellandii* too proved to be invalid. But with names like 'Alii' and 'Amstel King', etc., I now knew that I was dealing with a cultivar, and these names helped to refine my search on the Web.

I began to realize that I was dealing not with a 'normal' wild plant that had been tamed and bred in the garden as an ornamental, but one that was much more like a modern manufactured product – a proprietary trademark plant, confected and hybridized for the indoor potted plant market.

The highest-selling indoor plant in America is *Ficus benjamina*, which has a whole legion of cultivars and forms. While immensely popular, all benjaminas suffer from one apparently incurable habit – when moved from one part of a room to another, they tend to suddenly drop all their leaves. So the market had a crying need for a new, better-behaved indoor ficus. And if it had attractive, glossy foliage, it stood a better chance of carving out a niche in the indoor plant market.

The search for a good-looking, well-behaved ficus led to the 'Alii' form. I'm not certain when exactly it first hit the market, probably around 1995 or thereabouts. In the year 2000, 'Alii figs' were presented to the plant-buying public in Florida as one of the 'Figs with a Future', a trademark line that quickly captured a significant share of the indoor plant market. From then on, new forms of this plant have been introduced at regular intervals.

The original and most popular cultivar – called 'Alii' – bases its appeal on its glossy leaves and compact, bushy crown. Most advertising sites present it as an indoor fig especially suited for placing on the table or window sill. The 'Amstel' line is similar, but has wider and slightly larger leaves. Within 'Amstel' though, there are variations of leaf colour and form, and each has been given a different name like 'Amstel King', 'Amstel gold', and so on.

I finally stumbled on a Dutch and a German site that said that the Alii ficus is derived from *Ficus bennindijkii* from Thailand. But details of its hybridizing and development are still elusive. Did they irradiate its seeds? If *Ficus bennindijkii* was one parent, which was the other? What exactly is the genetic cocktail?

I must admit that I am somewhat unnerved by the Alii fig. I have become used to describing plants with a definite provenance and ecology, with so much history and, more often than not, such important uses and roles in human lives. Almost every one of the other fig trees in this book is a superb example of such trees. And then, suddenly, here I was dealing with a plant whose origins and botanical identity was almost incidental, if not altogether irrelevant – much less a natural plant than a trademark, off-the-shelf item of commerce.

Is this where we are headed? I hope not.

INDOOR RUBBERS

Rubber plants, with their big, glossy leaves and bright-pink leaf-buds, have been used as ornamental indoor plants (in the West) at least since Victorian times. They still account for a huge share of the trade in indoor plants in the United States. Of course, there's no such thing as an 'indoor plant' in nature – they are all wild plants that have been domesticated or genetically manipulated to make the transition from the outdoors into the particular conditions of our homes. In the West, this usually translates into lower light conditions, drier and staler air (because of air conditioning), and limited soil and space in which to grow (not to speak of an ambience replete with cat's hair, loud music and turpenoid smells).

The first task of domesticating the rubber tree was to shrink this giant of the rainforest into a compact form, and to breed it to adapt to lower light conditions. That done, plant breeders set out

to produce new leaf colours and forms. The earliest decorative leaves were simply variegated (yellow or white blotches on a green background) but it wasn't until the introduction of the hybrid form 'Decora' (from Belgium) in the 1950s that the indoor rubber tree became all the rage. 'Decora' had a wider leaf that was deep bronze-green, its leaf-bud long and startlingly red, and its form more compact and leafy. The huge spurt in 'Decora' sales spurred plant breeders to new exertions.

There have been lots of successful new forms since – one of the most dramatic was 'Doescheri', with a narrower leaf, strikingly variegated in patterns of green, greyish green, yellow and white, and a pink midrib and leaf stalk. Its downside was that it was a slow grower.

'Decora', meanwhile, subdivided into numerous forms like 'Decora Schryveriana', 'Decora rubra', 'Decora Honduras' and 'Decora Zulu Shield'. With bold colours, mottling, streaks and unusual patterns on their leaves, there is now a very long list of recognized – and in many instances, patented TM – ornamental forms. The list is far too long to reproduce here, but it is worth pointing out that these names are in danger of becoming hopelessly confused.

(Remember that when you render the name of a cultivar, it is standard practice not to use italics, and instead to capitalize its first letter and to use single inverts around its name. This way, you know that you're not dealing with a scientific name, but a plant breeder's product.)

THE LAUREL FIG AND ITS HYBRIDS

For a very long time, the laurel fig was known to botanists as *Ficus retusa*, but the epithet 'retusa' was a bit puzzling because the leaves of this tree are hardly ever 'retuse' (i.e. notched at the apex). E.J.H. Corner pointed out in the 1960s that this name was an error and that the 'real' *Ficus retusa* is a small 'strangler' of Malaysian swamp-forests.

Meanwhile, sometime in the 1960s or there-abouts, the laurel fig – especially 2 or 3 small-leaved garden varieties – became a big hit as an indoor plant in America, closely rivalling the weeping fig (*Ficus benjamina*) and its ornamental cultivars. Its newly won popularity, however, gave a new lease of life to the old mistaken name, and you still find many nurseries stubbornly sticking to the name 'Ficus retusa'.

To confuse matters further, there is now a long list of garden hybrid and cultivar names, such as 'Green Gem', 'Hawaii', 'Nitida' and so on, differing from each other mainly in the size, shape and colouring of their leaves. Incidentally, the plant that many Indian nurseries sell as 'Ficus panda' is also thought to be a cultivar of this tree, though its precise horticultural origins remain somewhat obscure.

What about natural varieties?

Here too, the taxonomic literature is a little confusing: it lists at least 9 separate varieties of Ficus microcarpa, most of which are Malesian or Australian. The only Indian variety seems to be Ficus microcarpa var. microcarpa. Some authors also cite Ficus microcarpa var. nitida as an Indian variety, with leaves that are distinctly narrower and slightly smaller than the former. It is also claimed that var. microcarpa is indigenous to the Deccan peninsula, while var. nitida is found in 'trans-Gangetic' India, but the identity of this second variety is by no means universally accepted.

OTHER SPECIES OF MORUS IN DELHI

For more than a century now, writers describing the mulberry in India have said that there are (at least) 2 species commonly found in the plains – the white and the Indian mulberry, or Morus alba and Morus indica (now known as Morus australis) respectively.

This is probably as true for Delhi as it is for Lucknow, Patna or Calcutta. The only trouble is that even though I am alert to their stated botanical differences, I cannot say with any confidence that I have held a specimen of Morus australis in my hand.

There are 2 factors that make it extremely hard to tell these 2 species apart. For one, the 'flagship' species – Morus alba or the white mulberry – is known to be spectacularly variable. Despite its name, the white mulberry produces fruit that range from white through red to the deepest purple. So the colour of the fruit is no good as a clue to its identity.

The problem really is that the species has been cultivated for so many millennia that it has led to the selection and breeding of a huge roster of forms. There are some 700 recognized varieties of Morus alba in Japan alone! And this is to say nothing of the natural variability of semi-wild specimens growing in different conditions on varied sites.

The other reason it is so difficult to isolate Morus alba from Morus australis is that the technical difference between the 2 species is slight, so much so that some botanists regard Morus australis as a mere variety of Morus alba. Combing through the literature, the following differences stand out:

Morus alba	Morus australis
Small or middle-sized tree	Usually smaller than Morus alba
Young shoots may be lightly downy	Young shoots are smooth, not downy
Apex of leaf short-pointy, seldom long	Apex of leaf usually pointier and stretched out longer
The styles (in the female flower) are short, smooth or only slightly hairy, and separate at their base	The styles are longer than Morus alba's and hairy, and are joined at their base
Fruit are extremely variable in size, range from white to purple in colour, and are usually sweet	Fruit are small, usually dark purple but scarcely edible

As you can imagine, looking for a specimen of Morus australis can be a frustrating task. The shape and size of the leaf are not reliable clues. Nor is the colour or size of the fruit. It might help if you look at the minute parts of a female flower with a hand lens. But it's a little like looking for a dwindling race of people whose only distinguishing character is that they all have peculiar shaped moles on the palms of their hands. You can't spot them merely by looking at their faces or figures. And how many people can you approach to look at their palms?

Actually it gets worse – it's possible that the impressive variability of the white mulberry masks the presence of some other closely related species in Delhi. The black mulberry (*Morus nigra*) may well be cultivated here, and so too the Himalayan mulberry (*Morus serrata*). They are a little easier to tell apart from *Morus alba* than *Morus australis*, but then, on the other hand, even a little hybridizing would go a long way towards hiding their true identity.

WHICH KOELREUTERIA?

I am going against the grain in identifying this Delhi tree as *Koelreuteria elegans* rather than *Koelreuteria paniculata*, but I am persuaded of its identity by the fact that the literature clearly states that *Koelreuteria paniculata* has feather-compound, not bi-pinnate leaves. Furthermore, its bladder fruits are much larger than those found on specimens in Delhi.

I should mention, however, that *Koelreuteria elegans* has 2 recognized subspecies in subsp. *elegans* and subsp. *formosana*, and I have not been able to determine which of these subspecies our trees in Delhi belong to.

THE LONG-FINGERED CHINAR

There are a few cultivated varieties of the chinar which are sold in nurseries. The most popular is a variety with long, deeply incised, pointy lobes in its leaf known in the nursery trade as 'Digitata', though botanists do not all agree on whether it is a cultivar or a species in its own right. Proponents of the cultivar theory call it *Platanus orientalis* 'Digitata', *Platanus orientalis* var. *acerifolia* or alternately, as a hybrid, *Platanus* x *acerifolia*. As a separate species, it is given the name *Platanus acerifolia*, but since there is little agreement about its origins, it is fair to use any one of these names!

MAKING SENSE OF THE FRANGIPANIS

Genus *Plumeria* pays a price for being so popular – it has so many (literally) hundreds of varied forms and hybrids that botanists have found it extremely difficult to separate them into species. Some years ago, most botanists believed that there

were some 50 species of *Plumeria*, sorted (mainly) by the form and colour of their flowers. Today, most botanists accept that there are not more than 7 or perhaps 8 species in all. This obviously means that a few species, at least, must contain a great and confusing diversity of forms. Here are a few diagnostic tips to help you tell them apart:

There are only 2 species of *Plumeria* grown in Delhi – *Plumeria rubra* and *Plumeria obtusa*. (It doesn't help that both of them are loosely referred to as 'temple trees', 'frangipanis' or 'champas', so I'll stick to their botanical names to avoid confusion.)

With a little practice, you can learn to tell these 2 species apart by their leaves. *Plumeria rubra* has a larger leaf that tapers narrowly at base and more gently at its apex. Its leaf is more or less smooth (at least when mature) with a hairless stalk. It also has relatively fewer pairs of secondary nerves branching out from the central nerve. Furthermore, it is usually matte green, without any gloss.

Plumeria obtusa's leaf is smaller, widest in the upper third or has parallel sides. It too has a V-shaped base, but the apex is broad and rounded, and is either notched or has only a minute little point. Some of its forms are densely woolly-hairy underneath, but this is extremely variable. Other forms may appear hairless, but if you look closely you can see minute hairs, especially on the leaf stalk and along the main nerve. Relative to *Plumeria rubra*, the leaf is darker on top, with a faint but distinct gloss.

There are other differences too – the long common stalk from which the individual flowers branch out is always pink in *Plumeria rubra*, green in *Plumeria obtusa*. The flowers exhibit slight differences too – the petals tend to be broader and more distinctly spiral in *Plumeria rubra* with some overlap between the petals. The petals of *Plumeria obtusa* are usually thinner, with little or no overlap. But it is dangerous to generalize about their flowers because of the sheer number and diversity of hybrids and cultivars.

Of the 2 species, *Plumeria rubra* is more common in Delhi, but it also has more hybrid forms and a greater diversity of flower colours. Remember that there are literally dozens of hybrids, and this breakdown only lists the broad categories or 'forma' to which the hybrids can be assigned. (The term 'forma' [= form] suggests that it is less distinct than a 'subspecies' or 'variety' within a species.)

Here's how *Plumeria rubra* breaks down:

Plumeria rubra	Predominant flower colour
...forma *acutifolia*	White petals with a yellow throat, often splashed on the base of the petals too – sometimes flushed with pink on the outside
...forma *rubra*	Petals rose or deep-red (of varying intensity) with a yellow throat
...forma *tricolor*	Petals half pink, half white, with yellow throat
...forma *lutea*	Predominantly yellow petals, flushed with pink on the outside

There are only 2 main sub-types of *Plumeria obtusa* and the main difference is seen in the hairiness of the leaf:

Plumeria obtusa	Leaf description
...var. *obtusa*	The leaf appears relatively smooth, pale green underneath; close inspection (with a hand lens) shows hairs on the leaf stalk and main nerve; distinctly broader towards the apex
...var. *sericifolia*	Densely woolly-hairy underneath, appearing dirty white; the leaves may have parallel sides for much of their length

PONGAMIA OR MILLETTIA?

Some years ago, there was a move to sink genus *Pongamia* under *Derris*, but this did not find favour with most taxonomists. Nevertheless, you may come across some references to this species as '*Derris indica*' that you can disregard now as a failed attempt at reclassification.

Less easy to ignore is a more recent attempt at merging *Pongamia* with *Millettia*, with which it shares much in common. One publication already lists *Pongamia pinnata* as *Millettia pinnata*, citing

Panigrahi as the author. This may well find more general acceptance in the near future, but for the moment we can stick with the more widely accepted name *Pongamia pinnata*.

NOT TABEBUIA ROSEA?

The nursery trade in Delhi and many botanists insist that Delhi's pink flowering tabebuia is *Tabebuia rosea*, but the attributes of *Tabebuia rosea* in the scientific literature do not quite square with this tree.

One of the easiest ways of telling *Tabebuia rosea* apart from *Tabebuia impetiginosa* is that the leaflets of the former, apart from being much larger, are glandular-scaly but never hairy, with plain, untoothed margins. *Tabebuia impetiginosa*, on the other hand, has smaller but variable leaflets that may be densely hairy on the underside and, at the very least, are hairy all along the principal veins. Furthermore, the edges of the leaflets are often (but not always) toothed (or serrulate).

Having said that, all the scientific literature agrees that *Tabebuia impetiginosa* is an extremely variable species with several forms. Some strains are paler pink than others, some more fragrant, others much more prominently toothed on their leaflets, and so on. To make matters worse, there are also now a number of nursery hybrids, including a few that are the product of crossing *Tabebuia impetiginosa* with yellow-flowered species of *Tabebuia*, and you can well imagine that it is now a risky business to try and identify a pink tabebuia by field characters alone.

However, it is some consolation to learn that the tabebuias from tropical mainland America and the West Indies – about a hundred species in all – have always been a botanist's nightmare and have a long history of name-changing and species-hopping. I think it would be fair to say that today the 'joiners' are having a field day, and a number of forms which were previously regarded as separate species (such as *Tabebuia ipe*, *Tabebuia palmeri* and *Tabebuia avellanedae*) are now regarded as variable forms of the one species, *Tabebuia impetiginosa*. But with gene-mapping around the corner, who is to say that the joiners will not soon bite the dust?

WHICH TAXODIUM?

You may come across the Montezuma baldcypress (*Taxodium mucronatum*) referred to as *Taxodium distichum* var. *mexicanum*, thus reducing it to a mere variety of the common baldcypress (*Taxodium distichum*). Botanists differentiate between 3 different kinds of *Taxodium*, but depending on which authority you consult, *Taxodium* is treated as a genus with either just a single species (with 3 varieties), or else 2 or 3 completely separate species. This kind of controversy is not at all unusual in taxonomy, and reflects uncertainty about a geographically widespread species where evolution has not yet wrought substantive changes.

The differences between *Taxodium distichum* and *Taxodium mucronatum* are in fact so small and indecisive that it has led to some difference of opinion among Indian botanists as to the identity of the *Taxodium* grown in Delhi. The leaf, flowers and fruit appear not to be strongly differentiated at all. One of the chief differences is that *Taxodium distichum* is reputedly deciduous while *Taxodium mucronatum* is reported to be evergreen or semi-deciduous, but that is hardly a crucial test and may merely indicate an adaptive response to the availability of moisture.

In the absence of decisive criteria and mainly on grounds of habitat, I believe that the species that grows in Delhi is much more likely to be the same as that which grows in dry parts of the Mexican plateaux than the one that is adapted to swamps and marshes.

WILL THE REAL TUN PLEASE STAND UP!

Trees like the tun which have a very wide geographic range are apt to exhibit considerable variation, and taxonomists have had a field day splitting the species up into various subspecies and into various varieties within the subspecies. The species is probably not important enough in Delhi to warrant a full explication, but it is worth knowing that the BSI, for example, treats the tun that we find in Delhi as *Toona ciliata* Roem. subsp. *ciliata* Bahadur var. *ciliata* Bahadur. That translates into variety *ciliata* of subspecies *ciliata* of the species *Toona ciliata*!

MAYTENUS SENEGALENSIS?

The scientific names of the kankera are in a bit of a mess. Part of the problem is that the species – or closely allied relatives – has a very wide distribution from Africa to Malesia, and different authors treat it in different ways.

Up to a few years ago, there seemed general consensus that the kankera found here and in the Thar desert is *Maytenus senegalensis*. Authors writing about the African species, meanwhile, preferred to sink *Maytenus* under *Gymnosporia*, and called the species *Gymnosporia montana*. Meanwhile, in the Malesian region, the species became differentiated as *Maytenus emarginata*, and it is this name that has been widely adopted by many Indian botanists today.

According to ('splitter') authors who make fine distinctions between different forms of the species, however, *Maytenus emarginata* is found only in SE India and Malesia, and so the correct name of the species in Delhi remains *Maytenus senegalensis*.

FAMILY NAMES

It can be useful to know which Family a tree belongs to – it draws attention to related species and genera and this information can help in identifying a tree.

I have avoided using scientific Family names on the species pages and have preferred instead to indicate which family a tree belongs to by citing representatives of that family that might be more familiar. This page links back from the informal names to the scientific ones. Notice that all modern, scientific Family names end in –aceae (pronounced 'ay-see'), making it simple to distinguish Family names from individual species or generic names.

Amla/castor family – *Euphorbiaceae*

Arjun family – *Combretaceae*

Arnatto family – *Bixaceae*

Barna family – *Capparaceae*

Barringtonia family – *Lecythidaceae*

Ber family – *Rhamnaceae*

Casuarina family – *Casuarinaceae*

Chalta family – *Dilleniaceae*

Chikoo family – *Sapotaceae*

Chilla family – *Flacourtiaceae*

Cinnamon family – *Lauraceae*

Coca family – *Erythroxylaceae*

Cocoa family – *Sterculiaceae*

Coffee/gardenia family – *Rubiaceae*

Cotton/hibiscus family – *Malvaceae*

Custard apple family – *Annonaceae*

Cypress family – *Cupressaceae*

Ebony family – *Ebenaceae*

Elm family – *Ulmaceae*

Frangipani/oleander family – *Apocynaceae*

Jacaranda family – *Bignoniaceae*

Jamun/eucalyptus family – *Myrtaceae*

Lasora family – *Boraginaceae*

Magnolia family – *Magnoliaceae*

Maharukh family – *Simaroubaceae*

Mango/cashew family – *Anacardiaceae*

Mangosteen/kokam family – *Clusiaceae*

Mehndi family – *Lythraceae*

Monkey-puzzle family – *Araucariaceae*

Mulberry/fig family – *Moraceae*

Neem/mahogany family – *Meliaceae*

Oak family – *Fagaceae*

Olive/jasmine family – *Oleaceae*

Orange family – *Rutaceae*

Palm family – *Arecaceae*

Paulownia family – *Scrophularaceae*

Pea family – cassia subfamily – *Caesalpiniaceae*

Pea family – mimosa subfamily – *Mimosaceae*

Pea family and subfamily – *Papilionaceae*

Peelu family – *Salvadoraceae*

Pine family – *Pinaceae*

Plane tree family – *Platanaceae*

Podocarpus family – *Podocarpaceae*

Pomegranate family – *Punicaceae*

Ramdhan champa family – *Ochnaceae*

Redwood family – *Taxodiaceae*

Reettha/litchi family – *Sapindaceae*

Rose/peach/cherry family – *Rosaceae*

Saffron family – *Celastraceae*

Salai/frankincense family – *Burseraceae*

Semal family – *Bombacaceae*

Silky oak family – *Proteaceae*

Sonjna family – *Moringaceae*

Sweetgum family – *Hamamelidaceae*

Tamarisk family – *Tamaricaceae*

Teak family – *Verbenaceae*

Willow/poplar family – *Salicaceae*

Wood-sorrel family – *Oxalidaceae*

LIST OF SPECIES

In an ideal world, every tree or plant would have a single, universally accepted, scientific name and there would be no confusion. In practice, many plants are known by competing names. This is mostly a legacy of the age of exploration, when botanists were discovering and naming plants in far-flung parts of the world. This was also an age of poor communications and often led to situations where the same plant was discovered and named by different authorities, leading to a multiplicity of names.

If this was all there was to the confusion of names, botany would probably have sorted it out long ago. Unfortunately, name changes are a continuing process, made necessary by the recognition of new (evolutionary) relationships – or sometimes, the absence of a relationship, where one was presumed. This leads to new genera being formed ('splitting'), or to two or more genera being merged ('joining'), to reflect this new understanding. In short, names are not immutable.

The full citation of a botanical name includes the name (or more usually, an abbreviation of the name) of the botanist – called the 'authority' – who is 'officially' credited with naming the plant. This name is usually omitted in the popular literature (such as nursery plant lists), but for botanists, the author citation is a useful means of verifying the identity of a plant.

I have included a few synonyms (indented) that are still in wide circulation. For example, *Drypetes roxburghii* is a relatively new and little known scientific name of a tree that we know better as *Putranjiva roxburghii*, and I felt it was important to list this synonym both here and in the index. I have not cited the authority for the synonyms.

In a few cases, the indented synonyms are placed within square brackets – this is to indicate that they are not valid synonyms, but are commonly used (incorrectly) to signify the tree whose name precedes it.

Acacia auriculiformis A.Cunn. ex Benth.
Acacia catechu (L.f.) Willd.
Acacia farnesiana (L.) Willd.
Acacia leucophloea (Roxb.) Willd.
Acacia modesta Wall.
Acacia nilotica (L.) Del. subsp. *indica* (Benth.)
    Brenan
       Acacia arabica
Acacia senegal (L.) Willd.
Acacia tortilis (Forssk.) Hayne subsp. *raddiana*
    (Savi)
Acrocarpus fraxinifolius Wt. ex Arn.
Adansonia digitata L.
Adenanthera microsperma Teijsm.& Binn.
       Adenanthera pavonina
Aegle marmelos (L.) Correa
Afrocarpus gracilior (Pilg.) Page
       Podocarpus gracilior
Agathis robusta (C.Moore ex F.Muell.) Bailey
Ailanthus excelsa Roxb.
Albizia amara (Roxb.) Boiv. subsp. *amara*
Albizia lebbeck (L.) Benth.
Albizia lucidior (Steud.) I.C.Nielsen ex H.Hara
       Albizia lucida
       Albizia lucidor
Albizia procera (Roxb.) Benth.
Aleurites moluccana (L.) Willd.
       Aleurites triloba
Alstonia macrophylla Wall. ex G.Don

Alstonia scholaris (L.) R.Br.
Annona squamosa L.
Anogeissus acuminata (Roxb. ex DC.) Guill.& Perr.
    var. *acuminata*
Anogeissus pendula Edgew.
Araucaria columnaris (G.Forst.) Hook.
       Araucaria cookii
Artocarpus heterophyllus Lam.
       Artocarpus integrifolia
       Artocarpus integra
       Artocarpus integer
Artocarpus lacucha Buch.-Ham.
       Artocarpus lakoocha
Atalantia monophylla (L.) DC.
Averrhoa carambola L.
Azadirachta indica A.Juss.
       Melia indica
       Melia azadirachta
Balanites roxburghii Planch.
       [*Balanites aegyptiaca* var. *roxburghii*]
       [*Balanites aegyptiaca*]
Barringtonia acutangula (L.) Gaertn.
Bauhinia x *blakeana* Dunn.
       Bauhinia blakeana
Bauhinia purpurea L.
Bauhinia racemosa Lam.
Bauhinia variegata L. var. *variegata*
Bauhinia variegata L. var. *candida* Voigt.

Bergera koenigii L.
    Murraya koenigii
Bischofia javanica Blume
Bixa orellana L.
Bolusanthus speciosus (Bolus) Harms.
Bombax ceiba L.
    Bombax malabaricum
    Salmalia malabarica
Borassus flabellifer L.
    Borassus flabbeliformis
Brachychiton australis (Schott.& Endl.) A.Terracc.
    Sterculia trichosiphon
Brachychiton gregorii F.Muell.
    Brachychiton acerifolius var. *gregorii*
Bridelia retusa (L.) A.Juss.
    Bridelia spinosa
Broussonetia papyrifera (L.) Vent.
    Morus papyrifera
Butea monosperma (Lam.) Taub.
    Butea frondosa
Caesalpinia ferrea Mart.ex Tul.
Callistemon viminalis (Soland. ex Gaertn.) G.Don.
Calpurnia aurea (Ait.) Benth. subsp. *aurea*
Capparis decidua (Forssk.) Edgew.
    Capparis aphylla
Carissa congesta Wt.
    Carissa carandas
Caryota urens L.
Casearia tomentosa Roxb. ex Hook.
Cassia fistula L.
Cassia grandis L.f.
Cassia javanica L. var. *javanica*
Cassia javanica L. var. *indochinensis* Gagnep.
    Cassia nodosa
    Cassia javanica subsp. *nodosa*
    Cassia javanica var. *agnes*
    Cassia agnes
Cassia renigera Wall. ex Benth.
    Cassia javanica subsp. *renigera*
Cassia roxburghii DC
Castanospermum australe A.Cunn. & C.Fraser
Casuarina equisetifolia L. ex J.R. & G.Forst.
Ceiba insignis (Kunth) P.E.Gibbs & Semir
    Chorisia insignis
Ceiba pentandra (L.) Gaertn.
    Eriodendron anfractuosum
Ceiba speciosa (A.St.Hil.) Ravenna
    Chorisia speciosa
Celtis tetrandra Roxb.
    [Celtis australis]
Chrysophyllum oliviforme L.
Chukrasia tabularis A.Juss. var. *tabularis*
Chukrasia tabularis A.Juss. var. *velutina* (M.Roem.) W.Theob.
Cinnamomum camphora (L.) J.Presl.

Clerodendrum phlomidis L.
    Clerodendron phlomoides
Colvillea racemosa Boj.
Cordia dichotoma Forst. f.
    Cordia myxa
    Cordia obliqua
Cordia gharaf (Forsk.) Ehrenb. & Aschers.
    Cordia rothii
    Cordia sinensis
Corymbia citriodora (Hook.) K.D.Hill & L.A.S.Johnson
    Eucalyptus citriodora
Crateva adansonii DC. subsp. *odora* (Buch.-Ham.) Jacobs
    [Crataeva nurvala]
    [Crataeva religiosa]
    [Crataeva magna]
Crescentia alata H.B.& K.
    Parmentiera alata
Croton roxburghii Balakr.
    Croton laevigatus
Cupaniopsis anacardioides (A.Rich.) Radlk.
    Cupania anacardioides
Cupressus sempervirens L.
Dalbergia lanceolaria L.f.
Dalbergia sissoo Roxb. ex DC.
Delonix regia (Bojer ex Hook.) Raf.
    Poinciana regia
Desmodium oojeinense (Roxb.) H.Ohashi
    Ougeinia oojeinensis
Dichrostachys cinerea (L.) Wt. & Arn.
Dillenia indica L.
    Dillenia speciosa
Diospyros cordifolia Roxb.
    Diospyros montana var. *cordifolia*
    [Diospyros montana]
Diospyros malabarica (Desr.) Kostel.
    Diospyros embryopteris
    Diospyros peregrina
Drypetes roxburghii (Wall.) Hurus.
    Putranjiva roxburghii
Dypsis lutescens (H.Wendl.) Beentje & Dransf.
    Chrysalidocarpus lutescens
    Areca lutescens
Ehretia acuminata (DC.) R.Br.
    Ehretia serrata
    Ehretia acuminata var. *serrata*
Ehretia laevis Roxb.
Enterolobium contortisiliquum (Vell.) Morong
    Enterolobium timbouva
Erythrina blakei Hort.
Erythrina suberosa Roxb.
    Erythrina stricta var. *suberosa*
    Erythrina sublobata
Erythrina variegata L.
    Erythrina variegata var. *orientalis*

Erythroxylum coca Lam.
Eucalyptus brownii Maid. & Camb.
Eucalyptus camaldulensis Dehnh.
    Eucalyptus rostrata
Eucalyptus microtheca F. Muell.
    Eucalyptus coolabah
Eucalyptus tereticornis Sm.
Euphorbia neriifolia L.
Fernandoa adenophyllum (Wall. ex G.Don) Steenis
    Haplophragma adenophyllum
Ficus amplissima Sm.
    Ficus tsiela
Ficus benghalensis L. var. *krishnae* C.DC.
    Ficus krishnae
Ficus benghalensis L.
Ficus benjamina L. var. *benjamina*
    Ficus nitida
Ficus benjamina L. var. *comosa* (Roxb.) G.Panig. &
    Murti
    Ficus comosa
Ficus benjamina L. var. *nuda* (Miq.) Barrett
    Ficus nuda
Ficus binnendijkii Miq. 'Alii'
    [*Ficus longifolia*]
    [*Ficus* 'Maclellandii']
    [*Ficus maclellandii*]
    [*Ficusa alii*]
    [*Ficus* 'Alii']
Ficus drupacea Thunb. var. *pubescens* (Roth)
    Corner
    Ficus mysorensis
Ficus elastica Roxb. ex Hornem.
Ficus lyrata Warb. ex De Wild. & Durand
    Ficus pandurata
Ficus microcarpa L.f.
    Ficus retusa
    Ficus retusa var. *nitida*
Ficus natalensis Hochst. subsp. *leprieurii* (Miq.)
    C.C.Berg
    Ficus triangularis
Ficus palmata Forssk. subsp. *virgata* (Roxb.)
    Browicz
Ficus racemosa L.
    Ficus glomerata
Ficus religiosa L.
Ficus virens Aiton. var. *virens*
    Ficus infectoria
    Ficus lacor
    Ficus lucescens
Filicium decipiens (Wt. & Arn.) Thwaites ex
    Hook.f.
Flacourtia indica (Burm. f.) Merr.
    Flacourtia ramontchii
Gliricidia sepium (Jacq.) Kunth ex Walp.
    Gliricidia maculata
Gmelina arborea Roxb.

Gmelina asiatica L.
Grevillea robusta A. Cunn. ex R.Br.
Guazuma ulmifolia Lam.
    Guazuma tomentosa
Gynocardia odorata R.Br.
Haldina cordifolia (Roxb.) Ridsdale
    Adina cordifolia
Hardwickia binata Roxb.
Hibiscus tiliaceus L. subsp. *tiliaceus*
Hibiscus tiliaceus L. subsp. *hastatus* (L.f.) Borss.
    Waalk.
Holoptelea integrifolia Planch.
Indopiptadenia oudhensis (Brandis) Brenan
    Piptadenia oudhensis
Ixora pavetta Andr.
    Ixora parviflora
Jacaranda mimosifolia D.Don
    Jacaranda ovalifolia
Jatropha curcas L.
Joannesia princeps Vell.
    Anda gomesii
Juniperus chinensis L.
Khaya senegalensis (Desr.) A.Juss.
    Swietenia senegalensis
Kigelia africana (Lam.) Benth.
    Kigelia pinnata
Koelreuteria elegans (Seem.) A.C.Sm.
    [*Koelreuteria paniculata*]
Lagerstroemia floribunda Jack
Lagerstroemia indica L.
Lagerstroemia microcarpa Wt.
    Lagerstroemia lanceolata
Lagerstroemia speciosa (L.) Pers.
    Lagerstroemia flos-reginae
    [*Lagerstroemia thorellii*]
Lagerstroemia tomentosa Presl.
Leucaena leucocephala (Lam.) de Wit
    Leucaena latisiliqua
    Leucaena glauca
Limonia acidissima L.
    Limonia elephantum
    Feronia limonia
Liquidambar formosana Hance
Livistona chinensis (Jacq.) R.Br. ex Mart.
Livistona rotundifolia (Lam.) Mart.
Madhuca longifolia (Koen.) MacBr. var. *latifolia*
    (Roxb.) Chev.
    Bassia latifolia
    Madhuca indica
    Madhuca latifolia
Madhuca longifolia (Koen.) MacBr. var. *longifolia*
    Bassia longifolia
Magnolia grandiflora L.
Mallotus philippensis (Lam.) Muell.-Arg.
Mangifera indica L.

Manilkara hexandra (Roxb.) Dubard
   Mimusops hexandra
Manilkara zapota (L.) P.Royen
   Achras zapota
   Achras zapotilla
   Sapota achras
Markhamia lutea (Benth.) K.Schum.
   Markhamia platycalyx
Maytenus senegalensis (Lamk.) Exell.
   Celastrus senegalensis
   Gymnosporia montana
   [Maytenus emarginata]
Melaleuca bracteata F.Muell.
   Melaleuca genistifolia
Melia azedarach L.
Mesua ferrea L. var. *ferrea*
   Mesua nagassarium
Michelia champaca L.
Millettia peguensis Ali
   Millettia ovalifolia
   Derris ovalifolia
Millingtonia hortensis L.f.
Mimusops elengi L.
Mitragyna parviflora (Roxb.) Korth.
   Nauclea parvifolia
Moringa oleifera Lam.
   Moringa pterygosperma
Morus alba L.
   [Morus indica]
Murraya paniculata (L.) Jack
   Murraya exotica
Neolamarckia cadamba (Roxb.) Bosser
   Anthocephalus cadamba
Nyctanthes arbor-tristis L.
Ochna obtusata DC.
   [Ochna squarrosa]
   [Ochna jabotapita]
Olea europaea L.
Oroxylum indicum (L.) Vent.
Paraserianthes falcataria (L.) I.C.Nielsen
   Albizia moluccana
   Albizia falcataria
   Falcataria moluccana
Parkia biglandulosa Wt. & Arn.
Parkinsonia aculeata L.
Paulownia tomentosa (Thunb.) Sieb. & Zucc. ex
   Steud.
Peltophorum africanum Sond.
Peltophorum pterocarpum (DC.) Back. ex K.Heyne
   Peltophorum inerme
   Peltophorum ferrugineum
Phoenix canariensis Hort. ex Chabaud
Phoenix roebelinii O'Brien
Phoenix rupicola T. Anders.
Phoenix sylvestris (L.) Roxb.

Phyllanthus emblica L.
   Emblica officinalis
Pinus roxburghii Sarg.
   Pinus longifolia
Pistacia chinensis Bunge subsp. *integerrima*
   (J.Stewart) Rech.f.
   Pistacia intergerrima
   [Pistacia khinjuk]
Pithecellobium dulce (Roxb.) Benth.
   Inga dulcis
Platanus orientalis L.
Platycladus orientalis (L.) Franco
   Thuja orientalis
   Biota orientalis
Plumeria obtusa L. var. *obtusa*
   Plumeria emarginata
   [Plumeria alba]
Plumeria obtusa L. var. *sericifolia* (Wright) Woods
   Plumeria sericifolia
Plumeria rubra L.
   Plumeria acuminata
   Plumeria acutifolia
   Plumeria rubra var. *acutifolia*
Plumeria rubra L. forma *lutea* (Ruiz & Pav.)
   Woods.
   Plumeria lutea
Plumeria rubra L. forma *tricolor* (Ruiz & Pav.)
   Woods.
   Plumeria tricolor
Polyalthia longifolia (Sonn.) Thwaites ex Benth. et
   Hook.f.
   Polyalthia longifolia var. *pendula*
Polyalthia longifolia 'Angustifolia'
   Polyalthia longifolia var. *angustifolia*
Pongamia pinnata (L.) Pierre
   Pongamia glabra
   Derris indica
   Millettia pinnata
Populus deltoides Bartr. ex Marsh. subsp. *deltoides*
Prosopis cineraria (L.) Druce
   Prosopis spicigera
Prosopis glandulosa Torr. var. *glandulosa*
   Prosopis juliflora var. *glandulosa*
   Prosopis chilensis var. *glandulosa*
Prosopis juliflora (Sw.) DC.
Protium serratum (Wall. ex Colebr.) Engl.
   Bursera serrata
Prunus dulcis (Mill.) D.A.Webb var. *dulcis*
   Amygdalus dulcis
   Prunus amygdalus
Prunus persica (L.) Batsch.
Pseudobombax ellipticum (H.B.& K.) Dug.
   Bombax ellipticum
   [Pachira rosea]
   Pachira fastuosa
Psidium guajava L.

Pterospermum acerifolium (L.) Willd.
Pterospermum xylocarpum (Gaertn.) Santapau & Wagh.
    Pterospermum heyneanum
Pterygota alata (Roxb.) R.Br.
    Sterculia alata
Punica granatum L.
Pyrus pyrifolia (Burm.f.) Nakai
    Pyrus serotina
    Pyrus sinensis
    [Pyrus communis]
Quercus leucotrichophora A.Camus
    Quercus incana
Reutealis trisperma (Blco.) Airy Shaw
    Aleurites trisperma
Roystonea regia (Kunth) O.F.Cook
    Oreodoxa regia
Sabal mauritiiformis (H. Karst.) Griseb. & H.Wendl.
    Sabal glaucescens
Sabal palmetto (Walt.) Lodd. ex Schult. & Schult.f.
Salix tetrasperma Roxb.
Salvadora oleoides Decne.
Salvadora persica L.
Sapindus mukorossi Gaertn.
    Sapindus detergens
Sapium sebiferum (L.) Roxb.
Saraca asoca (Roxb.) de Wilde
    Jonesia asoca
    [Saraca indica]
Schleichera oleosa (Lour.) Oken
    Schleichera trijuga
Senna siamea (Lam.) Irwin & Barneby
    Cassia siamea
Senna spectabilis (DC.) Irwin & Barneby
    Cassia spectabilis
Senna surattensis (Burm. f.) Irwin & Barneby
    Cassia surattensis
    Cassia glauca
Spathodea campanulata Beauv.
Spondias pinnata (J.G.Konig ex L.f.) Kurz
    Spondias mangifera
Sterculia foetida L.
Streblus asper Lour.
Suregada multiflora (A. Juss.) Baill.
Swietenia macrophylla King
Swietenia mahagoni L. (Jacq.)
Syzygium cumini (L.) Skeels
    Eugenia jambolana
    Syzygium jambolanum
Syzygium nervosum DC.
    Cleistocalyx operculata
    Eugenia operculata
    Syzygium operculatum

Tabebuia aurea (Manso) Benth.& Hook.f. ex S.Moore
    Tecoma argentea
    Tabebuia argentea
    Tabebuia caraiba
Tabebuia impetiginosa (Mart. ex DC.) Standl.
    Tabebuia avellanedae
    Tabebuia palmeri
    Tecoma impetiginosa
    Tecoma ipe
    [Tabebuia rosea]
Tabernaemontana divaricata (L.) R.Br. ex Roem. & Schult.
    Tabernaemontana coronaria
Tamarindus indica L.
Tamarix aphylla (L.) Karst.
    Tamarix articulata
Taxodium mucronatum Ten.
    Taxodium distichum var. *mucronatum*
    Taxodium distichum var. *mexicanum*
    [Taxodium distichum]
    Taxodium mexicanum
Tecoma castanifolia (D. Don) Melch.
    Tecoma gaudichaudii
Tecoma stans (L.) A.Juss. ex Kunth
Tecomella undulata (Sm.) Seem.
    Tecoma undulata
Tectona grandis L.f.
Terminalia arjuna (Roxb. ex DC.) Wt. & Arn.
Terminalia bellirica (Gaertn.) Roxb.
Terminalia chebula Retz.
Terminalia muelleri Benth.
Terminalia myriocarpa Heurck & Muell.-Arg.
Thespesia populnea (L.) Sol. ex Corr.
    Hibiscus populneus
Thevetia peruviana (Pers.) K.Schum.
    Thevetia neriifolia
    Cascabela thevetia
Toona ciliata M. Roem. subsp. *ciliata* Bahadur var. *ciliata* Bahadur
    Cedrela toona
Trewia nudiflora L.
Washingtonia filifera (Linden) H.Wendl.
Wrightia tinctoria R.Br.
Ziziphus mauritiana Lam.
    Ziziphus jujuba

INDEX